Economic Growth, Inequality and Migration

Economic Growth, Inequality and Migration

Edited by

Amnon Levy

University of Wollongong, Australia

and

João Ricardo Faria

University of Texas at Dallas, USA

Edward Elgar

Cheltenham, UK • Northampton, MA, USA

Published by
Edward Elgar Publishing Limited
Glensanda House
Montpellier Parade
Cheltenham
Glos GL50 1UA
UK

Edward Elgar Publishing, Inc.
136 West Street
Suite 202
Northampton
Massachusetts 01060
USA

A catalogue record for this book
is available from the British Library

Library of Congress Cataloguing in Publication Data

Economic Growth, inequality and migration / edited by Amnon Levy and João Ricardo Faria.
    p. cm.
Includes index.

    1. Economic development. 2. Income distribution. 3. Emigration and immigration–Economic aspects. I. Levy, Amnon. II. Faria, João Ricardo.

HD75 .E262 2003
338.9–dc21

2002072172

ISBN 1 85898 970 1

Printed and bound in Great Britain by MPG Books Ltd, Bodmin, Cornwall

Contents

Tables

Figures

Contributors

Jorge Thompson Araujo, *World Bank*

Jorge Saba Arbache, *Department of Economics, University of Brasilia, Brazil*

Akihito Asano, *Department of Economics, University of Melbourne, Australia*

Vani K. Borooah, *School of Public Policy, Economics and Law, University of Ulster, Northern Ireland*

Francisco Galrão Carneiro, *Universidade Católica de Brasília, Brazil*

João Ricardo Faria, *School of Social Sciences, University of Texas at Dallas*

Ross S. Guest, *School of Accounting and Finance, Griffith University, Australia*

Charles Harvie, *Department of Economics, University of Wollongong, Australia*

John S. Landon-Lane, *School of Economics, University of New South Wales, Australia*

Miguel A. León-Ledesma, *Department of Economics, Keynes College, University of Kent at Canterbury, Canterbury, Kent, UK*

Amnon Levy, *Department of Economics, University of Wollongong, Australia*

Marco A.C. Martins, *Federal Senate, Brazil*

Ian M. McDonald, *Department of Economics, University of Melbourne, Australia*

Luiz de Mello, *International Monetary Fund*

Rogério B. Miranda, *Universidade Católica de Brasília, Brazil, and the Institute of Applied Economic Research (IPEA)*

André Varella Mollick, *Department of Economics, ITESM-Campus Monterrey, Mexico*

Peter E. Robertson, *School of Economics, University of New South Wales, Australia*

Joan R. Rodgers, *Department of Economics, University of Wollongong, Australia*

John L. Rodgers, *Department of Economics, University of Wollongong, Australia*

Erwin Tiongson, *International Monetary Fund*

Yacov Tsur, *Department of Agricultural Economics and Management, The Hebrew University of Jerusalem, Israel*

James Xiaohe Zhang, *University of Newcastle, Australia*

Preface

This book features eighteen studies on economic growth, inequality and migration. These socio-economic factors are interlinked. During the growth process inequality may rise or decline, and the change in the level of inequality may, in turn, affect growth. An increase in inequality in one place and better prospects of growth and earnings in other places can trigger migration. Each study in this volume is concerned with at least two of these issues and classified into one of the three general parts in accordance with the theme that is mostly emphasised. The main focus of the papers appearing in the first part is inequality and its effects on growth, labour market integration and government policies. The second part deals mainly with migration, its determinants and its possible effect on the host country's output, employment and standard of living. The third part is concerned with economic growth and its relationship with trade, capital accumulation and internal and external debts.

The first part of the book contains studies on inequality and its implications for growth, labour market integration and public policy. Asano surveys the literature on the interrelationships between inequality and growth with an emphasis on the effect of inequality on growth. Guest reports the results of the tests of two-way causality between income inequality and economic growth in the case of an advanced, stable, capitalist economy such as Australia. Using the median-voter concept, Levy argues that when income is not equally, or symmetrically, distributed, median income may provide a better assessment of the society's economic well-being and a broader framework for assessing growth and convergence of incomès across countries than the commonly used per capita income. Zhang and Harvie assess the impact of the household registration regime on the urban–rural income differential and inter-provincial income inequality in the post-reform era in China by decomposing the overall Gini index.

The remaining studies in the first part consider the relation between government policies and income distribution. Carneiro, Mello and Tiongson test the hypothesis that the less equal the distribution of income the higher the government redistributive spending with panel data for a sample of 37 countries. They show that, in general, the countries where redistributive public spending is more needed were found to be the ones that are less likely to redistribute income through public policies. Borooah develops a theoretical model to investigate the role of fair-employment regulation in ensuring fair access to jobs in a fragmented society. His analysis is focused on the trade-off between the equity gains and the efficiency losses generated by the rising costs of hiring and firing. Miranda presents a model for the Brazilian economy in which the economic group in power attempts to increase its income share, and as a consequence of which inflation is generated, which in turn might adversely affect output.

The second part of the book deals mainly with migration and the related issues of unemployment, assimilation, expected returns and risk. Faria develops a model with two labour market scenarios: full employment in which industries pay market clearing wages and unemployment in which efficiency wages are paid. It is shown that governments can design a tax that corrects the distortion caused by non-clearing market wages and leads to a decline in both urban unemployment and migration from the rural sector to the urban sector. Levy develops a model of supply of and demand for migrants and proposes an immigration feedback rule which is aimed at stabilising the host country's unemployment level. Levy and Tsur analyse migration-timing by combining the concepts of expected earning differential, risk-bearing and assimilation costs into the individual expected lifetime utility maximisation problem. They classify migrants by age and career stage and consider the possible effect of the host country's ethnic composition on migrants' assimilation costs, earnings and social stability. Rodgers and Rodgers test the human-capital theory of internal migration with individual-level census data on Australian men. Landon-Lane and Robertson discuss the post-Second World War immigration inflow to Australia and develop a model of growth in an open economy with economies of scale. Their simulations indicate that the large immigration inflow during the period from 1947 to 1952 may have boosted growth for 15 years and resulted in a small but significant long-term effect on per capita income. Guest and McDonald show that the levels of foreign borrowing that support an optimal path of living standards through time for Australia depend on the demographic structure of the economy.

The third part starts with a set of studies on trade and its impacts on growth. While a higher degree of openness increases the volume of trade and, thereby, is expected to foster growth, it might increase both internal and international levels of inequality. Arbache presents a review of the theoretical and empirical literature on the debate about the effects of trade liberalisation on wage inequality. Mollick focuses on the case of Mexico and finds no support for the assertion that increased openness to international trade plays a significant role in increasing the wage gap between skilled and unskilled workers. Leon-Ledesman investigates whether R&D spillovers increase competitiveness in international markets in the case of OECD countries. His empirical findings suggest that the assertion that foreign innovation tends to harm skilled workers at home might be ignoring the possibility that spillovers can enhance the export performance of domestic sectors enjoying a comparative advantage. The rest of the papers in the third part deal with the relationship between capital accumulation, debts and growth. Martins and Araujo present an overlapping generations model with AK technology and bequest decisions and show that Ricardian equivalence is not generally valid. Levy expands the neoclassical intertemporal maximisation model of growth to include international trade and external debt and analyses the stationary levels of capital stock and external debt.

This collection of studies contributes to the growing debate on inequality, migration and growth. We believe that the included studies illuminate many important issues related to these topics both theoretically and empirically.

Amnon Levy and João Ricardo Faria
August 2001

PART ONE

Inequality: Implications for Growth, Labour Market Integration and Policy

1 Inequality and Economic Growth: A Review of the Literature

Akihito Asano

1.1 INTRODUCTION

Both reducing income inequality and achieving high economic growth have been very important policy issues, especially in developing countries and, unsurprisingly, there has been a long debate on the relationship between inequality and growth.

One strand of research, which was initiated by Kuznets (1955), has tried to uncover the effect of growth (or development) upon inequality. Kuznets (1955) conjectures that economic development is necessarily accompanied by an increase in inequality since only rich people can obtain benefit from it, but then after a while inequality will decline when eventually poor people catch up. This is known as the inverted-U hypothesis because a plot of income on the horizontal axis and the Gini coefficient on the vertical axis will look like an upside-down U. This inverted-U hypothesis has been challenged by a number of studies such as Anand and Kanbur (1993) since the mid-1970s.[1]

The other strand of research focuses upon the reverse causation, that is, it investigates the effect of initial inequality upon subsequent growth. Conventionally, inequality was thought to have a *positive* impact upon growth. This view is due to Kaldor (1961), Stiglitz (1969) and Bourguignon (1981). Kaldor (1961) postulates that the marginal propensity to save is higher for the rich than for the poor. An immediate conjecture that follows this, bearing in mind the Swan–Solow growth model, is that a more unequal economy reaches a higher steady state income level than a more equal economy does because its savings rate tends to be higher. Stiglitz (1969) shows, using a linear saving function, that aggregate capital accumulation behaviour, which determines the

This chapter is based upon Chapters 1 and 2 of the author's PhD dissertation, Asano (2001).

growth rate of aggregate output (in transition), is independent of the distribution of wealth. Bourguignon (1981) extends this analysis using a convex saving function and predicts under this situation that the growth rate of aggregate output (in transition) is dependent upon the distribution of wealth and that a more unequal economy will reach a higher steady state income level. If output is a linear function of capital,[2] the long-run growth rate will be higher for a more unequal economy.

In the 1990s, this conventional view was challenged by a number of theoretical and empirical studies, which are our main focus in this chapter. A number of empirical studies have provided evidence that inequality has a negative impact upon growth (Persson and Tabellini 1992a, 1992b, 1994; Alesina and Rodrik 1994; Benhabib and Spiegel 1994; Perotti 1994, 1996; Birdsall et al. 1995; Clarke 1995; Deininger and Squire 1998). Table 1.1 summarises the main results of the studies that have conducted a growth regression including a certain measure of inequality on the RHS.

Table 1.1
Reduced Form Regressions

Author(s) (year)	LHS variable[a]	Inequality index[b]	Sign of the coefficient[c]	∂LHS/∂SD[d]
Alesina and Rodrik (1994)	*gdp*	*Gini*	–	na
Benhabib and Spiegel (1994)	*gdp or GDP*	*–MID*	(–)	na
Birdsall et al. (1995)	*gdp*	*1–MID*	–	0.32
Clarke (1995)	*gdp*	*various*	–	1.3 (OLS), 2.5 (2SLS)
Deininger and Squire (1998)	*gdp*	*Gini*	–	0.5
Perotti (1994)	*INV*	*–ID*	–	na
Perotti (1996)	*gdp*	*–MID*	–	0.6
Persson and Tabellini (1992a)	*gdp*	*–MIDDLE*	–	at least 0.5

Notes:

a. *gdp*: the average annual growth rate of GDP per capita over the sample period; GDP: the average annual growth rate of GDP over the sample period; INV: the average of the ratio of investment to GDP over the sample period.

b. *Gini*: Gini coefficient; *MID*: the share of the third and fourth quintiles of distribution; *ID*: the share of the two bottom quintiles of the distribution; *MIDDLE*: the share of the third quintile of the distribution; *various*: Clarke (1995) uses various measures of inequality. Correlations amongst these measures are high, and the regression is found to be robust against the choice of the inequality measure. The Gini coefficient based upon land rather than income is used in Deininger and Squire (1998).

c. A sign in brackets means the estimated coefficient of the inequality measure is insignificant. Aside from Birdsall et al. (1995), estimates are significant at at least the 5-per-cent level.

d. ∂LHS/∂SD shows a percentage point increase of the LHS variable if inequality is reduced by one standard deviation.

Most of these studies show a negative and statistically significant correlation between inequality and economic growth. The magnitude of the effect of inequality upon growth differs among the studies: a one standard deviation decrease in a measure of inequality raises the annual growth rate of GDP per capita by 0.32–2.5 percentage points.

Two questions have to be asked. First, is this effect significant? In other words, is the magnitude of the effect large enough to call our attention? Secondly, regardless of the significance of the effect, what is the mechanism underlying it? That is, how might inequality affect growth?

A common way to analyse the effect of inequality upon growth is to see what happens if a measure of inequality changes by one standard deviation. Let us use Birdsall et al. (1995) as an example. A one standard deviation decrease in inequality leads to a 0.32 percentage point increase in the growth rate of GDP per capita. Considering that the standard deviation of the growth rate of GDP per capita is about 0.02, we can regard this effect as sizeable. If we compare two economies that are identical but for initial income distribution by one standard deviation, GDP per capita will be 8.2 per cent higher after 25 years in the economy with the lower inequality of initial income distribution.

Having checked the importance of the effect of inequality upon growth, our interest now is to consider the underlying mechanisms by which inequality affects growth, which are the focus of this chapter. One obvious drawback of the standard growth regression using the reduced form, that is, regressing the growth rate of GDP per capita on various economic variables including a measure of inequality, is that it is unable to discern the underlying mechanism. Given this, in the 1990s, some economists attempted to construct theoretical models in order to back up these empirical results from reduced-form studies (Bertola 1993; Galor and Zeira 1993; Alesina and Rodrik 1994; Persson and Tabellini 1994; Acemoglu 1995; Bénabou 1996c; Benhabib and Rustichini 1996; Grossman and Kim 1996; Galor and Zang 1997). In addition, some empirical studies using the structural form have been conducted to test these theoretical models. We classify these theoretical and empirical studies into four approaches according to Perotti (1996)[3] as follows.

In the first approach, which we call the endogenous fiscal policy approach (Bertola 1993; Alesina and Rodrik 1994; Persson and Tabellini 1994), income distribution affects economic growth via its effect upon government expenditure and taxation. In the models of this approach, the levels of taxation and expenditure are determined by a vote. Since the levels of taxation and expenditure preferred by an agent are inversely related to her income, if the crucial voter, the median voter, has less income than the mean income, government taxation will be strengthened. If we consider the ratio of the median voter's income to the mean as the measure of equality, applying the theory of endogenous policy, we can say that redistributive government expenditure and therefore distortionary taxation decrease as equality increases (political mechanism), In turn, government expenditure and taxation are negatively correlated to economic growth as agents lose their incentives to save and invest under high taxation (economic mechanism). As a result, economic growth increases as equality increases.

In the second approach (Tornell and Velasco 1992; Murphy et al. 1993; Grossman 1991, 1994; Acemoglu 1995; Alesina and Perotti 1996; Benhabib and Rustichini 1996; Grossman and Kim 1996; Perotti 1996), income distribution affects economic growth via its effect upon sociopolitical instability. In more unequal societies, agents are more likely to be involved in rent-seeking activities or other manifestations of sociopolitical instability, violent protests, assassinations and so on. In turn, sociopolitical instability harms growth through uncertainty and has an adverse effect upon productivity due to disruption in market activities. As a consequence, economic growth increases as equality increases.

In the third approach (Banerjee and Newman 1993; Bénabou 1993, 1996a, 1996b; Galor and Zeira 1993; Perotti 1993, 1996; Durlauf 1994; Fernandez and Rogerson 1996; Aghion and Bolton 1997; Piketty 1997; Saint-Paul and Verdier 1997), income distribution affects economic growth via its effect upon investment in human capital. This type of model is meaningful when agents are not able to borrow freely against future income, that is, when market imperfections are present in the capital market. Under this situation, initial income distribution matters as it affects the number of agents who can invest in human capital. The model generally concludes that, if wealth is distributed more equally, more agents are able to invest in human capital. Since economic growth is assumed to increase as investment in human capital increases, we obtain the same conclusion as above: economic growth increases as equality increases.

The fourth approach, which we call the endogenous fertility approach, takes fertility into account (Becker and Barro 1988; Kelley 1988; ; Barro and Becker 1989; Becker et al. 1990; Perotti 1996; Galor and Zang 1997; Dahan and Tsiddon 1998; Morand 1999; Asano 2001). In this approach, fertility and schooling decisions are made jointly, as they are interpreted as two alternative uses of parents' human capital. That is, fertility determines the parents' quantity of immediate descendants and schooling determines their quality. This model concludes that fertility decreases and investment in human capital increases as equality increases. Since growth is assumed to be negatively related to fertility and positively related to investment in human capital, the overall conclusion in is the same as above: economic growth increases as equality increases.[4]

In the following four sections (Sections 1.2 to 1.5), we look at these four approaches in turn. We review both the theoretical and the empirical literature and also provide a discussion for each of these approaches. Section 1.6 concludes this chapter. It introduces more recent studies that emphasise the non-monotonic nature of the effect of inequality upon growth, which casts doubt upon the seemingly common agreement that inequality is harmful to growth.

1.2   THE ENDOGENOUS FISCAL POLICY APPROACH

1.2.1   Theory

Here, we briefly review the model by Persson and Tabellini (1994). In their overlapping generations (OLG) model, agents have the same preferences but different incomes. The ith individual born in period $t-1$, indexed by t, maximises her utility:

$$v_t^i = U(c_{t-1}^i, d_t^i) \qquad \text{(PT1.1)}$$

subject to the budget constraints:

$$c_{t-1}^i + k_t^i = y_{t-1}^i \qquad \text{(PT1.2)}$$

$$d_t^i = r\left[(1-\theta_t)k_t^i + \theta_t k_t\right] \qquad \text{(PT1.3)}$$

where c is the consumption when young and d is the consumption when old. The utility function is concave, well-behaved and homothetic. k and k^i are the average and individual stock of an asset, respectively, and the asset yields exogenous return of r. θ is a redistributive policy variable. Equation (PT1.3) shows that the redistributive policy takes from individuals who accumulated the asset more than average and gives to those who accumulated less than average.

Next, the income when young is defined as:

$$y_{t-1}^i = (w + e^i)k_{t-1} \qquad \text{(PT1.4)}$$

where w is an average endowment of skills, which is given exogenously, and e is an individual specific endowment of skills, which is also given exogenously, with zero mean and nonpositive median.

This model assumes that there is one-period-ahead commitment of policy, that is, voters choose θ before investors choose k. A politico-economic equilibrium is defined as a policy and a set of private economic decisions such that:

1.   the economic decisions of all citizens are optimal, given the policy, and all markets clear (economic equilibrium); and

2.   the policy cannot be defeated by any alternative in a majority vote amongst the citizens who have the right to vote (political equilibrium).

The economic equilibrium is obtained by solving a utility maximisation problem. It deduces that the growth rate of income (g_t) is a function of θ and the other variables as in equation (PT1.5):

$$g_t = G(w,r,\theta_t) = wD(r,\theta_t) / [r + D(r,\theta_t)] - 1 \qquad \text{(PT1.5)}$$

where $D(r,\theta_t) = d_t^i / c_{t-1}^i$. It can be shown that $G_w > 0$ and $G_\theta < 0$. This implies that the higher the average skills are, the higher the growth rate is, and more importantly, the less θ is, the higher the growth rate is.

Regarding political equilibrium, we first deduce the following equation using equation (PT1.2), equation (PT1.4), and the solution for c_{t-1}^i, which is obtained through solving the individual's utility maximisation problem:

$$k_t - k_t^i = \frac{-D(\cdot)k_{t-1}}{D(\cdot) + r(1-\theta_t)} e_{t-1}^i \qquad \text{(PT1.6)}$$

Equation (PT1.6) says that individuals who are poorer (richer) than the average accumulate the asset less (more) than the average. Therefore, the level of θ preferred by individuals is inversely related to their initial endowments of individually specific skills e^i. The political equilibrium value of θ is characterised by the value of θ^m which is preferred by the median voter, who has the median endowment of specific skills, e^m.

Secondly, equation (PT1.5), equation (PT1.6) and the maximising condition:

$$\frac{\partial v_t^i}{\partial \theta_t} = U_d(\cdot)\left[(k_t - k_t^i) + \theta_t \frac{\partial k_t}{\partial \theta_t}\right] r = 0 \qquad \text{(PT1.7)}$$

yield the equilibrium value of q^*, which is a function of w, r and e^m, defined implicitly by:

$$-\frac{D(r,\theta)e^m}{D(r,\theta) + r(1-\theta)} + \theta D_\theta(r,\theta)\frac{wr}{[r + D(r,\theta)]^2} = 0 \qquad \text{(PT1.8)}$$

It is easy to verify $\theta_e^* < 0$. Combining equation (PT1.5) and equation (PT1.8), the growth rate in the politico-economic equilibrium is given as follows:

$$g^* = G(w,r,\theta^*(w,r,e^m)) \qquad \text{(PT1.9)}$$

From equation (PT1.9), using $G_\theta < 0$ and $\theta_e^* < 0$, we conclude that more equality increases growth:

$$\frac{dg^*}{de^m} = G_\theta \theta_e > 0 \qquad \text{(PT1.10)}$$

1.2.2 Evidence

Persson and Tabellini (1994) and Perotti (1996) are the only empirical studies that are classified into this approach. The model by Persson and Tabellini (1994) predicts that more equality leads to less distortion and thus higher investment and economic growth. The equations they have estimated are as follows:[5]

$$GROWTH = 4.874 - 0.00052GDP60 + 0.011PSCHOOL - 4.742TRANSF$$
$$\quad\quad (3.414)\ (-3.873) \quad\quad\quad (0.763) \quad\quad\quad (-0.970)$$

$$TRANSF = 0.203 - 0.011MIDDLE + 0.000018GDP60.$$
$$\quad\quad (1.790)\ (-1.286) \quad\quad\quad (1.756)$$

They do not treat these equations as a system, so both equations are estimated separately by OLS. *GROWTH* is the average annual growth rate of real GDP per capita over 1960–85. *GDP60* is real GDP per capita in 1960 and is in the first equation to capture the possible convergence effect. *PSCHOOL* is percentage enrolled in primary school out of the relevant age group in 1960, which is a proxy for the initial human capital. They measure government-induced redistribution by the average ratio of transfers (pensions, unemployment compensations and other social expenditures other than health and education) to GDP between 1960 and 1981 (*TRANSF*). Inclusion of this variable reduces the number of observations to 13, which is very small. The measure of inequality is *MIDDLE*, which is the share of pre-tax income received by the third quintile of the population. An increase in *MIDDLE* is regarded as more equality.

The data do not appear to support their hypothesis well. The estimate of the coefficient on *MIDDLE* of the second equation is negative as expected but is statistically insignificant. Also, the estimate of the coefficient on *TRANSF* of the first equation is negative as the model predicts but is statistically insignificant.

Perotti (1996) estimates a system of equations by the method of two-stage least squares. The simplest specification of his system is as follows:

$$GROWTH = 0.004 - 0.004GDP60 + 0.004MSE + 0.001FSE - 0.0005PPPI + 0.090MTAX$$
$$\quad\quad (0.47) \quad (-2.39) \quad\quad (0.38) \quad\quad (0.10) \quad\quad (-0.07) \quad\quad (3.61)$$

$$MTAX = 0.164 - 0.021GDP60 - 0.096MIDDLE + 3.047POP65.$$
$$\quad\quad (1.13)\ (-1.50) \quad\quad\quad (-0.19) \quad\quad\quad (3.78)$$

In this system, *GROWTH* and *MTAX* are the endogenous variables. *MTAX* is the average marginal tax rate between 1970 and 1985, and this variable is a proxy for the distortions caused by the redistributive policy. *MSE* (*FSE*) is average years of secondary schooling of the male (female) population in 1960, which is a proxy for the initial human capital, and *PPPI* is a proxy for the market distortions for which the PPP value for the investment deflator relative to the USA in 1960 is used. As for the *MTAX* equation, the share of population over 65 years of age, average of 1970, 1975 and 1985 values (*POP65*) is included, apart from *GDP60* and *MIDDLE*, in order to control for a higher distributive expenditure to those people.

The estimation result is not convincing in supporting the theory. The positive estimate of the coefficient on *MTAX* in the first equation is statistically significant, but is against the prediction of the model. The negative estimate of the coefficient on *MIDDLE* in the second equation is anticipated but is statistically insignificant. The basic picture of the estimation result does not change if other fiscal policy variables or inequality measures are used instead.

1.2.3   Discussion

We reviewed a one-sector OLG model by Persson and Tabellini (1994). Here we hastily note the fact that two-sector infinite horizon models by Alesina and Rodrik (1994) and Bertola (1993) arrived at the same conclusion: inequality will lower economic growth via the endogenous fiscal policy determination and the resulting distortion. It shows the robustness of this approach in the sense that two different theoretical frameworks predict the same result.

However, as we have reviewed, the empirical evidence appears to be against what the theory predicts. Note that the important assumption of this approach is that policies are determined endogenously by a vote. Perhaps, as a number of studies have pointed out, this approach might prevail only in democratic countries, where this assumption sounds plausible.

Perotti (1996) actually has conducted the same estimation only for the democratic country subsample,[6] but the result has not improved so much to support the theory.[7] In addition to this, some empirical studies that use reduced-form equations have found little support for the endogenous fiscal policy approach. For example, Deininger and Squire (1998) find that inequality affects growth in non-democratic countries, but not in democratic ones.

In summary, we conclude that the data have not supported the endogenous fiscal approach so far.

1.3   THE SOCIOPOLITICAL INSTABILITY APPROACH

1.3.1   Theory

Now we turn to review theoretical models of the second approach, which deals with sociopolitical instability. First, let us regard sociopolitical instability as a situation under which property rights are insecure, that is, we assume that more inequality leads to more sociopolitical instability that leads to less secure property rights. Under this situation, rent-seeking activities will be more likely to take place than otherwise, and this may harm economic growth. Murphy et al. (1993) capture this point.

Murphy et al. (1993) show how rent seeking is costly to economic growth. It is shown that agents tend to engage in rent-seeking activities when property rights are not protected, and the level of output is far lower than otherwise. This situation is referred to as the 'bad equilibrium', and since it is stable, it is difficult to escape from that equilibrium once an economy slides into it.

Consider a farm economy where each agent can engage in one of the following three activities: production of a cash crop; production of a subsistence crop; rent seeking. A cash crop is traded in the market and the level of output per agent is q_1. But a cash crop is subject to rent seeking. If an agent engages in rent seeking, he can expropriate a cash crop by the maximum amount of q_2. On the contrary, a subsistence crop is not subject to rent seeking and the level of output is q_3 ($q_3 < q_1$). Note that the agent's rent-seeking technology is subject to diminishing returns, in the sense of an upper bound on how much he can grab with limited time and abilities.

An equilibrium in this economy is an allocation of the population between cash crop production, subsistence crop production and rent seeking. Let us denote the ratio of people engaged in rent seeking and cash crop production by n. We can find an equilibrium by considering payoffs to production and rent seeking as a function of n. We first consider two extreme cases where property rights are extremely well protected and extremely poorly protected.

Case 1. Well protected property rights ($q_2 < q_3$): In this case, property rights are well protected because the return to rent seeking is even lower than that to subsistence crop production. At $n=0$, the return to cash crop production is q_1, since there is no rent seeking. As n rises, the return to cash crop production falls to $q_1 - nq_2$, until it hits the critical level $q_1 - n_1 q_2$, where $q_1 - n_1 q_2 = q_3$ (or $n_1 = (q_1 - q_3)/q_2$). As n rises above n_1, cash crop producers drop into subsistence crop production to keep their income level at q_3. As a consequence, the return to each rent-seeker will be $(q_1 - q_3)/n < q_2$. Figure 1.1 describes the situation.[8] The equilibrium is unique in this case. Every agent engages in cash crop production; there will be no rent-seekers or subsistence crop producers. Output per capita is q_1, which is the highest this economy can yield.

Case 2. Poorly protected property rights ($q_1 < q_2$): In this case, rent-seekers are able to grab more than the amount which cash crop producers can produce, hence property rights are not well protected at all. As shown in Figure 1.2, the ratio of population between rent-seekers and cash crop producers in the unique equilibrium, in this case, must be given by $n_2 = (q_1 - q_3)/q_3$, and in the equilibrium, every agent's income is equal to the subsistence level q_3, which is lower than q_1.

Next, let us consider the intermediate case where the economy has multiple equilibria.

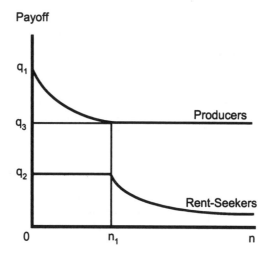

Figure 1.1   Well Protected Property Rights

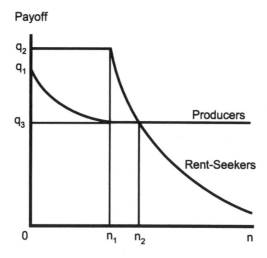

Figure 1.2   Poorly Protected Property Rights

Case 3. Intermediate Case – Multiple equilibria $(q_3 < q_2 < q_1)$: In this case, the return to rent-seeking is greater than that to subsistence crop production but is less than that to cash crop production. There are three equilibria, as shown in Figure 1.3. The first one corresponds to that in Case 1 in which every agent engages in cash crop production, and income per capita is q_1. The second one corresponds to that in Case 2 where agents are split up into three activities and the level of per capita output is driven down to the subsistence level q_3. In the third equilibrium, agents engage in either rent seeking or cash crop production and per capita income is q_2. In this equilibrium, $n = n_3 = (q_1 - q_2)/q_2$. However, this is not a stable equilibrium. An incremental increase in n beyond n_3 raises the return to rent seeking above that to cash crop production, and so leads to a further increase in rent-seeking activity. There are two stable equilibria, 'good' ($n = 0$) and 'bad' ($n = n_2$), and one unstable equilibrium ($n = n_3$).

Murphy et al. (1993) derive five implications from the model:

1. Well protected property rights (low q_2) eliminate the 'bad' equilibrium, whereas extremely poorly protected property rights (high q_2) eliminate the 'good' equilibrium.
2. Raising q_1 increases per capita income in the 'good' equilibrium but it also increases the possibility that this equilibrium exists. It also implies an increase in n in the 'bad' equilibrium since there are more rents to be disintegrated per producer before income falls to q_3.
3. Raising q_3 increases per capita income in the 'bad' equilibrium.

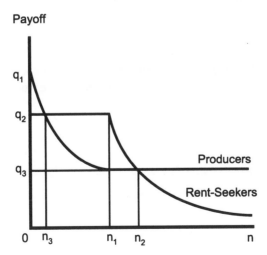

Figure 1.3   Multiple Equilibria

4. To get the best outcome, it is essential to provide enough property rights so that q_2 falls below q_3. To this end, a legal system, a rigid culture, or some other form of anti-rent-seeking ideology can play a role (North 1981) in decreasing q_2. Some protection of subsistence crop production, as well as raising productivity (rise in q_3), may also play an important role.

5. Whatever the strategy to protect property rights, it should be quite drastic, since the 'bad' equilibrium is stable and will not be affected by the minor improvement of property rights.

In this crude model, the degree of security of property rights is given exogenously by the relative level of q_2. Therefore, in order to link between inequality and lower economic growth, we need to assume that in more unequal societies, agents are more likely to be involved in rent-seeking activities. Some may say it is an acceptable assumption in modelling sociopolitical instability, but others may say it is too strong. So, let us look at another model by Benhabib and Rustichini (1996), who have dealt with sociopolitical instability in a different way.

Benhabib and Rustichini (1996) model sociopolitical instability by endogenising social conflict between two groups, namely the rich and the poor. In their game theoretic model, they characterise these groups as two players and show that the poor can undertake redistributive actions, which leads to lower investment and thus lower output in subsequent periods.

Consider the two players 1 and 2, who live for infinite periods. They have an identical utility function, with an identical discount rate β, which takes a value between 0 and 1:

$$U(c) = \frac{c^{1-\varepsilon}}{1-\varepsilon} \qquad (BR1.1)$$

where $0 < \varepsilon < 1$ and c is the level of consumption. The level of output (y) depends only upon the level of capital stock (k) in each period and the production function is given as follows:

$$y = ak \qquad (BR1.2)$$

where $a > 0$.

The current period's output (y_t) is either consumed by the two players (c_t^1, c_t^2) or invested to form the capital stock in the next period (k_{t+1}):

$$y_t - c_t^1 - c_t^2 \le k_{t+1} \qquad (BR1.3)$$

The total utility of each player among a first best equilibrium is derived by solving the following dynamic program:

$$\hat{v} = \underset{0 \le c \le \frac{y}{2}}{Max} \left[\frac{c^{1-\varepsilon}}{1-\varepsilon} + \beta \hat{v}(y - 2c) \right] \tag{BR1.4}$$

It follows that the first best consumption is given as follows:

$$\hat{c} = \hat{\lambda} y \tag{BR1.5}$$

where

$$\hat{\lambda} = \frac{1}{2} \left(1 - \beta^{\frac{1}{\varepsilon}} a^{\frac{1-\varepsilon}{\varepsilon}} \right) \ge 0 \tag{BR1.6}$$

For the first best $\hat{\lambda}$, the value function is given by:

$$\hat{v} = s(\hat{\lambda}) y^{1-\varepsilon} \tag{BR1.7}$$

where

$$s(\hat{\lambda}) = \frac{\hat{\lambda}^{1-\varepsilon}}{(1-\varepsilon)\left\{1 - \beta(a(1-2\hat{\lambda}))^{1-\varepsilon}\right\}} \tag{BR1.8}$$

This result shows that in a first best equilibrium, in each period, each agent will consume an equal share of output, but will not consume all output and invest the rest for the next period.

Next, let us consider the case where a player defects against a first best play by her opponent. If a player defects, the other player will take a grim trigger strategy, that is, all output will be consumed in equal shares by the two players after a defection. Therefore, this player must choose her consumption in the current period taking into account that a grim trigger strategy will be enacted subsequently.

Similar to the first best case, optimal defection value is given by:

$$v^D = \underset{0 \le c_D \le (1-\hat{\lambda})y}{Max} \left[\frac{c_D^{1-\varepsilon}}{1-\varepsilon} + \frac{\beta \left\{ a((1-\hat{\lambda})y - c_D) \Big/ 2 \right\}^{1-\varepsilon}}{1-\varepsilon} \right] \tag{BR1.9}$$

and the value of optimal defection from the first best (v^D) is derived as follows:

$$v^D = s_D y^{1-\varepsilon} \qquad \text{(BR1.10)}$$

where

$$s_D = \frac{1}{(1-\hat{\lambda})^{1-\varepsilon}(1-\varepsilon)M^\varepsilon} \qquad \text{(BR1.11)}$$

and

$$M = \frac{2a}{\left(\dfrac{\beta a}{2}\right)^{\frac{1}{\varepsilon}} + \dfrac{a}{2}} \qquad \text{(BR1.12)}$$

If $\hat{v} \geq v^D$ then the first best outcome prevails, but otherwise, a defection will take place. In the numerical example in Benhabib and Rustichini (1996), if the first best were sustained, capital stock would grow at 15 per cent. However, the economy would contract by 0.0015 per cent if there were a defection.[9]

Inequality is characterised by the disparity of the levels of consumption between two players. Therefore, when a defection is present, that is, $\hat{v} \leq v^D$, inequality is present because the player who defects consumes more than the other one. The disadvantaged player will undertake redistributive action, namely a grim trigger strategy. In this model, this leads to a slower accumulation of capital and hence slower economic growth.

1.3.2   Evidence

Alesina and Perotti (1996) and Perotti (1996) are the only empirical studies that have attempted to support this approach. Alesina and Perotti (1996) test the hypothesis that inequality affects *investment* via destabilising the sociopolitical situation. To this end, they specify a bivariate simultaneous equation model, with share of physical investment in *GDP* (*INV*) and the index of sociopolitical instability (*SPI*) as endogenous variables. In the simplest specification, variables on the RHS of the *INV* equation are as follows: *SPI*, the initial level of real GDP per capita to take the convergence effect into account, and indexes to capture domestic market price distortions (*PPPI* and *PPPIDE*: *PPPI* was defined previously; *PPPIDE* is a magnitude of the deviation of the PPP value for the investment deflator from the sample mean in 1960). On the RHS of the *SPI* equation, *INV*, the initial enrolment ratio in primary school as a proxy for human capital (*PRIM*), and the index of equality (*MIDCLASS*) are included. In this paper, this equality index is a share of the third and fourth quintiles of the population. The higher the value of this index is, the more equal is the economy. The simplest system of equations they have estimated is as follows:

$$\begin{cases} INV = 27.36 + 0.07GDP60 - 0.50SPI - 0.14PPPI + 0.04PPPIDE \\ \quad\quad (9.34) \;\; (1.09) \quad\quad\quad (-2.39) \quad (-2.39) \quad\quad (0.62) \\ \\ SPI = 37.43 - 0.23PRIM - 1.01MIDCLASS + 0.72INV \\ \quad\quad (4.54) \;\; (-2.45) \quad\quad (-3.42) \quad\quad\quad\quad (1.30) \end{cases}$$

The estimation is conducted by the method of two-stage least squares, which gives efficient and consistent estimates. The signs of all coefficients are as expected. Our interest is the estimate of the coefficient on *MIDCLASS*, which is negative and statistically significant. A one-standard-deviation increase in *MIDCLASS* decreases *SPI* by about 5.7, which corresponds to about 48 per cent of its standard deviation. This is associated with an increase in *INV* of about 2.85 percentage points. Provided that the standard deviation of *INV* is 7.49, the effect of initial inequality upon investment appears non-trivial. This estimation result is shown to be robust against different model specifications and a different measure of *SPI*.

Now we turn to look at Perotti (1996) who specifies the system slightly differently. The simplest specification of the system is as follows:

$$\begin{cases} GROWTH = 0.034 - 0.004GDP60 + 0.028MSE - 0.025FSE - 0.014PPPI - 1.495SPI \\ \quad\quad\quad\quad (3.46) \;\; (-1.81) \quad\quad\quad (2.63) \quad\quad (-2.05) \quad\quad (-1.32) \quad\quad (-2.27) \\ \\ SPI = 0.021 + 0.006MSE - 0.009FSE - 0.090MIDDLE \\ \quad\quad (3.26) \;\; (1.20) \quad\quad (-1.20) \quad\quad (-2.11) \end{cases}$$

The definitions of the variables are the same as before. The difference from Alesina and Perotti (1996) is that *GROWTH* instead of *INV* is used in the first equation of this system. Perotti (1996) does not explicitly justify why he has used the growth rate instead of the investment ratio, and this could be a problem. We will discuss this issue in the next subsection.

In any case, let us analyse the above estimation results. The estimate of the coefficient on *MIDDLE* in the second equation is negative as anticipated and is statistically significant. In addition, the estimate of the coefficient on *SPI* in the first equation is negative as the model predicts and is statistically significant. This estimation predicts that a one-standard-deviation increase in *MIDDLE* decreases *SPI* by about 0.005 and, in turn, leads to an increase in *GROWTH* of about 0.7 percentage point.

Inclusion of regional dummies does not change the picture much. The estimate of the coefficient on *MIDDLE* falls to –0.071 but is still statistically significant, which implies that the variation in *SPI* is explained by the continental differences, but only partly. This case, a one-standard-deviation increase in *MIDDLE*, leads to an increase in *GROWTH* of about 0.56 percentage point. In any event, the effect of inequality upon growth appears to be sizeable.

1.3.3   Discussion

The basic intuition behind this approach is that, in an unequal society, there is a strong incentive for the different groups to engage in unproductive activities in order to deprive other groups' output, and this results in uncertainty on the final distribution of output, which induces a decrease in investment in physical capital. Therefore, the relationship between inequality and *investment* is derived quite rigorously from the theoretical model. The empirical study by Alesina and Perotti (1996) has tested this link and supports it quite well, as we have seen. Inequality has a sizeable impact upon *investment*.

However, we are still not sure about the effect of inequality upon *growth*. Many of the studies have found a strongly positive and statistically significant relationship between investment and growth. However, as is well known, Barro and Sala-i-Martin (1995) report the opposite evidence that investment does not have much explanatory power for growth. Therefore, we need to be a little cautious when we link investment and growth.

A possible way to get around this problem could be to estimate a three-equation system. In addition to two equations of a system in Alesina and Perotti (1996), if we add a typical growth equation with the growth rate on the LHS and investment on the RHS as the third equation, we can estimate the effect of inequality upon *growth*, indirectly through *investment*.

Perotti (1996) skips this procedure and just replaces *INV* with *GROWTH*. This slight departure from the theoretical model makes the interpretation of the results very difficult. That is, from his estimation, we cannot really observe how sociopolitical instability affects growth.

Despite the problem raised above, Perotti (1996) provides us with an interesting finding. In his estimation, *SPI* is used to capture sociopolitical instability, but the question as to what *SPI* is really capturing is an awkward one – it might be just a proxy variable for Latin American/African countries where sociopolitical instability is often present. Interestingly, as we have seen, inclusion of regional dummies to Perotti (1996) does not change the result much. This shows that the variation in *SPI* is only partly explained by regional differences. Furthermore, the estimate on the coefficient of *MIDDLE* remains statistically significant.

This contrasts to some reduced-form regressions such as those of Birdsall et al. (1995). When regional dummies are introduced to their reduced-form regression, inequality becomes statistically insignificant. Ravallion and Chen (1997) report a similar finding. While these findings suggest that the relationship between inequality and growth might be spurious, Perotti (1996) presents the opposite result.

1.4 THE HUMAN CAPITAL AND BORROWING CONSTRAINT APPROACH

1.4.1 Theory

The third approach is characterised by two assumptions. One is that the credit market is imperfect and the other is that investment in human capital is indivisible, that is, there is a decision whether or not to invest in human capital but there is no decision on how much to invest. Galor and Zeira (1993) show that under this circumstance, an economy that has a larger middle class is likely to grow faster. A brief review of their model follows.

We consider a small open economy. There is only one good that can be used for either consumption or investment. There are two ways to produce this good. One is to utilise both capital (K_t) and skilled labour (L_t^s) and the other is to utilise only unskilled labour (L_t^n). The levels of output Y_t^s and Y_t^n are given as follows:

$$Y_t^s = F(K_t, L_t^s) \qquad \text{(GZE1.1)}$$

$$Y_t^n = w_n L_t^n \qquad \text{(GZE1.2)}$$

where w_n is the competitive wage rate determined in the unskilled labour market and F is a concave CRS production function.

We consider individuals who live for two periods. In the first period, each individual decides whether to work or to invest in human capital. If she invests in human capital, she can work as a skilled labourer in the second period, but if she does not invest in human capital she works as an unskilled labourer in the second period. Each individual consumes only in the second period and bequeaths something for her child. The utility function is given as follows:

$$U = \alpha \log c + (1 - \alpha) \log b \qquad \text{(GZE1.3)}$$

where c is consumption in the second period, b is the bequest and α is a parameter which takes a value between 0 and 1.

Capital is assumed to be perfectly mobile and the constant world interest rate is given by $r > 0$. It follows that:

$$\frac{\partial F}{\partial K_t} = r \qquad \text{(GZE1.4)}$$

and this equation determines the wage rate for skilled labour, w_s.

Now we turn to the capital market. Individuals can lend any amount at the world interest rate r. We assume that borrowers are able to evade paying the debt by all means and lenders are trying to keep track of borrowers. If it costs z to keep track of borrowers, it costs βz to evade paying the debt, where $\beta > 1$. If an individual borrows an amount d at the interest rate i_d, a zero profit condition in the competitive financial sector yields:

$$di_d = dr + z \qquad\qquad \text{(GZE1.5)}$$

Taking into account that lenders choose z high enough to make the default disadvantageous, we obtain the following result:

$$i_d = i = \frac{1 + \beta r}{\beta - 1} > r \qquad\qquad \text{(GZE1.6)}$$

This equation says that the borrowing interest rate, i, is higher than the lending interest rate, r. In this sense, the capital market is imperfect.

Now let us analyse optimal decisions by individuals. Individuals are identical except that they inherit a different amount of wealth, and we can think of three types of individual; individuals who remains unskilled; individuals who lend and invest in human capital; individuals who borrow and invest in human capital. Solving the utility maximisation problems for these three types of individual who inherit an amount x in the first period gives the optimal amount of bequest for each type, respectively, as follows:

$$b_n = (1 - \alpha)\left[(1 + r)(x + w_n) + w_n\right] \qquad\qquad \text{(GZE1.7)}$$

$$b_{sl} = (1 - \alpha)[w_s + (x - h)(1 + r)] \qquad\qquad \text{(GZE1.8)}$$

$$b_{sb} = (1 - \alpha)\left[w_s + (x - h)(1 + i)\right] \qquad\qquad \text{(GZE1.9)}$$

where h is the cost of investing in human capital. Therefore in equation (GZE8), $(x-h)$ is non-negative, but is negative in equation (GZE9). We confine our analysis to the case where lenders prefer to invest in human capital, that is, we assume that the following relationship holds:

$$w_s - h(1 + r) \geq w_n(2 + r) \qquad\qquad \text{(GZE1.10)}$$

This relationship can be easily derived by comparing utilities of an unskilled individual and a skilled individual who lends. It can also be shown that borrowers prefer to invest in human capital as long as the resulting utility is higher than otherwise, that is, they invest in human capital as long as the following relationship holds:

$$x \geq f = \frac{w_n(2-r) + h(1+i) - w_s}{i-r} \qquad \text{(GZE1.11)}$$

The important implication here is that education is limited to individuals with high enough initial wealth (above f). This is due to a higher interest rate for borrowers.

Now we turn to analyse the dynamics of the model. The distribution of inheritances in the next period (x_{t+1}) is described as follows:

$$x_{t+1} = \begin{cases} b_n = (1-\alpha)\big[(1+r)(x_t + w_n) + w_n\big], & \text{if } x_t < f \\ b_{sb} = (1-\alpha)\big[w_s + (x_t - h)(1+i)\big], & \text{if } f \leq x_t < h \\ b_{sl} = (1-\alpha)\big[w_s + (x_t - h)(1+r)\big], & \text{if } h \leq x_t \end{cases} \qquad \text{(GZE1.12)}$$

Figure 1.4 describes the situation.[10] The curves describe the dynamic relationships between inheritance and bequest (inheritance for the next generation) for three types of individual.

Points A and B are locally stable and they correspond to the long-run levels of inheritance for skilled individuals ($\bar{x}_s$) and unskilled individuals ($\bar{x}_n$), respectively. The critical point in Figure 1.4 is C. Individuals who inherit less than g in period t may invest in human capital, but eventually their descendants will become unskilled and their inheritances will converge to $\bar{x}_n$. On the other hand, individuals who inherit more than g in period t invest in human capital and their descendants will become skilled throughout the subsequent generations. Their inheritances will converge to $\bar{x}_s$.

Therefore, in the long run, this economy is divided into two groups – skilled individuals who have wealth $\bar{x}_s$ and unskilled individuals who have wealth $\bar{x}_n$. The relative size of these groups depends upon the initial wealth distribution since the number of (un)skilled individuals in the long run is the same as the number of individuals who inherit less than g initially in period t.

Galor and Zeira (1993) then argue the following. If we assume that productivity of unskilled individuals (w_n) grows at a certain rate and productivity of skilled individuals (w_s) and human capital (h) grows at a higher rate, then the growth rate of output per capita is a weighted average of these rates where initial wealth distribution is used as the weight. Therefore, initial wealth distribution can affect the rate of growth. The more there are individuals who inherit more than g, in other words, the larger the share of the middle class, the higher the growth rate will be. This argument is, however, problematic. We come back to this after reviewing a related empirical study.

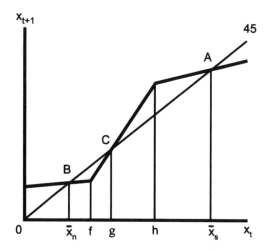

Figure 1.4   Bequest and Inheritance

1.4.2   Evidence

Perotti (1996) is the only empirical study that is based upon this approach. The simplest specification of a simultaneous equation system is as follows:

$$\begin{cases} GROWTH = 0.002 - 0.013GDP60 + 0.111FSEC \\ \quad\quad\quad (0.26)\ (-4.68) \quad\quad\quad (5.24) \\ \\ FSEC = -0.212 + 0.088GDP60 + 0.235MSE - 0.155FSE + 1.078MIDDLE \\ \quad\quad (-1.61)\ (5.86) \quad\quad\quad (2.95) \quad\quad (-1.80) \quad\quad (2.51) \end{cases}$$

Perotti (1996) chooses *FSEC*, the female secondary school enrolment ratio (average of 1965 and 1985 values), as a proxy for investment in human capital since the opportunity cost of secondary education is likely to be higher than that of primary education. The result is basically the same if *MSEC*, the male secondary school enrolment ratio (average of 1965 and 1985 values), is used instead of *FSEC*.

The estimation result appears to be consistent with what the theoretical model predicts. The positive estimate of the coefficient on *MIDDLE* in the second equation implies that in a more equal society investment in human capital will be higher, and the positive estimate of the coefficient on *FSEC* in the first equation implies a positive effect of investment in human capital on growth. A one-standard-deviation increase in *MIDDLE* leads to about a 0.63 percentage point increase in *GROWTH*. Again, we emphasise that this effect is sizeable. A standard deviation of *GROWTH* in this sample is 0.017.

However, this estimation has nothing to do with the borrowing constraint, that is, the imperfect capital market. In order to take this into account, a measure that can capture the degree of imperfection in the capital market is needed. Perotti (1996) reports that no ideal data exist for this purpose at present.

1.4.3   Discussion

We have reviewed a model by Galor and Zeira (1993), but it is problematic in at least two respects. One is their argument in deriving the implication for the effect of inequality upon growth in transition. In deriving the implication, they impose an assumption that both the wage rates for two types of worker and the cost investment in human capital grow. However, the model has been solved without this assumption. The optimal behaviour of individuals will change if this assumption is imposed, so strictly speaking the model should be constructed and solved with this assumption imposed from the beginning.

The other problem is their definition of inequality. We have kept it a little vague what is meant by inequality in their model, but they use the share of unskilled individuals in the total population (l^u) to define inequality. They define that an economy is more unequal if this share is higher. This definition, however, is obviously different from the ordinary inequality definitions such as the Gini coefficient. If every individual is unskilled and has the same income, the Gini coefficient will be zero, showing complete *equity* of an economy. But according to the definition by Galor and Zeira (1993), this economy is completely *unequal* because the share of unskilled individuals is unity.

Let us turn to discuss a possible extension of the model – including endogenous fertility. Becker et al. (1990) point out that investment in human capital is jointly determined by individuals, as they are interpreted as two alternative uses of parents' human capital. Parents face a trade-off between investing in the number of children and investing in children's education, given their budget constraint. In fact, fertility has been treated as an endogenous variable in some growth models (Barro and Becker 1989; Becker and Barro 1988; Becker et al. 1990).

The empirical evidence also gives us a fair reason to incorporate fertility into a growth model. Brander and Dowrick (1994), using a 107-country panel data set covering 1960–85, detect strong negative fertility effects upon per capita income growth. Their study also points out the significant negative relationship between fertility and human capital. Barro (1991) also finds a strong negative relationship between fertility and investment in human capital.

This leads us to investigate the fourth approach – the endogenous fertility approach.

1.5   THE ENDOGENOUS FERTILITY APPROACH

1.5.1   Theory

A theoretical model that captures the idea best can be found in Galor and Zang (1997), in which they incorporate *exogenous* fertility into a model by Galor and Zeira (1993) reviewed above.[11]

In Galor and Zeira (1993), each individual has only one child as in other typical OLG models. In order to incorporate the fertility rate, Galor and Zang (1997) assume that each individual has *n* children and that the bequest from their ancestor is equally allocated to them. By virtue of this, we are able to analyse the effect of the change in *n*, although it is given exogenously.

Unlike in Galor and Zeira (1993) individuals cannot work as unskilled labour in the first period. It is assumed that in the first period individuals only make a choice whether or not they invest in human capital. In the model, imperfection of the capital market is characterised by the assumption that individuals cannot borrow at all to finance their education. Hence, if an individual inherits wealth that is less than the cost of investing in human capital, she is not able to be a skilled worker in the second period. And the model focuses on the situation where individuals who inherit more than the cost of investing in human capital are better off if they invest in human capital. An assumption that investment in human capital is indivisible is present in this model as well.

The dynamics of bequest per child in the model of Galor and Zang (1997) is described as follows:

$$\frac{b_{t+1}}{n} = \begin{cases} \dfrac{1}{n}(1-\alpha)\left[\dfrac{b_t}{n}(1+r)+w_n\right], & \text{if } \dfrac{b_t}{n} < h \\[3mm] \dfrac{1}{n}(1-\alpha)\left[\left(\dfrac{b_t}{n}-h\right)(1+r)+w_s\right], & \text{if } \dfrac{b_t}{n} \geq h \end{cases} \quad \text{(GZA1.1)}$$

where the definitions of all symbols are the same as in the previous section. Since the assumption on the capital market is stronger, we only have to consider two cases. Figure 1.5 describes the situation.[12] As in Galor and Zeira (1993), in the long run this economy is divided into two groups of individuals, and the relative size of these groups depends upon initial wealth distribution.

From here they go one step further than Galor and Zeira (1993). In order to examine the effect of inequality and family size upon growth, they derive the growth rate between two consecutive periods during transition.

After some tedious calculation from equation (GZA1.1), it can be shown that per-family income (*y*) in period *t*+1 is:

$$y_{t+1} = \left[(1-\alpha)(1+r)\frac{y_t}{n} + w_n\right] + l_{t+1}^s\left[(w_s - w_n) - h(1+r)\right] \quad \text{(GZA1.2)}$$

where l_{t+1}^s is the share of skilled workers in period $t+1$. The growth rate of per-family income (g) is therefore:

$$g_t \equiv \frac{y_{t+1} - y_t}{y_t} = \frac{(1-\alpha)(1+r)}{n} - 1 + \frac{w_n}{y_t} + \frac{l_{t+1}^s}{y_t}\left[(w_s - w_n) - h(1+r)\right] \quad \text{(GZA1.3)}$$

The share of skilled workers in period $t+1$, l_{t+1}^s, is determined by the distribution of inheritances per child born in period t, and it depends upon the per-family income (y), the family size or fertility (n), the income distribution (Q) and the cost of human capital investment (h). Q is a measure of inequality and higher Q implies greater inequality.[13] Now we have the following relationship:

$$l_{t+1}^s = l_{t+1}^s(y_t, n, Q, h) \quad \text{(GZA1.4)}$$

Together with equation (GZA3), it follows:

$$g_t = G(y_t, n, Q, e, h) \quad \text{(GZA1.5)}$$

where e is 'basic' education that every individual obtains when they are young, so both w_n and w_s depend positively upon e.

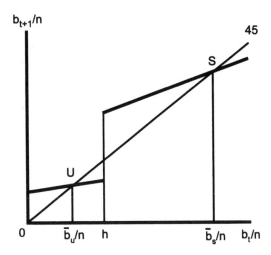

Figure 1.5   The Dynamics of Bequest

Taking first-order approximation of Equation (GZA1.5) yields the following:

$$g_t = G_n n + G_Q Q + G_{y_t} y_t + G_{en} e + G_h h + u_t. \qquad \text{(GZA1.6)}$$

Galor and Zang (1997) then mathematically show that $G_Q < 0$, that is, the growth rate of an economy, is higher, the more equally initial income is distributed. They also show that $G_n < 0$, that is, the growth rate of an economy, is higher, the lower the rate of fertility is.

1.5.2   Evidence

Following equation (GZA1.6), Galor and Zang (1997) specify their econometric model as follows:

$$GROWTH = 3.2038 - 0.2547FERT - 3.9620GINI - 0.2011GDP60$$
$$(3.190)\ (-2.182)\qquad (-2.211)\qquad (-6.056)$$

$$+ 0.0293PSCHOOL + 0.1785PUBEDU$$
$$(4.806)\qquad\qquad (1.820)$$

where *GINI* is the Gini coefficient and *PUBEDU* is the average public expenditure ratio relative to GNP for the period 1960–83. The estimation results are consistent with the empirical implication of the model: given the rate of fertility, the more equal an economy is, the higher is the growth rate; given income distribution, the lower the rate of fertility is, the higher is the growth rate. Estimates of all the coefficients have anticipated signs and are statistically significant at at least 5 per cent.

Regarding the magnitude of the effect of fertility and inequality upon growth, a reduction of the net fertility rate by a point leads to an increase in *GROWTH* of about 0.25 percentage point, and a one-standard-deviation decrease in *GINI* leads to an increase in *GROWTH* of 0.32 percentage point. Again, let us emphasise that these effects are not negligible.

Their estimation shows that both fertility and inequality have a significant effect upon economic growth. However, they do not deal with a system of equations as fertility is given exogenously in their model. In this sense, their result does not tell us anything about the joint decision on fertility and investment in human capital.

Perotti (1996) goes one step further in this respect and estimates the following system of equations.

$$GROWTH = 0.101 - 0.010GDP60 + 0.011PPPI - 0.016FERT$$
$$(6.27)\ (-4.45)\qquad\quad (1.29)\qquad (-5.10)$$

$$FERT = 8.903 - 0.466GDP60 - 1.380MSE + 1.368FSE - 10.310MIDDLE$$
$$(11.92)\ (-5.63)\qquad\quad (-3.19)\qquad (2.92)\qquad (-4.24)$$

where *FERT* is the net fertility rate average of 1965 and 1985 values.[14] The estimation results appear consistent with what the theory predicts. The negative estimate of the coefficient on *MIDDLE* in the second equation is as anticipated and is statistically significant. The estimate of the coefficient on *FERT* in the first equation is negative and statistically significant, which implies that the growth rate will be higher, the lower the fertility rate is. A one-standard-deviation increase in *MIDDLE* decreases *FERT* by about 0.55, which in turn increases *GROWTH* by approximately 0.87 percentage point. This magnitude is about a half of its standard deviation, which is not negligible.

Perotti (1996) then adds female secondary school enrolment ratio (*FSEC*) to the second equation. When *FSEC* is controlled for, the estimate of the coefficient on *MIDDLE* falls by approximately 40 per cent to −5.858. Perotti (1996) argues that this implies the joint determination of fertility and the secondary school enrolment ratio (investment in human capital) as the model suggests, because this shows that a significant part of *FERT* is explained by the effect of *MIDDLE* through *FSEC*. Perotti (1996) also estimates the system where the first equation includes *FSEC* instead of *FERT* and the dependent variable of the second equation is *FSEC*. In this case, when *FERT* is controlled for in the second equation, *MIDDLE* has no explanatory power for *FSEC*.

1.5.3   Discussion

Theoretical contribution of Galor and Zang (1997) is twofold. First, they derived the growth rate between two periods during transition, in order to observe the effect of inequality upon growth. This allows them to overcome the first problem in Galor and Zeira (1993) we previously pointed out. Secondly, more importantly, Galor and Zang (1997) have attempted to incorporate fertility into the model by Galor and Zeira (1993). This has allowed them to come up with an econometric model including the fertility rate, which has enabled them to see the effect of fertility upon growth. The rate of fertility is, however, still given exogenously, in which case neither their theoretical nor their econometric model captures the idea of the *joint* fertility and education *decision*.

Furthermore, Galor and Zang (1997) have not overcome the second problem in Galor and Zeira – the problem of defining inequality. They use inequality variable Q in their paper and mathematically show that growth is negatively related to this variable. However, this hinges upon the assumption they impose:[15]

$$\frac{\partial l_{t+1}^s}{\partial Q} < 0 \qquad\qquad (GZA1.7)$$

In order for this to hold in general, we need to use the same definition of inequality as in Galor and Zeira (1993). A model by Asano (2001) attempts to overcome these problems, but before we review it, let us turn to discuss the empirical side.

Aside from Galor and Zang (1997), we have reviewed a study by Perotti (1996). He specifies a system of equations in an ad hoc manner and has attempted to support the endogenous fertility approach. However, his estimation is problematic in the following sense. In specifying his econometric model, Perotti (1996) has a strong prior belief that fertility and investment in human capital are jointly determined. However, the way he has controlled for *FSEC* contradicts this prior belief, that is, *FSEC* is treated as *exogenous* to the system. If fertility and schooling decisions are made jointly, the system should be estimated with both *FERT* and *FSEC* being treated as *endogenous* variables.

Aside from this, a couple of issues regarding human capital are worth discussing. Note that female education is used in all estimations we introduced. However, it is under dispute which variable should be used as a proxy for human capital. In fact, Perotti (1996) also estimates the system using male education and reports that, rather surprisingly, some significant changes are observed between the estimation results.

Note also that in all the empirical studies we have reviewed, the flow of human capital, that is, the enrolment ratio, is used in the growth equation. In other empirical studies such as Barro and Lee (1994), in contrast, the stock of human capital, that is, the average years of schooling, is used in the growth equation. The choice of which variable to use usually has to do with the theoretical model underlying the econometric model. In Galor and Zang (1997), the flow of human capital *e* is used since they try to explain growth between two periods in transition. However, it is not clear why the flow of human capital is employed in Perotti (1996) in which the econometric model is specified in an ad hoc manner.

1.6   IS INEQUALITY REALLY HARMFUL TO GROWTH?

So far we have reviewed both the theoretical and the empirical literature that has attempted to show the negative inequality effects upon growth. The idea that reducing inequality will lead to higher growth appears to have become a common one in the literature. However, more recently, some studies have challenged this common agreement suggesting that the relationship could be non-monotonic. In addition, some evidence has been found supporting the idea that inequality *fosters* growth. Let us conclude this chapter by reviewing these studies and suggest possible further research directions.

To begin with, we review a study by Asano (2001).[16] Instead of incorporating *endogenous* fertility into the model of Galor and Zeira (1993), Asano (2001) incorporates inequality into a model by Ehrlich and Lui (1991) in which they dealt *simultaneously* with *endogenous* fertility, human capital accumulation and growth. While Ehrlich and Lui (1991) look at a country as a whole, Asano (2001) focuses upon a number of heterogeneous individuals within a country in order to incorporate inequality. Since the fertility decision is *endogenised* in this study, it has overcome one of the shortcomings in Galor and Zang (1997) we pointed out previously. Furthermore, instead of using a problematic definition of inequality in Galor and Zeira (1993) or Galor and Zang (1997),[17] Asano (2001) uses the coefficient of variation of income as a measure of inequality, which is common in the literature on inequality. This introduction of a more serious measure of inequality makes the analysis much more complicated, so Asano (2001) resorts to numerical simulations in order to observe how initial inequality can affect subsequent growth. Using numerical simulations, Asano (2001) conjectures that the effect of inequality upon growth may not be non-monotonic, that is, it depends upon an economy's demographic stage of development.[18]

Economies are classified into two types according to whether or not they have already begun the demographic transition, which is reflected in the observed rate of fertility, *FERT*. Asano (2001) estimates the following system of equations in order to test his conjecture:

$$\begin{cases} GROWTH = 0.121 - 0.012GDP65 - 0.005PPPI + 0.025FSEC \\ \qquad\quad (4.42) \quad (-3.26) \qquad\; (-0.85) \qquad\quad (2.02) \\[6pt] FSEC = 2.108 - 0.443FERT + 0.094FSE - 0.030GINI + 0.007FERTGINI \\ \qquad\;\; (3.68) \;\; (-3.14) \qquad\quad (3.33) \qquad (-2.08) \qquad\quad (2.16) \end{cases}$$

It is crucially different from Perotti's (1996) estimation in that both fertility (*FERT*) and investment in human capital (*FSEC*) are treated as endogenous variables in the system. A formal test for endogeneity confirms that fertility and education are determined jointly. The key in understanding the non-monotonic nature of the effect of inequality upon growth is the interactive term in the second equation, *FERTGINI*, which is a product of *FERT* and *GINI*. From a negative coefficient on *GINI* in the second equation and a positive coefficient on *FSEC* in the first equation, we know the effect of inequality upon growth would be negative if fertility were low. However, if fertility is high enough, the direction of the effect will be the other way round.

Another study, which is empirical, that suggests a non-monotonic nature according to democracy and non-democracy is Deininger and Squire (1998), in which they find a significant negative relationship between inequality and growth in non-democratic societies, but not in democratic ones. They claim that this finding undermines the plausibility of the first mechanism we reviewed – the endogenous fiscal policy approach – where democratic voting plays an important role. They separate their samples into two according to the values of the Gastil index of civil liberties (a country is democratic if the value of the index is below two) and in a growth regression for democratic countries, inequality does not have statistically significant effects upon growth, whereas for non-democratic ones it does.[19]

Barro (2000) also finds the non-monotonic nature of the effect of inequality upon growth according to how wealthy a country is. He finds that for poor countries inequality tends to retard growth but for rich countries inequality fosters growth, implying that the conventional argument prevails in rich countries but not in poor countries. Two remarks should be made. One remark is that the time period it deals with is different from the studies we have reviewed so far. The studies we have reviewed look at the effect of inequality upon growth *in the long run* (around 25 to 30 years), whereas Barro (2000) looks at it *in the short run*. This became possible due to the availability of better inequality data compiled by Deininger and Squire (1996). Barro (2001) has constructed his panel data set for a number of countries over three time periods, where each time period is 10 years. The other remark is related to the use of panel data. The estimator reported in the study is the random effect estimator. However, since a lagged value of a dependent variable is one of the independent variables in his regression, the estimator will be biased and inconsistent.[20] Hence we should be careful in interpreting his estimation results.

Empirical studies by Forbes (2000) and Li and Zou (1998) are both similar to Barro (2000) in that they use panel data and look at growth in the short run (one period is five years for both studies). Their regressions also include the lagged dependent variable as one of the independent variables, but they employ the GMM estimation that gives the consistent estimator. Their estimation results show that inequality fosters growth, which sounds like a revival of the conventional idea. Does this imply that developing countries will inevitably have to face a dilemma whether to reduce inequality or to achieve high economic growth? How can we explain the difference between these results and previous results supporting negative inequality upon growth? One answer to these questions is found in Forbes (2000). As she notes, the short-run inequality effect upon growth might be positive, but this effect may be weakened or even reversed in the longer run. Her estimation shows that the effect over 10-year periods is smaller than that for five-year periods. However, lack of data prevents us from checking the relationship for more than 10 years. Forbes (2000) also notes that her estimation still suffers from problems of omitting variables and measurement errors. In any case, reduced-form regressions by Forbes (2000), Barro (2000) and Li and Zou (1998) prompt us to further research into this matter.

The other issue where further research should be directed is uncovering the linkage between inequality and growth. Some research has been done on this issue as we have seen in the previous section, but theories possess shortcomings that have to be overcome and empirical studies that estimate a system of equations are rare. Furthermore, estimation results do not particularly favour the theories they are intended to support and some estimations appear to contain serious problems, such as an inappropriate definition of inequality, as discussed. Asano (2001), which we reviewed earlier in this section, is an attempt to overcome some of the problems in this area, and more research of this type would be welcome.

NOTES

1 For a more detailed survey on this causation, see Aghion et al. (1999) and Ray (1998).
2 In this case, the economy will be approaching the balanced growth path in the long run instead of approaching the steady state.
3 Bénabou (1996c) is also a survey paper on this topic. But his paper does not cover the fourth approach.
4 However, this result depends upon how inequality is defined. We discuss this issue in due course.
5 All values in the brackets are *t* statistics for the all regression results hereafter.
6 A democracy index by Jodice and Taylor (1988) is used to classify economies into democratic and non-democratic countries. If an average value over 1960–85 is 0.5, then a country is classified as democratic.
7 Persson and Tabellini (1994) have only 13 observations for their estimation, so a similar kind of analysis is meaningless.
8 Figures 1.1, 1.2 and 1.3 are taken from Murphy et al. (1993), pp. 410–11.
9 The following parameter values are used: $a=3.3$, $b=0.325$, $e=0.5$.
10 Figure 1.4 is taken from Galor and Zeira (1993), p. 41.
11 Asano (2001) attempts to incorporate *endogenous* fertility into a model by Galor and Zeira (1993) and also arrives at the conclusion that inequality is harmful to growth. An economy in his model, however, turns out to be destined to exhibit negative growth in any case, which is unrealistic. Asano (2001) also addresses another model in which he deals simultaneously with inequality, endogenous fertility, human capital and growth, which will be introduced in the concluding section of this chapter.
12 Figure 1.5 is taken from Galor and Zang (1997), p. 205.
13 This definition is problematic. We will discuss this issue shortly.
14 The net fertility rate is constructed as the total fertility rate multiplied by (1 minus infant mortality rate in the first year of life).
15 This is equation (33) in Galor and Zang (1997).
16 In fact, Dahan and Tsiddon (1998) and Morand (1999) also examine models in which fertility is endogenously determined with investment in human capital. Both studies discuss a very interesting relationship between demographic transition, income distribution and growth. However, neither

study addresses the question of how the initial inequality affects subsequent economic growth.

17 Dahan and Tsiddon (1998) use this definition as well.

18 This is slightly different from an implication that is derived by Dahan and Tsiddon (1998) and Morand (1999). They have emphasised the implication of the demographic transition for distribution of income, which ultimately affects growth.

19 One problem here, however, is that they give no justification for separating samples into two on statistical grounds. In fact, this problem can be observed in many growth studies; see discussion of this issue in Asano (2001).

20 Discussion of the dynamic panel estimation can be found in Arellano and Bond (1991) and Caselli et al. (1996).

REFERENCES

Acemoglu, Daron (1995), 'Reward Structures and the Allocation of Talent', *European Economic Review*, **39**, 17–33.

Aghion, Philippe and Patrick Bolton (1997), 'A Theory of Trickle-Down Growth and Development', *Review of Economic Studies*, **64**, 151–72.

Aghion, Philippe, Eve Caroli and Cecilia García-Peñalosa (1999), 'Inequality and Economic Growth: The Perspective of the New Growth Theories', *Journal of Economic Literature*, **37**, 1615–60.

Alesina, Alberto and Roberto Perotti (1996), 'Income Distribution, Political Instability, and Investment', *European Economic Review*, **40**, 1203–28.

Alesina, Alberto and Dani Rodrik (1994), 'Distributive Politics and Economic Growth', *Quarterly Journal of Economics*, **109**, 465–90.

Anand, Sudhir and R.S.M. Kanbur (1993), 'Inequality and Development: A Critique', *Journal of Development Economics*, **41**, 19–43.

Arellano, Manuel and Stephen Bond (1991), 'Some Tests of Specification for Panel Data: Monte Carlo Evidence and an Application to Employment Equations', *Review of Economic Studies*, **58**, 277–97.

Asano, Akihito (2001), 'Inequality and Economic Growth', PhD dissertation, The Australian National University.

Banerjee, Abhijit V. and Andrew F. Newman (1993), 'Occupational Choice and the Process of Development', *Journal of Political Economy*, **101**, 274–98.

Barro, Robert J. (1991), 'Economic Growth in a Cross Section of Countries', *Quarterly Journal of Economics*, **106**, 407–43.

Barro, Robert J. (2000), 'Inequality and Growth in a Panel of Countries', *Journal of Economic Growth*, **5**, 5–32.

Barro, Robert J. and Gary S. Becker (1989), 'Fertility Choice in a Model of Economic Growth', *Econometrica*, **57**, 481–501.

Barro, Robert J. and Jong-Wha Lee (1994), 'Sources of Economic Growth', *Carnegie-Rochester Conference Series on Public Policy*, **40**, 1–46.

Barro, Robert J. and Xavier Sala-i-Martin (1995), *Economic Growth*, McGraw-Hill.

Becker Gary S. and Robert J. Barro (1988), 'A Reformulation of the Economic Theory of Fertility', *Quarterly Journal of Economics*, **103**, 1–25.

Becker Gary S., Kevin M. Murphy and Robert Tamura (1990), 'Human Capital, Fertility, and Economic Growth', *Journal of Political Economy*, **98**, S12–37.

Bénabou, Roland (1993), 'Working of a City: Location, Education, and Production', *Quarterly Journal of Economics*, **108**, 619–52.

Bénabou, Roland (1996a), 'Equity and Efficiency in Human Capital Investment: The Local Connection', *Review of Economic Studies*, **63**, 237–64.

Bénabou, Roland (1996b), 'Heterogeneity, Stratification, and Growth: Macroeconomic Implications of Community Structure and School Finance', *American Economic Review*, **86**, 584–609.

Bénabou, Roland (1996c), 'Inequality and Growth', *NBER Macroeconomics Annual*, 11–74.

Benhabib, Jess and Aldo Rustichini (1996), 'Social Conflict and Growth', *Journal of Economic Growth*, **1**, 125–42.

Benhabib, Jess and Mark M. Spiegel (1994), 'The Role of Human Capital in Economic Development: Evidence from Aggregate Cross-Country Data', *Journal of Monetary Economics*, **34**, 143–73.

Bertola, Giuseppe (1993), 'Factor Shares and Savings in Endogenous Growth', *American Economic Review*, **83**, 1184–98.

Birdsall, Nancy et al. (1995), 'Inequality and Growth Reconsidered: Lessons from East Asia', *World Bank Economic Review*, **9**, 477–508.

Bourguignon, François (1981), 'Pareto Superiority of Unegalitarian Equilibria in Stiglitz' Model of Wealth Distribution with Convex Saving Function', *Econometrica*, **49**, 1469–75.

Brander, James A. and Steve Dowrick (1994), 'The Role of Fertility and Population in Economic Growth', *Journal of Population Economics*, **7**, 1–25.

Caselli, Francesco, Gerardo Esquivel and Fernando Lefort (1996), 'Reopening the Convergence Debate: A New Look at Cross-Country Growth Empirics', *Journal of Economic Growth*, **1**, 363–89.

Clarke, George R.G. (1995), 'More Evidence on Income Distribution and Growth', *Journal of Development Economics*, **47**, 403–27.

Dahan, Momi and Daniel Tsiddon (1998), 'Demographic Transition, Income Distribution, and Economic Growth', *Journal of Economic Growth*, **3**, 29–52.

Deininger, Klaus and Lyn Squire (1996), 'A New Data Set Measuring Income Inequality', *The World Bank Economic Review*, **10**, 565–91.

Deininger, Klaus and Lyn Squire (1998), 'New Ways of Looking at Old Issues: Inequality and Growth', *Journal of Development Economics*, **57**, 259–87.

Durlauf, Steven N. (1994), 'Spillovers, Stratification, and Inequality', *European Economic Review*, **38**, 836–45.

Ehrlich, Isaac and Francis T. Lui (1991), 'Intergenerational Trade, Longevity, and Economic Growth', *Journal of Political Economy*, **99**, 1029–59.

Fernandez, Raquel and Richard Rogerson (1996), 'Income Distribution, Communities, and the Quality of Public Education', *Quarterly Journal of Economics*, **111**, 135–64.

Forbes (2000), 'A Reassessment of the Relationship Between Inequality and Growth', *American Economic Review*, **90**, 869–87.

Galor, Oded and Joseph Zeira (1993), 'Income Distribution and Macroeconomics', *Review of Economic Studies*, **60**, 35–52.

Galor, Oded and Hyoungsoo Zang (1997), 'Fertility, Income Distribution, and Economic Growth: Theory and Cross-country Evidence', *Japan and the World Economy*, **9**, 197–229.

Grossman, Herschel I. (1991), 'A General Equilibrium Model of Insurrections', *American Economic Review*, **81**, 912–21.

Grossman, Herschel I. (1994), 'Production, Appropriation, and Land Reform', *American Economic Review*, **84**, 705–12.

Grossman, Herschel I. and Minseong Kim (1996), 'Predation and Accumulation', *Journal of Economic Growth*, **1**, 333–50.

Jodice, D. and D.L. Taylor (1988), *World Handbook of Social and Political Indicators*, Connecticut: Yale University Press.

Kaldor, Nicholas (1961), 'Capital Accumulation and Economic Growth', in D.C. Hague (ed.), *The Theory of Capital*, London: Macmillan.

Kelley, Allen C. (1988), 'Economic Consequences of Population Change in the Third World', *Journal of Economic Literature*, **26**, 1685–728.

Kuznets, Simon (1955), 'Economic Growth and Income Inequality', *American Economic Review*, **45**, 1–25.

Li, Hongyi and Heng-fu Zou (1998), 'Income Inequality Is Not Harmful for Growth: Theory and Evidence', *Review of Development Economics*, **2**, 318–34.

Morand, Olivier F. (1999), 'Endogenous Fertility, Income Distribution, and Growth', *Journal of Economic Growth*, **4**, 331–49.

Murphy, Kevin M. et al. (1993), 'Why is Rent-Seeking So Costly to Growth?' *American Economic Review*, **83**, 409–13.

North, Douglass C. (1981), *Structure and Change in Economic History*, New York: Norton.

Perotti, Roberto (1993), 'Political Equilibrium, Income Distribution, and Growth', *Review of Economic Studies*, **60**, 755–76.

Perotti, Roberto (1994), 'Income Distribution, and Investment', *European Economic Review*, **38**, 827–35.

Perotti, Roberto (1996), 'Growth, Income Distribution, and Democracy: What the Data Say', *Journal of Economic Growth*, **1**, 149–87.

Persson, Torsten and Guido Tabellini (1992a), 'Growth, Distribution and Politics', in Cukierman et al. (eds), *Political Economy, Growth, and Business Cycles*, Cambridge, MA: MIT Press.

Persson, Torsten and Guido Tabellini (1992b), 'Growth, Distribution and Politics', *European Economic Review*, **36**, 593–602.

Persson, Torsten and Guido Tabellini (1994), 'Is Inequality Harmful for Growth?' *American Economic Review*, **84**, 600–21.

Piketty, Thomas (1997), 'The Dynamics of Wealth Distribution and the Interest Rate with Credit Rationing', *Review of Economic Studies*, **64**, 173–89.

Ravallion, Martin and Shaohua Chen (1997), 'What Can New Survey Data Tell Us about Recent Changes in Distribution and Poverty?', *World Bank Economic Review*, **11**, 357–82.

Ray, Debraj (1998), *Development Economics*, Princeton, NJ: Princeton University Press.

Stiglitz, J.E. (1969), 'Distribution of Income and Wealth among Individuals', *Econometrica*, **37**, 382–97.

Saint-Paul, Gilles and Thierry Verdier (1997), 'Power, Distributive Conflicts, and Multiple Growth Paths', *Journal of Economic Growth*, **2**, 155–68.

Tornell, Aaron and Andrés Velasco (1992), 'The Tragedy of the Commons and Economic Growth: Why Does Capital Flow from Poor to Rich Countries?', *Journal of Political Economy*, **100**, 1208–31.

2 Growth and Income Inequality in Advanced, Capitalist, Stable Economies: Evidence from Australia

Ross Guest

2.1 INTRODUCTION

The traditional view that an economy faces a trade-off between equity and economic growth has been called into question by recent empirical evidence and new developments in growth theory and political economy research. Cross-country studies by Persson and Tabellini (1994) and Perotti (1996) find that reducing inequality in income distribution boosts economic growth, contrary to the traditional view that reducing inequality inhibits incentives and therefore growth. This new evidence and the theoretical developments that help explain the evidence are evaluated in detail by Aghion, Caroli and Garcia-Penalosa (1999). They conclude that while reducing inequality does boost growth, higher growth may well increase inequality at least in the short term. This implies the need for sustained income redistribution in order to maintain growth. However, Aghion et al. (1999) call for further empirical evidence – especially time series evidence – on the existence and direction of causality between growth and inequality. This is echoed by Forbes (2000) who points out that typical cross-country regressions cannot address the important policy question of how changes in inequality for a particular country affect the growth rate for that country. In response to these calls for time series evidence, this study uses annual time series data for Australia to test for a bi-directional relationship between economic growth and income inequality. The study is a replication, with some differences in variables and data, of that in Hayes et al. in Bergstrand et al. (1994) for the US economy for the period 1948–90. They find that the relationship between growth, more precisely productivity growth, and income inequality runs both ways and they conclude that policies designed to affect productivity growth and income inequality should be considered simultaneously.

There are likely to be differences in the relationship between growth and inequality in advanced, capitalist, stable economies and that in LDCs and economies in transition. The reasons can be traced to differences in their rates of technical progress and level of development of their capital markets (see Section 2.2). This study refers to the former group of countries, illustrated by evidence from Australia, and thus compares to the study of the USA in Hayes et al. (1994).

The question of whether a relationship between growth and inequality exists, and if so whether the causality (Granger 1969) runs from growth to inequality or from inequality to growth, or in both directions, is more than an academic curiosity. It is important for macroeconomic policy and redistributive policy. In particular, the existence of bi-directional causality of the type found by Aghion et al. (1999) could considerably complicate the policy assignment currently adopted in Australia. The current assignment of policies to objectives in Australia can be summarised as follows. Monetary policy is assigned the role of achieving sustained low-inflationary growth (RBA 2000, p. 1), while the primary objective of fiscal policy is to achieve fiscal balance over the economic cycle (Commonwealth Budget Paper No. 1, 2000, Statement 1, p. 1). In the case of both monetary and fiscal policy economic growth and 'full' employment are ultimate goals to be achieved through the medium-term target of low (that is, 2–3 per cent) inflation (monetary policy) and an appropriate level of public sector saving (fiscal policy). Neither monetary policy nor fiscal policy, in terms of its overall stance, is currently assigned any redistributive role. So whilst growth is an important consideration in the overall setting of monetary and fiscal policy, income distribution is not. Rather, distributional objectives are achieved through other public policies – in particular, the tax mix, government expenditures and transfers. These distributive objectives are much more controversial than the appropriate rates of growth, inflation and national saving. For example, the focus of the Senate Select Committee on a New Tax System was mostly on the redistributive effects of the GST package (Australian Senate 1999). Other examples include the debates over the targeting of welfare and minimum wages.

Aghion et al. (1999) suggest that the appropriate policy response to the particular bi-directional causality between growth and inequality that they found, in which reducing inequality boosts growth but this in turn raises inequality, is to adopt a sustained redistributive policy. But one could go further, as do Hayes et al. (1994), and argue for macro policy and redistributive policy to be modelled simultaneously, because policies aimed at the growth rate will affect income distribution and vice versa. In that case both the monetary and the fiscal authorities would need to formulate policies jointly in achieving the simultaneous objectives of inflation (and growth), national saving and income distribution.

This could in turn have implications for the independence of the central bank and could amount to a quite radical change in the conduct of economic policy.

The remainder of the chapter is organised as follows. Section 2.2 outlines the old and new views on the growth–inequality relationship and the recent empirical evidence. Section 2.3 describes the data and methodology adopted in this study. Section 2.4 presents the results and Section 2.5 concludes the chapter.

2.2   THE OLD AND NEW VIEWS: THEORY AND EVIDENCE

The old view that the causality runs from inequality to growth, with greater inequality leading to higher growth, was based on three main arguments (Aghion et al. 1999). The first argument, formalised by Stiglitz (1969) in the context of a Solow growth model, is based on the observation that the marginal propensity to save of the rich is higher than that of the poor. Hence a redistribution of income to the rich is growth-enhancing because the resulting increase in saving leads to higher growth. A modern version of this view is based on an extension of the life-cycle saving hypothesis (LCH) to include bequests.[1] If bequests are a luxury, saving rates should be higher for wealthier people and hence greater inequality implies higher aggregate saving and hence growth (Schmidt-Hebbel and Serven 1999, p. 152).[2] The second argument applies to economies without a well-functioning capital market, especially for shares, and so applies to transition economies such as those in Eastern Europe rather than to advanced capitalist economies such as Australia (Aghion et al. 1999, p. 1620). This argument is that much investment is lumpy, such as a new industrial activity, and therefore requires significant individual or family wealth to finance it. Therefore greater inequality of income and wealth implies greater availability of investment finance. The third argument for the old view derives from the principle that the return to saving depends on the after-tax interest rate. Hence, higher taxes required to reduce inequality also reduce the return to saving and therefore reduce investment and growth (Aghion et al. 1999, p. 1620).

The traditional trade-off view was reinforced by the Kuznets hypothesis (Kuznets 1963). Kuznets (1963) found an inverted U-shaped relation between inequality and GNP per head for a cross-section of countries over time. He explained this by the shift in population from mainly rural to mainly industrial/ urban activities during the process of development. Given that industrial activity generates a more unequal distribution of income than does rural activity, the population shift during the development phase leads to greater income inequality. The Kuznets hypothesis has been extended and modelled more formally by Anand and Kanbar (1993). However, the recent empirical study by Deininger and Squire (1998) found little support for the Kuznets hypothesis.

Further theoretical and empirical evidence on the effect of growth on inequality is provided by Aghion et al. (1999). They find that the increase in income inequality experienced by many developed countries, including Australia, in the last one to two decades can be traced to technical progress; because it raises the premium for skilled labour and therefore increases income inequality. Although they do note that this increased inequality may taper off once the new technologies are sufficiently spread among workers so that nearly all workers have had some experience with it.[3]

The new view is that there is no growth–equity trade-off. Rather, reducing inequality enhances growth. There are two main strands to this view. One derives from developments in political economy research in which fiscal policy is modelled as endogenous and determined by majority voting rule (Alesina and Rodrik 1994; Persson and Tabellini 1994, Diekmann 1996). In these models greater inequality leads to political pressure for redistributive taxation, on capital in particular, which reduces growth. Also, inequality can create political instability and therefore macroeconomic volatility which inhibits investment (Perotti 1996). The second strand to the new view draws on developments in new growth theory that emphasise heterogeneous consumers and imperfect capital markets (Aghion et al. 1999, p. 1621). As with the old view, there are several mechanisms that may operate. One mechanism, given the assumption of restrictions on borrowing and lending, is that the rich have a lower marginal product of capital than the poor and therefore a redistribution away from the rich to the poor can create investment opportunities. A second mechanism is based on incentive effects in the case of limited liability companies. Limited liability means that the more wealth a borrower/investor has, the greater the incentive to supply effort to make the investment succeed because the more the investor can keep of the marginal returns from effort. Therefore redistributing wealth towards relatively poor investors will have a positive effect on their effort incentives and therefore on growth (Banerjee and Newman 1993; Aghion and Bolton 1997). A third mechanism is that greater inequality may cause greater dispersion in the distribution of investments in human capital. This increases the variance of workers' skills and therefore workers may not 'mesh' as efficiently, reducing labour productivity (Hayes et al. 1994).

On the effect of inequality on growth, the latest empirical evidence tends to support the new view that inequality is harmful for growth (Persson and Tabellini 1994; Alesina and Rodrik 1994; Perotti 1996). The contrary view, that inequality has a positive effect on growth, is found in the recent study by Forbes (2000). With respect to the effect of growth on inequality, some studies have found that growth reduces inequality, implying a virtuous circle in which redistributive policies to reduce inequality not only boost growth but the resulting growth further reduces inequality (Perotti 1996; Easterly and Rebelo 1993). The method of capturing this simultaneity is a two-stage least squares regression using growth and a measure of redistribution (for instance, the marginal income tax rate) as the two endogenous variables. On the other hand, these cross-country regressions have been criticised for their ad hoc specifications and the lack of robustness of the results (Temple 1999 in Aghion et al. 1999). The structural equation modelling in the two-stage least squares framework can also be criticised for the potentially incorrect assumptions it imposes on the true data generating process (Hayes et al. 1994).

This criticism is overcome by using a vector autoregression (VAR) framework. For example, Hayes et al. (1994) test for bi-directional causality between income inequality and changes in productivity for the USA from 1948 to 1990. This is done by estimating a bivariate and a multivariate VAR model to search for feedback between productivity change and inequality. They find that feedback does in fact exist and conclude that this has clear public policy implications of the kind discussed in the introduction.

The study here can also be seen as an extension of the single equation model for Australia in Guest and Doraisami (1994). The aim of that study was to determine the impact of both cyclical and secular influences on income inequality for Australia, including a disaggregation of the income distribution by gender. However, the model did not allow for the possibility of endogeneity in the macroeconomic variables on the right hand side of the equation – that is, the possibility of a bi-directional relationship. Nor did it include productivity growth explicitly, in the context of the debate about the new and old views of the growth– inequality relationship.

2.3   DATA AND METHODOLOGY

The data consist of annual observations from 1950–51 to 1998–99.[4] The two dependent variables are the growth rates of average labour productivity and the Gini coefficient of the distribution of after-tax income of individuals, where income is taxable income. The data on taxable incomes is available from Taxation Statistics published by the Australian Taxation Office. The advantages and limitations of using taxable income of individuals in determining a measure of income inequality, compared with more conventional measures such as gross market income of households as measured in the ABS Income Survey, are discussed in Guest and McDonald (1999) and Guest and Doraisami (1994). These can be summarised as follows. The advantages are: (i) Taxation Statistics data are not subject to the sampling error inherent in the ABS Income Survey data and exacerbated by the voluntary nature of the survey; (ii) taxable income gives a better measure of living standards than gross market income to the extent that necessary expenses incurred in earning gross income are deducted to arrive at taxable income; (iii) taxable income data are available as an annual series rather than four yearly as is the case for the ABS data. The added information from annual observations is useful for analytical purposes such as the regression analysis conducted in this study. The disadvantages are: (i) using the individual as the income unit can lead to an overestimate of inequality in living standards compared with using the household as the income unit. This occurs to the extent that larger households imply lower housing costs and other living expenses per household member; and to the extent that individuals with low taxable incomes are more likely to share housing and other living expenses with others in a household;[5] (ii) some individuals whose incomes are below the income tax threshold may not be required to submit a tax return and therefore will not be recorded in the data; (iii) taxable income data are subject to both the vagaries of the tax laws and tax avoidance/evasion, which tends to lead to understatement of high incomes which in turn implies an underestimate of income inequality. These advantages and disadvantages suggest that there is a case both for and against the use of annual taxable income data for individuals in the analysis of relationships between income inequality and other variables.

After-tax income is defined as taxable income less income tax payable. Income tax is deducted in arriving at the adopted income measure because taxation is one of several macroeconomic phenomena which influence both inequality and productivity and which therefore must be controlled for in analysing the relationship between those two variables. Using after tax income controls for the effect of taxation on disposable income directly. This is arguably better than adopting some pre-tax measure of income and controlling for tax indirectly by including a tax variable in the regression model, such as the marginal tax rate, as done in Hayes et al. (in Bergstrand et al. 1994).

The Gini coefficient is adopted as the measure of inequality since it is widely accepted in the literature (including in Hayes et al. in Bergstrand et al. 1994) and it generates inequality outcomes for Australia that differ very little from those derived from measures of income inequality (see, for example, Guest and McDonald 1999). The (interpolated) after-tax Gini coefficient is calculated from the distribution of after-tax income in deciles, as follows:[6]

$$Gini = 0.9 - 0.2 \sum_{i=1}^{9} S_i \qquad (2.1)$$

where S_i is the cumulative share of total after-tax income received by the lowest *i*th decile of taxpayers ranked by their after-tax income.

Figure 2.1 presents time series of the Gini coefficients of the distribution of taxable incomes and after-tax incomes of individuals and the growth of real GDP per capita for the sample period 1950–51 to 1998–99.[7] The gap between the Gini coefficients for the taxable and after-tax incomes indicates the degree of progressivity of the tax system. This is also plotted in the figure. The apparent upward trend in the series, GINI-ATGINI, indicating tax progressivity, is

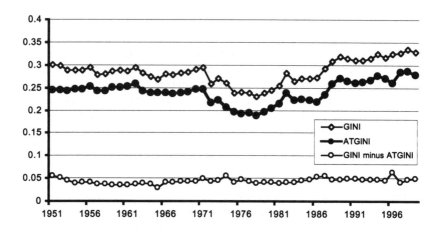

Figure 2.1   Distribution of Income in Australia, 1950–51 to 1998–99

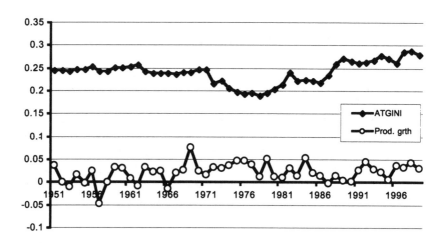

Figure 2.2   Productivity Growth and After-Tax Income Distribution

confirmed by an ordinary least squares regression (not reported) of the series on a time trend which shows a positive parameter estimate on the trend variable significant at 1 per cent. Hence, the tax system has become more progressive over time, which has tended to reduce the degree of after-tax income inequality relative to inequality before tax.

The indicator of economic growth adopted here is the growth rate of average labour productivity, following Hayes et al. in Bergstrand et al. (1994). This is defined as real GDP per hours worked.[8] Figure 2.2 plots the after-tax Gini coefficient and the growth rate of average labour productivity. Inspection of Figure 2.2 does not reveal a clear relationship between these two variables.

Several types of model have been applied in prior studies of the relationship between growth and inequality. The most restrictive type of model is the OLS model, adopted in Alesina and Rodrik (1994), Persson and Tabellini (1994), Perotti (1996), Anand and Kanbur (1993), Deininger and Squire (1998) and, for Australia, Guest and Doraisami (1994). In these models either growth or inequality is the dependent variable and the other of these two variables is one of several independent variables, where the other independent variables are included to avoid omitted variable bias. Most of these studies do recognise endogeneity of both growth and inequality as a problem in the OLS model and therefore also report the results of simultaneous equation estimation typically using two-stage least squares. A less restrictive methodology is the VAR approach which overcomes the criticism of the simultaneous equations structural model that it is difficult to find appropriate exogenous variables in order to identify each equation. The VAR approach is used in Hayes et al. in Bergstrand et al. (1994) and their approach is followed closely in this study. The main difference lies in the alternative measures of income and average labour productivity. Their income unit is the family and their data are derived from 'Current Population Reports' and hence is not taxable income. Also, their measure of labour productivity uses employees whereas hours worked is used here.

Their approach, followed here, is to begin with a simple bivariate VAR, using the Gini coefficient and labour productivity as the two variables, and then test for Granger causality. This is followed by a multivariate VAR model, in which several macroeconomic variables are included to attempt to control for factors that are likely to influence growth and inequality. These variables are the unemployment rate, income transfers from government, and marginal tax rates (not required here as discussed above). Hayes et al. find, using the bivariate model, evidence that productivity growth 'Granger causes' income inequality growth (at 5 per cent) and that income inequality growth 'Granger causes' productivity growth (at 10 per cent). They find that greater productivity growth tends to lead to lower inequality growth but the coefficient signs on the first and second lags of inequality growth were mixed in the regression with productivity growth as the dependent variable.

Dickey-Fuller tests for stationarity were conducted for all variables, with a constant and trend term included in the regressions. Productivity growth and transfers[9] were found to be the only stationary variables. However, the growth rates of all variables were found to be stationary and so all variables in the VAR model are measured in growth rates.

The VAR model is specified as

$$Z_t = \sum_{k=1}^{m} A_k Z_{t-k} + \mu_t \qquad (2.2)$$

where Z is a (nx1) vector of endogenous variables, and A is a (nxn) vector of parameters. Tests are conducted for the lag length m and the exogeneity of the variables in Z. The test adopted here for exogeneity is a multivariate extension of the Granger causality test. This is done by estimating (2.2) with all variables included and then re-estimating (2.2) by excluding each of the variables, one at a time. The test is to compare the likelihood ratio statistic (LRS), based on the variance–covariance matrix of residuals of the restricted and unrestricted models, with the critical value from a χ^2 distribution. The value of LRS is given by $(T-c)\left(\log|\Sigma_r| - \log|\Sigma_u|\right)$, where T is the number of usable observations, $|\Sigma|$ is the determinant of the variance/covariance matrix of the residuals, and c is the number of parameters estimated in each equation of the unrestricted system. The null hypothesis is exogeneity of the omitted variable. The appropriate lag length is chosen by estimating models with various lag lengths and choosing the model with the lowest value of the Akaike Information Criterion statistic which is given by $T \log|\Sigma| + 2N$, where $|\Sigma|$ is the determinant of the variance/ covariance matrix of the residuals and N is the total number of parameters estimated in all equations.

2.4   RESULTS

Tables 2.3 and 2.4 (Appendix) present the results of the bivariate and multivariate models respectively. In each table the far right-hand columns give the corresponding results in Hayes et al. in Bergstrand et al. (1994) for comparison. In the bivariate model results are presented for one-, two- and three-period lags. The value of the AIC statistic is extremely close in each case, especially for the one- and two-period lags for which the AIC values are higher than for the three-lag model; and there is no qualitative difference in results between the models with different lags (as expected). The same pattern was observed for the one-, two- and three-lag versions of the multivariate model. For consistency with Hayes et al., and for parsimony, we focus the discussion on the results of the two-period lag, which is the only case reported in Hayes et al.

There is no evidence from the bivariate model that productivity growth 'Granger causes' inequality growth. This differs from Hayes et al. who found Granger causality from productivity growth to inequality growth. There is, however, evidence (p value=0.00) that inequality growth 'Granger causes' (lower) productivity growth. In this case the coefficient sign on the first lag is negative. The coefficient sign on the second lag is positive but smaller and not significant at 5 per cent. This is a similar result to that in Hayes et al., including the mixed signs on the first and second lags. However, in their results the p values on the two lags were above 0.1 and of approximately the same size (see comparison in Table 2.3). The result here then is somewhat stronger than that in Hayes et al. with respect to Granger causality from inequality growth to lower productivity growth. This supports the new view that inequality is harmful for growth and that reductions in inequality tend to boost growth. The lack of evidence for causality in the opposite direction – from productivity growth to inequality – supports neither the old nor the new view. However, given the evidence that inequality is harmful for growth, the overall results from the bivariate model favour the new view. The main qualification here is that the equation fit is poor where productivity growth is the dependent variable, as indicated by the low R^2, suggesting the possibility of omitted variable bias. On the other hand, the equation fit is not much worse than in Hayes et al. and, indeed, for the other regression it is much better, 0.77 compared with 0.10 in Hayes et al.

Tests of exogeneity in the multivariate model resulted in rejection of the null hypothesis (at 1-per-cent significance) of exogeneity for each of the four variables. The values of the LRS were: 192.58 for transfers/GDP, 104.51 for unem, 228.33 for ATGini, 267.47 for prod. grth. This supports the case for a multivariate analysis due to feedback from the other economic variables, growth in unemployment and transfers, on both productivity growth and inequality growth. Hayes et al. came to the same conclusion based on their exogeneity tests. As in the bivariate model, the values of the AIC statistic for lags of one, two and three are extremely close and, for comparison with Hayes et al., the discussion is restricted to the results of the two-lag model.

The qualitative results in the bivariate model carry over to the multivariate model with respect to the ˙growth–inequality relationship (Table 2.4). There is no evidence in the multivariate model that productivity growth leads to either higher or lower inequality. Although the coefficients on productivity growth are negative, suggesting that higher productivity growth lowers inequality growth, the p values are 0.20 and 0.35 on the first and second lags, respectively. As in the bivariate model, the fit of this equation (with growth in after-tax Gini as the dependent variable) is much higher (adj. $R^2 = 0.81$) than for the other equations and much higher than that found in Hayes et al. ($R^2 = 0.34$). There is evidence, in the equation with productivity growth as the dependent variable, that greater inequality growth leads to lower productivity growth as found in the bivariate model. The coefficient on the first lag of inequality growth (for the two lag model) is –0.19 (p = 0.06). The coefficient on the second lag is positive but smaller and with a higher p value (0.10), as in the bivariate model. Again, this finding is qualified by the low adj. R^2.

2.5   CONCLUSION

This study was motivated by recent empirical and theoretical developments that cast doubt on the traditional view that policy makers face a trade-off between the goals of equity and economic growth. A new view is emerging that inequality may be harmful for growth and that growth may not increase inequality. The new view is based on cross-country empirical studies and developments in growth theory and political economy theory. The approach adopted here is a close replication of that in Hayes et al. (1994) for the US economy over a similar period. The conclusions here and in Hayes et al. are more likely to apply to advanced, capitalist, stable economies than to LDCs and economies in transition because the nature of the relationship between growth and inequality is likely to differ between the two types of economy.

The results of the two studies are is some respects parallel and in other respects divergent. Most importantly, while Hayes et al. find a significant bi-directional relationship between inquality growth and productivity growth, the results here support a one-way relationship running from inequality to growth. The sign of that relationship is negative in both studies, meaning that greater inequality growth leads to lower productivity growth. Both studies support the new view of the growth–inequality relationship that inequality is harmful for growth rather than the old view that there is a positive relationship between inequality and growth.

However, because the results here do not support a bi-directional relationship, the conclusion in Hayes that policies designed to affect inequality and growth ought to be considered simultantaneously is not supported in this study. Rather, the conclusion here is that policies that reduce inquality are win–win policies in the sense that they can also be expected to boost productivity growth. This does have implications for policies that shift the tax mix from income to consumption with the aim of achieving efficiency gains. If such policies result in greater inequality it is likely that the gains in productivity will be offset to some extent. There are also implications for the debate about high marginal tax rates in Australia. The evidence here is that lowering the top marginal tax rate, ceteris paribus, would tend to lower productivity growth.

NOTE

1   The LCH was first introduced by Modigliani and Brumberg (1954). For a review see Deaton (1992).

2   On the other hand, if the poor face greater uncertainty, are more risk-averse, or have less access to risk diversification than the rich, they may have higher precautionary saving than the rich. In this case a redistribution

from the rich to the poor could boost aggregate saving and growth (Schmidt-Hebbel and Serven 1999, p. 153).

3   This suggests a kind of alternative Kuznets effect.

4   1998–99 is the latest year for which taxable income data are available at the time of writing.

5   Also, as Ternowetsky (1979, p. 18) points out, we cannot say whether the individual's income is supplementing family income or whether it is derived by some income splitting mechanism to ease the spouse's tax burden.

6   This is derived from the following approximation for the Gini coefficient (see, for example, Yao 1997, 1999): $Gini = 1 - \sum_{i=1}^{n} p_i \left(2 \sum_{k=1}^{i} S_i - w_i \right)$ where w_i is the income share of the ith group, p_i is the relative population frequency of the ith group and S_i is as defined above.

7   Data on GDP at constant prices are from ABS Catalogue 5204.0.

8   Data sources are: real GDP from ABS Cat. No. 5206; hours worked from ABS Cat. No. 5204.

9   Transfers are defined as total social assistance benefit payments from government as a proportion of GDP (ABS Cat. No. 5206). The unemployment rate is sourced from ABS Cat. No. 6203.

APPENDIX: TABLES OF DATA AND RESULTS

Table 2.1
Various Data, 1951–99: Gini, After-Tax Gini, Productivity Growth, Transfers to GDP Ratio and Unemployment Rate

	GINI	ATGINI	Prod. grth	Trf/GDP	Unem rate
1951	0.3020	0.2454	0.0373	0.0052	0.0040
1952	0.2986	0.2457	0.0015	0.0042	0.0147
1953	0.2901	0.2436	−0.0088	0.0044	0.0200
1954	0.2887	0.2480	0.0181	0.0042	0.0080
1955	0.2904	0.2477	−0.0011	0.0043	0.0067
1956	0.2964	0.2542	0.0262	0.0044	0.0107
1957	0.2804	0.2425	−0.0462	0.0043	0.0173
1958	0.2814	0.2425	0.0004	0.0046	0.0227
1959	0.2869	0.2506	0.0333	0.0047	0.0227
1960	0.2886	0.2518	0.0310	0.0046	0.0160
1961	0.2880	0.2525	0.0082	0.0061	0.0347
1962	0.2958	0.2585	−0.0075	0.0067	0.0280
1963	0.2841	0.2437	0.0331	0.0065	0.0253
1964	0.2759	0.2387	0.0242	0.0067	0.0147
1965	0.2685	0.2386	0.0255	0.0067	0.0120
1966	0.2824	0.2398	−0.0144	0.0069	0.0120
1967	0.2785	0.2371	0.0222	0.0069	0.0160
1968	0.2840	0.2401	0.0268	0.0069	0.0170
1969	0.2845	0.2409	0.0772	0.0069	0.0160
1970	0.2917	0.2479	0.0252	0.0073	0.0150
1971	0.2964	0.2469	0.0180	0.0075	0.0140
1972	0.2603	0.2168	0.0326	0.0082	0.0170
1973	0.2704	0.2234	0.0318	0.0099	0.0250
1974	0.2623	0.2063	0.0373	0.0118	0.0180
1975	0.2397	0.1970	0.0475	0.0160	0.0240
1976	0.2412	0.1938	0.0481	0.0211	0.0460
1977	0.2395	0.1958	0.0406	0.0265	0.0470
1978	0.2305	0.1894	0.0140	0.0312	0.0570
1979	0.2384	0.1965	0.0521	0.0323	0.0620
1980	0.2458	0.2041	0.0122	0.0339	0.0590
1981	0.2558	0.2147	0.0101	0.0367	0.0590
1982	0.2824	0.2402	0.0319	0.0407	0.0560

(continued)

Table 2.1 (continued)
Various Data, 1951–99: Gini, After-Tax Gini, Productivity Growth,
Transfers to GDP Ratio, and Unemployment Rate

	GINI	ATGINI	Prod. grth	Trf/GDP	Unem. rate
1983	0.2653	0.2225	0.0154	0.0514	0.0670
1984	0.2704	0.2251	0.0537	0.0575	0.0990
1985	0.2711	0.2227	0.0216	0.0590	0.0850
1986	0.2729	0.2182	0.0155	0.0607	0.0790
1987	0.2925	0.2353	−0.0014	0.0635	0.0800
1988	0.3093	0.2602	0.0145	0.0650	0.0780
1989	0.3188	0.2713	0.0056	0.0659	0.0680
1990	0.3156	0.2649	0.0025	0.0694	0.0570
1991	0.3115	0.2622	0.0281	0.0809	0.0700
1992	0.3125	0.2636	0.0463	0.0937	0.0950
1993	0.3156	0.2673	0.0287	0.0983	0.1050
1994	0.3251	0.2772	0.0224	0.1019	0.1070
1995	0.3185	0.2718	0.0063	0.1019	0.0920
1996	0.3258	0.2618	0.0376	0.1045	0.0810
1997	0.3275	0.2858	0.0329	0.1066	0.0850
1998	0.3349	0.2875	0.0441	0.1033	0.0830
1999	0.3302	0.2803	0.0320	0.1049	0.0760

Table 2.2
Dickey Fuller Tests for Stationarity
Including Constant and Trend Term

Variable	p value
ATGINI	0.3991
PROD. GRTH	0.0000
TRF/GDP	0.3778
UNEM RATE	0.0621

Table 2.3
Bivariate Causality Model

Growth in After-Tax Gini as Dependent Variable

Variable	Coeff.	P-value	Coeff.	P-value	Coeff.	P-value	Coeff.	P-value
							Hayes et al.*	
	No. of lags = 1		No. of lags = 2		No. of lags = 3		No. of lags = 2	
Constant	−0.21	0.14	−0.30	0.06	−0.36	0.05	0.01	0.04
ATGini (−1)	0.87	0.00	0.94	0.00	0.91	0.00	−0.14	0.41
ATGini (−2)			−0.13	0.45	−0.01	0.98	0.09	0.55
ATGini (−3)					−0.13	0.50		
Prod. (−1)	−0.36	0.24	−0.43	0.18	−0.40	0.27	−0.40	0.01
Prod. (−2)			−0.36	0.26	−0.39	0.26	−0.05	0.78
Prod (−3)					−0.15	0.66		
Adj. R^2	0.77		0.77		0.76		0.10	
Prob. (F-stat.)	0.02		0.00		0.00		0.11	
S.E. of est.	0.04		0.04		0.04		0.01	
Log likelihood	76.79		75.49		73.45		118.65	
AIC	−583.00		−581.9		−576.37			
Granger-	F	P value	F	P value	F	P value	F	P value
Causality test	0.72	0.40	0.52	0.60	0.28	0.84	3.97	0.03

*   Hayes et al. (1994) used before-tax income for families in calculating their Gini coefficient. They also use run regressions for two alternative measures of productivity growth. Their results reported here are for the productivity measure that generates the better regression fit.

Prod. Grth as Dependent Variable

Variable	Coeff.	P-value	Coeff.	P-value	Coeff.	P-value	Coeff.	P-value
							Hayes et al. (1994)	
	No. of lags = 1		No. of lags = 2		No. of lags = 3		No. of lags = 2	
Constant	−0.12	0.12	−0.08	0.32	−0.11	0.23	0.01	0.09
ATGini (−1)	−0.09	0.06	−0.22	0.02	−0.24	0.01	0.24	0.15
ATGini (−2)			0.16	0.09	0.11	0.41	−0.26	0.11
ATGini (−3)					0.05	0.59		
Prod. (−1)	−0.10	0.54	−0.09	0.60	−0.08	0.64	0.33	0.04
Prod. (−2)			−0.11	0.53	−0.16	0.35	0.19	0.27
Prod (−3)					−0.19	0.29		
Adj. R^2	0.05		0.07		0.06		0.15	
Prob. (F-stat.)	0.18		0.18		0.25		0.04	
S.E. of est.	0.02		0.02		0.02		0.02	
Log likelihood	100.10		100.27		98.76		117.16	
AIC	−583.03		−581.94		−576.37			
Granger-	F	P value	F	P value	F	P value	F	P value
Causality test	23.23	0.00	9.9	0.00	5.11	0.01	2.83	0.07

Table 2.4
Multivariate Causality Model

After-tax Gini as Dependent Variable

Variable	Coeff.	P-value	Coeff.	P-value	Coeff.	P-value	Coeff.	P-value
							Hayes et al.	
	No. of lags = 1		No. of lags = 2		No. of lags = 3		No. of lags = 2	
Constant	−0.34	0.05	−0.64	0.00	−0.74	0.004	0.01	0.06
ATGini (−1)	0.80	0.00	0.78	0.00	0.73	0.00	0.08	0.65
ATGini (−2)			−0.16	0.31	−0.05	0.83	−0.03	0.87
ATGini (−3)					−0.14	0.45		
Prod. (−1)	−0.34		−0.40	0.20	−0.46	0.21	−0.27	0.11
Prod. (−2)			−0.30	0.35	−0.37	0.30	−0.19	0.29
Prod. (−3)					−0.26	0.47		
Trf/GDP(−1)	−0.10		−0.10	0.26	−0.11	0.31	−0.06	0.15
Trf/GDP(−2)			−0.16	0.03	−0.16	0.17	0.08	0.02
Trf/GDP(−3)					−0.05	0.58		
Unem rate(−1)	−0.00		0.01	0.74	0.03	0.27	−0.01	0.72
Unem rate(−2)			−0.01	0.49	−0.10	0.70	−0.01	0.33
Unem rate(−3)					0.02	0.19		
Adj. R^2	0.77		0.81		0.80		0.34*	
Prob. (F-stat.)	0.00		0.00		0.00		0.18	
S.E. of est.	0.04		0.03		0.03		0.01	
Log likelihood	75.60		71.17		78.91			
AIC	−592.37		−584.37		−576.37			

Prod. Grth as dependent variable

Variable	Coeff.	P-value	Coeff.	P-value	Coeff.	P-value	Coeff.	P-value
Constant	−0.08	0.36	−0.04	0.69	−0.10	0.46	0.00	0.33
ATGini (−1)	−0.06	0.25	−0.19	0.06	−0.24	0.06	−0.22	0.15
ATGini (−2)			0.15	0.10	0.13	0.38	−0.02	0.92
ATGini (−3)					0.03	0.79		
Prod. (−1)	−0.05	0.77	−0.05	0.76	−0.10	0.65	0.28	0.05
Prod. (−2)			−0.12	0.50	−0.17	0.41	0.44	0.00
Prod. (−3)					−0.21	0.33		
Trf/GDP(−1)	0.01	0.73	0.06	0.24	0.07	0.30	0.02	0.57
Trf/GDP(−2)			−0.02	0.65	−0.03	0.70	−0.06	0.06
Trf/GDP(−3)					−0.02	0.65		
Unem rate(−1)	0.01	0.28	−0.00	0.72	0.00	0.98	0.04	0.00
Unem rate(−2)			0.01	0.22	0.01	0.46	0.01	0.40
Unem rate(−3)					0.00	0.85		
Adj. R^2	0.02		0.05		0.01		0.58*	
Prob. (F-stat.)	0.36		0.32		0.62		0.00	
S.E. of est.	0.02		0.02		0.02		0.01	
Log likelihood	99.16		99.81		97.83			
AIC	−592.37		−584.37		−576.37			

* The statistic reported in Hayes et al. is 'R^2', whereas both R^2 and adjusted R^2 are reported in the bivariate model.

Table 2.4 (continued)
Multivariate Causality Model

Unemployment Rate as Dependent Variable

	Coeff.	P-value	Coeff.	P-value	Coeff.	P-value	Coeff.	P-value
							Hayes et al.	
Variable	No. of lags = 1		No. of lags = 2		No. of lags = 3		No. of lags = 2	
Constant	−1.79	0.23	−0.01	0.99	−1.82	0.34	0.06	0.38
ATGini (−1)	−1.11	0.21	−1.59	0.28	−2.96	0.08	−4.64	0.06
ATGini (−2)			1.62	0.24	3.72	0.07	1.69	0.48
ATGini (−3)					−1.80	0.22		
Prod. (−1)	−4.33	0.13	−2.27	0.39	−0.19	0.95	−6.53	0.00
Prod. (−2)			5.19	0.06	4.66	0.11	2.42	0.30
Prod. (−3)					0.56	0.85		
Trf/GDP(−1)	0.06	0.92	−0.22	0.78	0.03	0.97	0.70	0.21
Trf/GDP(−2)			0.74	0.21	0.14	0.88	0.28	0.54
Trf/GDP(−3)					−0.59	0.39		
Unem rate(−1)	0.00	0.99	0.08	0.68	−0.03	0.90	−0.10	0.64
Unem rate(−2)			−0.33	0.01	−0.20	0.32	−0.06	0.73
Unem rate(−3)					−0.22	0.15		
Adj. R^2	0.01		0.24		0.03		0.53*	
Prob. (F-stat.)	0.46		0.04		0.41		0.00	
S.E. of est.	0.32		0.28		0.27		0.19	
Log likelihood	−7.71		0.16		3.47			
AIC	−592.37		−584.37		−576.37			

Transfer Payments as Dependent Variable

	Coeff.	P-value	Coeff.	P-value	Coeff.	P-value	Coeff.	P-value
Constant	−0.53	0.16	−0.19	0.66	−0.39	0.49	0.05	0.01
ATGini (−1)	−0.33	0.14	−0.35	0.39	−0.47	0.34	−1.00	0.21
ATGini (−2)			0.24	0.53	0.70	0.24	−0.77	0.31
ATGini (−3)					−0.46	0.29		
Prod. (−1)	0.20	0.78	0.76	0.30	1.18	0.18	−2.52	0.00
Prod. (−2)			0.78	0.31	0.57	0.50	1.66	0.03
Prod. (−3)					−0.21	0.81		
Trf/GDP(−1)	0.33	0.03	0.56	0.01	0.65	0.02	0.23	0.18
Trf/GDP(−2)			−0.01	0.97	−0.19	0.51	−0.03	0.83
Trf/GDP(−3)					0.01	0.94		
Unem rate(−1)	−0.01	0.75	−0.06	0.24	−0.07	0.33	−0.01	0.94
Unem rate(−2)			−0.03	0.42	0.00	0.96	0.00	0.94
Unem rate(−3)					−0.02	0.70		
Adj. R^2	0.25		0.31		0.22		0.47 *	
Prob. (F-stat.)	0.01		0.01		0.11		0.19	
S.E. of est.	0.08		0.08		0.08		0.06	
Log likelihood	44.94		47.54		47.28			
AIC	−592.37		−584.37		−576.37			

* The statistic reported in Hayes et al. is 'R^2', whereas both R^2 and adjusted R^2 are reported in the bivariate model.

REFERENCES

Aghion, P. and P. Bolton (1997), 'A Trickle-Down Theory of Growth and Development with Debt Overhang', *Review of Economic Studies*, **64** (2), 151–62.

Aghion, P., E. Caroli and C. Garcia-Penalosa (1999), 'Inequality and Economic Growth: The Perspective of the New Growth Theories, *Journal of Economic Literature*, **37**, 1615–60.

Alesina, A. and D. Rodrik (1994), 'Distributive Politics and Economic Growth', *Quarterly Journal of Economics*, **109** (2), 465–90.

Anand, S. and S.M.R. Kanbar (1993), 'The Kuznets Process and the Inequality–Development Relationship', *Journal of Development Economics*, **40** (1), 25–52.

Australian Senate (1999), *Senate Select Committee on a New Tax System. Main Report*, Canberra: Commonwealth of Australia.

Banerjee, A. and A.F. Newman (1993), 'Risk-Bearing and the Theory of Income Distribution', *Review of Economic Studies*, **58** (2), 211–35.

Blinder, A.S. and H.Y. Esaki (1978), 'Macroeconomic Activity and Income Distribution in the Post-War United States', *The Review of Economics and Statistics*, **60**, 604–609.

Deaton, A. (1992), *Understanding Consumption*, Oxford: Oxford University Press.

Deininger, K. and L. Squire (1998), 'A New Data Set Measuring Income Inequality', *World Bank Economic Review*, **10** (3), 565–91.

Diekmann, O. (1996), 'Income Inequality and Economic Growth in an Open Economy', *International Advances in Economic Research*, **2** (3), 270–78.

Easterly, W. and S. Rebelo (1993), 'Fiscal Policy and Economic Growth: An Empirical Investigation', *Journal of Monetary Economics*, **46**, 107–78.

Engle, R. and C. Granger (1987), 'Cointegration and Error Correction: Representation, Estimation and Testing', *Econometrica*, **55**, 251–76.

Forbes, K. (2000), 'A Reassessment of the Relationship Between Inequality and Growth', *American Economic Review*, **90** (4), 868–87.

Granger, C. (1969), 'Investigating Causal Relations by Econometric Methods and Cross-Spectral Methods', *Econometrica*, **37**, 424–38.

Guest, R. and A. Doraisami (1994), 'The Impact of Inflation, Unemployment and Secular Influences on the Distribution of Personal Taxable Incomes in Australia', *Economics Papers*, **13** (4), 11–22.

Guest, R. and I.M. McDonald (1999), 'The Effect of Population Ageing on the Distribution of Taxable Incomes of Individuals in Australia', *Economic Papers*, **18** (3), 34–48.

Harris, R. (1995), *Using Cointegration Analysis in Econometric Modelling*, Wheatsheaf: Prentice Hall/Harvester.

Hayes, K., M. Nieswiadomy, D. Slottje, M. Redfearn, and E. Wolff (1994), 'Productivity and Income Inequality Growth Rates in the United States', in J.H. Bergstrand, T.F. Cosimano, J.W. Houck, and R.G. Sheehan (eds), *The Changing Distribution of Income in an Open US Economy*, Amsterdam: North-Holland.

Johansen, S. (1988), 'Statistical Analysis of Cointegration Vectors', *Journal of Economic Dynamics and Control*, **12**, 231–54.

Kuznets, S. (1963), 'Quantitative Aspects of the Economic Growth of Nations', *Economic Development and Cultural Change*, **11** (2), 1–80.

Modigliani, F. and R. Brumberg (1954), 'Utility Analysis and the Consumption Function: Interpretation of Cross-Section Data', in Kenneth K. Kurihara (ed.), *Post-Keynesian Economics,* New Brunswick, NJ: Rutgers University Press, pp. 388–436.

Perotti, R. (1996), 'Growth, Income Distribution and Democracy: What the Data Say', *Journal of Economic Growth*, **1** (2), 149–87.

Persson, T. and G. Tabellini (1994), 'Is Inequality Harmful for Growth?', *American Economic Review*, **84** (3), 600–21.

Reserve Bank of Australia (2000), 'A Medium-Term Perspective on Monetary Policy', *Reserve Bank of Australia Bulletin*, 1–6 September.

Schmidt-Hebbel, K. and L. Serven (eds), (1999), '*The Economics of Saving and Growth*', Cambridge: Cambridge University Press.

Stiglitz, J. (1969), 'The Distribution of Income and Wealth Among Individuals', *Econometrica*, **37** (3), 382–97.

Temple, J. (1999), 'The New Growth Evidence', *Journal of Economic Literature*, **37** (1), 112–56.

Ternowetsky, G. (1979), 'Taxation Statistics and Income Inequality in Australia: 1955–56 to 1974–75', *ANZJS*, **15** (2), 17–24.

Yao, S. (1997), 'Decomposition of Gini Coefficients by Income Factors: A New Approach and Application', *Applied Economics Letters*, **4**, 27–31.

Yao, S. (1999), 'On the Decomposition of Gini Coefficients by Population Class and Income Source: A Spreadsheet Approach and Application', *Applied Economics*, **31**, 1249–64.

3 Median Income: Modelling and Implications for Assessing Growth and Convergence

Amnon Levy

When the distribution of income is skewed, median income is a richer statistic and a better indicator of the well being of the majority of people than the commonly used per capita income. Median income is linked to per capita income and the disparity in income-generating assets ownership. While ownership identity is only important in the determination of the size of the change in per capita income, it is crucial for determining both the direction and the magnitude of changes in median income and, thereby, the prospects of growth and convergence in median-income centred analyses.

3.1 INTRODUCTION

Following Solow's (1956) and Swan's (1956) seminal ad hoc growth model and Cass's (1965), Koopman's (1965) and Phelps's (1966) refinement of Ramsey's (1928) optimal growth model, economic growth and international comparative studies have been centred on per capita income and per capita productive assets and have used them as the prominent indicators of the earnings, production potential and wealth of representative members of society. The focus on per capita measures and indicators has also been a characteristic of the convergence controversy between neoclassical growth theories and endogenous growth studies (for example, Baumol 1986; Barro 1991; Mankiw, Romer and Weil 1992; Barro and Sala-i-Martin 1992; Romer 1994; Pack 1994; Ortigueira and Santos 1997).

There are considerable analytical and measuring advantages in using per capita indicators. However, ownership of productive assets is unlikely to be equally distributed among people and the distribution of income is usually skewed, with per capita income considerably larger than the median. That is, a majority of people earns income levels lower than per capita income. The greater the skewness of the distribution of income the less reliable the per capita income in assessing the well being of a majority of people. Although not an idle indicator, median income provides a better assessment of the economic well being of any majority, that includes the lowest 50-per-cent income earners with each receiving an equal weight, than per capita income.

The objective of this essay is fourfold. First, to justify and promote the use of median income in assessing growth and convergence. Secondly, to offer a method for modelling median income and to link median income to per capita income and the variances and covariances of ownership of income-generating assets. Thirdly, to compare conceptually the growth rates of median income and per capita income and to highlight the effects of asset accumulation and ownership identity on these rates and on the prospects of convergence, or divergence, of incomes across countries. Fourthly, to compare the golden rule of capital accumulation advocated by per-capita-income-centred models and the golden rule stemming from a median-income-centred model.

Correspondingly, the analysis is organised in four sections as follows. Using the notion of aggregate deprivation, it is argued in Section 3.2 that the greater the skewness of the distribution of income the greater the likelihood that the ordering of policies affecting the distribution of income by majority vote is closer to the preferences of the median-income earners than to the preferences of the per-capita-income earners. It is therefore sensible to consider median income and its determinants and explore the implications of median-income centred models for growth and convergence of income across countries. The relationship between median income, per capita income and ownership of income-generating assets is developed in Section 3.3. This relationship is used in Section 3.4 for analysing the growth rate of median income and modifying the condition of cross-country income–convergence. It is also used in Section 3.5 for modifying the neoclassical per-capita-income-centred golden rule of capital accumulation to the case where the representative agent's income is taken as being equal to the median income. A summary of the main analytical findings is provided in Section 3.6.

3.2   WHY MEDIAN INCOME?

Observed distributions of income are leftwardly skewed with per capita income (y_{pc}) considerably larger than the median (y_{med}). The greater the skewness of the distribution of income the larger the gap between y_{pc} and y_{med}. The ratio of y_{med} to y_{pc} may serve as a proxy of this skewness. The smaller this ratio the lower the popularity of per-capita-income-centred policies.

Moreover, under certain circumstances y_{med} affects, and is affected by, the distribution of political power and is a relevant statistic for designing income-redistribution policies. Let the distribution of income ($y_\ell \le y \le y_h$) within a population of N people, all income earners and eligible voters, be represented by a leftwardly skewed density function $\varphi(y)$, and suppose that people suffer from deprivation from having incomes lower than an equal share of the total income (that is, per capita income), then the argument can be formalised as follows.

Proposition: If

i. rulers are elected by majority voting,

ii. voting is compulsory,

iii. bribes are eliminated,

iv. all people have the same deprivation function $v(y_{pc} - y)$, $v' > 0$, for $y < y_{pc}$, and zero otherwise,

v. people collude in order to reduce their personal level of deprivation and agree to minimise their collective average deprivation, and

vi. the greater the initial average deprivation (*IAD*) within a coalition the more aggressive the coalition and the less diluted its income redistribution policy,

then the ruling coalition comprises all people with incomes smaller than or equal to $y_{med} + \xi$, where ξ satisfies $\varphi(y_{med} + \xi)N = 1$.

The proof of this proposition can be sketched as follows. Condition (iv) implies that among all possible majority groups, the group of the lowest 50-per-cent-plus-one income earners has the highest level of initial average deprivation:

$$IAD = \frac{1}{0.5N + 1} \int_{y_\ell}^{y_{med} + \xi} v(y_{pc} - y)\varphi(y)dy \qquad (3.1)$$

Conditions (i)–(iii), (v) and (vi) ensure that the lowest 50-per-cent-plus-one income earners have the incentive and ability to form a ruling coalition. Since they must vote, they are the majority of voters. In the absence of bribes their political position cannot be swayed and their mutual interest in reducing their level of deprivation leads them to collude and form a minimum majority coalition that can reduce the deprivation level for each member and minimise the aggregate deprivation level for its members. In this sense, the coalition of the lowest 50-per-cent-plus-one income earners implements the least diluted income redistribution policy. This policy reduces the initial average deprivation level of members most effectively. Since the coalition's *IAD* rises with y_{pc} but declines with y_{med}, both statistics are relevant for designing a policy that minimises *IAD*, subject to the requirement that every coalition member's depression level is reduced and subject to feasibility and constitutional constraints.

Another argument in favour of median income is that its formula provides a richer description and analysis of growth and convergence than the use of per capita income as a single statistic. As is shown in the next section median income can be formulated as a function of both per capita income and the weighted sum of the variances and covariances of income-generating assets within a population.

3.3   MEDIAN INCOME AND ITS RELATIONSHIP WITH PER CAPITA INCOME AND ASSET OWNERSHIP

Unlike the analysis of per capita income, the modelling of median income employs assumptions about the distribution of income and income-generating assets within a society rather than the aggregate production function. The provision of a theory of income distribution in which the joint distribution of income-generating assets is treated as endogenous is beyond the scope of the present essay. Hence, ad hoc specifications are used. A sensible choice of an ad hoc personal-income equation should be consistent with a density function that provides a reasonable approximation of observed income distributions. As argued by Adelman and Levy (1984) and Levy (1987), a personal-income equation satisfying this requirement displays the income of the *i*-th person, y_i, as a product of a positive scalar θ and an exponential dispersion factor:

$$y_i = \theta \exp(\varepsilon_i) \qquad (3.2)$$

where ε is assumed to be normally distributed among the members of the society with zero mean and a finite variance. Recalling that y is exponentially related to ε, this specification suggests the lognormal distribution as an approximation of the distribution of income within a population.

Among the distribution functions that do not obey the weak Pareto law the lognormal distribution is the most extensively used one for approximating the distribution of income. It was introduced to the study of income distribution by Gibart (1931). As indicated by Aitchison and Brown (1954, 1957), Yotopoulos and Nugent (1976), and Kakwani (1980), the wide use of lognormal distribution in empirical studies of income distribution can be attributed to its attractive properties. Its relationship with normal distribution provides a convenient access to statistical inference and efficient estimation methods. Similarly to observed income data it is positively skewed. It also fits reasonably the middle range of observed income data accruable to about 60 per cent of the population of income earners.

Since ε is assumed to be normally distributed, its median is equal to its mean. Recalling that the latter is assumed to be equal to zero, ε is equal to zero for a person receiving the median income and hence his income is equal to θ. That is, θ can be interpreted as the median income (y_{med}) and the aforementioned personal-income equation can be rendered as

$$y_i = y_{med}\exp(\varepsilon_i) \qquad (3.3)$$

Furthermore, personal income is linked to the possession of income-generating assets such as various types of human capital and physical capital, perishable inputs and access to technology, production systems and markets. Recalling that e_i indicates the degree of dispersion of the income accruable to person i from the median income (that is, $\ln(y_i/y_{med})$) and that is assumed to be normally distributed in a population with a zero mean, it is reasonable to express e_i as a function of the deviations of person i's endowments of these assets from their average stocks in the population that preserves the equality of the mean of e to zero. A simple linear specification of such a function is given by the following weighted sum:

$$\varepsilon_i = \Phi'(e_i - \mu_e) \qquad (3.4)$$

where e_i is a Kx1 vector of person i's endowments of material and non-material income-generating assets, μ_e is a Kx1 vector of the average endowments of these income-generating assets in the population, and Φ is a Kx1 vector of positive scalars (weights) indicating the rates of change of the income of person i, relative to the median income, induced by an infinitesimal growth in person i's stocks of the income-generating assets.

The weighted sum specified in equation (3.4) has zero mean and a variance $\Phi'\Sigma\Phi$, where Σ is a KxK matrix of the variances and covariances of the personal endowments of income-generating assets in the population. It is worth noting that if the degree of aggregation of the income-generating assets is sufficiently low and accommodating for a very large number (K) of material and non-material assets, each independently distributed (that is, Σ is diagonal) and having a high probability of making a small contribution to the weighted sum, then the central limit theorem lends support to the aforementioned assumption that ε is normally distributed.

By taking the mean of equation (3.3), the per capita income (y_{pc}) can be rendered as the product of the median income and the moment-generating function (*mgf*) of ε. That is,

$$y_{pc} = E[y_{med}\exp(\varepsilon)] = y_{med}E[\exp(\varepsilon)] = y_{med}\,mgf(\varepsilon) \qquad (3.5)$$

Recalling further that

$$\varepsilon \sim \aleph(0, \Phi' \Sigma \Phi) \qquad (3.6)$$

then

$$mgf(\varepsilon) = \exp(0.5\Phi'\Sigma\Phi) \qquad (3.7)$$

and by substituting this equality into equation (3.5) and rearranging terms

$$y_{med} = \frac{y_{pc}}{\exp(0.5\Phi'\Sigma\Phi)} \qquad (3.8)$$

Equation (3.8) suggests that the relationship between median income and per capita income depends on the weighted sum of the variances and covariances of income-generating assets within the population under consideration, where the weights correspond to the effects of these assets on personal earning. Recalling that the variance–covariance matrix Σ is positive semi-definite, the denominator is convex. That is, the median income is obtained by *discounting* the per capita income in accordance with the overall degree of ownership inequality in the distribution of income-generating assets among people.

3.4   GROWTH RATE AND CONVERGENCE IN A MEDIAN-INCOME-CENTRED MODEL

Equation (3.8) can be equivalently rendered as:

$$\ln\left(\frac{y_{pc}}{y_{med}}\right) = 0.5\Phi'\Sigma\Phi \qquad (3.9)$$

which by differentiating with respect to time implies that the rate of change of the median income is equal to the rate of change of per capita income minus: 1. the weighted sum of the changes in the variance and covariances of income-generating assets ownership, and 2. the weighted sum of the changes in the contribution of these assets to personal income:

$$\frac{\dot{y}_{med}}{y_{med}} = \frac{\dot{y}_{pc}}{y_{pc}} - (\Phi'\dot{\Sigma}\Phi + \Phi'\Sigma\dot{\Phi}) \qquad (3.10)$$

Equations (3.10) and (3.8) reveal the fundamental difference between per capita income and median income and their response to the accumulation of income-generating assets. An increase in the stock of any of the income-generating assets, as long as it is employed and all other things remaining the same, raises the aggregate output and thereby per capita income regardless of the identity of the owners of the new stock. Recalling equations (3.2) and (3.4), ownership identity is only important in the determination of the size, but not the direction, of the change in aggregate output and per capita income – the larger the stocks of all other income-generating factors owned by an individual, the higher the rise of the aggregate output and per capita income induced by an additional unit of an income-generating factor accumulated by that person. In contrast, ownership identity is crucial for determining both the direction and the size of the change in the median income because the contributions of the new capital stock or market-access to the aggregate income is discounted by its effect on the variance of ownership of that asset and the covariances of ownership between that asset and the rest of the income-generating assets. When the increase in the stock of an income-generating asset is accompanied by increased overall equality in the distribution of assets ownership (that is, when it reduces the denominator of the right-hand-side term in equation (3.8)) median income rises more than per capita income. However, when the increase in the stock of an income-generating asset raises the overall asset-ownership inequality, median income rises at a lower rate than per capita income. Moreover, if the increase in the overall asset-ownership inequality dominates the contribution of the new stock of the asset to the aggregate income-generation process, median income declines.

Equation (3.10) also has interesting implications for the prospects of convergence of incomes across countries. Let A and B denote two countries, or groups of countries, with A having initially a higher per capita income than B. In this case, the per-capita-income-centred economic growth literature considers

$$\frac{\dot{y}_{pc}^{B}}{y_{pc}^{B}} - \frac{\dot{y}_{pc}^{A}}{y_{pc}^{A}} > 0 \qquad (3.11)$$

as the condition for convergence. In contrast, equation (3.10) suggests that when the median income in country A is also higher than the median income in country B the condition for convergence in a median-income-centred growth model is:

$$\frac{\dot{y}_{pc}^{B}}{y_{pc}^{B}} - \frac{\dot{y}_{pc}^{A}}{y_{pc}^{A}} > (\Phi'_{B} \Sigma_{B} \Phi_{B} + \Phi'_{B} \Sigma_{B} \dot{\Phi}_{B})$$

$$- (\Phi'_{A} \Sigma_{A} \Phi_{A} + \Phi'_{A} \Sigma_{A} \dot{\Phi}_{A}) \qquad (3.12)$$

That is, convergence can occur even when the per capita growth rate differential between B and A is negative, so long as this differential exceeds the change over time in the difference between the variances of the income dispersion degree ε between B and A. Conversely, divergence occurs if the change over time in the difference between the variances of ε between B and A exceeds the per capita growth rate differential between B and A even when this growth rate differential is positive.

Moreover, when the distribution of income-generating assets in country B is sufficiently more equal than in country A, it is possible that the median income in country B exceeds the median income in country A

A. In this case, convergence of these countries' median incomes occurs if the change over time in the difference between the variances of the income dispersion degree between B and A exceeds the per capita growth rate differential between B and A:

$$\frac{\dot{y}^{B}_{pc}}{y^{B}_{pc}} - \frac{\dot{y}^{A}_{pc}}{y^{A}_{pc}} < (\Phi'_{B}\dot{\Sigma}_{B}\Phi_{B} + \Phi'_{B}\Sigma_{B}\dot{\Phi}_{B})$$

$$(3.13)$$

$$- (\Phi'_{A}\dot{\Sigma}_{A}\Phi_{A} + \Phi'_{A}\Sigma_{A}\dot{\Phi}_{A})$$

3.5 THE GOLDEN RULE STEMMING FROM A MEDIAN INCOME CENTRED MODEL

Using a simple version of the neoclassical per capita income centred optimal growth model (Ramsey 1928; Phelps 1966) as a benchmark, the *modified golden rule* of capital accumulation is modified for the case where people are not identical and the representative agent's income is equal to the median income. It is assumed, for simplicity, that capital and labour are the only production inputs and that they are fully employed in a Cobb-Douglas production process generating a single homogeneous good that can be either consumed or invested. Capital ownership is assumed to be unequally distributed among people with a finite instantaneous variance $\sigma^2(t)$. Labour is taken, for convenience, as an homogenous and equally distributed input. The extension of the analysis to a broader and endogenous growth framework may consider the effects of human capital on production and satisfaction from leisure and the issue of time allocation along the lines of Ortigueira and Santos (1997), for example.

Consequently, and in view of equation (3.8), the instantaneous median income accruing to the representative household is:

$$y_{med}(t) = f(k(t)) \exp\{-0.5\phi(t)\sigma^2(t)\} \tag{3.14}$$

where k is the capital–labour ratio, $f(k)$ is a concave function measuring the per capita output generated by k, and ϕ is a positive weight associated with the deviation of capital stock from the mean value in constructing ε (or the natural logarithm of the change of the income accruing to person i, relative to the median income, induced by an infinitesimal increase in person i's stock of capital).

A convenient conceptualisation of the social planner's intertemporal decision problem, which also allows a straightforward comparison with the golden rule of capital accumulation stemming from the conventional, neoclassical and per capita income centred model, treats the instantaneous saving rate, $s(t)$, as the control variable, assumes that it is identical for all members of society, and takes the planning horizon to be infinite. Note, however, that despite having an identical saving rate, individuals may possess different amounts of capital stock because of differences in their initial endowments. That is, the assumption of different initial endowments does not preclude different levels of saving and investment across individuals.

Formally, the trajectory of s is chosen so as to maximise

$$U = \int_0^\infty e^{-\rho t} u((1 - s(t))y_{med}(t)) dt \tag{3.15}$$

subject to the median-income equation (3.14) and the conventional law of motion of the capital–labour ratio

$$\dot{k}(t) = s(t)f(k(t)) - (\delta + n)k(t) \tag{3.16}$$

where U is the overall utility of the median-income earner from consumption over the planning horizon, taken for simplicity as the sum of the discounted instantaneous utilities (or felicities), u, with $u' > 0$, $u'' < 0$ and a constant rate of time preference ρ; and where δ and n are fixed rates of capital depreciation and population growth, respectively.

The Hamiltonian associated with the intertemporal decision problem described above is

$$H(t) = e^{-\rho t} u((1 - s(t))e^{-0.5\phi(t)^2\sigma^2(t)} f(k(t))) + \lambda(t)[s(t)f(k(t)) - (\delta + n)k(t)] \tag{3.17}$$

where the co-state variable λ can be interpreted as the shadow price of (per capita) capital. The evolution of λ is obtained by differentiating $-H$ with respect to k and depicted by the following first-order differential (adjoint) equation:

$$\dot{\lambda} = -e^{-\rho t} u'(c_{med})(1-s)[f'(k)e^{-0.5\phi^2 \sigma^2}$$

$$-0.5\phi^2 \sigma_k^2 e^{-0.5\phi^2 \sigma^2} f(k)] - \lambda[sf'(k) - (\delta + n)] \tag{3.18}$$

where c_{med} denotes the consumption level of the median-income earner and σ_k^2 the derivative of the variance of k with respect to k. Moreover, the optimality condition

$$\frac{\partial H}{\partial s} = -e^{-\rho t} u'(c_{med})e^{-0.5\phi^2 \sigma^2} f(k) + \lambda f(k) = 0 \tag{3.19}$$

implies that along the optimal capital-accumulation path the shadow price of capital is equal to the marginal utility from consumption discounted by both the rate of time preference and the degree of inequality in the distribution of capital. That is,

$$\lambda = e^{-(\rho t + 0.5\phi^2 \sigma^2)} u'(c_{med}) \tag{3.20}$$

The evolution of the optimal level of the median-income earner's consumption is found by differentiating the optimality condition (3.19) with respect to t. The singular control equation describing this evolution can be simplified by substituting the right-hand sides of equation (3.18) and equation (3.20) for $\dot{\lambda}$ and λ, respectively, dividing both sides of the resultant equality by the right-hand side of equality 3.20, and isolating $\dot{c}_{med}$. That is,

$$\dot{c}_{med} = \left[\frac{f'(k) - (\rho + \delta + n)}{-u''(c_{med})/u'(c_{med})} \right] -$$

$$\left[\frac{0.5(1-s)\phi^2 \sigma_K^2 f(k) + \phi\sigma^2 \dot{\phi} + 0.5\phi^2 \sigma^2}{-u''(c_{med})/u'(c_{med})} \right] \tag{3.21}$$

where the time index t is omitted for brevity.

The first term on the right-hand side of equation (3.21) is the familiar no-arbitrage rule obtained with the conventional per capita income centred model. It states that the instantaneous change in consumption corresponds to the difference between the marginal product and the user cost of capital but discounted by the degree of concavity of the instantaneous utility function. The second term modifies this conventional no-arbitrage rule for the case where the median income is taken as the representative household's income by altering the marginal product and user cost differential in accordance with the changes in the variance of the distribution of capital within the population. The underlying rationale for this modification is that, as indicated in equation (3.14), the variance of capital stock affects adversely the median income.

The modified no-arbitrage rule (3.21) indicates further that the change in the variance of the distribution of capital induced by the accumulation of capital makes the difference between the stationary capital–labour ratios in the median-income centred model and the conventional per capita income centred model. By setting $\dot{c}_{med}$ to be equal to zero the stationary level of the capital–labour ratio in the conventional per capita income centred model should satisfy the golden rule

$$f'(k_{ss}^{conventional}) = \rho + \delta + n \tag{3.22}$$

whereas in the median-income centred model it should satisfy

$$f'(k_{ss}) = (\rho + \delta + n) + 0.5(1-s)f(k_{ss})\phi^2\frac{\partial\sigma^2}{\partial k} \tag{3.23}$$

Recalling that f is concave, the golden stationary capital-labour ratio in the median-income centred model is smaller than, equal to, or larger than the golden stationary capital–labour ratio in the per capita income centred model if a rise in capital stock is accompanied by an increase, no change, or decline, in the variance of the distribution of capital ownership among people, respectively. Moreover, while the steady state in the conventional per capita income centred model is a saddle point, it is not necessarily so in the median-income centred model. Information about the relationship between capital-ownership inequality and capital accumulation, and the second derivative of s with respect to capital in particular, is essential for assessing the asymptotic properties of the modified system's stationary point.

3.6   SUMMARY AND CONCLUSION

When the distribution of income is skewed, median income indicates the earnings of the representative member of society better than the commonly used per capita income, in the sense that the income levels accruing to a majority of the population are closer to the median level than to the per capita level. A method of modelling median income and its determinants was offered. Median income was related to per capita income and to the variances and covariances of the distribution of ownership of income-generating factors. Differences between the effects of income-generating factors on median income and per capita income were highlighted. The difference between the rates of change of per capita income and median income was expressed as the weighted sum of the changes in the variance and covariances of the distribution of the ownership of income-generating factors within the population plus the weighted sum of the changes in the contribution of these factors to personal income. It was shown that while ownership identity is only important in the determination of the size of the change in per capita income, ownership identity is crucial for determining both the direction and the size of the change in the median income. It was consequently shown that a positive per capita income growth rate differential between a relatively low-income country and a relatively high-income country is neither a sufficient condition for convergence of the incomes accruing to their representative agents, nor a necessary one. In addition, the conventional neoclassical golden rule of capital accumulation was modified by using a median income centred optimal growth model, and the role of changes in the variance of capital ownership in the determination of the socially optimal trajectory of consumption and capital stock was highlighted.

REFERENCES

Adelman, I. and A. Levy (1984), 'The Equalizing Role of Human Resource Intensive Growth Strategies: A Theoretical Model', *Journal of Policy Modeling*, **6**, 271–87.

Aitchison, J. and J.A.C. Brown (1954), 'On Criteria for Description of Income Distribution', *Metroeconomica*, **6**, 88–107.

Aitchison, J. and J.A.C. Brown (1957), *The Lognormal Distribution*, Cambridge: Cambridge University Press.

Barro, R.J. (1991), 'Economic Growth in a Cross-Section of Countries', *Quarterly Journal of Economics*, **106** (2), 407–43.

Barro, R.J. and X. Sala-i-Martin (1992), 'Convergence', *Journal of Political Economy*, **100** (2), 223–51.

Baumol, W. (1986), 'Productivity Growth, Convergence, and Welfare: What the Long-Run Data Show', *American Economic Review*, **76** (5), 1072–85.

Cass, D. (1965), 'Optimum Growth in an Aggregative Model of Capital Accumulation', *Review of Economic Studies*, **32**, 233–40.

Deaton, A. and J. Muellbauer (1980), *Economics and Consumer Behaviour*, Cambridge: Cambridge University Press.

Gibart, R. (1931), *Les inégalités économiques*, Paris: Sirely.

Kakwani, N. (1980), *Income Inequality and Poverty*, Oxford: Oxford University Press.

Koopman, T. (1965), 'On the Concept of Optimal Economic Growth', in *The Econometric Approach to Development Planning*, Amsterdam: North Holland.

Levy, A. (1987), 'Income Inequality and the Distribution of Ownership of Productive Resources: Theory and Application with Lognormal Distribution', *Journal of Policy Modeling*, **9**, 321–36.

Mankiw, G.N., D. Romer and D.N. Weil (1992), 'A Contribution to the Empirics of Economic Growth', *Quarterly Journal of Economics*, **107** (2), 407–37.

Ortigueira, S. and M.S. Santos (1997), 'On the Speed of Convergence in Endogenous Growth Models', *American Economic Review*, **87** (3), 383–99.

Pack, H. (1994), 'Endogenous Growth Theory: Intellectual Appeal and Empirical Shrtcomings', *Journal of Economic Perspectives*, **8** (1), 55–72.

Phelps, E.S. (1966), *Golden Rules of Economic Growth*, New York: W.W. Norton.

Ramsey, F. (1928), 'A Mathematical Theory of Saving', *Economic Journal*, **38**, 543–59.

Romer, P. (1994), 'The Origins of Endogenous Growth', *Journal of Economic Perspectives*, **8** (1), 3–22.

Solow, R.M. (1956), 'A Contribution to the Theory of Economic Growth', *Quarterly Journal of Economics*, **70**, 65–94.

Swan, T.W. (1956), 'Economic Growth and Capital Accumulation', *Economic Record*, **32**, 334–61.

Yotopoulos, P.A. and J.B. Nugent (1976), *Economics of Development: Empirical Investigation*, New York: Harper & Row.

4   Income Inequality among Different Regions in China's Post-Reform Era

James Xiaohe Zhang and Charles Harvie

4.1   INTRODUCTION

China is one of the few countries in the world that uses a household registration (*hukou*) regime to prohibit migration not only from rural to urban areas, but also from one province to another. Although it has not been well acknowledged and discussed by academics and policy makers in China the impact of the *hukou* on overall income inequality is significant, as found in the present study. Despite this registration system the country has achieved remarkable double-digit annual economic growth in the last two decades of economic reform, and the *hukou* regime and the corresponding migration restrictions remain effective. As a result, income differentials among different regions and between rural and urban sectors have been growing (World Bank 1997, p. 27).

Even measured by official unadjusted data the urban–rural income ratio is larger than 2, a gap that is greater than for most countries. In real terms, the ratio is believed to be 3.09 in 1980, 2.26 in 1984 and 3.27 in 1993 (Zhao 1999, p. 768). Notwithstanding the fact that agricultural reform has been successful, and that the township and village enterprises have achieved impressive growth over the last two decades, poverty in China is still a rural phenomenon. Zhao and Li (1997, p. 22) reported that almost all of the poorest 5 per cent of the population were located in rural areas,[1] whereas urban residents accounted for about 80 per cent and more than 75 per cent of the wealthiest 10 per cent of the population in 1988 and 1995 respectively.

Although income distribution issues have attracted considerable attention in recent years, a continuous time series measurement of overall nation-wide income inequality in China is still not available. This is mainly due to the lack of appropriate data. Reliable household survey data covering a reasonably long period of time are generally absent in China. In addition, the publicly available data are usually some kind of average aggregate income at the provincial level at best. This has forced most of the measurements of income inequality into sub-groups of the aggregate population: for example, within a particular sector (rural or urban).[2] Given the fact that sector inequality is usually different from overall inequality, if not contradictory, the policy implications derived from sectoral measurements must be different from those attained from overall measurements. For instance, when the rural sector alone is considered the development of the township and village enterprises is responsible for increasing income inequality in the sector (Yao 1997b, p. 108), yet at the overall China level this same factor is obviously inequality alleviating. Hence when the urban-rural income gap is large, income inequality is overwhelmingly determined by inter-sector factors rather than intra-sector factors.[3]

This study provides a measurement of a nation-wide Gini index on the basis of officially published provincial income data. Although this index is different from the conventional Gini index where the fundamental unit of measurement is the household, the index is an overall measurement that reflects the inequality created mainly by the institutional segmentation of China's labour markets. This index has several special policy implications. First, it is an overall index that reflects income disparities not only among different provincial-level administrative units,[4] but also between rural and urban sectors. Secondly, since it is at the provincial level where the *hukou* is created the index mainly reflects how and to what extent the *hukou* regime contributed to the country's inequality level.[5] Thirdly, the Gini index is further decomposed into different components so the impact of inter-sector and intra-sector factors can be clearly detected. This helps to identify the main source of income inequality among different regions and sectors, and to design different policy packages to reduce the overall income inequality.

The study is organised as follows. In the following section the nature of the *hukou* regime in China and its likely impact on personal income distribution, namely the enlargement of income gaps between rural and urban sectors and among different provincial administration units, is identified. How the Gini index is measured and the corresponding results are reported in Section 4.3. In Section 4.4, the Gini index is further decomposed into its inter-sector and intra-sector components. Section 4.5 concludes the chapter and presents some policy implications.

4.2   HOUSEHOLD REGISTRATION IN CHINA

Since the communists came to power in 1949, social welfare policy in China has mainly favoured the urban workers in terms of job security, free medical treatment, hospitalisation, disability, education, and retirement coverage. The differentiation in real living standards created an incentive for the population to migrate from rural areas to urban areas in the 1950s. Starting from 1955 the government implemented a *hukou* regime that virtually prohibited inter-sector migration (Cheng and Selden 1994). The population was, therefore, broadly divided into two groups: rural and urban residents. The *hukou* regime differentiated not only between rural and urban residents but also between urban residents in different provincial administrative units, and consequently the mobility among different provincial units was also prohibited. The *hukou* regime, in conjunction with an elaborate rationing mechanism that restricted food and housing supply merely to urban dwellers, froze and formalised sector positions and eliminated the possibility of change in residential status. A hierarchical economic structure with big cities at the apex, provincial administered and smaller cities in the middle, and the poorest rural areas at the base, was created thereafter in China.

As part of China's industrialisation strategy the *hukou* regime was developed elaborately to establish a strong industrial base in the urban areas at the expense of the rural residents. The regime was further enforced by a 'reversed migration' of city youth to rural areas when they graduated from middle school in the late 1960s and early 1970s, during the period of the cultural revolution. It is reported that more than 48 million people were sent to the countryside during 1960–76 (Selden 1993, p. 166). This ruralisation process was maintained for a period of more than 10 years until the death of Mao Zedong in 1976.

Since the start of economic reforms from 1978, restrictions on labour mobility have been partially eased. The farmers who subsequently flocked into the cities and towns in order to find some temporary jobs in urban areas are known as 'blind floating people'. Holding a rural *hukou,* the floating people can neither have access to employment opportunities in the state owned enterprises, nor enjoy the state subsidies on housing, health care, and education. The total blind floating population reached 80 million in the late 1980s (Chai and Chai 1997, p. 1040). While the emergence of the floating population may have relieved rural poverty, its impact on income inequality so far appears to have been limited.

The rural–urban migration restrictions have had a significant impact on income distribution in China. Figure 4.1 shows a ranking of personal income in ascending order among all of the thirty provincial-level administrative units in 1996, where the rural and urban sectors in each unit are separately classified. The 30 urban units are numbered from 1 to 30 while the 30 rural units are numbered from 31 to 60. The figure clearly shows that when all but one (Shanghai) of the rural units was located at an income level of less than 3 600 *yuan* per annum, all urban units, except Inner Mongolia, were above that level. This indicates that income inequality in China is overwhelmingly determined by urban–rural income differentials, while regional disparities are responsible for only a smaller portion. As a comparison, Figure 4.2 (a and b) presents the income disparity among the 51 states in the USA in 1990 and 1999. The comparison shows that the capitalist USA had a more equal income distribution pattern than that of the socialist People's Republic of China at the provincial (state) level.

The income gaps between rural and urban sectors are demonstrated more clearly in Table 4.1. When China's economic reform started in 1978 the income differential ratio between urban and rural sectors was 2.57. The ratio initially declined to 1.7 in 1983, then increased to 2.86 in 1994 and decreased thereafter to 2.51 in 1998. The figures are likely to be understated due to a lack of comparability in the income data between the two sectors. According to the World Bank (1997, p. 19) the standard of living in urban areas is much higher than that suggested by the official per capita income data as a result of the provision of considerable state subsidies. Including the value of these subsidies and in-kind benefits raises urban income by 78 per cent in 1990 and 72 per cent in 1995. Taking this into account, the real urban–rural income gap may have increased from around twofold to about 3.5-fold on average over the period of the 1980s. This indicates that the urban–rural income gap was higher in China in the 1980s than that in some of the other low-income countries, for instance India (1.4), Bangladesh (1.5), Philippines (2.1), Thailand (2.2), Brazil (2.3) and Colombia (2.3) in the 1970s (World Bank 1983, p. 86).

4.3   A MEASUREMENT OF INCOME INEQUALITY

Among the measurements of income inequality the Gini index is the most well known since it is distribution free and ranges between zero and one, and therefore has broad international comparability. Despite this, owing to difficulties in gaining access to reliable statistical data, its application has been limited in China. In this study, official statistical provincial data are used but the urban sector and rural sector are separately classified. There are 30 provincial-level administrative units in China, and each unit is further divided into its own rural and urban parts. Hence there are 60 units in total. Since each unit has its own *hukou* system that restricts permanent population mobility from one unit to another, the computed Gini indexes reflect income inequality not only among different provinces but also between the rural and urban sectors.[6]

The official survey data published by the State Statistical Bureau annually are adjusted by using the consumer price index to remove the effects of inflation over the observed period. The data were obtained by a routine sample survey conducted by the State Statistical Bureau every year and published in the China Statistical yearbooks. The earliest year in which the data were compiled is 1981, hence that year is used as the base of the price adjustment. Since the data are not quintiles, the following equation, introduced by Yao (1997a), is used in the computation of the Gini index.

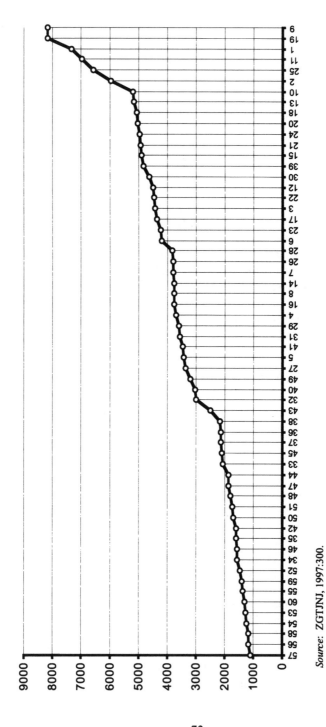

Source: ZGTJNJ, 1997:300.

Figure 4.1   The Ranking of Personal Disposable Income by Provinces and Sectors, 1996, China

(See next page for Note on this figure)

Note (for Figure 4.1):   The 30 urban units are numbered from 1 to 30 while the 30 rural units are numbered 31 to 60. The corresponding provincial administrative units shown in the figure are numbered as follows:

Urban	Rural	Province	Urban	Rural	Province	Urban	Rural	Province	Urban	Rural	Province
1	31	Beijing	9	39	Shanghai	17	47	Hubei	25	55	Tibet
2	32	Tianjin	10	40	Jiangsu	18	48	Hunan	26	56	Shaanxi
3	33	Hebei	11	41	Zhejiang	19	49	Guangdong	27	57	Gansu
4	34	Shanxi	12	42	Anhui	20	50	Guangxi	28	58	Qinghai
5	35	Inner Mongolia	13	43	Fujian	21	51	Hainan	29	59	Ningxia
6	36	Liaoning	14	44	Jiangxi	22	52	Sichuan	30	60	Xinjiang
7	37	Jilin	15	45	Shangdong	23	53	Guizhou			
8	38	Heilongjiang	16	46	Henan	24	54	Yunnan			

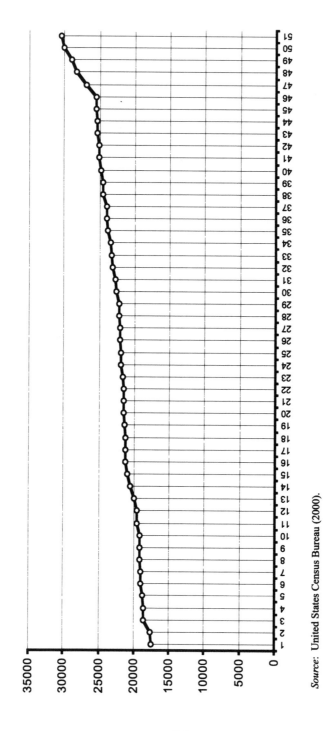

Source: United States Census Bureau (2000).

Figure 4.2a   Disposable Income by State, 1999, USA

(A State Index for this figure appears on the following page)

State Index (for Figure 4.2a)

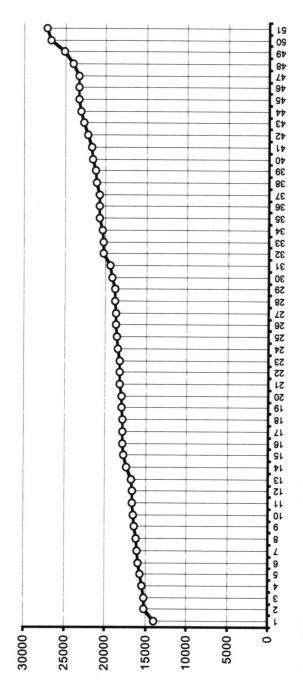

Source: United States Census Bureau (2000).

Figure 4.2b Disposable Income by State, 1990, USA

(A State Index for this figure appears on the following page)

State Index (for Figure 4.2b)

1 Mississippi	21 Georgia	41 Delaware
2 Arkansas	22 Texas	42 California
3 West Virginia	23 Missouri	43 Hawaii
4 Utah	24 Wisconsin	44 Maryland
5 New Mexico	25 Vermont	45 New York
6 Kentucky	26 Oregon	46 Massachusetts
7 Louisiana	27 Kansas	47 Alaska
8 Montana	28 Nebraska	48 Colorado
9 Idaho	29 Wyoming	49 New Jersey
10 Alabama	30 Ohio	50 District of Columbia
11 South Carolina	31 Michigan	51 Connecticut
12 Oklahoma	32 Minnesota	
13 North Dakota	33 Virginia	
14 South Dakota	34 Pennsylvania	
15 Tennessee	35 Florida	
16 Arizona	36 Washington	
17 North Carolina	37 Rhode Island	
18 Iowa	38 Illinois	
19 Indiana	39 Nevada	
20 Maine	40 New Hampshire	

Table 4.1
Income Differential between Rural and Urban Sectors, 1981–96

| Year | Personal income | | Income differential |
	Rural (1) RMB yuan	Urban (2) RMB yuan	Ratios (2)/(1)
1978	133.6	343.4	2.57
1980	223.4	477.6	2.14
1981	223.4	458.0	2.05
1982	270.1	494.5	1.83
1983	309.8	526.0	1.70
1984	355.3	607.6	1.71
1985	398.0	739.0	1.86
1986	423.8	899.6	2.12
1987	462.6	1 002.2	2.17
1988	544.9	1 181.4	2.17
1989	601.5	1 375.7	2.29
1990	686.3	1 510.2	2.20
1991	709.0	1 700.6	2.40
1992	784.0	2 026.6	2.58
1993	921.6	2 577.4	2.80
1994	1 221.0	3 496.2	2.86
1995	1 577.7	4 283.0	2.71
1996	1 926.0	4 838.9	2.51
1997	2 090.1	5 160.3	2.47
1998	2 162.0	5 425.1	2.51
1999	2 210.3	5 854.0	2.65

Note: RMB: Renmibi, unit of Chinese currency.

Sources: ZGTJNJ (1998) p. 78; (1996) p. 53; (1999) p. 318; (2000).

$$G = \sum_{i=1}^{n} p_i(2Q - w_i) \qquad i = 1 \text{ to } n \qquad (4.1)$$

where G is the Gini index and p_i is the population share of unit i, and $w_i = (p_i m_i)/m$, where m_i is income of unit i and m is the population mean income. Given

$\sum_{i=1}^{n} p_i = 1$, $\sum_{i=1}^{n} w_i = 1$, $Q = \sum_{k=1}^{i} w_k$ is the cumulative income share from unit 1 to

unit k, and p_i and w_i follow an ascending order of m_i.

Three Gini indexes, rural (G_r) (30 units), urban (G_u) (30 units) and overall (G) (60 units), were computed for the period 1981–96. The computations are summarised in Table 4.2.

Several insights can be generated from the results. First, bearing in mind that the computed indexes represent mainly the 'institutionally created' income inequality at the provincial level, and they are supposed to be trivial in a

Table 4.2
Computed Regional Gini Indexes in China, 1981–96

Year	G	G_r	G_u
1981	0.1655	0.0829	0.0717
1982	0.1571	0.1049	0.0795
1983	0.1531	0.1309	0.0778
1984	0.1781	0.1541	0.0835
1985	0.1629	0.1050	0.0798
1986	0.1881	0.1197	0.0809
1987	0.2030	0.1260	0.0855
1988	0.2108	0.1333	0.0874
1989	0.2101	0.1358	0.0864
1990	0.2028	0.1304	0.0908
1991	0.2225	0.1467	0.0968
1992	0.2339	0.1520	0.1074
1993	0.2578	0.1665	0.1198
1994	0.2796	0.1738	0.1500
1995	0.2700	0.1870	0.1312
1996	0.2529	0.1839	0.1310
1997	0.2466	0.1397	0.1339
1998	0.2540	0.1243	0.1172
Annual growth			
1981–89	2.26	5.03	2.62
1990–96	2.50	−0.53	2.84
1981–98	2.38	2.25	2.73
The USA counterpart			
1990	0.073		
1999	0.063		

Sources: Calculated by using statistical data of the ZGTJNJ (1991–98), ZGRKTJNJ (1994–97), LSTJZLHB (1990), and United States Census Bureau (2000).

circumstance of perfect population mobility, the figures presented in the table are significantly large. Taking Zhao's and Li's (1997) estimation of the corresponding rural, urban and overall household Gini indexes (0.340, 0.286 and 0.445 respectively in 1995) as a benchmark, the corresponding provincial counterparts reported in the table are: 0.187, 0.131 and 0.270, respectively. The computed level of income inequality between the urban and rural sectors could be lower had incomes been adjusted to the costs of living, which are, overall, substantially lower in the rural areas of China than in the cities.[7] Taking the difference between these two estimates as 'normal' income inequality, the 'institutionally created' inequality may account for 56.4, 47.7 and 61.9 per cent of the overall inequality in rural, urban, and China as a whole respectively in 1995. The Chinese regional Gini index can be compared with its US counterpart which ranged between 0.063 to 0.073 in 1990 and 1999 respectively (see Table 4.2). This suggests implicitly that had the *hukou* regime been abolished, about 0.20 of income inequality would have been removed from the national Gini index level in the 1990s.

Secondly, income inequality is higher in the rural sector than it is in the urban sector. This is in sharp contrast with other communist economies, and developing countries, where the opposite is usually observed. This is likely to be a consequence of the *hukou* regime that restricts the low-income rural residents moving out of the poorest rural areas. The difference between urban inequality and rural inequality is about 5 percentage points on average.

Thirdly, the computation indicates that all income inequality indexes (G, G_r and G_u) increased substantially over time. This is consistent with the studies of Griffin and Zhao (1993), Hussain et al. (1994), Tsui (1993, 1996), Wei (1996), and Zhao and Li (1997), among others. It is also worth noting that the rate of increase of the Gini index is faster in the rural sector than that in the urban sector during the observed period. If the observed period of 17 years is divided into two stages the increase of inequality was faster in the rural sector in the first stage (1981–88), whereas this pattern reversed in the second stage (1989–96). The growth in inequality is thus consistent with the deepening of economic reforms. More importantly, this trend is in sharp contrast to the urban–rural income gaps reported in Table 4.1, which show that the income differential between the two sectors declined during the first half of the 1980s but increased after 1985. This seems to suggest that the narrowing of the income gap between the two sectors in the first half of the 1980s was created by increases in both income and inequality in the rural sector, while the urban sector remained egalitarian. When the reform process incorporated the urban areas in the late 1980s, income and inequality had grown mainly in the urban sector so that the gap between the two sectors enlarged and the overall Gini index increased.

All these seem to suggest that overall income inequality increased in China when economic reform deepened, and the inequality is overwhelmingly determined by the urban–rural income gaps. A question raised is the extent to which the separation between the urban and rural sectors contributes to the provincial income inequality, and whether there are other factors involved. These questions cannot be answered without a decomposition of the Gini indexes.

4.4   DECOMPOSITION OF THE GINI RATIOS

Income inequality can be decomposed in several ways, but the Gini index is decomposable only in some circumstances (Pyatt 1976; Fei et al. 1979; Lambert and Aronson 1993). In this study we decompose the Gini ratio into three components (see Yao and Liu 1996; and Yao 1997a, 1997b).

As shown by Pyatt (1976), the Gini index at the overall level can be decomposed into its inter-sector, intra-sector and overlapped components, as follows:

$$G = G_A + G_B + G_O \qquad (4.2)$$

where G_A, G_B and G_O are the intra-sector, inter-sector, and overlapped components respectively of an overall Gini coefficient G. In our case the inter-sector component represents the rural and urban income differential; the intra-sector component indicates the income variations among provinces within either urban or rural sectors. The remainder, the overlapped component, reflects a circumstance where people living in the poorest urban area (such as a city in Inner Mongolia) can still feel better off than people living in the wealthiest rural area (such as a suburb of Shanghai), even if the income level is lower in the former than that in the latter. Yao and Liu (1996) developed a simple four-step procedure to conduct this decomposition. Using their method the 60 provincial-level administrative units are merely divided into two groups: the urban and rural sectors. Using the same data as used to compute the Gini indexes, the decomposition of the indexes into their inter-sector, intra-sector and overlapped components is computed and reported in Table 4.3.

The overall Gini indexes are shown in column 1 and the decomposed components of inter-sector, intra-sector and an overlapped term are shown in columns 2 to 4. The contribution of each factor, defined as the percentage of inequality generated from each component to the overall Gini index, is displayed in columns 5 to 7. Accounting for more than 61 per cent of the overall inequality, on average, the inter-sector component dominates the overall Gini index. The remainder, 37 per cent and 2 per cent respectively, can be allocated to the intra-sector component and the overlapped component. This decomposition attributes a similar proportion of the rural–urban income gap to overall inequality as estimated by the World Bank (World Bank 1997, p. 15), but the proportion is larger than that reported by Tsui (1993, 1996) and Wei (1996, p. 76) who decomposed a different index of income inequality, the Theil index.[8] We believe that our decomposition represents a lower bound of the inter-sector inequality since only part of the state subsidies to the urban residents are included in the official data. Even evaluated at this low limit, China's urban–rural income inequality is among the highest in the world. In contrast, for example, urban–rural income inequality contributed a mere 13 per cent of overall inequality in Malaysia (Tsui 1993, p. 617), 50 percentage points lower than that of China, as shown in Table 4.3.

The figures also indicate that inter-sector inequality increased over time when intra-sector inequality decreased. If the 15-year samples are divided into two stages, the inter-sector inequality increased by more than 11 percentage points and intra-sector inequality decreased by nearly 7 percentage points between the first stage (1981–88) and the second stage (1989–96). The balance is filled by a decrease in the overlapped term. This is consistent with the pattern of change in urban–rural income gaps shown in Table 4.1, indicating that overall income inequality is created mainly by the urban–rural income gaps that firstly narrowed but eventually enlarged after 1985. Using a different methodology in decomposing the Theil index, Wei (1996, p. 72) obtained a similar result.

4.5   CONCLUSIONS AND POLICY IMPLICATIONS

One distinctive feature of overall income distribution in China is that income inequality has increased along with the country's rapid economic growth over the past two decades. An administratively implemented household registration regime that prohibits rural–urban and inter-provincial migration is responsible for the particular pattern of inequality in personal income distribution in China. Since the income level in the urban sector is significantly higher and more equally distributed than that in the rural sector, overall income inequality in China is overwhelmingly determined by income differentials between the two sectors. The inter-sector inequality accounts for about 61 per cent while the intra-sector inequality accounts for merely 37 per cent of the overall income inequality. While the former mainly indicates an isolation effect between rural and urban areas, the latter captures the impact of the *hukou* regime on provincial disparities within each sector.

Given the fact that the 'institutionally created' income inequality accounts for over 60 per cent of the overall income inequality, this study tends to suggest that the overall income inequality would be greatly reduced (roughly by 0.20 from its computed Gini index) if the *hukou* regime was abolished. However, since the abolition of the *hukou* is a complicated and politically sensitive issue, it should be carried out gradually and with a great deal of caution.

In the short run the following measures may be implemented. First, the policy bias in transfer payments toward the urban sector can be removed. The

Table 4.3
Decomposition of the Gini Indexes by Sector

Year	[1] Overall Gini	[2] Inter-sector com-ponent	[3] Intra-sector com-ponent	[4] Overlap term	[5] Inter-sector (%)	[6] Intra-sector (%)	[7] Overlap term (%)
1981	0.1655	0.0889	0.0578	0.0188	53.74	34.91	11.36
1982	0.1571	0.0900	0.0663	0.0008	57.26	42.23	0.51
1983	0.1531	0.0653	0.0818	0.0059	42.67	53.45	3.88
1984	0.1781	0.0707	0.0985	0.0089	39.68	55.32	5.01
1985	0.1613	0.0940	0.0662	0.0011	58.29	41.04	0.67
1986	0.1912	0.1207	0.0701	0.0004	63.12	36.66	0.22
1987	0.1844	0.0918	0.0773	0.0153	49.80	41.92	8.28
1988	0.2108	0.1135	0.0780	0.0193	53.85	36.99	9.16
1989	0.2101	0.1336	0.0768	−0.0003	63.57	36.55	−0.12
1990	0.2033	0.1280	0.0744	0.0009	62.95	36.61	0.45
1991	0.2225	0.1394	0.0823	0.0007	62.67	37.00	0.33
1992	0.2339	0.1492	0.0840	0.0007	63.80	35.90	0.30
1993	0.2578	0.1685	0.0887	0.0007	65.35	34.39	0.26
1994	0.2796	0.1873	0.0920	0.0004	66.98	32.89	0.13
1995	0.2700	0.1729	0.0967	0.0005	64.02	35.81	0.17
1996	0.2529	0.1558	0.0962	0.0009	61.61	38.05	0.34
Mean							
1981–88	0.1752	0.0919	0.0745	0.0088	52.30	42.82	4.89
1989–96	0.2413	0.1543	0.0864	0.0006	63.87	35.90	0.23
1981–96	0.2325	0.1440	0.0846	0.0039	61.46	36.61	1.93

Sources: Same as for Table 4.2.

new reform programmes may redress the bias on housing, food, credit, education, employment, and other policies that provide *de facto* subsidies to urban residents. The implementation of this reform may be accompanied by some other reforms, for instance private issuance services and commercialisation of the housing allocation system, to overcome the political difficulties and provide executive feasibility.

Secondly, by using either pricing or fiscal tools the government may facilitate rural household farming. The self-sufficiency policy in grain production and price control on grain and cotton sales may be abolished. Rural nonagricultural activities may be encouraged, especially in the inland provinces where it has been proved that the development of township and village enterprises is the main source of poverty alleviation. Any policy package that facilitates reducing rural poverty, for instance the increase in investment in rural infrastructure, tax deductions for agricultural produce and an increase in state relief resources, may also reduce overall income inequality. By the same token the recent government decision to further extend the lease of land use for up to 30 years may certainly be a good move. If the restriction on land trade is further removed, rural income can be expected to increase from an emerging rural land market. This in turn may also help in reducing the rural–urban income gaps.

However, these short-run measures can only alleviate, but not eliminate, the regional income differentials. In the long run the rural–urban income gaps cannot be removed without abolishing the *hukou* regime and encouraging rural to urban (and cross-provincial) migration. Since the isolation between a capital intensive and high-income urban sector and a labour surplus and low-income rural sector represents a misallocation of resources, more could be produced when the immobility is lessened. Although migration may create problems, particularly to the fragile state-owned sector that is suffering from labour abundance, so far its impact on overall income distribution has been positive (Chai and Chai 1997). According to a study by Zhao (1999, p. 776) shifting one worker from farm to local non-farm work increases family income by 13 per cent, while shifting one worker from farm to migratory work increases family income by 49.1 per cent. Migration alleviates the pronounced inequality between poor rural people and relatively wealthy urbanites when the migrants send significant portions of their earnings back to their families in rural areas. When the urban sector absorbs surplus labour from the rural sector until the value of the marginal product is equalised in the two sectors, the total product of the country will be maximised and income will be more equally distributed among its people.

So far there are more restrictions than incentives in the process of rural to urban migration in China. The explicit cost, along with implicit costs, such as discrimination in the education and health system, expensive urban living standards for migrants, and psychological hardship, all deter the willingness to migrate (Zhao 1999, p. 778). Should income distribution be a major goal of China's economic development in the new century a far-sighted policy may remove these deterrents and encourage further migration.

NOTES

1   The World Bank's cut-off of the poorest 10 per cent of low-income receivers were all located in rural areas (World Bank 1997, p. 44).

2   See for example Cheng (1996), Yao (1997b) and Wan (1998) for a recent analysis of the rural sector.

3   For instance, while the Gini index ratios were 0.338 and 0.233 for the rural and urban sectors respectively in 1988, the overall Gini index ratio was 0.382. These ratios were raised to 0.429, 0.286, and 0.445 respectively in 1995 (Zhao and Li 1997, p. 21).

4   These units include three municipalities, five minority autonomous regions and 22 provinces in the pre-reform era. Since 1997 the combination has been extended to four municipalities, five minority autonomous regions, 22 provinces and one special administrative region (Hong Kong).

5   However, caution should be applied when interpreting this ratio since it is based on provincial data rather than household data.

6   Here we interpret each provincial unit as representative of identical households within the province, a common assumption used in most empirical studies and referred to as the linear interpolation method (Kakwani 1980, p. 96). Obviously, this method may lead to substantial underestimation of real overall inequality, especially when the income groups are widely dispersed.

7   However, there are some forces that might invert this commonsense assertion. For instance, general price indexes have been higher in the rural areas than in the urban areas. Also general rural retail price indexes of industrial products have been higher than general retail price indexes, which in turn have been higher than general purchasing price indexes of farm products since 1996 (ZGTJNJ 1999, p. 293).

8   Tsui (1993, 1996) and Wei (1998) decompose an index of the general entropy and report that about half of the overall income inequality is attributable to the inter-sector contribution. Their results cannot be compared with ours since the data and period of evaluation are different.

REFERENCES

Adelman, Irma and David Sunding (1987), 'Economic Policy and Income Distribution in China', *Journal of Comparative Economics*, **11**, 444–61.

Atkinson, Anthony B. and John Micklewright (1992), *Economic Transformation in Eastern Europe and the Distribution of Income*, Cambridge: Cambridge University Press.

Adams, R. (1994), 'Non-farm Income and Inequality in Rural Pakistan: A Decomposition Analysis', *Journal of Development Studies*, **31** (1), 10–33.

Barmail, Chris and Marion E. Jones (1993), 'Rural Income Inequality in China Since 1978', *The Journal of Peasant Studies*, **21** (1), 41–70.

Chai, Joseph C.H. and B. Karin Chai (1997), 'China's Floating Population and

Its Implications', *International Journal of Social Economics*, **24** (7/8/9), 1038–51.

Chen Zongsheng (1994), *Income Distribution in Economic Development*, Shanghai: Shanghai Sanlian Press.

Cheng Yuk-shing (1996), 'A Decomposition Analysis of Income Inequality of Chinese Rural Household', *China Economic Review*, **7** (2), 155–67.

Cheng, Tiejun and Mark Selden (1994), 'The Origins and Social Consequences of China's Hukou System', *The China Quarterly*, **139** (September), 644–68.

Cornia, Giovanni Andrea (1994), 'Income Distribution, Poverty and Welfare in Transitional Economies: A Comparison Between Eastern Europe and China', *Journal of International Development*, **6** (5), 569–607.

Fei, J. G. Ranis and Shirley Kuo (1979), *Growth with Equity: The Taiwan Case*, A World Bank Research Publication, Washington, DC: Oxford University Press.

Feng Wenrong, Lai Desheng and Li You (1996), *Issues of Distribution of Personal Income in China*, Beijing: Beijing Normal University Press.

Griffin, Keith and Zhao Renwei (eds) (1993), *The Distribution of Income in China*, New York: St Martin's Press.

He Qinglain (1997), *The Trap of Modernization*, Beijing: China Today Press.

Hussain, Athar, Peter Lanjouw and Nicholas Stern (1994), 'Income Inequalities in China: Evidence from Household Survey Data', *World Development*, **22** (12), 1947–57.

Kakwani, Nanak, C. (1980), *Income Inequality and Poverty: Methods of Estimation and Policy Applications*, A World Bank Research Publication, Washington, DC: Oxford University Press.

Khan, Azizur Rahman, Keith Griffin, Carl Riskin and Zhao Renwei (1993), 'Household Income and its Distribution in China', in Keith Griffin and Zhao Renwei (eds), *The Distribution of Income in China*, New York: St Martin's Press.

Khan, Azizur Rahman and Carl Riskin (1998), 'Income and Inequality in China: Composition, Distribution and Growth of Household Income', *China Quarterly*, **154** [June], 221–53.

Kuznets, S. (1955), 'Economic Growth and Income Inequality', *American Economic Review*, **45**, 1–28.

Lambert, P.J. and J.R. Aronson (1993), 'Inequality Decomposition Analysis and the Gini Coefficient Revisited', *Economic Journal*, **420**, 221–7.

Lewis, W. Arthur (1954), 'Economic Development with Unlimited Supplies of Labor', *The Manchester School*, (May) 139–91.

LSTJZLHB (*Lishi Tongji Ziliao Huibian*, Encyclopaedia of Historical Statistical Materials), China Statistical Press.

Nolan, P. and J. Sender (1992), 'Death Rates, Life Expectancy and China's Economic Reforms', *World Development*, **20** (9), 1279–304.

Putterman, Louise (1992), 'Dualism and Reform in China', *Economic Development and Cultural Change*, **40** (3), 467–94.

Pyatt, G. (1976), 'On the Interpretation and Desegregation of Gini Coefficient', *Economic Journal*, **86**, 243–55.

Ranis, G. and J. Fei (1961), 'A Theory of Economic Development', *American Economic Review*, September, 533–65.

Riskin, Carl (1987), *China's Political Economy: The Quest for Development Since 1949*, New York: Oxford University Press.

Schwarze, J. (1996), 'How Income Inequality Changed in Germany Following Reunification: An Empirical Analysis Using Decomposable Inequality Measures', *Review of Income and Wealth*, **42** (1), 1–11.

Selden, Mark (1993), *The Political Economy of Chinese Development*, Armont, NY: M.E. Sharpe.

Tsui, K.Y. (1993), 'Decomposition of China's Regional Inequalities', *Journal of Comparative Economics*, **17**, 600–27.

Tsui, K.Y. (1996), 'Economic Reform and Inter-Provincial Inequalities in China', *Journal of Development Economics*, **50**, 353–68.

United States Census Bureau (2000), 'Statistical Abstract of the United States', Section 1 (1–76) and 14 (715–766). Available from <www.census.gov/prod/www/statistical-abstract-us.html>.

Wan, Guanghua (1998), 'An Empirical Analysis on Inter-Regional Income Inequality in China and its Changes', *Jingji Yanjiu* (*Economic Research Journal*), **5**, 36–41.

Wei Houkai (1996), 'Inter-Regional Income Inequality in China and Its Decomposition', *Jingji Yanjiu* [Economic Research Journal], **11**, 66–73.

World Bank (1983), *Socialist Economic Development*, Volume I: *The Economy, Statistical System and Basic Data*, Washington, DC: The World Bank.

World Bank (1997), *Sharing Rising Incomes*, China 2020 Series, Washington, DC: The World Bank.

Yao, Shujie (1997a), 'Decomposition of Gini Coefficients by Income Factors: A New Approach and Application', *Applied Economic Letters*, **4**, 27–31.

Yao, Shujie (1997b), 'Industrialization and Spatial Income Inequality in Rural China, 1986–92', *Economics of Transition*, **5** (1), 97–112.

Yao, Shujie (1999), 'Economic Growth, Income Inequality and Poverty in China under Economic Reforms', *The Journal of Development Studies*, **35** (6), 104–30.

Yao Shujie and Liu Jirui (1996), 'Decomposition of Gini Coefficients by Income Factors: A New Approach', *Applied Economic Letters*, **3**, 115–9.

ZGRKTJNJ [*Zhongguo Renkou, Tongji Nianjian*, Statistical Yearbook of Population in PRC], 1994–97, Beijing: Chinese Statistical Press.

ZGTJNJ [*Zhongguo Tongji Nianjian*, Chinese Statistical Yearbook], many issues.

ZGTJZY [*Zhongguo Tongji Zhaiyao*, A Statistical Survey of China], 1998.

Zhang, Xiaohe (1992), 'Urban-Rural Isolation and Its Impact on China's Production and Trade Pattern', *China Economic Review* (USA), **3** (1), 85–105.

Zhang, Xiaohe (1998), 'Growth Without Development: A Paradox of Urban-Rural Income Gaps in China', paper presented at an international conference on 'China's Economic Reform and Social Development', held at Hong Kong Baptist University, Kowloon Tong, Hong Kong, 11–12 May.

Zhao Renwei (1993), 'Three Features of the Distribution of Income during the Transition of Reform', in Keith Griffin and Zhao Renwei (eds), *The Distribution of Income in China*, New York: St Martin's Press.

Zhao Renwei and Li Shi (1997), 'The Enlargement and Reasons of Income Differential of Chinese Citizens', *Jingji Yanjiu* [Economic Research Journal], **9**, 19:28.

Zhao Xiaohui (1999), 'Labor Migration and Earnings Difference: The Case of Rural China', *Economic Development and Cultural Change*, **47** (4), 767–83.

5   Income Inequality and Redistributive Government Spending: Theory and Panel Data Evidence

Francisco Galrão Carneiro, Luiz de Mello and Erwin Tiongson

5.1   INTRODUCTION

An important debate on the international development policy agenda is the extent to which economic growth contributes to poverty alleviation. There is widespread recognition that periods of sustained economic growth are associated with reductions in the incidence of poverty, measured by the share of the population living below the poverty line, for example, but not necessarily with improvements in the distribution of income.[1] The weak correlation between economic growth and changes in income distribution has been used to justify government intervention in the form of publicly-financed income redistribution programmes. However, paradoxically, casual observation suggests that governments in more unequal societies tend to redistribute less, not more, than those in more egalitarian parts of the world. Against this background, it can be argued that the countries where redistributive public spending is more needed are the ones that are less likely to allocate public resources to these programmes.

An equally important debate in the literature has been on the impact of inequality on growth. Economists since at least Simon Kuznets in the 1950s, and Nicholas Kaldor in the 1960s, have explored the tradeoff between reduced inequality and faster growth. The phenomenal post-war growth of East Asian economies and the advent of endogenous growth models have led to renewed interest in the inequality/growth nexus and its institutional and political channels. This rapidly growing literature is surveyed in Perotti (1996), Alesina and Perotti (1994), and Bénabou (1996). A series of papers have explored the channels through which inequality affects growth, including what Perotti (1996) refers to as the 'endogenous fiscal policy' channel. In brief, this argues that inequality leads to greater redistribution, following the median voter hypothesis. Redistribution is financed by greater distortionary taxation and this, in turn, reduces growth. Inequality, therefore, is harmful to growth. In practice, however, inequality has not led to greater redistribution.

Several studies have aimed at shedding light on the reasons why unequal societies are less willing to spend public funds on redistribution but the empirical literature on redistribution and inequality, to be surveyed below, is not clear-cut. The correlation between inequality and redistribution is sensitive to the choice of countries in the sample, the time period under examination, and the definition of redistributive spending and income distribution indicators. This will be discussed in some detail in what follows.

Specifically, this chapter will focus on three questions. In particular:

- What is the sign of the correlation between income inequality and redistributive government spending? If the correlation is negative, more unequal societies spend less on redistribution than their more egalitarian counterparts, and the median voter hypothesis is rejected.

- Is the relationship between redistributive spending and income inequality linear? Under the median voter hypothesis, the political science literature shows that redistributive spending increases linearly with income inequality. However, the possibility of a nonlinear relationship between redistribution and inequality has been motivated by recent work, such as Bénabou (2000), who has identified two steady states associating high (low) income inequality with low (high) redistributive spending. Although intellectually appealing, the hypothesis of a nonlinear association between redistribution and inequality has not yet been tested in the empirical literature.

- What are the main channels through which inequality affects redistribution? It has been argued that capital market imperfections affect the inequality/ redistribution nexus (Bénabou 2000). The key argument is that inequality is perpetuated over time when people do not have access to capital markets to insure themselves against adverse economic shocks or to make the long-term investment needed to improve their future earnings capacity. In the presence of capital market imperfections, the argument goes, egalitarian societies are willing to spend on redistributive programmes to avoid the rise of inequality.

This chapter is organised as follows. Section 5.2 surveys the theoretical literature. Section 5.3 reviews the main findings in the empirical literature. Section 5.4 describes the data and the estimation techniques, and reports the results of the empirical analysis. Section 5.6 concludes.

5.2   THE THEORETICAL BACKGROUND

The theoretical rationale for an association between inequality and redistribution is provided by the median voter hypothesis. The seminal work by Meltzer and Richard (1981) develops a model of voting over redistribution in which income is imperfectly distributed so that the median voter is poorer than the mean voter. The key argument is that, assuming that the preferences of the median voter are taken into account in the political process under majority voting and that taxation is progressive, the median voter is better off exerting political pressure for redistributive government intervention. This is because, as long as taxation is progressive, the benefit to the median voter of redistributive transfers from the government outweighs the costs of taxation (borne by the median voter) to finance redistribution.

A large literature, surveyed by, for instance, de Mello and Tiongson (2001), followed Meltzer's and Richard's work. Interestingly, the hypothesis that inequality could be associated with less, not more, redistributive spending was originally put forward in the empirical, rather than the theoretical, literature. This was motivated primarily by the failure reported in many empirical studies, to be surveyed below, to find empirical support for the median voter hypothesis. Theoretical arguments for a negative correlation between inequality and redistribution were not available until, more recently, Bénabou (2000) developed a stochastic growth model in which capital market imperfections play a key role in the association between inequality and redistributive government spending. The argument is that, when capital and insurance markets are imperfect and individuals are heterogeneous, popular support for redistributive policies decreases with inequality.

Bénabou argues that low inequality creates wide political support for redistribution so as not to allow income disparities to grow over time as a result of capital market imperfections. In support of this line of argument, Furman and Stiglitz (1998, p. 222) argue that 'capital market imperfections imply that consumption fluctuations induced by business fluctuations are far greater than they would be with perfect capital markets, with correspondingly large effects on welfare'. Thus, if capital markets are imperfect, investment opportunities differ between individuals with low and high initial wealth and these unequal investment opportunities generate income inequalities that persist over time. Additionally, Bénabou (2000) shows that nonlinearities in the model lead to two steady states defined for low inequality and high redistribution, on the one hand, and for high inequality and low redistribution, on the other hand. In the long run, a negative relationship is expected to prevail between redistribution and inequality.

The role of capital market imperfection in perpetuating income inequality can easily be illustrated. Consider to begin with the example of private spending on education. Human capital investment has long-term maturity and individuals may not be able to borrow to finance spending on education and therefore increase their future earnings possibilities. Even when individuals can borrow against future earnings, investment in education is risky, returns are uncertain, and, in the absence of insurance markets, poorer individuals may be unwilling, and unable, to incur these risks. Poor households may therefore be caught in a poverty trap, as suggested by Galor and Zeira (1993), and inequality may be perpetuated across generations in the presence of imperfect capital markets. A similar argument is put forward by Lee and Roemer (1998): when a class of individuals is unable to invest in education, due to capital market imperfection, a Kaldorian channel works against the median voter hypothesis. While the median voter hypothesis assumes a negative relationship between inequality and private investment, due to higher tax rates, the Kaldorian channel assumes that because the rich save more, inequality favours accumulation.

Agricultural risk is another example of how imperfections in capital and insurance markets may perpetuate income inequality, particularly in the developing world. In the absence of well-functioning capital markets, poor households may fail to insure themselves against adverse states of nature, such as bad weather conditions and fluctuations in commodity prices. Poor individuals may also be denied access to credit markets, and financial intermediation in general, that would allow them to smooth consumption and to finance housing acquisition and upgrading, trade, small manufacturing, service activities, and investment in existing, often small enterprises.

The association between inequality and redistribution has also been shown to depend on political economy factors, as argued by Persson and Tabellini (1999). These factors have been shown to weaken the median voter hypothesis and, therefore, to justify a negative correlation between inequality and redistribution. For instance, Rodriguez (1999b) shows that inequality may be negatively associated with redistribution via rent-seeking and political influence. In his analysis, greater inequality translates into an increased share of public resources accruing to individuals who are in a position to influence policymakers. This is also the argument used by Olson (1965) to illustrate how pressure groups can affect the path of economic growth. As shown by the political economy–growth literature, in unequal societies, organised individuals pursue their interests outside the usual channels of political representation (Alesina and Perotti 1994, 1996). Similarly, Lee and Roemer (1999) show that, with greater inequality, a given tax rate yields less revenues for the same tax base, which then induces less public spending.

5.3   THE EMPIRICAL LITERATURE

The empirical literature has focused on estimating the sign of the correlation between inequality and redistributive government spending, and on testing the median voter hypothesis. Rather than estimating the correlation between inequality and redistribution directly, the median voter hypothesis has been tested almost exclusively in the political economy–growth literature. As surveyed in Bénabou (1996), Panizza (1999), and Milanovic (2000), among others, income distribution has been shown to affect economic growth through its impact on government spending and taxation. Redistributive spending financed by distortionary taxation reduces the incentive for capital accumulation and investment, and therefore output growth (Alesina and Rodrik 1994; Perotti 1996). Persson and Tabellini (1994), for example, report a negative relationship between income inequality and growth in which government transfers constitute a key mechanism.

The empirical literature has focused on industrial economies. Data availability is an important limitation to the estimation of the association between redistribution and inequality for a large enough sample of countries. More importantly, the industrial country bias is justified on the grounds that the median voter argument is only valid in democracies (Perotti 1996). Moreover, because of the limited variance over time in the data, given that inequality indicators, such as income shares and the Gini coefficient, are not likely to change significantly in short periods of time, most empirical studies have focused on cross-sectional data. In recent empirical studies, the cross-sections have often been constructed using 10-year averages, rather than annual data. This is the case in Perotti (1992, 1994, 1996), and Persson and Tabellini (1994), among others. Panel data studies are few and typically use US state data, such as the study by Partridge (1997), Gouveia and Masia (1998), and Rodriguez (1999a). Lindert (1996) and Milanovic (2000) are among the few empirical studies using panel data for a cross-section of industrial economies.

Cross-country studies typically regress aggregate or redistributive government spending on a measure of income distribution and control for other determinants of public expenditure. Government spending data are drawn from the IMF's Government Finance Statistics (GFS), often combined with information from other sources. Until 1996, data on income distribution had been drawn from different data sets. Cross-country studies conducted after 1996 have relied on data collected by Deininger and Squire (1996), noting their superior reliability to data collected earlier. Notwithstanding the improvement in the quality of data on income distribution, researchers (Panizza 1999; Atkinson and Brandolini 2000) have recently criticised the data compiled by Deininger and Squire (1996).

The association between inequality and redistributive government spending has conventionally been estimated in cross-sectional equations such as:

$$\frac{T_i}{Y_i} = a_0 + a_1 I_i + a_2 C_i + u_i \tag{5.1}$$

where T denotes government-financed redistributive transfers to individuals/ households, Y is GDP, I is a measure of inequality (that is, income shares, Gini coefficient), C is a vector of control variables, u is an error term, and i identifies the countries in the sample.

The standard control variables are initial per capita income and the dependency ratio, measured as the share of the population aged 65 and over. Initial per capita income, proxying for ability to pay for redistributive programmes, is associated with a larger share of redistributive spending in GDP.[2] Additional control variables have been experimented with in the literature. An index of democracy has been used as an additional control variable and as an interaction with the inequality indicator to test the median voter hypothesis, as in Perotti (1996) and de Mello and Tiongson (2001). For the median voter hypothesis to hold, most, if not all, individuals are assumed to vote. Thus, the relationship between inequality and redistribution must be stronger in democracies.

As shown in Table 5.1, reproduced from de Mello and Tiongson (2001), the parameter estimates reported in the empirical literature have been, in general, insignificant. The earliest test of the inequality–redistribution hypothesis, carried out by Meltzer and Richard (1983), has been criticised on methodological grounds (Tullock 1983). More recently, Gouveia and Masia (1998) replicated the Meltzer and Richard (1983) equations using panel data for the US states covering the period 1979–91 and found little evidence to support the hypothesis. Moffitt, Ribar, and Wilhelm (1998) test the hypothesis that the decline in welfare benefits in the USA is related to the increase in wage inequality and to the decline of real wages at the lower end of the income distribution. That is, voters prefer welfare benefits that are tied to low-skill wages. Using US state panel data for 1962–92, the authors indeed find support for the hypothesis.

The cross-state study by Bassett, Burkett and Putterman (1999) is one of the empirical studies reporting a negative association between inequality and redistribution, based on data for up to 54 countries in the period 1970–85. Inequality is measured as the share of income accruing to the third quintile to proxy for the median voter. A positive association is reported between inequality and redistribution only when the inequality variable is redefined as the income share of the very rich (highest 5-per-cent bracket of the income distribution). The explanation proposed by the authors is based on a 'soak-the-rich' effect due to a large concentration of income at the top of the country's income

Table 5.1

Summary of Recent Studies: Inequality and Redistribution

Source	Sample size	Period	Data structure	Measures		Correlation	
				Redistribution[a]	Inequality	Sign[b]	Significance
Bassett, and others, 1999	Up to 54 countries	1970–85	Cross-country average	Social security and welfare	Mostly Q3 in 1960s[c]	Generally negative	Inconsistent
Easterly and Rebelo, 1993	Not available	1970–88	Cross-country average	Spending variables	Gini, various income shares	Positive	Significant
Figini, 1998	Up to 63 countries	1970–90	Cross-country average	Tax rates, total revenue and total spending	Gini coefficient in 1970	Nonlinear	Significant
Gouveia and Masia, 1998	50 US states	1979–91	Panel	Spending variables	Ratio of mean to median income	Generally negative	Generally significant
Lindert, 1996	14 OECD countries	1962–81	Panel	Spending variables	Income gap index	Negative	Generally insignificant
Meltzer and Richard, 1983	US average	1937–77	Time series	Spending variables	Ratio of mean to median income	Positive	Significant
Milanovic, 2000	24 mostly OECD countries	1967–97[d]	Panel	Gain by poorest quintile or poorest half	Pre-transfer Gini coefficient	Positive	Significant
Panizza, 1999	46 US states	1970–80	Cross-state average	Tax, tax progress-ivity, and spending variables	Q3 in 1970[c]	Generally positive	Inconsistent
Partridge, 1997	48 US states	1960–90[e]	Panel	Tax, employment & spending variables	Pre-tax Gini, Q3	Inconsistent	Generally significant
Perotti, 1992	40 democracies	1970–85	Cross-country average	Spending variables	Q3 in 1970[c]	Negative	Insignificant

(continued)

95

Table 5.1 (continued)

Summary of Recent Studies: Inequality and Redistribution

Source	Sample size	Period	Data structure	Measures		Correlation	
				Redistribution[a]	Inequality	Sign[b]	Significance
Perotti, 1994	52 countries	1970–85	Cross-country average	Transfers	Q3 in 1960[c]	Negative	Insignificant
Perotti, 1996	49 countries	1970–85	Cross-country average	Tax rates and spending variables	Q3 and Q4 in 1960[c]	Generally positive	Generally insignificant
Persson and Tabellini, 1994	13 OECD countries	1960–81	Cross-country average	Transfers	Q3 in 1965[c]	Positive	Insignificant
Rodriguez, 1999a	50 US states	1984–94	Time series and cross-state average[f]	Spending variables	Distribution skewness	Inconsistent	Insignificant
Tanninen, 1999	Up to 45 countries	1970–88	Cross-country average	Spending variables	Adjusted Gini co-efficient in 1970s[g]	Inconsistent	Generally insignificant

Source: de Mello and Tiongson (2001).

Notes:

a   In percentage of GDP unless otherwise indicated.
b   Negative means greater inequality is associated with less spending.
c   A higher Q3 means greater income equality. For consistency with other studies in the reporting of main results, Q3 and Q4 are taken to mean – Q3 and – Q4.
d   Total number of observations is 79.
e   Total number of observations is 144.
f   Refers to national time series.
g   Adjusted for variations in the Gini definition.

distribution. Accordingly, in societies where the income distribution is highly skewed, the median voter is substantially poorer than the 'decisive voter', who controls the political process. Incidentally, in his theoretical model, Bénabou (1996) assumes that the pivotal agent has a higher income than the median voter to show that inequality can lead to less redistribution.

An important discussion in the empirical literature is the measure of income to be used in the inequality indicator. In principle, following the political economy argument, support for redistributive policies depends on pre-redistribution income. Detailed information on pre-tax, pre-transfer income (factor income) is only available for more developed countries, as well as data on the incidence of redistributive programmes. A recent test of the theory reported by Milanovic (2000) uses factor income data available from the Luxembourg Income Study (LIS). Based on this data set, a positive and statistically significant association is reported between redistribution and inequality. The results reported by Milanovic (2000) nevertheless do not lend support to the median voter hypothesis, according to which redistribution is pursued in unequal societies through its increased benefits to the middle class. In the same vein, to better control for the determinants of disposable income, Panizza (1999) uses an index of tax progressivity for the US states as an additional explanatory variable in his regional growth regressions.

The hypothesis of nonlinearities in the relationship between inequality and redistribution, as put forward by Bénabou (2000), has been tested by de Mello and Tiongson (2001) by re-estimating equation (5.1) as follows:

$$\frac{T_i}{Y_i} = a_0 + a_1 I_i + a_2 I_i^2 + a_3 C_i + u_i \qquad (5.2)$$

When the inequality indicator used in the estimating equations is the Gini coefficient, the authors cannot reject the null hypothesis that $a_1 < 0$ and $a_1 \neq 0$ in equations (5.1) and (5.2). A preliminary test of nonlinearity was carried out by Figini (1998), using aggregate spending variables. The U-shaped relationship holds for different definitions of inequality: the Gini coefficient, the income share of the lowest quintile, and the income share of the middle quintile.[3]

De Mello and Tiongson (2001) also argue that equations (5.1) and (5.2) do not allow for testing the hypothesis that the association between inequality and redistribution is affected by capital market development, as hypothesised by Bénabou (2000), among others. In this case, they re-estimate equations (5.1) and (5.2) together with equation (5.3) below:

$$I_i = \alpha_0 + \alpha_1 M_i + \alpha_2 C_i + e_i \qquad (5.3)$$

where M is a proxy for capital market development.

When the inequality indicator used in the estimating equations is the Gini coefficient, the authors cannot reject the null hypothesis that $\alpha_1 < 0$ in equation (5.3). Parameter estimates are negatively signed and statistically significant, as above, and greater in magnitude than those estimated by OLS. The results also hold when the quadratic term and the share of the population aged 65 and over are included in the regressions.

The endogeneity of the inequality variable had not been addressed in the literature on the grounds that it is difficult to find adequate instruments for income distribution in inequality/growth equations (Perotti 1998). Bourguignon and Morrisson (1998) use an indicator of economic dualism, constructed as the ratio of labour productivity in the non-agricultural sector and in the agricultural sector, as a determinant of inequality. Perotti (1996) suggests the inclusion of the urbanisation rate in the inequality regressions because urban areas tend to have higher levels of inequality.

Conventional proxies for capital deepening are used as the instruments for capital market imperfection, including credit to the domestic economy and to the private sector. The ratio of credit to GDP, where credit is measured by M2, is a standard proxy for capital deepening. The higher this ratio, ceteris paribus, the more sophisticated the financial intermediation instruments in the economy. In addition, although credit measures differ significantly across countries, the measurement of M2 is fairly standard, hence facilitating cross-country comparability. De Mello and Tiongson (2001) also experimented with different proxies for capital market development, including the black market premium and the interest rate spread. The results for both transfers and welfare spending hold when credit to the domestic market is used as an instrument, together with the black market premium, instead of the M2/GDP ratio.

5.4   DATA AND EMPIRICAL ANALYSIS

The data we use a span from 1972 to 1987 for a sample of 37 industrialised and developing countries.[4] Table 5.2 provides descriptive statistics of the data and Table 5.3 lists the countries included in our sample.

We use data on government transfers (government expenditures on social security and welfare), available from the IMF's *Government Finance Statistics* (GFS) and the United Nations' *System of National Accounts* (SNA). Income inequality data (Gini coefficient) are available from Deininger and Squire (1996). The share of the population aged 65 and over, GDP per capita, and instruments for capital market imperfection, including credit to the domestic economy, credit to the private sector, and the share of broad money (M2) to GDP, are available from the World Bank's 2000 *World Development Indicators* (WDI). Data on the black market exchange rate premium are available from the *Global Development Network* database. The indicator of democracy is available from

Table 5.2
Descriptive Statistics

	Mean	Std. dev.	Min.	Max.	Source
Population over 65 years of age (in % of total)	8.2	4.4	2.6	17.9	WDI
Gini coefficient	38.3	10.2	20	62.5	UNU-WIDER
Government spending (in % of GDP)	13.8	12.4	0.3	54.8	GFS-SNA
PPP real GDP per capita (US dollars)	9 431.1	8 335.8	189	31 588.5	WDI
Democracy index	5.8	3.7	0	10.0	La Porta, et al. (1999)
Money and quasi money (M2) (in % of GDP)	24.1	21.2	11.9	91.9	WDI
Domestic credit by banking sector (in % of GDP)	59.1	35.8	9.1	223.5	WDI
Credit to private sector (in % of GDP)	43.9	29.1	4.1	152.2	WDI

La Porta, Lopez-de-Silanes, Shleifer, and Vishny (1999). It is scaled from 0 to 10, with lower values indicating a less democratic environment.

5.5   THE RESULTS

Against the background of the survey of the empirical literature above, we have opted for estimating equation (5.1) directly and testing for the nonlinearity of the inequality variable in equation (5.2). The baseline estimations of equations (5.1) and (5.2) are reported in Table 5.4. Models (1) to (4) were estimated by OLS. The dependent variable is the sum of government spending on social security and welfare programmes in relation to GDP. Model (5) was estimated by two-stage least squares (2SLS) and the inequality variable was instrumented by conventional proxies for capital deepening such as credit to the domestic economy and to the private sector, as well as the share of broad money (M2) in GDP. In all models, the parameter estimates show that more inequality, measured by the initial Gini coefficient, is associated with less redistribution. The control

Table 5.3
Countries in the GFS and SNA Samples for Which There Were Data
Available for Our Estimating Period, 1972–87

Australia	Japan
The Bahamas	Korean Republic
Bangladesh	Malaysia
Belgium	Mexico
Brazil	Netherlands
Bulgaria	New Zealand
Canada	Norway
Chile	Panama
Colombia	Philippines
Costa Rica	Portugal
Denmark	Romania
Finland	Singapore
France	Spain
Germany	Sri Lanka
Honduras	Sweden
Hungary	Thailand
India	United Kingdom
Ireland	United States
Italy	Venezuela

Note: Estimating sample (NT) contains 592 observations as the result of 37 countries (N) and 16 time periods (T).

variable is correctly signed as initial income per capita is associated with a larger share of redistributive spending in GDP.[5]

Since we are dealing with significantly different cross-sections, including developed and developing countries, particular attention is focused on controlling for cross-country differences in the allocation of public expenditures. We have done this by including country-specific dummies in the model, which are supposed to control for all proportional differences in government expenditures across the different country groups. Furthermore, as argued by Greene (2000), the fixed effects model is a reasonable approach when we can be confident that the differences between the cross-sections can be viewed as parametric shifts of the regression function.[6]

As discussed above, a particularly disturbing regularity in the literature based on cross-section estimates is that inequality becomes statistically insignificant when the dependency ratio (the share of the population aged 65 and over) is controlled for. Exclusion of demographics would bias parameter estimates, given that the age composition of the population is a powerful determinant of public

Table 5.4
Inequality and Redistribution – Fixed Effects Estimation Dep. Variable:
Social Security and Welfare Spending in % of GDP, 1972–87

Variables	(1)	(2)	(3)	(4)	(5)
Constant	56.3458	17.7183	23.7176	14.3114	na
	(10.690)	(3.402)	(4.209)	(2.208)	
GDP Per Capita	0.0078	0.0004	0.0004	0.0003	0.0002
	(15.391)	(8.075)	(6.809)	(5.183)	(3.003)
Gini Coefficient	−2.4062	−1.3193	−1.6295	−1.3007	−1.5554
	(−8.957)	(−5.472)	(−6.131)	(−4.521)	(−10.003)
(Gini Coefficient)2	0.0269	0.0181	0.0214	0.0019	0.0293
	(8.041)	(6.215)	(6.809)	(5.939)	(9.856)
Population over 65		1.7563	1.6363	1.6233	2.2476
years of age		(14.766)	(12.952)	(12.920)	(15.814)
Democracy Index			0.0079	1.2649	3.3425
			(2.708)	(2.883)	(6.969)
Democracy Index x				−0.0219	−0.0651
Gini Coefficient				(−2.042)	(−6.128)
F–Statistics	195.21	254.95	207.63	176.57	152.90
Adjusted R-Squared	0.4964	0.6322	0.6361	0.6406	0.5624
Sargan Test (df = 1)					3.31
N*T	592	592	592	592	592
Estimation Method	OLS	OLS	OLS	OLS	2SLS

Note: Numbers in parentheses are t-statistics. The instruments used in the 2SLS regression are measures of financial development: credit provided by banks to the domestic sector, credit provided to the private sector, and M2 as percentage of GDP.

spending on social security and welfare programmes, which are the most common transfer payments. Indeed, according to our results reported for models (1) and (2), the age composition of the population appears to be an important determinant of public spending. More importantly, our panel data results do not confirm the regularity reported in the cross-section literature; the parameters reported in Table 5.4 show that inequality remains negatively associated with redistribution, even in the presence of a nonlinear term.

Our panel estimations also confirmed the nonlinearity hypothesis put forward by Bénabou (2000), and validated in the cross-sectional regressions reported by de Mello and Tiongson (2001). The inequality parameter remains statistically significant and negatively associated with redistribution. The statistical regularity noted above, that the parameter estimate of the measure of inequality loses significance when demographics is controlled for, does not hold when the quadratic term is included as an additional regressor. The inequality indicator remains negatively signed and statistically significant even if demographics and the quadratic term are included in the estimating equation.

Given the limitations of the data, additional robustness checks were performed. We experimented with including an index of democracy as an additional control variable and as an interaction with the inequality indicator to test the median voter hypothesis, as in Perotti (1996). The democracy index proxies for political participation and therefore the likelihood that the preferences of the median voter will be taken into account in the political process. The interaction term takes into account the fact that political representation may be dominated by a decisive voter who is significantly richer than the median voter in polarised societies, as discussed above (Models 3 and 4). The parameter estimate of the inequality coefficient remains correctly signed and statistically significant and our panel regressions are in line with the cross-sectional evidence reported in de Mello and Tiongson (2001).

The findings reported above support the two hypotheses put forward by Bénabou (2000), namely that more inequality is associated with less redistributive spending and that the association between the two variables is nonlinear. The channel through which these results hold true in the theoretical model developed by Bénabou (2000) is capital market imperfections. Inequality depends on whether people have access to insurance instruments, as discussed above. This provides a good candidate for an instrument in the otherwise reduced-form equations used for estimating the association between inequality and redistribution. The endogeneity of the inequality variable had not been addressed in the literature on the grounds that it is difficult to find adequate instruments for income distribution in inequality/growth equations (Perotti 1998).

The results of the two-stage least squares estimation of equations (5.1) and (5.3) are reported in Model (5). Conventional proxies for capital deepening are used as the instruments for capital market imperfection, including credit to the domestic economy and to the private sector, as well as the share of broad money (M2) in GDP. Parameter estimates are negatively signed and statistically significant, as above, and roughly the same in magnitude as those estimated by OLS. The results hold when the quadratic term and the share of the population aged 65 and over are included in the regressions. We tested for the over-identifying restrictions resulting from the chosen set of instrumental variables using the standard Sargan test, which is reported at the bottom of Table 5.4. The test for the validity of instruments, the t-ratios for each variable and the other summary statistics were all satisfactory and confirmed the robustness of the estimates.

5.6   CONCLUSIONS AND POLICY IMPLICATIONS

This chapter has surveyed the literature on the association between income inequality and redistribution. Emphasis was placed on the literature on political economy and growth, in which the median voter hypothesis plays a critical role in justifying a positive relationship between inequality and redistribution; namely that in countries where income is more unevenly distributed, the government is called upon to provide a larger share of total government expenditure in the form of income transfers to individuals and households. Failure to provide empirical support for the median voter hypothesis has motivated closer scrutiny of the reasons why the correlation between inequality and redistribution may be negative, rather than positive, as predicted under the median voter hypothesis.

This chapter also provides some empirical analysis. Rather than testing the median voter or the decisive voter hypotheses discussed in the political economy literature, we focused on estimating the sign of the correlation between inequality and redistribution, and testing the nonlinearity of the inequality variable, as well as the capital market imperfections as a channel through which inequality is associated with redistributive public spending. Conventional wisdom is that inequality is perpetuated over time when people, particularly the poor, do not have access to capital markets to insure themselves against adverse economic shocks or to make the long-term investment needed to improve their future earnings capacity.

Our main findings, based on a panel of 37 industrial and developing countries in the period 1972–87, show that, in general, the countries where redistributive public spending is more needed were found to be the ones that are less likely to redistribute income through public policies. We also provide empirical support to the hypothesis of nonlinearity in the inequality–redistribution correlation. Our empirical results are by no means conclusive but confirm the cross-sectional evidence reported by de Mello and Tiongson (2001).

Several important policy implications follow from the empirical findings. First, increasing redistributive spending implies confronting well-entrenched constituencies whose tax burden is increased to finance public programmes that are designed not to reach them (Haussman 1998). This complicates the politics of policy reform and can lead to policy reversals. Secondly, if redistributive spending is somehow carried out, it may still be inefficient as an instrument to reduce poverty and to improve income distribution because the benefits of public spending are often captured by the non-poor. There is, in fact, a large literature on benefit incidence of government expenditure and middle class capture (Castro-Leal et al. 1999).

More importantly, because capital market imperfection plays a role in the association between redistributive spending and inequality, government policies could focus on measures to protect the poor from shocks or to assist them in smoothing consumption. Social safety nets, for example, could help mitigate the adverse impact of fluctuations in income. Microfinance can also enhance the access of the poor to some types of financial intermediation and allows them to finance housing acquisition and upgrading, trade, small manufacturing, service activities, and agriculture, as well as investment in existing, often small enterprise.[7]

NOTES

1   The recent literature on the association between economic growth, poverty and income distribution includes, inter alia, Chen and Ravallion (1997), Dollar and Kraay (2000), Ravallion (2000), and Foster and Székely (2001). The literature shows that the correlation between economic growth and income distribution is particularly weak in countries where income is less evenly distributed. For example, Easterly (2000) shows that the poor are hurt less by falling standards of living in countries where the distribution of income is more unequal because the poor have a lower share of income to begin with.

2   A particularly disturbing regularity in the literature is that inequality becomes statistically insignificant in cross-sectional equations when the dependency ratio is controlled for (Perotti 1996; Bassett, Burkett, and Putterman 1999). Exclusion of a variable capturing demographic trends would bias parameter estimates, given that the age composition of the population is a powerful determinant of public spending on social security and welfare programmes, which are the most common transfer payments.

3   As noted by de Mello and Tiongson (2001), when the quadratic term is included as an additional regressor in the estimating equation, the inequality indicator does not lose significance when the dependency ratio is controlled for.

4   The countries and the time period we use were selected based on data availability.

5   To avoid reverse causality, the initial, rather than current, level of income is used as the control variable in the estimating equations.

6   We have also estimated the models using a random effects estimator, but this alternative model was always rejected against a one-way fixed-effects model.

7   See Khandker (1998), Ledgerwood (1998) and Zaman (1999) for more information.

REFERENCES

Alesina, A., and D. Rodrik (1994), 'Distributive Politics and Economic Growth', *Quarterly Journal of Economics*, **109**, 465–90.

Alesina, A., and R. Perotti (1994), 'The Political Economy of Growth: A Critical Survey of the Recent Literature, *World Bank Economic Review*, **8**, 351–71.

Alesina, A., and R. Perotti (1996), 'Income Distribution, Political Instability, and Investment', *European Economic Review*, **40**, 1203–28.

Atkinson, A.B., and A. Brandolini (2000), 'The Promise and Pitfalls in the Use of "Secondary" Data-Sets: Income Inequality in OECD Countries', Banca D'Italia Temi di discussione No. 379, Rome: Banca D'Italia.

Bassett, W., J.P. Burkett, and L. Putterman (1999), 'Income Distribution, Government Transfers, and the Problem of Unequal Influence', *European Journal of Political Economy*, **15**, 207–28.

Bénabou, R. (1996), 'Inequality and Growth', NBER Working Paper No. 5658.

Bénabou, R. (2000), 'Unequal Societies: Income Distribution and the Social Contract', *American Economic Review*, **90**, 96–1 29.

Bourguignon, F., and C. Morrisson (1998), 'Inequality and Development: The Role of Dualism', *Journal of Development Economics*, **57**, 233–57.

Castro-Leal, F., J. Dayton, L. Demery, and K. Mehra (1999), 'Public Social Spending in Africa: Do the Poor Benefit?', *The World Bank Research Observer*, **14**, 49–72.

Chen, S., and M. Ravallion (2000), 'How Did the World's Poorest Fare in the 1990s?', Policy Research Working Paper No. 2049, Washington: World Bank.

De Mello, L., and E. Tiongson (2001), 'Income Inequality and Redistributive Government Spending', mimeo, Washington: International Monetary Fund.

Deininger, K., and L. Squire (1996), 'A New Data Set Measuring Income Inequality', *The World Bank Economic Review,* **10**, 565–91.

Dollar, D., and A. Kraay (2000), 'Growth Is Good for the Poor', mimeo, Washington: World Bank.

Easterly, W. (2000), 'The Effect of IMF and World Bank Programs on Poverty', mimeo, Washington: World Bank.

Easterly, W., and S. Rebelo (1993), 'Fiscal Policy and Economic Growth: An Empirical Investigation', *Journal of Monetary Economics*, **32**, 417–58.

Figini, P. (1998), 'Inequality and Growth Revisited', mimeo, Trinity College Dublin.

Foster, J.E., and M. Székely (2001), 'Is Economic Growth Good for the Poor? Tracking Low Incomes Using General Means', unpublished manuscript.

Furman, J., and J.E. Stiglitz (1998), 'Economic Consequences of Income Inequality', in *Income Inequality: Issues and Policy Options*, Kansas City: Federal Reserve Bank of Kansas City.

Galor, O., and J. Zeira (1993), 'Income Distribution and Macroeconomics', *Review of Economic Studies*, **60**, 33–52.

Gouveia, M., and N.A. Masia (1998), 'Does the Median Voter Explain the Size of Government? Evidence from the States', *Public Choice*, **97**, 159–77.

Greene, W. (2000), *Econometric Analysis*, New Jersey: Prentice Hall.

Hausmann, Ricardo (1998), 'Comments', in Vito Tanzi and Ke-young Chu (eds), *Income Distribution and High-Quality Growth*, Cambridge: MIT Press.

Khandker, Shahidur R. (1998), *Fighting Poverty with Microcredit: Experience in Bangladesh*, Washington: World Bank.

La Porta, R., F. Lopez-de-Silanes, A. Shleifer, and R. Vishny (1999), 'The Quality of Government', *Journal of Law, Economics, and Organization*, **15**, 222–79.

Ledgerwood, Joanna (1998), *Microfinance Handbook: An Institutional and Financial Perspective*, Washington: World Bank.

Lee, W., and J.E. Roemer (1998), 'Income Distribution, Redistributive Politics and Economic Growth', *Journal of Economic Growth*, **3**, 217–40.

Lee, W., and J.E. Roemer (1999), 'Inequality and Redistribution Revisited', *Economics Letters*, **65**, 339–46.

Lindert, P.H. (1996), 'What Limits Social Spending?', *Explorations in Economic*, **33**, 1–34.

Meltzer, A.H., and S.F. Richard (1981), 'A Rational Theory of the Size of Government', *Journal of Political Economy*, **89**, 914–27.

Meltzer, A.H., and S.F. Richard (1983), 'Tests of a Rational Theory of the Size of Government', *Public Choice*, **41**, 403–18.

Milanovic, B. (2000), 'Do More Unequal Countries Redistribute More? Does the Median Voter Hypothesis Hold?', *European Journal of Political Economy*, **16**, 367–410.

Moffitt, R., D. Ribar, and M. Wilhelm (1998), 'The Decline of Welfare Benefits in the US: The Role of Wage Inequality', *Journal of Public Economics*, **68**, 421–52.

Olson, M. (1965), *The Logic of Collective Action*, Cambridge: Harvard University Press.

Panizza, U. (1999), 'Income Inequality and Economic Growth: Evidence from American Data', Inter-American Development Bank Working Paper WP-404.

Partridge, M. (1997), 'Is Inequality Harmful for Growth? Comment', *American Economic Review*, **87**, 1019–32.

Perotti, R. (1992), 'Income Distribution, Politics and Growth', *American Economic Review*, **82**, 311–16.

Perotti, R. (1994), 'Income Distribution and Investment', *European Economic Review*, **38**, 827–35.

Perotti, R. (1996), 'Growth, Income Distribution, and Democracy: What the Data Say', *Journal of Economic Growth*, **1**, 149–87.

Persson, T., and G. Tabellini (1994), 'Is Inequality Harmful for Growth? Theory and Evidence', *American Economic Review*, **84**, 600–21.

Persson, T., and G. Tabellini (1999), 'Political Economics and Public Finance', NBER Working Paper No. 7097.

Ravallion, M. (2000), 'Growth, Inequality and Poverty: Looking Beyond Averages', mimeo, Washington: World Bank.

Rodriguez, F.C. (1999a), 'Does Distributional Skewness Lead to Redistribution? Evidence from the United States?', *Economics and Politics*, **11**, 171–99.

Rodriguez, F.C. (1999b), 'Inequality, Redistribution, and Rent-Seeking', University of Maryland Department of Economics Working Paper.

Tanninen, H. (1999), 'Income Inequality, Government Expenditures, and Growth', *Applied Economics*, **31**, 1109–17.

Tullock, G. (1983), 'Further Tests of a Rational Theory of the Size of Government', *Public Choice*, **41**, 419–21.

Zaman, Hassan (1999), 'Assessing the Impact of Micro-Credit on Poverty and Vulnerability in Bangladesh', Policy Research Working Paper No. 2145, Washington: World Bank.

6 Employment Inequality, Employment Regulation and Social Welfare

Vani K. Borooah

6.1 INTRODUCTION

An important concern of public policy is to ensure that persons of different sex, ethnic background, religion, colour and so on, are treated fairly in the labour market. The existence of bodies in the United Kingdom like the Equal Opportunities Commission, the Commission for Racial Equality and the Fair Employment Commission (coupled with the prominence given by the media to their findings) and the existence in the USA of the Civil Rights Act (coupled with the prominence given by the media to judgments based on the Act), bears testimony to this. There are two aspects to this concern. The first is whether differences in the remuneration to different persons fully reflect disparities in their productivity or whether such differences are, wholly or in part, the result of 'earnings discrimination'. The disparity in the USA between the earnings of Southern Blacks and equally educated Whites prompted Title VII of the 1964 Civil Rights Act banning discrimination in employment on grounds of race, sex and religion. The second aspect relates to the differential chances, of persons from different groups, of finding suitable employment. Here the concern is whether the different degrees of success that persons from different groups have in finding jobs can be justified by inter-group differences in worker attributes, or whether they are the result of 'employment discrimination'. The disparity in Northern Ireland between the proportion of the Catholic and Protestant labour

This chapter was written while I was a Fellow at the International Centre for Economic Research at Turin. I am grateful to the Centre and to the Department of Economics, University of Turin, for supporting his work. However, I alone am responsible for its deficiencies and for the views expressed in it.

forces that were employed led to the 1989 Fair Employment (NI) Act. This Act put in place legislation to secure fair participation in employment for the two communities in Northern Ireland and created a Fair Employment Commission (FEC) to oversee its implementation.

This chapter is concerned with the second issue. As Arrow (1998) has observed, although this is the more important of the two issues – in the sense of occurring more frequently in the 'real world' – it is also the more neglected. The question most frequently asked in the literature on discrimination concerns the effect of segregated employment on the wages of the group discriminated against. However, as Higgs (1977) and Whately and Wright (1994) have argued in the context of the US labour market, black and white wages for the same job rarely differed by much. Instead, discrimination took the form of restricting the range of jobs to which Black persons were hired.[1] In similar fashion, Catholics in Northern Ireland were excluded from a range of industrial jobs, particular those relating to the Harland and Wolf shipyards – Northern Ireland's largest employer – Belfast (Smith and Chambers 1991).

The usual line of explanation, in economics, for employment discrimination follows the argument of Becker (1971): some White (or Protestant) employers, by attaching a special disutility to contact with Black (or Catholic) workers, have a 'taste for discrimination' and this leads them to either exclude the offending persons from their workforce or to greatly restrict their numbers. In effect, the maximand of such employers contains, in addition to profits, a 'taste-related' argument. Discriminating employers, by indulging their taste for discrimination, would earn a lower level of profits than their non-discriminating counterparts (who maximised only on profits) and would, therefore, eventually be driven out of business. Many economists have concluded from this analysis that market forces would lead discrimination to die a natural death and that, therefore, the helping hand of the legislative physician was not required. In addition, as Donohue (1998) points out, Becker's work strengthened the resolve of those who, philosophically, were opposed to state regulation. For example, Friedman (1962) argued that anti-discrimination legislation was conceptually no different from legislation (for example, like Hitler's Nuremberg laws) requiring employers to impose special disabilities on certain groups.

Another explanation for discrimination (Krueger 1963; Lewis 1979; McAdams 1995) is that its practice may accord with the collective interest of a group: the discriminating group – Whites in apartheid South Africa; Hutus in Burundi – acquires (economic, political and social) status by restricting the job opportunities of other groups and it imposes these restrictions by discriminating against them. In this 'status-production' model, the forces generating discrimination stem not from the preferences of (some) individuals but from the collective preference of the group. Individuals within the group, who seek to break the group's injunctions against association with members of other groups, risk being penalised by their peers through *inter alia*: economic boycott; social ostracism; and violence against them and their property.

The third explanation for discrimination which is important in the economics literature is based on 'statistical discrimination' (Phelps 1972). Suppose that two groups, on average, do differ in terms of productivity – or that employers believe that they do – where these productivity differences are due to differences in some work-related attribute which is difficult, if not impossible, to observe (say, quality of education). In such situations, employers may use some observable quality (say, ethnicity) as a surrogate for these unobservable differences in attributes. Consequently, members of a particular group may be denied employment because employers feel that, on the balance of probabilities, they are likely to get better workers from other groups. This is a market-based explanation for discrimination which does not require tastes for discrimination.

The objections to Becker's (1971) model are well-known and have been set out succinctly by Arrow (1998). Briefly, they are that: (i) the introduction of additional variables into the maximand risks turning the theory into a tautology; (ii) a large fraction of the workforce is hired by large corporations and it is difficult to ascribe discriminatory tastes to impersonal entities; (iii) the theory does not explain discrimination by occupation; (iv) the theory predicts the demise of precisely the phenomenon it is meant to explain (Arrow 1972). The McAdams (1995) model has been criticised by Epstein (1995): the relevance of discrimination based on social norms has diminished considerably in the modern world and many of the examples cited in support of the model – apartheid laws in South Africa; segregation laws in the Southern US states; the Protestant hegemony over jobs and housing in Northern Ireland – are defunct. The problem with statistical discrimination is that it can become a self-fulfilling prophecy. The rejection of applicants from a particular group by employers, who mistakenly believe that group identity and worker ability are correlated, could discourage members of the rejected group from making the human capital investments needed to be a good worker thus fulfilling employers' expectations that persons from this group do not make good workers (Elmslie and Sedo 1996).[2]

Against this background, this chapter develops a model which explains the unequal employment outcomes of two groups (Blacks and Whites) defined as their, respective, likelihoods of successfully filling job vacancies without resorting to the assumption that (some) employers, as individuals, have a taste for discrimination or to the assumption that prevailing social norms support discrimination and that individual employers depart from these norms at their peril. Nor does the model assume that (some) employers believe that group identity and worker quality are correlated. Instead, 'discrimination' in the model arises, in the first instance, because information about vacancies is a private good which is available in unequal measure to Blacks – who receive less of it – and to Whites – who receive more of it.

This occurs because a proportion of jobs are filled through informal recruitment methods so that, as a first step, information about vacancies only becomes available by word-of-mouth; as a second step, appointments are based on the recommendations of existing employees. If society is fragmented then members of one group will have little or no contact with – or, if they do have contact, little or no sympathy for – members of the other group. In such a situation, the power to inform and to recommend is inordinately concentrated in the group that dominates the workforce. If this group happens to be Whites, then Blacks have a lower chance of filling vacancies because, relative to White job-seekers, they lack both information about vacancies and sponsors to support their applications. The two forces that drive the model are, therefore, informal recruitment methods and social fragmentation and these two forces acting in concert result in a jobs-network (Rees and Schultz 1970; Granovetter 1974 and 1988; White 1995). The central point of the model is to show that because Black job-seekers do not have the same degree of access to the jobs-network as do White job-seekers, their employment outcomes are worse than those of Whites.

The purpose of fair-employment regulation is to afford fairer participation in employment for members of the disadvantaged group. This involves emasculating the jobs-network by insisting that all information about vacancies be publicly available and that the ensuing recruitment process be both transparent and accountable.[3] The result of these interventions is equity-gain. However, these statutory requirements, taken collectively, could significantly raise hiring (and firing) costs and, compared to the pre-regulatory situation, lead to fewer vacancies being announced. This is identified in the model as the efficiency-loss from regulation. Whether fair-employment regulation leads to a net increase in welfare or not depends on comparing the welfare-magnitudes of the gains and losses. The model proposes a method, based on Atkinson's (1970) analysis of income inequality, for effecting such a comparison.

6.2   THE ANALYTICAL FRAMEWORK

There are M economically active persons in a region, of whom a proportion α (> 0.5) are White, the remainder, $1 - \alpha$, being Black. There is a single employer (call it a firm) in the region. This firm has E employees all of whom do a particular type of job and all of whom are paid the same wage, s. A proportion β ($> \alpha$) of the employees are White, the remainder, $1 - \beta$, being Black. The profits of the firm are:

$$\pi = ry(E) - sE \qquad (6.1)$$

where: $y(E)$ is the firm's production function ($y'(E) > 0$ and $y''(E) < 0$) and r is the output price. By assumption, both the product and the labour markets are competitive so that r and s are invariant with respect to, respectively, changes in output and in employment.

By definition, there are $U = M - E$ unemployed persons in the region, of whom $U_W = \alpha M - \beta E$ are White and $U_B = U - U_w = (1 - \alpha)M - (1 - \beta)E$ are Black. The unemployment rates for Whites and Blacks are, respectively:

$$u_W = \frac{\alpha M - \beta E}{\alpha M} = 1 - \frac{\beta}{\alpha}(1 - u) = \frac{\alpha - \beta}{\alpha} + \frac{\beta}{\alpha}u \qquad (6.2a)$$

$$u_B = \frac{(1-\alpha)M - (1-\beta)E}{(1-\alpha)M} = \frac{\beta - \alpha}{1 - \alpha} + \frac{1 - \beta}{1 - \alpha}u \qquad (6.2b)$$

where: $u = (M - E)/M$ is the overall unemployment rate. The three unemployment rates – u, u_W and u_B – are linked by the relationship:

$$\alpha u_W + (1 - \alpha)u_B = u \qquad (6.3)$$

A vacancy now occurs in this firm. This vacancy may be filled by informal or by formal methods. Informal methods comprise filling the vacancy on the basis of recommendations by existing employees. Formal methods, on the other hand, involve filling the vacancy by means of a process which *inter alia* involves: publicly advertising the job, scrutinising applications, taking up references, and conducting job interviews.

6.2.1   Informal Recruitment Methods

Each employee knows at least one person who is unemployed and who would like to fill this vacancy and he informs one, and only one, of these persons of the vacancy. In effect, every employee 'votes' for a person on the unemployment list with a view to informing him of the vacancy. Consequently, E votes are cast – two, or more, voters may vote for the same person – and E^* ($\leq U$) unemployed persons are informed of the vacancy (receive votes). These E^* persons (the 'successful candidates') constitute the pool of applicants for the vacancy. Since they were made aware of the vacancy through the strength of their contacts with existing employees, they may be regarded as belonging to a job-network, where a job-network is defined as the set of unemployed persons, each of whom is the preferred choice (for filling the vacancy) of at least one employee.

The firm, which has to fill the vacancy from one of these E^* applicants, has no reason to prefer one applicant over another. However, it would like to place suitable weight on the number of votes received by each applicant and, in order to do so, it enters each applicant's name on as many separate slips of paper as the number of votes received by the applicant. Then, from this collection of E slips of paper, it picks one at random: the person whose name appears on the slip gets the job.

Assume that γ_B and γ_W are the respective probabilities that Black and White employees recommend someone of the same colour, $1 - \gamma_B$ and $1 - \gamma_W$ being the respective probabilities that they recommend someone of a different colour. Then, of the total number of slips of paper (E) in the hat, the expected proportions that have the names of White and of Black persons (denoted q_W and q_B, respectively) are:

$$q_W = [\beta\gamma_W + (1 - \beta)(1 - \gamma_B)] \tag{6.4a}$$

$$q_B = [\beta(1 - \gamma_W) + (1 - \beta)\gamma_B] \tag{6.4b}$$

where: $q_W + q_B = 1$. Since all the applicants are viewed equally favorably by the employer, q_W and q_B may be regarded as the respective likelihoods of a White and of a Black person filling the vacant position, when the vacancy is filled using informal methods. The values of γ_B and γ_W measure the degree to which society is 'fragmented' along racial lines, with lower values of γ_B and γ_W reflecting smaller degrees of fragmentation or, equivalently, higher degrees of integration. Note that $\partial q_W / \partial \gamma_W > 0$, $\partial q_B / \partial \gamma_B > 0$. Two cases may be highlighted: complete fragmentation and complete integration.

Complete fragmentation
If $\gamma_B = \gamma_W = 1$, so that Black employees would never recommend for the vacancy an unemployed person who was White, and vice versa, then society is completely fragmented by race and $q_W = \beta$ and $q_B = (1 - \beta)$: the likelihood of a Black person filling a vacancy depends entirely on the proportionate presence of Black workers on the firm's payroll. On the other hand, if all the employees in the firm are White, then $\beta = 1$ and $q_W = \gamma_W$ and $q_B = (1 - \gamma_W)$: the likelihood of a Black person filling a vacancy depends entirely on the likelihood of White workers recommending Black persons. If society is completely fragmented and all employees are White, then $q_W = 1$ and $q_B = 0$: vacancies will never be filled by Black persons.

Complete integration
The counterpoint to complete fragmentation is complete integration. This occurs when recommendations are 'colour-blind' so that the likelihood of an employee, irrespective of his colour, recommending a Black or a White person is given by the respective proportions of Black and White job-seekers in the total of unemployed persons. More formally, under complete integration:

$$\gamma_W = \frac{\alpha M - \beta E}{U} = \alpha \frac{M}{U} - \beta \frac{M-U}{U} = \frac{\alpha - \beta}{u} + \beta = 1 - \gamma_B \quad (6.5a)$$

$$\gamma_B = 1 - \gamma_W = \frac{\beta - \alpha}{u} + (1-\beta) = 1 - \gamma_W \quad (6.5b)$$

so that, substituting the expressions for γ_W and γ_B from equations (6.5a) and (6.5b) into equations (6.8a) and (6.8b) yields:

$$q_W = \beta \gamma_W + (1-\beta)(1-\gamma_B) = \beta \gamma_W + (1-\beta)\gamma_W = \frac{\alpha - \beta}{u} + \beta \quad (6.6a)$$

$$q_B = \beta(1-\gamma_W) + (1-\beta)\gamma_B = \beta \gamma_B + (1-\beta)\gamma_B = \frac{\beta - \alpha}{u} + (1-\beta) \quad (6.6b)$$

6.2.2 Formal versus Informal Recruitment Methods

The alternative to filling the vacancy by informal methods is to fill it using formal methods. These involve, as a first step, the public advertisement of the vacancy. Suppose that this attracts applications from all the $U = M - E$ unemployed persons in the region. Subsequent steps in the process of filling the vacancy using formal methods involve, as noted above, such activities as scrutinising applications, taking up references, and conducting interviews.

The disadvantages to the firm of using formal methods are two. First, formal methods are more costly – if the costs of filling a vacancy by informal and formal methods are, respectively, c_E and c_F, then, by assumption, $c_E < c_F$. Assume without loss of generality that $c_E = 0$ so that $c_F > 0$. The second disadvantage is that formal methods require time to implement – by assumption, there is a delay of $\tau > 0$ periods between the decision to fill the vacancy and the new employee starting work and the cost of this delay is reflected in lost production of $\tau y'(E)$ and in lost profits of $\tau[ry'(E) - s]$. By contrast, under informal methods, the new worker can start as soon as the vacancy is to be filled.

The advantage to the firm of using formal methods is that these would lead to a larger number of applicants: under informal methods, only $E^* \leq U$ persons would be considered for the vacant position but, under formal methods, there would be an additional $F = U - E^*$ applicants. Consequently, the firm may end up with a 'better' worker. Let ρ_E and ρ_F denote, respectively, the firm's expectation of the marginal product of a worker recruited through informal and through formal methods, $\rho_E \leq \rho_F$.

Then the expected net advantage, A, to the firm, of filling the vacancy using formal, instead of informal, methods is:

$$A = \int_{\tau}^{T} (\rho_F - \rho_E) e^{-it} dt - \int_{0}^{\tau} (\rho_E - w) e^{-it} dt - c_F \qquad (6.7)$$

where T in equation (6.7) represents the number of periods the job is expected to last (the 'life' of the job) and i is the discount rate. The first term in the above expression is the present value of the additional profit stream expected from employing a worker through formal methods. The second term is the present value of the forgone profits arising from the delay, arising from formal methods, in the new employee starting work: this is the additional profit the firm could have earned if the worker had, instead, been recruited informally. The last term is simply the fixed cost associated with filling the vacancy through formal methods. It is assumed that the firm is risk-neutral so that the different terms in equation (6.7) can be directly compared.

From equation (6.7), the firm will fill its vacancy using informal methods if $A < 0$, and fill it using formal methods if $A > 0$. For routine jobs – with a high degree of specificity in terms of performance and standards, which are easily supervised and monitored, in which the worker's flair and enterprise is not likely to be of importance, and for which the quality of training is fairly uniform – there would not be much difference between ρ_F and ρ_E. Opening up such vacancies – in general connected with unskilled, semi-skilled, skilled manual/non-manual or technical jobs – to public competition would not be likely to yield better workers and the firm would prefer to recruit using informal methods. On the other hand, where standards of job performance vary according to the quality of training received by the worker and according to his skill, initiative and enterprise, the firm might expect that the public advertisement of the vacancy would attract a better class of applicant than that supplied by the recommendations of existing employees: a significant difference between ρ_F and ρ_E would lead the firm to prefer formal methods.

6.3   EMPLOYMENT CHANCES UNDER FORMAL AND INFORMAL RECRUITMENT METHODS

Under formal methods of recruitment all unemployed persons in a region learn of a vacancy and apply for it. Of these unemployed persons, a proportion p_w are White and p_B are Black, where:

$$p_W = \frac{\alpha M - \beta E}{U} = \alpha \frac{M}{U} - \beta \frac{M - U}{U} = \frac{\alpha - \beta}{u} + \beta \qquad (6.8a)$$

$$p_B = 1 - q_W = \frac{\beta - \alpha}{u} + (1 - \beta) \tag{6.8b}$$

where $p_W + p_B = 1$ and $\partial p_W / \partial \beta = 1 - 1/u < 0$ and $\partial p_W / \partial \beta = 1/u - 1 > 0$, if $u < 1$. If skills and abilities are equally distributed between Blacks and Whites, then p_W and p_B may be regarded as the respective likelihoods of a White and of a Black person being appointed to the vacant position, when the vacancy is filled using formal methods.

Whether Blacks would be more likely to get employment under formal, compared to informal, methods of filling vacancies would depend on the degree of social fragmentation (by race) as measured by the values of the parameters γ_B and γ_W. If $\gamma_B = \gamma_W = 1$, so that society is completely fragmented, then (remembering that $\alpha < \beta$), from equations (6.4a) and (6.8a),

$$p_W = \beta + \frac{\alpha - \beta}{u} < \beta = q_W \Rightarrow p_B > q_B \tag{6.9}$$

so that the likelihood of a Black person filling a job-vacancy would be higher if the firm adopted formal, instead of informal, methods of recruitment.

However, if society were completely integrated, so that the values of γ_B and γ_W were given by equations (6.5a) and (6.5b), respectively, then $p_W = q_W$ and $p_B = q_B$. In other words, formal recruitment methods produce the same result in terms of the chances of Blacks and Whites filling a vacancy as would informal recruitment methods in societies that were completely integrated.

However, complete integration is a sufficient but not a necessary condition for the likelihood of a Black or a White person filling a job-vacancy[4] to be invariant with respect to the method of recruitment adopted. Suppose that $\gamma_B = \gamma_W$. Then from equations (6.4a) and (6.8a) a necessary and sufficient condition for $p_W = q_W$ and for $p_B = q_B$ is:

$$\gamma = 1 + \frac{\alpha - \beta}{u(2\beta - 1)} < 1 \tag{6.10}$$

Comparing the expression for γ from equation (6.10) with that of γ_W from equation (6.5a) it is evident that:[5]

$$\gamma = 1 + \frac{\alpha - \beta}{u(2\beta - 1)} \geq \beta + \frac{\alpha - \beta}{u} = \gamma_W \Rightarrow \gamma \geq 1 - \gamma_B \tag{6.11}$$

Equation (6.11) shows that the probability of White employees recommending a White person is greater than what would be implied by complete integration: notwithstanding this, the probability of a Black or a White person filling the vacancy would not depend upon the method of recruitment. Consequently, it is possible, even under conditions of less than complete integration, for Blacks, in terms of their likelihood of filling a vacancy, to be as well off under informal, as under formal, recruitment methods. However, in practice, from equation (6.10a), the 'break-even' value of γ is unlikely to be realised. For example, if one imposed the constraint $\gamma \geq 0.5$, then from equation (6.10):

$$\gamma = 1 + \frac{\alpha - \beta}{u(2\beta - 1)} \geq 0.5 \Rightarrow u \geq \frac{2(\beta - \alpha)}{2\beta - 1} \qquad (6.12)$$

If, for example, $\beta = 0.7$ and $\alpha = 0.6$, then, for the break-even degree of social fragmentation to be achieved, $u \geq 0.5$. Realistically, therefore, with less than complete integration, Blacks would be more likely to fill a vacancy if the firm adopted formal, as opposed to informal, methods of recruitment.

6.4   FAIR EMPLOYMENT POLICIES

Suppose that, against the background of the basic model outlined above, the firm has $V (< U)$ vacancies and of these it decides to fill a proportion θ using formal methods and the remainder, $1-\theta$, by informal methods. That is, in terms of equation (6.7), $A > 0$ for a fraction θ of these vacancies, $A < 0$ for the remainder. Then the likelihood of White and Black persons filling these vacancies, represented by π_W and π_B respectively, are:

$$\pi_W(\theta) = \theta p_W + (1 - \theta) q_W \qquad (6.13a)$$

$$\pi_B(\theta) = \theta p_B + (1 - \theta) q_B \qquad (6.13b)$$

where: $d\pi_W/d\theta < 0$, $d\pi_B/d\theta > 0$, the values of $\pi_W(\theta)$ and $\pi_B(\theta)$ being, respectively, minimised and maximised when $\theta = 1$.

The government, observing the small number of vacancies filled by Blacks, sets up a Fair Employment Commission (FEC) to redress the racial imbalance in employment. The FEC, acting under powers assigned to it by Fair Employment legislation, imposes transparency in recruitment on the firm by requiring that *all* vacancies be filled using formal methods. It requires that the firm publicly advertise all its vacancies and it specifies detailed procedures – perhaps more rigorous than the firm acting on its own would have followed – that need to be followed before a vacancy can be filled. As a consequence the firm is forced to eschew informal methods of recruitment so that $\theta = 1$.

6.5   SOCIAL WELFARE AND INEQUALITY

6.5.1   The Social Welfare Function

For a given number of vacancies, V, that are filled, let V_B and V_W represent, respectively, the numbers of vacancies filled by Blacks and by Whites and let $v = V/U$, represent the proportion of unemployed persons in the region who were able to find employment while $v_B = V_B/U_B$ and $v_W = V_W/U_W$ represent, respectively, the proportion of Black, and of White, job-seekers who obtained employment. Then v, v_B and v_W may be thought of (and are referred to in this paper as) the likelihood of successful job-search of, respectively: all jobseekers; Black job-seekers; White job-seekers. The relationship between the three likelihoods is given by:

$$v = \frac{V}{U} = \frac{V_B}{U} + \frac{V_W}{U} = \frac{V_B}{U_B}\frac{U_B}{U}\frac{M}{M_B}\frac{M_B}{M} + \frac{V_W}{U_W}\frac{U_W}{U}\frac{M}{M_W}\frac{M_W}{M}$$

$$= v_B(u_B/u)(1-\alpha) + v_W(u_W/u)\alpha \tag{6.14}$$

Suppose that social welfare, J, can be written, for $k = B, W$, in additively separable form, as:

$$J = J(v_B, u_W) = \sum_{k=B}^{W} U_k F(v_k) \tag{6.15}$$

The function $F(.) \geq 0$ in equation (6.15) represents society's valuation of the gain (to it) arising from persons in group k having a likelihood, v_k, of successful job-search, with higher values of the group-specific function, $F(.)$ representing higher levels of gain. The sum of the group-specific gains is the social welfare associated with a given overall likelihood of successful job-search, v.

The change in the value of the social welfare function (SWF) of equation (6.15), following a change in v_k, is:

$$\Delta J = \sum_{k=B}^{W} a_k U_k \Delta v_k \tag{6.16}$$

where: $a_k = \partial F(v_k)/\partial v_k > 0$ is the social marginal gain attached to a change in the likelihood of successful job-search of members of group k. If it is assumed that the function $F(.)$ is strictly concave, then social marginal gain decreases for increases in v_k. Consequently, for a given overall likelihood, v, social welfare is maximised, when the likelihood of successful job-search is the same for persons in the different groups, that is when: $v_B = v_W$.

The SWF has constant elasticity if, for $\varepsilon \geq 0$, $F(.)$ can be written as:

$$F(v_k) = \frac{v_k^{1-\varepsilon} - 1}{1-\varepsilon} \qquad (6.17)$$

since then: $a_k = \partial F(v_k)/\partial v_k = v_k^{-\varepsilon} \Rightarrow (\partial a_k/\partial v_k)/(v_k/a_k) = -\varepsilon < 0$.

Consequently, the percentage change in the welfare weights, following a percentage change in the likelihood of successful job-search, is both negative and constant. The greater the value of ε, the greater the proportional decrease in the welfare weights in response to a proportional increase in the likelihood. The parameter ε represents, as shown below, society's aversion to inter-group inequality in the likelihood of successful job-search.

6.5.2   Inequality Aversion

From equation (6.14), the change in the overall likelihood of successful job-search, Δv, is related to the changes in the group likelihoods since:

$$\Delta v = \Delta v_B (u_B/u)(1-\alpha) + \Delta v_W (u_W/u)\alpha \qquad (6.18)$$

and if, in the above equation, $\Delta v = 0$, then:

$$-\Delta v_W = \Delta v_B \frac{u_B}{u_W} \frac{1-\alpha}{\alpha} = \Delta v_B \delta \mu \qquad (6.19)$$

where: $\delta = u_B/u_W$ and $\mu = (1-\alpha)/\alpha$ are, respectively, the ratios of unemployment rates, and of labour force shares, of Blacks and Whites.

From equation (6.16), and its accompanying properties, the change in the value of J, following changes in the Black and White likelihoods of successful job-search, is:

$$\Delta J = a_B U_B \Delta v_B + a_W U_W \Delta v_W = \lambda^{-\varepsilon} v_W^{-\varepsilon} U_B \Delta v_B + v_W^{-\varepsilon} U_W \Delta v_W \qquad (6.20)$$

where: $v_B/v_W = \lambda$ and since, by assumption, the likelihood of successful job-search for Blacks is not greater than that for Whites, $\lambda \leq 1$. Setting $\Delta J = 0$ in equation (6.20) implies:

$$-\Delta v_W = \Delta v_B \lambda^{-\varepsilon} (U_B/U_W) = \Delta v_B \frac{u_B}{u_W} \frac{1-\alpha}{\alpha} \lambda^{-\varepsilon} = \Delta v_B \delta \mu \lambda^{-\varepsilon} \qquad (6.21)$$

Suppose $\Delta v_B = 1$, so that the likelihood of successful job-search by Blacks is increased by 1 percentage point (pp). If the reduction in the likelihood of successful job-search by Whites is $\Delta v_w > \delta u \lambda^{-\epsilon}$, then social gain would decrease since $\Delta J < 0$ and if $\Delta v_w < \delta u \lambda^{-\epsilon}$, then social gain would increase since $\Delta J > 0$.

From equation (6.21), if $\epsilon = 0$, $\Delta v_w = \delta u$. This implies that society, in response to the fact that the likelihood of successful job-search is disproportionately high for White job-seekers, would be prepared to increase the likelihood of successful job-search by Blacks by 1 pp, and to reduce that of Whites by an appropriate amount (δu), provided that in this redistribution the overall likelihood, v, did not change.

If $\epsilon > 0$, then, in order to increase the Black likelihood by 1 pp, society would be prepared to lower the White likelihood by $\Delta v_w = \delta u \lambda^{-\epsilon}$. Since $\lambda < 1$, $\lambda^{-\delta} > 1$ (so that $\delta u \lambda^{-\epsilon} > \delta u$) and the overall likelihood of successful job-search falls. Since $\delta \Delta v_w / \delta \epsilon > 0$, associated with higher values of ϵ, is society's willingness to accept a smaller number of vacancies (or, equivalently, a smaller overall likelihood of successful job-search)[6] than that which currently exists, provided this smaller number of vacancies was filled more equitably than hitherto by Blacks and Whites. In this sense, the value of ϵ represents the degree to which society is averse to inequality, between Blacks and Whites, in the likelihood of successful job-search, with higher values of ϵ representing greater degrees of aversion.

6.5.3 A Welfare-Based Measure of Inter-Group Inequality in the Likelihood of Successful Job-Search

Let $v^* \leq v$ represent the overall likelihood of successful job-search which, if also the likelihood for Blacks and Whites, would yield the same level of social welfare as the existing distribution of likelihoods. Then v^* may be termed the equally distributed equivalent likelihood of successful job-search. Following from this, Atkinson's (1970) inequality index applied to the distribution of likelihoods between Blacks and Whites yields:[7]

$$I = 1 - (v^* / v) = 1 - \left[\sum_{k=B}^{W} \frac{U_k}{U} \left(\frac{v_k}{v} \right)^{1-\epsilon} \right]^{1/(1-\epsilon)} \tag{6.22}$$

When $\epsilon = 0$, society is indifferent as to how a given overall likelihood is distributed: $v^* = v$ and $I = 0$. For $\epsilon > 0$, $v^* < v$ and $I > 0$. The higher the value of the inequality aversion parameter, ϵ, the smaller will be the value of v^* and, therefore, the higher will be the value of the inequality index, I.

6.6 FAIR EMPLOYMENT REGULATION AND WELFARE IMPROVEMENT

From equation (6.22), the 'equally distributed equivalent' likelihood of successful job-search, v^*, remains unchanged for equi-proportionate changes in the Black and White likelihoods. This, however, does not imply that social welfare remains unchanged. Indeed, an equi-proportionate increase (decrease) in the likelihoods, by raising (lowering) the overall likelihood by the same proportion, would lead to an equi-proportionate increase (decrease) in social welfare.[8] To see this more clearly observe that in order to make comparisons of loss (or gain) across different overall likelihoods of successful job-search, a specific transformation, linking the inequality measure, I to different overall likelihoods, v, is needed. One obvious transformation is the reverse of the Atkinson transformation, which yields the social welfare function:

$$J = v(1 - I) \tag{6.23}$$

which is homogenous of degree one in the likelihood rate. The social welfare function in equation (6.23) has a natural interpretation: the welfare from an overall likelihood of successful job-search (v) is reduced by the extent of inequality in the distribution of this likelihood between Blacks and Whites.

Given an overall likelihood of successful job-search, v, equation (6.23) says that the value of the Atkinson index (I) is a measure of the social welfare (J) associated with this overall likelihood. This welfare depends upon the distribution of this overall likelihood between Blacks and Whites (that is, in terms of their respective likelihoods of successful job-search, v_B and v_w) and upon the degree to which society is averse to inequality in the distribution of this likelihood (that is, the value of the inequality aversion parameter, ε).

Under fair employment regulation, for a given overall likelihood of successful job-search, $v = V/U$, the likelihoods of successful job-search by Blacks and Whites are, respectively, $v_B^p = V_B/U_B = p_B V/U_B$ and $v_W^p = V_W/U_W = p_W V/U_W$ while, in the absence of regulation, they were, respectively, $v_B^\pi = V_B/U_B = \pi_B V/U_B$ and $v_W^\pi = V_W/U_W = \pi_W V/U_W$, where: $v_W^p \leq v_W^\pi$ and $v_B^p \geq v_B^\pi$ with $v_W^p < v_W^\pi$ and $v_B^p > v_B^\pi$ if $q < 1$ (equations (6.13a) and (6.13b)). Consequently, J^p and J^π denote, respectively, the social welfare associated with fair-employment regulation, and with the absence of fair-employment regulation, then, from equation (6.23):

$$J^p - J^\pi = v(1 - I^p) - v(1 - I^\pi) = v(I^\pi - I^p) \tag{6.24}$$

where I^p and I^π are the values of the inequality index in equation (6.22) when, respectively, $v_k = v_k^P$ and $v_k = v_k^\pi, k = B, W$. Since, $v_B^P = v_W^P = v$, $I^P = 0$. However, since $I^\pi \geq 0$, $J^P - J^\pi \geq 0$, with $J^P - J^\pi > 0$, $\theta < 1$. As long as some vacancies, in the absence of fair-employment regulation, were filled using informal methods of recruitment, fair-employment regulation will increase social welfare. The amount by which regulation will increase social welfare will depend upon four factors:

- the proportion of vacancies, θ, that were, in the pre-regulation state, filled using formal methods: the lower the value of θ, the greater will be the impact of regulation on welfare, the maximum impact occurring when $\theta = 0$ and the minimum (zero) impact occurring when $\theta = 1$.
- the proportion of employees, β, that are White: *ceteris paribus*, the higher the value of β the greater will be the rise in welfare following regulation, the rise being greatest when $\beta = 1$.
- the degree to which society is fragmented: the higher the degree of fragmentation (that is, the larger the value of γ), the more will social welfare rise after regulation: the increase will be greatest when $\gamma = 1$ and will be zero when γ is defined by equation (6.10).
- the degree to which society is inequality-averse: the smaller the value of the inequality-aversion parameter ε, the smaller will be the impact of regulation on welfare, with $\varepsilon = 0$ resulting in no increase in welfare.

6.7   FAIR-EMPLOYMENT REGULATION AND EFFICIENCY LOSS

As a consequence of the regulatory activities of the FEC, the firm, for two reasons, incurs additional costs. First, costs go up because vacancies which earlier would have been filled through informal methods (the cost of which is zero) must now be filled using formal methods. Secondly, the cost of FEC-determined formal procedures may be higher than the cost of such procedures as determined by the firm. For example, the FEC may attach financial penalties to faulty compliance and, in order to avoid these penalties, the firm may have to make additional investments in acquiring appropriate expertise for its human resources department. The desire on the part of the firm to avoid error may also combine with the (possibly) more elaborate recruitment procedures laid down by the FEC so as to stretch out the recruitment process. Consequently, it is conceivable that the fixed cost of recruiting to a vacancy, and the lag between the decision to fill the vacancy and the new employee starting work, rise from c_F and τ, respectively, under the formal procedures devised by the firm, to c^*_F and τ^*, respectively, under FEC-determined procedures.

As a result of FEC regulations the costs to a firm, per vacancy, arising from its need to comply with FEC regulations in filling its vacancies, rise by:

$$\theta\left[(c*_F - c_F) + \int_\tau^{\tau^*}(\rho_E - s)e^{-rt}dt\right] + (1-\theta)\left[c*_F + \int_0^{\tau^*}(\rho_E - s)e^{-rt}dt\right] \quad (6.25)$$

The first and second terms in the *first* set of square brackets in equation (6.25) are, respectively, the additional cost from filling a vacancy using formal procedures, and the increased opportunity cost arising from the longer delay in filling a vacancy, under FEC regulations. The first and second terms in the *second* set of square brackets in equation (6.25) are, respectively, the fixed cost that has now to be paid on vacancies that, in the absence of the FEC, would have been filled informally, and the forgone profits from the delay, resulting from the use of formal methods of recruitment, in appointing a worker.

Because the FEC, for the two reasons discussed above, raises the cost of filling vacancies, fewer vacancies will be filled under its regulatory regime. Some vacancies which were worth filling in the pre-regulation period (particularly those that, in the absence of regulation, would have been filled through informal methods) may no longer be worth filling under FEC-approved recruitment procedures. This, more often than not, will be the invidious result of the higher costs of filling vacancies and the longer delays in filling them, combined with the fact that some vacancies have a very short life-span.

Suppose that, as a consequence of the higher recruitment costs imposed by FEC regulations, the number of vacancies that are filled falls from V^π to V^p with a concomitant decline in the likelihood of successful job-search from $v^\pi = V^\pi/U$ to $v^p = V^p/U$. Then, the net change in social welfare, as a consequence of fair-employment regulation, is from equation (6.23):

$$\Delta J = v^p(1 - I^P) - v^\pi(1 - I^\pi) = (I^\pi - I^P)v^\pi + (v^P - v^\pi)(1 - I^P) \quad (6.26)$$

From equation (6.26), fair-employment regulation will, in the net, increase or decrease social welfare ($\Delta J > 0$ or $\Delta J < 0$) if the positive effects on welfare of greater equality between Blacks and Whites in their likelihoods of successful job-search outweigh or are outweighed by the negative effects on welfare of a lowering in the overall likelihood of successful job-search. The term $(v^P - v^\pi)$ $(1 - I^P)$ in equation (6.26) represents the efficiency loss from fair-employment regulation while, as noted earlier, the term $(I^\pi - I^P)v^\pi$ represents the equity gain.

Under regulation, the overall likelihood is equally distributed so that $v^P = v^P_B = v^P_W$ and $I^P = 0$. So, by the argument of the previous section, $\Delta J > 0$ if $v^P > v^*$ and $\Delta J < 0$ if $v^P < v^*$, where v^* is the 'equally distributed equivalent likelihood' that is, the overall likelihood of successful job-search which, if equally distributed between Blacks and Whites would yield the same amount of social welfare as the distribution of likelihoods in the preregulatory state. In turn, the value of v^*, depends on how averse society is to inequality with higher degrees of aversion leading to lower values of v^*. If the inequality aversion parameter, $\varepsilon = 0$, then $v^* = v^\pi$ and society would not be prepared to tolerate any efficiency loss in exchange for equity gains. On the other hand, for high degrees of inequality aversion, society would be prepared to accept relatively high efficiency losses in exchange for the equity-gains that fair-employment regulation confers.

6.8   DIAGRAMMATIC REPRESENTATION

It may be useful to present an intuitive understanding of the approach to measuring employment inequality, set out in the previous sections, in terms of a diagram. Figure 6.1 portrays a world of Black (B) and White (W) who 'share' a given overall likelihood of successful job-search, v, to obtain, respectively, their likelihoods of v_B and v_W. The horizontal axis measures v_W and the vertical axis measures v_B. The sharing equation (6.14) may be simplified as:

$$v = v_B \phi_B + v_W \phi v_W \qquad (6.27)$$

where: $\phi_W = U_W / U$ and $\phi_B = U_B / U$ are the respective proportions of White

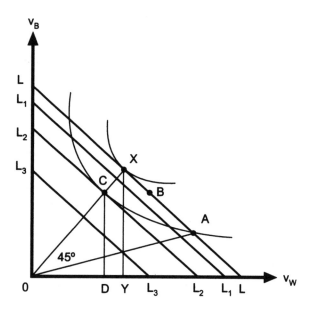

Figure 6.1   Employment Inequality Between Equal Quality Black and White Workers

and Black persons in the total of unemployed persons. Equation (6.18) is represented by the 'likelihood–possibility' line *LL* in Figure 6.1. The slope of *LL* is ϕ_W / ϕ_B. Each point on *LL* represents a (v_B, v_W) combination that yields the value v. At the point X, which lies on the 45° line passing through the origin, $v_B = v_W$.

Labour market outcomes may be viewed as a mapping from the parameters of the system, v, u_B, u_W, u, α (which define *LL*) to a point on *LL*. Different outcomes will locate at different points on *LL*. Those that locate closer to the point X (for example, at B) will be more egalitarian in terms of the distribution of the likelihood of successful job-search between Blacks and Whites than those which locate further away from X (for example, at A). For a given constellation of parameter values, Whites (at L on the horizontal axis) and Blacks (at L on the vertical axis) can 'buy' $v/[\alpha u_W /u]$ and $v/[(1 - \alpha)u_B/u]$ as their, respective, likelihoods of successful job-search. The quantities ϕ_B and ϕ_W may be interpreted as the 'prices' attached to the likelihood of successful job-search by, respectively, Blacks and Whites. The lower the proportion of White (Black) persons in the total of unemployed persons, the lower will be the price of the likelihood of successful job-search by Whites (Blacks).

Superimposed upon the likelihood–possibility line in the diagram are the welfare indifference curves: each curve shows the different v_B, v_W combinations that yield the same level of social welfare. From equation (6.15), the slope of any indifference curve is:

$$\frac{\partial J / \partial v_B}{\partial J / \partial v_W} = \frac{\phi_B a_B}{\phi_W a_W}$$

and social welfare is maximised when the slope of the indifference curve = slope *LL*, that is, when:

$$\frac{\dot{\phi}_B a_B}{\phi_W a_W} = \frac{\phi_B}{\phi_W} \Rightarrow a_B = a_W$$

and since the marginal utilities a_B and a_W diminish with increases in, respectively, v_B and v_W:

$$a_B = a_W \Rightarrow v_B = v_W$$

so that X is the point at which the likelihood–possibility line, *LL*, is tangential to an indifference curve. If the labour market outcome is at the point A, with $v_W = OF$ and $v_B = AF$ then this is equivalent, in welfare terms, to $v_W = v_B = CD$. The degree of inequality in labour market outcomes is, from equation (6.22): $1 - (CD/XY)$.

A decrease in the number of vacancies filled, following a (fair-employment regulation induced) increase in the cost of filling vacancies, causes a parallel, inward shift in the likelihood–possibility line, *LL*. The extent of the shift will depend on the size of the efficiency-loss: the greater the loss, the more the likelihood–possibility line will shift inwards: at L_1L_1, fair-employment regulation yields a net welfare gain; at L_3L_3 it yields a net welfare loss; and at L_1L_1 the net gain (loss) is zero.

6.8.1   Differences in Black–White Worker Quality

The fact that the likelihood of successful job-search by Blacks is less than that of Whites may be due to two reasons: (i) Blacks have less access to job-networks than do Whites; (ii) Whites, on average, are better (or perceived by employers to be better) workers than Blacks. In the preceding analysis the second point was assumed away: the labour market outcome, in terms of the different likelihoods of successful job-search, was at *A* in Figure 6.1 entirely because Blacks had an 'access problem'; fair-employment regulation, by removing this problem, would shift the outcome from *A* to *X*. In the process, efficiency losses would cause an inward parallel shift in the likelihood–possibility line but, as long as this shift stopped short of L_2L_2, fair-employment regulation would confer a net welfare benefit. In this subsection the assumption of equal worker quality is relaxed and it is assumed that Blacks, in terms of their likelihood of filling vacancies, suffer from the further handicap that, on average, they are not perceived (by employers) to be as good workers as Whites.

In terms of Figure 6.2, this quality constraint means that fair-employment regulation – by offering Blacks fair access to jobs – can only move the outcome from its pre-regulation point *A* to the post-regulation point *B*. The segment *BX* along the likelihood–possibility line, *LL*, is inaccessible: even if information on vacancies was available to all, and even if recruitment practices were entirely fair and above-board, differences in average worker quality would mean that the likelihood of successful job-search by Blacks could not be raised beyond *B*. The point *B*, by eliminating one difficulty that Blacks faced, offers a higher level of welfare than *A*. In welfare terms, point *A* is equivalent to point *G*. At *G*, the relative likelihoods of successful job-search by Blacks and Whites is the same as at *B*, but the fact that the overall likelihood is lower at *G* than at *B* means that it offers a lower level of welfare. The overall likelihood of successful job-search associated with *G* is *EF* where the point *E* lies at the intersection of *L'L'* and the 45° line, *OX*. This overall likelihood, *EF*, if distributed between Blacks and Whites according to the ratio given by the slope of *OB*, would yield the same level of welfare as obtained at point *A*.

Now if fair-employment regulation led to a decrease in the number of vacancies such that the likelihood–possibility line was shifted from (its original

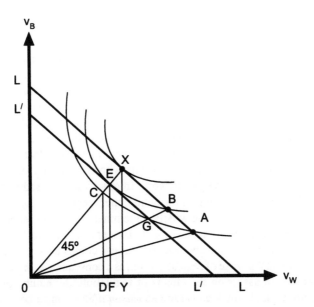

Figure 6.2 Employment Inequality Between Blacks and Whites with Perceived Quality Differential

position of) *LL* to the left of *L'L'* then such regulation would lead to a net welfare loss. Indeed, the greater the bite of the quality-constraint – so that the closer B was to *A* – the more likely it would be that fair-employment regulation would lead to a welfare loss. Conversely, the closer *B* was to *X* – that is, the less serious was the quality constraint – the more likely would fair-employment regulation be to lead to welfare gain. In the final analysis, therefore, the likelihood that fair-employment regulation would increase welfare would depend upon the 'human-capital gap' between Black and White workers. Nor could this gap be by-passed by interpreting fair-employment as positive discrimination rather than simply as affirmative action. Under positive discrimination a Black worker would fill a vacancy even in the presence of a superior White applicant: consequently, a move from *A* to *X* would be feasible. However, the employment, under positive discrimination, of less efficient workers than are available would lead the likelihood–possibility line to shift even further inwards: efficiency loss would now stem from the high post-regulatory cost of filling vacancies and from the fact that, owing to regulation, jobs are taken by less efficient (Black) workers while more able (White) workers remain unemployed.

6.9   CONCLUSIONS

The central conclusion of this chapter is that any employment disadvantage that members of a particular group (or groups) suffer from may not necessarily stem from 'discrimination' as it is usually understood in the literature. That is to say, this disadvantage is not necessarily the outcome of employer distaste towards, or social norms that restrict contact with, persons from that group. Nor need this disadvantage be based upon any perceived inferiority in terms of worker quality. Instead, as this chapter suggests, the recruitment and selection procedures for filling vacancies disadvantages persons who are not part of, or are only peripherally attached to, the job-network. In other words, disadvantage is the result of a lack of access to jobs. Fair-employment regulation, by insisting that information about vacancies be widely disseminated and that recruitment and selection procedures are transparent and accountable, tries to ensure that all persons have fair access to jobs. But fair access comes at a cost. Hiring and firing costs rise in the wake of regulation and, as a consequence, fewer vacancies are advertised. In assessing the effects of regulation, the equity gains which follow from it – and which constitute its *raison d'être* – must be compared to the concomitant efficiency losses, where both the gains and losses are measured in terms of social welfare. This paper suggested a method for making this comparison. It argued that the likelihood of a net social gain emerging from regulation would be less the greater the quality gap between the groups. Indeed, it may be that the redressal of this quality gap should be at least as important a component of policy as regulation to improve minority access to jobs.

NOTES

1   As Arrow (1998) points out, this form of discrimination was similar to residential segregation: Black persons were excluded from certain areas rather than being charged higher rents for living in those areas.

2   See Kirschenman and Neckerman (1991) for evidence on employer attitudes in Chicago towards the worker-quality of Hispanics and Blacks.

3   The FEC for Northern Ireland, for example, sees it as a measure of its success that, as a result of its enforcing the statutory obligations on the province's employers under the 1989 Fair Employment (NI) Act, most vacancies are publicly advertised and that a greater degree of formality has been introduced into recruitment and selection procedures (Fair Employment Commission for Northern Ireland, *Annual Report*, 1999).

4   Indeed, if the value of γ was low enough, the likelihood of Blacks filling a vacancy would be higher under informal, rather than formal, methods of recruitment.

5   Since $\beta \leq 1$ and $(2\beta - 1) \leq 1$.
6    $\delta\log\Delta v_w/\delta\varepsilon = -\log\lambda > 0$ since $\lambda < 1$.
7   By definition of J, $F(.)$ and

$$v^* : UF(v^*) = \sum U_k F(v_k) \Rightarrow (v*/v)^{1-\varepsilon} = \sum(U_k/U)(v_k/v)^{1-\varepsilon}$$

8   That is, the social welfare function is homogenous of degree one in the likelihoods.

REFERENCES

Arrow, K.J. (1972), 'Some Mathematical Models of Race in the Labor Market', in A.H. Pascal (ed.), *Racial Discrimination in Economic Life*, Lexington, MA: Lexington Books.

Arrow, K.J. (1998), 'What Has Economics to Say About Racial Discrimination?', *Journal of Economic Perspectives*, **12**, 91–100.

Atkinson, A.B. (1970), 'On the Measurement of Inequality', *Journal of Economic Theory*, **2**, 244–63.

Becker, G.S. (1971), *The Economics of Discrimination*, (2nd edition), Chicago: University of Chicago Press.

Donohue, J. (1998), 'Discrimination in Employment', in P. Newman (ed.), *The New Palgrave Dictionary of Economics and the Law*, London: Macmillan.

Elmslie, B. and S. Sedo (1996), 'Discrimination, Social Psychology and Hysterisis in Labor Markets', *Journal of Economic Psychology*, **17**, 465–78.

Epstein, R. (1995), 'The Status-Production Side-Show: Why the Antidiscrimination Laws are Still a Mistake', *Harvard Law Review*, **108**, 1085–109.

Friedman, M. (1962), *Capitalism and Freedom*, Chicago: Chicago University Press.

Granovetter, M. (1974), *Getting a Job: A Study of Contacts and Careers*, Cambridge: Cambridge University Press.

Granovetter, M. (1988), 'Economic Action and Social Structure', in B. Wellman and S.D. Berkowitz (eds), *Social Structures: A Network Approach*, Cambridge: Cambridge University Press.

Higgs, R. (1977), *Competition and Coercion: Blacks in the American Economy, 1865–1914*, New York: Columbia University Press.

Kirschenman, J. and K. Neckerman (1991), '"We'd love to hire them, but...": The Meaning of Race for Employers', in C. Jencks and P.E. Peterson (eds), *The Urban Underclass*, Washington, DC: The Brookings Institution.

Krueger, A.O. (1963), 'The Economics of Discrimination', *Journal of Political Economy*, **79**, 481–86.

Lewis, W.A. (1979), 'The Dual Economy Revisited', *The Manchester School*, **47**, 211–29.

McAdams, R.H. (1995), 'Cooperation and Conflict: The Economics of Group Status Production and Race Discrimination', *Harvard Law Review*, **108**, 1005–84.

Phelps, E.S. (1972), 'The Statistical Theory of Racism and Sexism', *American Economic Review*, **62**, 659–61.

Rees, A. and G.P. Schultz (1970), *Workers and Wages in an Urban Labor Market*, Chicago: University of Chicago Press.

Smith, D. and G. Chambers (1991), *Inequality in Northern Ireland*, Oxford: Clarendon Press.

Whatley, W. and G. Wright (1994), 'Race, Human Capital, and Labour Markets in American History', in G. Grantham and M. MacKinnon (eds), *Labour Market Evolution*, New York: Routledge.

White, H.C. (1995), 'Social Networks Can Resolve Actor Paradoxes in Economics and Psychology', *Journal of Institutional and Theoretical Economics*, **151**, 58–74.

7   Oligarchy Power and Inflation in Brazil

Rogério B. Miranda

7.1   INTRODUCTION

One of the most puzzling phenomena in Latin American countries is the fact that, although inflation is viewed by the majority of the population as the most serious economic problem, it has been frequently very difficult to stabilise prices.

This chapter offers an explanation as to why third world countries, especially Brazil, sometimes develop a chronically high inflation rate, which is perceived by the majority of the population as noxious. We aim to show that this phenomenon is derived from the choices made by the economic groups in power rather than by irrationality or lack of expertise. In this context, we describe the main function of economic and political populism and how it has been used to ensure the status quo in Latin American countries.

Thus, the episodes of chronic high inflation with large variance are seen as the optimal response by the leading political groups to shocks in output.

This chapter does not intend to revive the tradition of economic thought of the CEPAL,[1] in which there should be a distinct economic theory for third world countries; it only recognises that it is necessary to take into consideration the institutional characteristics of each country in order to explain or forecast economic outcomes. In this sense the political arrangements and distributive characteristics of Brazilian society[2] should have a major impact on the economic outcomes which interest us here.

A variety of other approaches have been utilised to explain persistent inflation in the third world, and in Latin America especially. The early explanations are based on economic and political populism (Dornbusch and Edwards 1991).

The author would like to thank João R.O. Faria and Jeremy Harris for their constructive comments. He accepts any remaining errors as his own.

These kinds of approach usually appeal to some degree of irrationality or lack of competence in order to explain why policymakers implement clearly inconsistent policies, adopted in this case by mistake.[3] The problem here is that it seems impossible to reconcile these hypotheses with rational agents or even with agents with adaptive expectations, since it is supposed that policy makers not only fail to anticipate the outcome of the model they implement, but also cannot learn (or learn only very slowly) from past experiences.

Because of this difficulty, the literature has moved to alternatives where delay or inaction can appear as the result of maximising decisions. In this way Alesina and Drazen (1991) argue that a 'war of attrition' among different socioeconomic groups may lead to situations in which infeasible policies can arise. This 'war of attrition' would result from the fact that the reform or policy correction can be viewed as a public good and no group would have incentives to be the first to supply it by accepting a cut in its budget share.

In Labán and Sturzenegger (1994), delayed stabilisation comes as a result of a model in which there exists distributional conflict between two groups of risk averse agents. This model supposes that the expected economic benefit from reform is positive for both groups, but not for certain. In this environment the optimal decision may be to postpone the reform, even for the group which suffers the most by not reforming.

Arbache and Faria (1996) developed a model with 'reversible sclerosis'. There, pressure groups demand inflationary policies, which gradually disorganise the economy. This disorganisation leads to a loss of power of these groups and then to reform. The final outcome is cyclical inflation, since the economic recovery strengthens the pressure groups once again.

In this chapter we evaluate the existence of an optimal inflation response in a two-group oligarchic economy in which the government cares only about one of the groups, and infinity-lived agents maximise their discounted flow of utility. We show that the average level of inflation is negatively associated with the income share of the oligarchic group and that if this share is big enough the optimal inflation will be zero. The model also shows a negative correlation between inflation and exogenous shocks.

One natural question that may arise in this context is how this oligarchic group can remain in power, since it is by supposition a minority. In order to answer this question this chapter explores the fact that minorities may actually be very powerful if their members hold key positions in the government, positions that allow them to use populism to control electoral outcomes.

7.2   ECONOMIC ENVIRONMENT

7.2.1   Long-run Phillips Curve

The positive correlation between inflation and output (and employment) was the centre of a classical debate in the 1970s (Lucas 1973 and Friedman 1976, among others), and it is still difficult to scorn the practical implications of the Phillips curve, at least in the short run.

But in the long run, one could expect a true negative relationship between inflation and economic growth, as Friedman (1976) points out. In what he calls the '3rd stage of the professional analysis' of the relation between inflation and unemployment, he claims that:

> [i]n recent years high inflation has often been accompanied by higher, not lower, employment, especially for periods of several years in length. A simple statistical Phillips curve for such periods seems to be positively sloped ...[4]

In this chapter we implement a conciliatory approach: the real effects of inflation in the short run are not dismissed, but in the long run persistent inflation will hurt effective output.

Many are the reasons why the persistence of inflation undermines the productive capability of the real sector. Fischer (1993) argues empirically that inflation reduces growth by reducing investment and productivity growth. Investments would tend to shrink in a chronically inflationary economy since the variance of the rate of return in this case would probably be high enough to discourage some investors. Besides, the longer the maturity of the investment, the higher the variance, which means those long-run investments would be rare. Without these long-term projects it is plausible that productivity will fall.

But for these negative effects to take place it is necessary for inflation to be persistent; what matters here is the inflationary history of the economy rather than the present inflation rate. So it is necessary to define some quantitative measure of this history in order to formulate the problem. In this way, we define *inflationary memory* as follows:

$$\Psi_t = \varphi \Psi_{t-1} + \pi_{t-1} \qquad (7.1)$$

where Ψ_t is the inflationary memory in period t, π_{t-1} is the inflation rate at time $t-1$ and $\varphi \in (0,1)$ is a persistence factor (*memory factor*). Although this formulation may look like an adaptive expectation formula, one should realise that it is not a psychological rule to update expectations, but a physical constraint on the production capability of the economic system, as will be seen. Thus, there is no inconsistency between this assumption and perfect economic rationality.

To perform a simple test of the applicability of this specification, equation (7.1) is re-written as:

$$\Psi_t = \varphi^t \, \Psi_0 + \sum_{i=0}^{t-1} \varphi^i \pi_{t-1-i} \qquad (7.2)$$

where ψ_0 is given.

Then, supposing $\Psi_0 = 0$ and using Brazilian inflation data from 1944 to 1999, a series of inflationary memory was built and then regressed together with a time trend against the yearly gross domestic product (in billions). This regression was performed with the data from 1968 to 1998 because, as we only have Brazilian inflation data from 1944 and the initial value for Ψ was arbitrarily chosen, that series needed some time 'to mature'.

Using $\varphi = 0.942$,[5] the following results were obtained:

$$\log(GDP) = 19.47 + \underset{(16.12)}{0.0537} \, time - \underset{(-5.34)}{0.0047} \, \Psi \qquad (7.3)$$

This regression has a $R^2 = 0.948$ and a negative coefficient associated with Ψ, which is significant at the 99.5 per cent level. If one directly regress inflation (instead of inflationary memory) and the time trend against GDP within the same data set the coefficient associated with inflation is still negative (–0.0003), but not significant even at the 90 per cent level, as one can see in Figure 7.1, in which the values of the t-statistic for φ between 0 and 1 are shown. Thus, we believe that inflationary memory is a better variable in order to explain deviations of output from its time trend than inflation is.

The regression as a whole is significant at the 99 per cent level. This simple exercise was done to highlight the fact that inflationary memory may be a good factor in explaining deviations of output from its natural trend.[6]

Thus, the long-run Phillips curve can be written as:

$$y_t = G(\Psi_t) y_t^p \qquad (7.4)$$

where $G' < 0$ and y_t^p is the potential output in period t, which is determined by other economic factors.

7.2.2   Distributive Impact of Inflation in Brazil

Aside from the effect that persistent inflation may have over production it has perhaps a more dramatic and perverse consequence for income distribution. There are various channels through which these effects can act.

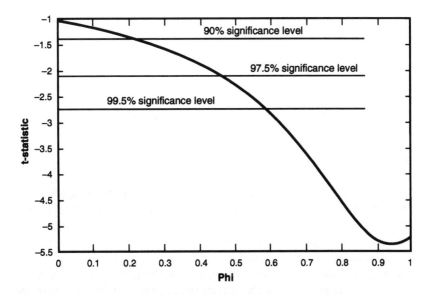

Figure 7.1   The Significance of the Inflation-Memory Coefficient

First, it has been recognised that inflationary taxation in Latin America is strongly regressive[7] since the lower classes have no access to financial protection against the corrosion of their income by inflation. On the other hand, the upper and upper-middle classes have available highly sophisticated financial markets, where the inflation tax can be avoided almost entirely.

Secondly, public expenditure mostly benefits the upper and upper-middle classes. This seems quite evident when one looks for some specific examples; in Brazil, resources destined for free public universities are five times higher than the amount allocated to elementary and high schools. But the typical college student in that country comes from the richest classes, because only they can afford private high schools and the state of elementary public education is very poor – as one could expect given this expenditure structure.

Finally, some groups have directly benefited from inflation. That is the case in the bank sector. Models such as Ostrup (2000) have been developed to show how a bank's earnings are positively correlated to inflation.[8] Although the literature is poor in relation to the performance of Brazilian banks and the factors which can affect it, the huge expansion of this sector during the 1970s and 1980s and its rapid decline after inflation was tamed in the 1990s may serve as empirical evidence of the profit obtained from 'floating'.

In summary, inflation has three major redistributive consequences: it erodes the wages of the poor, it is a tax revenue used for the benefit of the upper classes and it is a direct source of profit for some sectors.

Based on the above reasoning one can suppose that the income share of the inflation-protected groups in output is an increasing function of inflation. Thus:

$$y_t^h = [\alpha + \phi(\pi_t)]y_t = [\alpha + \phi(\pi_t)]G(\Psi_t)y_t^p \qquad (7.5)$$

where y_t^h is the income of the inflation protected groups, α is that group's share of total income if there were no inflation, $\phi \in (0, 1-\alpha)$, $\phi(0) = 0$ and $\phi' > 0$.

7.2.3   Oligarchy Power and Populism

If the lower classes, presumably the majority, suffer from inflation, one could expect that they would elect politicians committed to terminating inflation. But, under some circumstances, the story (or the history) may be quite different.

Sometimes the group in power governs just to promote their own interest and this situation, although broadly viewed as unfair, will be sustained for a long period. In Latin America, the two major forms through which the oligarchies manage to retain power are authoritarianism and populism. In the former, the government is taken by force, in general with the support of the military and in some cases, by the military alone. Once in power the oligarchy will implement policies in their own interest.[9] In the latter case, in spite of the democratic system, power is 'bought' from voters.

In its authoritarian form, oligarchy power is in general supported by a coalition, which is very well coordinated, and any opposing group formation is forbidden and suppressed, when necessary, by force.

In this tyrannical-type government it is not so hard to see that it is very difficult to replace the group in power, and in most cases it happens only when another oligarchy coalition is powerful enough to take the government for itself.

A more complicated process occurs when the political system is democratic. As seen by Ferejohn (1986) if the electorate has a retrospective vote rule and is sufficiently heterogeneous, the incumbent can assure his reelection by playing the voters against each other. In this way, he can 'buy' the votes with redistributive promises which, given the competition among electors, may become as small as the power-holding politician wants.

In this context, populism can be viewed as a political or electoral strategy rather than an economic doctrine. It works both as a smoke scream, which avoids coordination among voters, and as political propaganda in which the message is clear: 'vote for your own interest because others will do so also'. So, apparently inconsistent economic concessions for certain groups might make sense as a strategy for the incumbent (or for the status quo) to achieve the minimum necessary coalition.

This result only holds if the electorate votes selfishly. The sociotropic voting criterion, that is, the situation in which voters' choice is based on aggregate economic performance, precludes this 'buying' scheme. Although there is evidence that sociotropic motives are an important factor in elections in developed countries, one may suspect that the low level of coordination and, in some cases, the hopeless economic state of third-world voters may induce them to vote only based on their own short-run interest.

7.3   THE MODEL

Suppose an economy with two groups of agents where the central planner maximises, in principle, the weighted sum of the two groups' discounted utility. Thus, he faces the following function:

$$U(c^h, c^l) = \sum_{t=0}^{\infty} \beta^t E\left[\delta u(c_t^h) + (1-\delta)u(c_t^l)\right] \tag{7.6}$$

where c^h and c^l are the consumption flows of the groups H and L, respectively, $\beta \in (0,1)$ is a discount factor, $\delta \in (0,1)$ is the weight the central planner assigns to the utility of the group H and $u(\bullet)$ is a non-decreasing, concave function.

The main supposition here is that inflation works as a distributive mechanism as described in Section 7.2.2. Since there is no alternative use of income apart from consumption, each group constraint can be written as:

$$c_t^h = y_t^h = [\alpha + \phi(\pi_t)]G(\Psi_t, A_t)y_t^p \tag{7.7}$$

and

$$c_t^l = y_t^l = [1 - \alpha - \phi(\pi_t)]G(\Psi_t, A_t)y_t^p \tag{7.8}$$

where A_t is a random shock to the Phillips curve ($G_A > 0$).

Notice that, without inflation, each group collects a fixed proportion of the income determined purely by economic factors. In this way, it is supposed that inflation is the only mechanism available to redistribute income.

If the central planner only cares about the welfare of group H, then $\delta = 1$ and the problem can be written as:

$$\begin{cases} Max: U(c^h) = \sum_{t=0}^{\infty} \beta^t E[u(c_t^h)] \\ s.t.: c_t^h = [\alpha + \phi(\pi_t)]G(\Psi_t, A_t)y_t^p \\ \quad \Psi_t = \delta \Psi_{t-1} + \pi_{t-1} \\ \quad \Psi_0 \text{ given} \\ \quad \pi_t > 0, \forall t \end{cases} \qquad \text{(P7.1)}$$

The *Bellman equation* associated with (P7.1) is:

$$V(\Psi, A) = u([\alpha + \phi(\pi_t)]G(\Psi, A)y^p) + \beta EV(\hat{\Psi}, \hat{A}) \qquad (7.9)$$

where $y_t^p = y_{t+1}^p = y^p$ is fixed across time and $\hat{\Psi}$ and A are the next period values for Ψ and A.

The first order condition implies that:

$$\beta EV_\Psi(\hat{\Psi}, \hat{A}) = -u'(c)\phi'(\pi)G(\Psi, A)y^p) \qquad (7.10)$$

and the envelope theorem condition:

$$V_\Psi(\Psi_t, A_t) = u'(c)(\alpha + \phi(\pi_t))G_\Psi(\Psi_t, A_t)y^p + \beta\varphi EV_\Psi(\Psi_t, A_t). \qquad (7.11)$$

Then, taking the combination of equations (7.10) and (7.11) :

$$V_\Psi(\Psi, A) = u'(c)[(\alpha + \phi(\pi))G_\Psi(\Psi, A)y^p - \varphi\phi'(\pi)G(\Psi, A)]y^p \qquad (7.12)$$

Leading equation (7.12) by one period:

$$V_\Psi(\hat{\Psi}, \hat{A}) = u'(\hat{c})[(\alpha + \phi(\hat{\pi}))G_\Psi(\hat{\Psi}, \hat{A})y^p - \varphi\phi'(\hat{\pi})G(\hat{\Psi}, \hat{A})]y^p \qquad (7.13)$$

Finally, combining equations (7.10) and (7.13), one obtains the following Euler equation:

$$u'(c) = -E\left[\frac{\beta u'(\hat{c})[(\alpha + \phi(\hat{\pi}))G_\Psi(\hat{\Psi}, \hat{A})y^p - \varphi\phi'(\hat{\pi})G(\hat{\Psi}, \hat{A})]}{\phi'(\pi)G(\Psi, A)}\right] \qquad (7.14)$$

7.3.1 Steady State and Encompassing Interest

In this economy, although group H has the political control and chooses its preferred level of inflation,[10] it faces a trade-off: the higher the inflation, the higher its share of the product, but the lower the expected income in the next period. Intuitively, the greater α is, the lower should be the preferred rate of inflation. In this case, α is a measure of the encompassing interest of group H.[11] To see this formally, consider a deterministic[12] version of equation (7.14) at the steady state:

$$\frac{\phi'(\pi^*)G(\Psi^*,\overline{A})}{\beta[(\alpha+\phi(\pi^*))G_\Psi(\Psi^*,\overline{A})-\varphi\phi'(\pi^*)G(\Psi^*,\overline{A})]} = -1 \qquad (7.14a)$$

which imples

$$\phi'(\pi^*)G(\Psi^*,\overline{A})+\beta(\alpha+\phi(\pi^*))G_\Psi(\Psi^*,\overline{A})-\beta\,\varphi\phi'(\pi^*)G(\Psi^*,\overline{A})=0 \quad (7.14b)$$

and, in turn,

$$\frac{\partial\pi^*}{\partial\alpha} = -\beta G_\Psi(\Psi^*,\overline{A})\left\{\left[\beta+(1-\beta\varphi)\frac{\partial\Psi^*}{\partial\pi^*}\right]\phi'(\pi^*)G_\Psi(\Psi^*,\overline{A})+ \right.$$

$$\left. \beta(\alpha+\phi(\pi^*))G_{\Psi\Psi}(\Psi^*,\overline{A})\frac{\partial\Psi^*}{\partial\pi^*}+(1-\beta\varphi)\phi''(\pi^*)G(\Psi^*,\overline{A})\right\}^{-1} \qquad (7.14c)$$

If $G_{\Psi\Psi}$ and $\phi''<0$, then $\partial\pi^*/\partial\alpha<0$ since $\partial\Psi^*/\partial\pi^*>0$.[13] Observe further that, as there is no possibility of deflation in this model (that is, $\pi_t\geq 0\;\forall t$), one question that may arise is under what conditions this group will have a *superencompassing* interest, in the sense defined by McGuire and Olson (1996).

In the context of this model, the superencompassing interest would be a situation in which inflation would be set equal to zero and all inflationary transferences would cease. The benefit of abolishing inflation, measured in terms of an increase in future output, would offset the benefit of the inflationary transfers.

The question, then, is under what conditions the benefits of reducing inflation would be greater that the potential inflationary transfers. If π^* and Ψ^* are the steady-state values for the inflation rate and inflationary memory, respectively:

$$\phi(\pi^*) = \frac{(\beta\varphi-1)\phi'(\pi^*)G_\Psi(\Psi^*,\overline{A})}{\beta G_\Psi(\Psi^*,\overline{A})}-\alpha \qquad (7.15)$$

Then,

$$\bar{\alpha} = \left\{ \frac{(\beta\varphi - 1)\phi'(\pi^*)G_\Psi(\Psi^*,\overline{A})}{\beta G_\Psi(\Psi^*,\overline{A})} \right\} \Rightarrow \{\pi^* = 0\} \qquad (7.16)$$

since

$$\{\phi'(\pi^*) = 0\} \Leftrightarrow \{\pi^* = 0\} \qquad (7.17)$$

First notice that $\bar{\alpha} > 0$ since $\beta, \varphi < 1, G$ and $G_\Psi < 0$ and $\phi' > 0$. It means that, if group H's pre-inflation share of output is greater than $\bar{\alpha}$, there will be a superencompassing interest and inflation will be zero.

7.4   SIMULATING THE MODEL

7.4.1   Functions and Parameters

In most cases, equation (7.14) does not have an analytical solution. One alternative method of examining the properties of this dynamic model is to simulate it using numerical techniques. In order to do that, one must specify all the necessary functions.

The utility function is a CES function since it allows temporal substitutability, thus:

$$u(c) = \frac{c^{1-\sigma}}{1-\sigma} \qquad (S7.1)$$

The *inflationary memory* function was specified as:

$$y_t = G(\Psi_t, A_t) = A_t \bar{y} e^{-\gamma\Psi_t} \qquad (S7.2)$$

In this way, income in time t depends both on the inflationary memory and a stochastic shock A_t in that period. This specification was chosen in respect of the good explanatory power it showed in the exercise with the Phillips curve.

The redistributive impact of the same period's inflation was modelled as follows:

$$\phi(\pi_t) = e^{\lambda\pi_t} \qquad (S7.3)$$

Then (P7.1) can be rewritten as:

$$\left\{ \begin{array}{l} Max: U(c^h) = \sum_{t=0}^{\infty} \beta^t E\left[\dfrac{c_t^{1-\sigma}}{1-\sigma}\right] \\[3ex] s.t.: c_t^h = [\alpha + e^{\lambda \pi_t}]A_t \bar{y} e^{-\gamma \Psi_t} \\[2ex] \Psi_t = \delta \Psi_{t-1} + \pi_{t-1} \\[2ex] \Psi_0 \text{ given} \\[2ex] \pi_t > 0, \forall t \end{array} \right. \qquad (P7.2)$$

Another necessary thing to simulate the model is, of course, setting the parameter values. Table 7.1 shows the chosen values for diverse parameters.

Some of these parameters may need further explanation. At first glance α, group H's pure productive share of income, may appear to have been set too high. But if one considers that the capital share of the income in Brazil is around 63 per cent, this number makes sense. The measure of the negative impact of inflationary memory over income, γ, came from the regression in Section 7.2.1 as well as the parameter for inflation memory propagation, φ.

The discount factor, β, looks too small, but this number is consistent with a real interest rate of 12 per cent per year, which is the bottom level for interest rates in Brazil in the last 30 years.

Table 7.1
Parameter Values

Parameter	Value	Meaning
σ	2	Elasticity of intertemporal substitution
α	0.6	Group H pure productive income share
λ	6	Measure of the redistributive effect of inflation
γ	0.0047	Measure of the impact of inflationary memory on income
φ	0.942	Inflationary memory propagation parameter
β	0.89	Discount factor
$\bar{y}$	100	Normalised average of the potential product

7.4.2   Income Shocks

The idiosyncratic shock to income, A_p is modelled as a nine-state Markov chain with high persistence. This model is supposed to reproduce the external shock to which the Brazilian economy has been subjected. The possible values go from 0.6 to 1.4, with variations of 0.1. The transition matrix for this process was built in a way such that the probability of going to an adjacent state (that is, of going from state 4 to state 3 or 5, for example) is one-half of the probability of staying in the same state. The probability of shifting two states (to the state next to the adjacent) is one-fourth and so on.

Later this shock will be associated with the performance of the US economy, since it is the best proxy for the Brazilian economy's external environment.

7.4.3   Simulation Results

Figure 7.2 compares the inflation rate path obtained using the functions and parameters described above and simulating the model for 55 periods against the logarithm of the real Brazilian inflation rate.[14] Some features are particularly worth noting.

First, although in the simulation the inflation rate (or its logarithm) was not allowed to be negative, the similarities between the two diagrams are evident. The variance of the logarithm of the actual Brazilian inflation rate is 2.65 while the variance of the simulated inflation is 1.84.

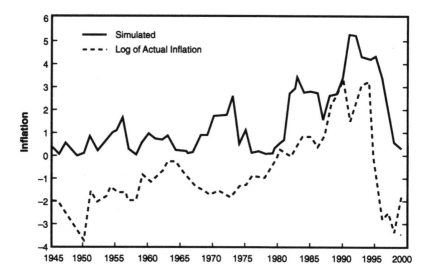

Figure 7.2   Simulated and Actual Inflation

Secondly, the simulated inflation rate shows a high negative correlation with the exogenous shock, –0.982. If one takes the variations of US GDP as a measure of the exogenous shock, and then calculates the correlation between this and the actual Brazilian inflation the result will also be negative. Table 7.2 shows correlations between real Brazilian inflation and variations in US GNP for various lags.

The utilisation of US GDP as a measure of exogenous shock makes sense because a decrease in US income would have not only a direct impact on the Brazilian economy, since it is the principle purchaser of Brazil's exports, but also indirect effects. The latter would come from the fact that most of the other countries which are significant importers of Brazilian products, that is, Latin American countries, also have the USA as main buyer of their own products. This means that a decrease in US income would lead not only to a decrease in US imports, but also to a decrease in Latin America countries' purchases from Brazil.

The high negative correlation shown by the model may be explained by the fact that, although American economic performance is the best proxy for the Brazilian economy's exogenous condition, it is absolutely not the only one. For example, in 1995 the Mexican currency devaluation (an exogenous factor) drove up the Brazilian inflation rate. In this particular case, the US economy was not a good measure of the relevant Brazilian external environment.

7.4.4 Optimal Inflation: The Brazilian Case

With these results in hand, one can try to establish the causality between inflation and growth in the Brazilian economy. The starting point is the potential product, which is a function of such economic factors as capital stock, labour force available, technology and so on. How much of this potential output will be effectively produced depends on the inflationary memory, which is, as we saw above, a discounted average of past inflation rates. Given the effective output, the oligarchy will choose the inflation rate for the current period, this rate is supposed to maximise the discounted flow of future consumption of that group.

Table 7.2
Correlation between Brazilian Inflation and American GDP,
% Variation

Lag in Years	1	2	3	4	5	6	Simm.
Correlation	–.0995	–.0960	–.1189	–.1270	–.0172	–.0010	–.9824

In short, the past inflation history determines what is going to be the effective income and then what is going to be the current inflation.

Under this perspective, it is not the current inflation rate that determines economic growth, but rather the opposite: the level of income together with the past inflation will set the current rate.

Another important factor is that the external shocks, which also influence the effective output, are negatively correlated to the inflation rate. This means that deteriorating external conditions will lead to an increase in the inflation rate: if income goes down the group in power increases its share of the diminishing product by increasing inflation.

But what in fact happened in the Brazilian economy starting in 1995 that slowed inflation down? Three explanations are consistent with this model.

The most optimistic explanation would attribute the fall in Brazilian inflation to the development of true democracy in that country. The maturity of the democracy would break the 'Ferejohn situation' described in Section 7.2.3 and allow the central planner to consider also the welfare of the non-oligarchy group, that is, to decrease the value of δ (until supposed equal to 1). It would cause a decline in inflation, since this group does not get any benefit from it. One could argue that since the *Real Plan* (1994) the Brazilian government has acted in order to close the inflationary channels in spite of some parliamentary resistance. Both the new economic policy and parliamentary opposition are consistent with this explanation. The change in economic policy can be associated with the 'new objective function' faced by the social planner and the parliamentary opposition embodies the struggle of the oligarchy to keep its interests running.

Another explanation would appeal to the fact that the technology for avoiding the negative impact of inflation has become more broadly available than before. In fact, during the 1980s not even monthly passes for public transportation were available, which forced the poor to face a new price rise almost every week. Towards the end of the 1980s the expansion of computerised banking systems led to a decrease in the transaction costs of banking, which allowed much of the population to get inflation-indexed chequing accounts. An estimate of the Brazilian Bank Association says that Brazilians use proportionally twice as many cheques as Americans do.[15] This decrease in the ability of the oligarchy to transfer income to itself would reduce the benefits of inflation without a corresponding reduction of its cost. Therefore the oligarchy would reduce inflation because inflationary transfers would become too expensive.

A third alternative explanation within this model would come from the external front. As seen above the model predicts a negative correlation between external events and Brazilian inflation. If one chooses the US economic performance as a proxy for the external factors, it is easy to observe that the decline of Brazilian inflation has happened during one of the greatest booms in the American economy. In that way, one could say that favourable external conditions are truly responsible for the decline in inflation.

Of course, a mix of these three explanations is possible if they are not mutually exclusive. Thus, more representation of the poor, a smaller transfer base and favorable external conditions acting together would lead to a decrease in the inflation rate.

7.5 CONCLUSIONS AND EXTENSIONS

This chapter has presented a model in which inflation comes from the maximising behaviour of the economic group in power. This group faces a trade-off since inflation reduces output and increases its income share.

The relationship between inflation and growth has two directions: first the past inflationary history, here called *inflationary memory*, affects negatively the overall product, and then variations of the effective output – caused, for example, by external shocks – will lead to variations in the current inflation rate. The latter is then added to the overall history to determine the next period's output.

In this context, there are three non-mutually exclusive explanations for the fall in Brazilian inflation during the 1990s. First, the maturity of democracy may have led to a redistribution of power among the various interest groups that reduced the ability of the inflation-benefited group to pursue inflationary policies. Secondly, advances in technology may have decreased the costs of protecting oneself against inflation, shrinking significantly the transfer base and thus increasing the opportunity cost of inflation. Finally, the favourable external scenario may have been a positive aspect, keeping Brazilian inflation down.

The inflation rate path generated by the model presented in this chapter has properties in common with the real Brazilian inflation path, especially in respect of its variance. The obtained correlation between the inflation rate and exogenous shocks is negative as in the actual case, although its absolute value is larger.

Several improvements can be made to this basic model. First, one may want to recalculate the entire model for cases where $\delta \neq 1$ and evaluate the effects on the inflation rate.

But a more interesting modification would be to include a reaction function for group L. In such a way, one could suppose that group L is the labour provider and that this group's efforts are increasing its income share. If group L maximises its own welfare function, then they would have a reaction function to be considered by the central planner when maximising the welfare of group H.

NOTES

1   In English, Economic Commission for Latin America and the Caribbean, ECLAC.

2   The focus of this chapter on Brazil is due to the fact that I have a 'comparative advantage' in obtaining data and institutional information about this country. I believe that this analysis, with some modifications, could fit well with other Latin American countries.

3   'At the end of the road one cannot avoid wondering whether the mistakes of the past populist regimes can be internalized by policymakers, politicians, and the population at large and, thus, be avoided in the future.' (Dornbusch and Edwards 1991).

4   Friedman (1976), bottom of p. 459.

5   The choice of the parameter j was made by numerical methods. The computer did a comparison of 10 000 values between 0 and 1 and picked out from among them the one which produced the best result in the regression.

6   Of course a much more sophisticated regression analysis, which may include capital, labour, productivity and so on, would be required to develop this point.

7   Labán and Sturzenegger (1994).

8   This chapter provides some empirical evidence for the Danish bank sector.

9   'When an individual has much more power than another, he may be better able to serve his interests by threatening to use – or by using – force than by voluntary exchange: he may be able to obtain for free what would otherwise be costly' (Olson 2000, p. 60).

10   In this model we are supposing that the policy maker is able to choose his desired level of inflation. We recognise that in real economies this level could never be precisely achieved, but for our purposes it is enough to assume that the policy maker may choose among inflationary policies of diverse degrees.

11   See Olson (2000) and McGuire and Olson (1996).

12   In this version, $A_t = \overline{A}$ with probability 1 for all t.

13   $\Psi^* = \pi^* + \varphi\pi^* + \varphi^2\pi^* \ldots \Rightarrow \Psi^* = \pi/(1-\varphi) \Rightarrow \partial\Psi^*/\partial\pi^* > 0.$

14   Brazilian inflation, Fundação Getúlio Vargas 1945–99.

15   See FEBRABAN (1993).

REFERENCES

Alesina, A. and A. Drazen (1991), 'Why are Stabilizations Delayed?', *American Economic Review*, **81** (5), 1170–88.

Arbache, J. and J. Faria (1996), 'Pressure Groups and Inflation: a Cyclical Model', *Revista de Economia Politica*, **16** (3), 129–35.

Bernanke, B.S., T. Laubach, F.S. Mishkin and A.S. Posen (1999), *Inflation Targeting: Lessons from the International Experience*, Princeton, NJ: Princeton University Press.

Dornbusch, R. and S. Edwards (eds) (1991), 'The Macroeconomics of the Populism', in *The Macroeconomics of Populism in Latin America*, Chicago, IL: University of Chicago Press.

Drazen, A. (2000), *Political Economy in Macroeconomics*, Princeton NJ: Princeton University Press.

FEBRABAN (1993), *Relatório Técnico*, São Paulo, Brazil: Federação Brasileira de Bancos.

Ferejohn, J. (1986), 'Incumbent Performance and Election Control', *Public Choice*, **50**, 5–26.

Fischer, S. (1993), 'Socialist Economy Reform: Lessons of the First Three Years', *Economic Review*, **83** (2), 390–5.

Friedman, M. (1976), 'Nobel Lecture: Inflation and Unemployment', *Journal of Political Economy*, **85** (3), 451–72.

Judd, K. (1998), *Numerical Methods in Economics*, Cambridge, MA: MIT Press.

Labán, R. and F. Sturzenegger (1994), 'Distributional Conflict, Financial Adaptation and Delayed Stabilizations', *Economics and Politics*, **6** (3), 257–76.

Ljungqvist, L. and T. Sargent (2000), 'Recursive Macroeconomic Theory', unpublished manuscript, Stanford University.

Lucas, R. (1973), 'Some International Evidence on Inflation–Output Tradeoffs', *American Economic Review*, **63** (3), 326–34.

McGuire, M and M. Olson (1996), 'The Economics of Autocracy and Majority Rule: The Invisible Hand and the Use of Force', *Journal of Economic Literature*, **34**, 72–96.

Olson, M. (2000), *Power and Prosperity*, New York: Basic Books.

Ostrup, F. (2000), *Money and the Natural Rate of Unemployment*, Cambridge, UK: Cambridge University Press.

Sturzenegger, F. (1991), 'Description of a Populist Experience: Argentina, 1973–1976', in R. Dornbusch and S. Edwards (eds), *The Macroeconomics of Populism in Latin America*, Chicago, IL: University of Chicago Press.

PART TWO

Migration: Unemployment, Assimilation,
Expected Returns and Risk

8 Migration, Unemployment and the Optimal Tax: Implications for Growth and Income Distribution

João Ricardo Faria

8.1 INTRODUCTION

The assumption of a dual economy is common in development economics. Two sectors are assumed, one modern and dynamic, using the state of the art technology generating high productivity and wages. The second sector is the traditional, where technology level is low and labour productivity is at the subsistence level. It is also used to relate the first sector to the industrial sector and the second to agriculture. As industries concentrate in cities the modern sector is also associated with the urban sector. Another important difference is that in the traditional rural sector full employment prevails, while the modern urban sector can be at or below the full employment equilibrium.

Due to the productivity gap and wage differentials between these sectors there is an opportunity cost for migration in this dual economy. The dual economy model is particularly suitable to describe internal migration and it is consistent with the human capital model of migration. The human capital model assumes that rational agents compare the expected gains from migration to expected costs.[1] In the context of a dual economy, workers in the traditional sector compare the present value of their prospective wages (and other positive externalities such as schooling and health care) in both sectors and decide to migrate to cities whenever the earning differential, netting out any migration costs, is positive.

Assuming that in the modern sector the labour market clears with no unemployment, it is possible to show that migration increases total output, and, often, will lead to remittances of income to the families of migrants that remain

---

The author would like to thank, without implicating, Miguel León-Ledesma for valuable comments.

in the traditional sector. Thus migration generates economic growth and increases social welfare through an improvement in income distribution.

There are two problems with this approach. On the one hand, by dropping the assumption of full employment in the modern urban sector, instead of generating growth and prosperity, it is possible to show that migration can lead to urban unemployment and poverty (for example, Todaro 1969). On the other hand, even in the presence of remittances of income from the modern to the traditional sector, there is a case that the loss in human capital, population, and other factors in the traditional sector offsets the gains from remittances, leading to net losses for the source sector creating regional imbalances. That is, migration can worsen income distribution.

This essay addresses these issues in a simple framework. It is shown that there is an optimal tax levied by the government that leads to an optimal migration path. This optimal tax corrects the distortions caused by non-clearing wages in the urban sector, leading to a fall in urban unemployment and a decrease in the rural–urban migration rate. This policy is also growth enhancing and can be seen as an income distribution instrument.[2]

The article is organised as follows. The next section presents the basic model. Section 8.3 discusses two types of labour market equilibrium in the modern sector. Section 8.4 presents the optimal tax. Section 8.5 describes the optimal path created by the introduction of the optimal tax, and finally section 8.6 brings the concluding remarks.

8.2   THE MODEL

Assume that total population (L) is fixed and normalised to unity. A zero population growth highlights the role of migration in the model:

$$L_I + L_A = 1 \equiv L \qquad (8.1)$$

where the subscripts I and A stand for industry and agriculture. L_I is urban population and L_A is rural population. Migration (M) corresponds to the flux of population from the rural to the urban sector, that is, from agriculture to industry. This implies that the urban population is a positive function of migration:

$$L_I = L_I(M), L_I'(M) > 0 \qquad (8.2)$$

As discussed above, the time path of migration increases with the net gains of migration. The net gains of migration correspond to the wage differential between industry and agriculture ($W_I - W_A$), and decrease with the costs of migration:

$$\dot{M} = [1 - \tau(M)]W_I - W_A \qquad (8.3)$$

For the sake of simplicity it is assumed that the only cost of migration is a tax that employed urban workers pay. That is, the government chooses a tax rate, τ, relating the migrating population to urban wages. This way to model migration costs and taxes allows us a high degree of flexibility; we can capture many cases and problems with this formulation (see Faria and Mollick 1996). One can think of it as a way to provide city infrastructure and amenities (such as better schools and hospitals), or to finance anti-pollution activities (Batabyal 1998), or to pay for unemployment benefits and so on. One can look at the term on the right hand side of equation (8.3) as $W_I - [W_A + \tau(M)W_I]$, that is, as a 'supplementary' wage in the rural sector as well. That is, the government can redistribute income from cities to the countryside as if it was a remittance or a subsidy.[3]

The migration of the rural population to cities decreases labour supply in agriculture. Other things being constant, one should expect that the shift in the labour supply curve in the rural sector leads to an increase in wages:

$$\dot{W}_A = \Omega(M,W_A), \Omega_M > 0, \Omega_A < 0 \qquad (8.4)$$

The adoption of new technologies in the traditional sector depends on wages, capital stock (K), and actual level of technology (H):

$$\dot{H} = \Psi(W_A,K,H) \qquad (8.5)$$

In order to characterise the threshold level of technology, let us assume that in the steady state ($\dot{H} = 0$) the level of technology can be written as a function of wages and the capital stock in the traditional sector:

$$H = H(W_A,K) \qquad (8.6)$$

Given a critical level of wage ($\overline{W}_A$), that can be the one at the subsistence level, any wage rate above this level leads to an increase in the use of more capital intensive technologies, that is:[4]

$$H = H(W_A,K), H_{W_A} > 0, H_K > 0, \text{ if } W_A \geq \overline{W}_A$$
$$H = \overline{H}, \text{ if } W_A < \overline{W}_A \qquad (8.7)$$

One can associate the variable H with human capital. In this case, equations (8.5)–(8.7) describe the formation of human capital as a function of new technologies that become economically viable whenever the opportunity cost of labour decreases. This is in line with Schultz's (1964) argument that new technology creates a demand for the ability to analyse and evaluate new production possibilities, which will raise the return to education (see also Galor and Weil 2000).

It is assumed that the traditional sector (agriculture) can increase its productivity after some critical level of technology. This threshold technological level is related to the evolution of wages in agriculture. The idea is that when rural population migrates to cities, it decreases the labour supply in the traditional sector, pushing up its wages. After a given level of wages it pays producers in this sector to substitute labour with capital. This is another way of seeing that the increase in the wages in the traditional sector increases the return to education and accelerates the adoption of new and more productive technologies. This movement leads to an increase in productivity and output in agriculture, generating overall growth in the economy.

The output in the traditional sector is described by the following production function:

$$Y_A = F(L_A, H) \tag{8.8}$$

One can think of Y_A as a consumption good (C).

The modern sector is responsible for the production of capital through new investments:

$$I = \dot{K} = G(N, K) \tag{8.9}$$

where N stands for employed urban population. Total production of capital is therefore a function of the work force employed in this sector and the existing capital stock. This can be written simply as:

$$K = g(N) \tag{8.10}$$

The government is assumed to maintain a balanced budget, in which its expenditures, G, are equal to its revenue, $\tau(M)W_I$:

$$G = \tau(M)W_I \tag{8.11}$$

Finally the value of total output in terms of the consumption good is given by:

$$Y = Y_A + pI + G = C + pI + G \tag{8.12}$$

8.3   MARKET CLEARING AND EFFICIENCY WAGES

The model presented in the last section is able to capture two different types of labour market equilibrium in the modern urban sector. It is consistent with urban unemployment and full employment. The literature commonly associates unemployment with the presence of efficiency wages (for example, Akerlof and Yellen 1986). Firms in the modern sector aiming at increasing loyalty and labour productivity pay wages above the market-clearing wage. These wages are called efficiency wages, and they are a source of wage rigidity and unemployment. Market clearing wages, by definition, generate full employment in the labour market.

Thus let us assume two types of wage regime in the industrial sector: (1) $W_I = W\,^*$, the efficiency wage, and (2) $W_I = W(K,L_I) = W\,^{**}$, the market clearing wage. Of course, the efficiency wage is greater than the market-clearing wage:

$$W^* \geq W^{**} \tag{8.13}$$

Moreover, if the market clearing wage, W^{**}, prevails, there is full employment in the urban sector. Therefore, the level of industrial employment corresponding to full employment that is consistent with

$$W^{**} = W(K,L_I^{**}) = W(K,N^{**})$$

is:

$$N^{**} = L_I^{**} \tag{8.14}$$

The level of employment related to the efficiency wage is given by:

$$N^* = \alpha L_I^*, 0 < \alpha < 1 \tag{8.15}$$

and it should be less than L_I^{**}:

$$N^* \leq L_I^{**} \tag{8.16}$$

In order to analyse the behaviour of the model with both types of wage, let us consider the steady state equilibrium, characterised by:

$$\dot{W}_A = \dot{M} = \dot{H} = \dot{K} = 0$$

As already seen, equation (8.6) holds when $\dot{H} = 0$. When $\dot{K} = 0$, it follows equation (8.10), and from equation (8.12) one obtains:

$$Y = C + G \tag{8.12'}$$

Equations (8.4) and (8.3) can be rewritten as:

$$\Omega(M,W_A) = 0 \Rightarrow W_A = \theta(M), \theta'(M) > 0 \tag{8.4'}$$

$$W_A = [1 - \tau(M)] \, W_I \qquad (8.3')$$

The cases of efficiency and market clearing wages are analysed below.

8.3.1   Efficiency Wages: $W_I = W^*$

In this case the modern industrial sector pays efficiency wages, and there is urban unemployment. The model is block recursive. The equilibrium values [denoted by an asterisk] of W_A^* and M^* are found simultaneously through (8.3') and (8.4'). Then the equilibrium values of L_I^* and G^* are determined by equations (8.2) and (8.11). The equilibrium L_A^* and N^* follow by equations (8.1) and (8.15), respectively. Given N^* the value of K^* is found by equation (8.10). Then, if $W_A^* \geq \overline{W}_A$, equation (8.7) determines H^*, and $H^* = \overline{H}$ otherwise. Given the equilibrium value of H^*, one can find the value of $Y_A^* = C^*$ by equation (8.8). Finally, equation (8.12') determines total output, Y^*.

8.3.2   Market Clearing Wages: $W_I = W(K,L_I)$

In this case, there is full employment in the modern urban sector. The model is block recursive as well, however its recursiveness differs from the previous case. The equilibrium values [denoted by double asterisk] of $W_A^{**}, M^{**}, L_I^{**}$, N^{**} and K^{**} are found simultaneously through equations (8.2), (8.3') (8.4'), (8.10) and (8.14). Then the equilibrium L_A^{**} and G^{**} follow by equations (8.1) and (8.11); and if $W_A^{**} \geq \overline{W}_A$, equation (8.7) determines H^{**}, and $H^{**} = \overline{H}$ otherwise. As before, given the equilibrium value of H^{**}, one can find the value of $Y_A^{**} = C^{**}$ by equation (8.8). Finally, equation (8.12') determines total output, Y^{**}.

8.3.3   The Workings of the Model

When the government applies the same tax rate for both industrial wage regimes, the workings of the model can be described as follows. Migrants assume (for reasons not explored here, such as lack of information, myopia, and social networks) that the probability of finding a job in the cities is one. If industries pay efficiency wages, they attract more migrants from the rural sector than in the case of market clearing wages [$M^* > M^{**}$]. So the urban population in the case of efficiency wages is higher than in the case of market clearing wages [$L_I^{**} \leq L_I^*$]. Efficiency wages create unemployment, and the unemployment can be associated with the excess of urban population [$N^* \leq L_I^{**}$]. Conversely, rural population is smaller under efficiency wages than with market clearing wages [$L_A^* \leq L_A^{**}$].

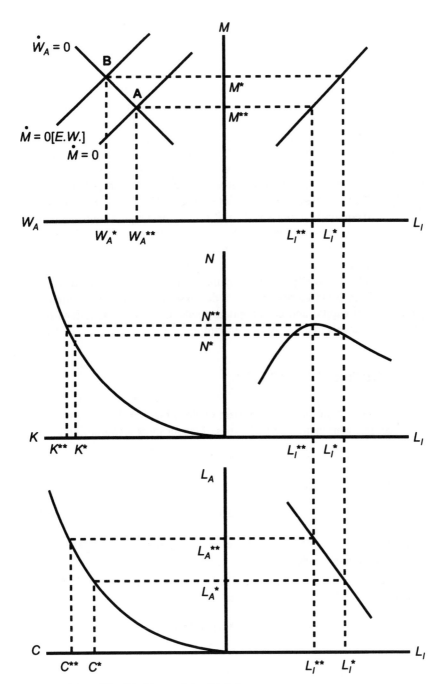

Figure 8.1   The Workings of the Model

The capital stock is lower when the level of industrial employment is lower, so $[K^* < K^{**}]$. Rural wages should increase more when migration is greater, thus rural wages are higher when efficiency wages are paid in industry $[W_A^* > W_A^{**}]$. The human capital is assumed to be the same with this combination of rural wage and capital: $H^* = H(W_A^*,K^*) = H^{**} = H(W_A^{**},K^{**})$. This assumption allows us to make output in the rural sector higher, the greater the rural population: $L_A^* \le L_A^{**} \Rightarrow C^* \le C^{**}$. Government revenue increases with migration and industrial wage, which happens to be the case in the efficiency wage regime, $G^* \ge G^{**}$. Finally, if government expenditures correspond to a small fraction of total output, one has: $C^* + G^* = Y^* \le Y^{**} = C^{**} + G^{**}$. That is, output is higher when there is full employment.

Figure 8.1 illustrates the workings of the model. The dynamics of M and W_A provide two equilibria. Point A is the full employment equilibrium and point B is the efficiency wage equilibrium [denoted in the figure as E.W.]. Notice that there is an increasing relationship between migration and urban population, which leads to a rise in industrial employment up to the full employment equilibrium $[N^{**} = L_I^{**}]$. As total population is held constant, an increase in the urban population corresponds to a decrease in the rural population. The production of capital and consumption goods are positive functions of the employment levels in industry and agriculture.

8.4   OPTIMAL TAXATION

A fiscal policy is optimal in the present model whenever the government can find a tax rate consistent with both types of labour market equilibrium:

$$[1-\tau_E(M^*)]W^* = [1-\tau_C(M^{**})]W(K^{**},L_I^{**}) \qquad (8.17)$$

One necessary condition for equation (8.17) to hold is:

$$\tau_E(M^*) \ge \tau_C(M^{**}) \qquad (8.18)$$

where $\tau_E(M^*)$ is the tax rate when there is unemployment and $\tau_C(M^{**})$ the tax rate in full employment.

In order to make the point more clearly, let us assume that $\tau_C(M^{**}) = 0$. So equation (8.17) can be rewritten as:

$$[1-\tau_E(M^*)]W^* = W(K^{**},L_I^{**}) \qquad (8.17')$$

That is, the government chooses $\tau_E(M^*)$ so as to make the efficiency wage net of tax equal to the market clearing wage. Therefore, the optimal tax is:

$$\tau_E(M^*) = 1 - \frac{W^{**}}{W^*} \qquad (8.19)$$

One can see the optimal tax as a migration policy. It describes the government's efforts to affect urban wages in such a way as to decrease migration to the level consistent with full employment. If the implementation of this optimal tax is successful the economy will converge to the market clearing wage equilibrium.

8.5   THE TRANSITION PATH

The transition path describes the convergence process towards the full employment equilibrium. One can understand the transition path generated by the optimal tax by departing from two different initial conditions. If the initial condition is given by the efficiency wage case, urban population is above the equilibrium urban population consistent with full employment, N. The transition from the efficiency wage to the market clearing wage equilibrium is characterised by a decrease in migration and urban population in conjunction with an increase in urban employment. In addition, capital stock and rural population will grow, and rural wages will fall, while human capital in agriculture remains constant. The output in agriculture will increase and government revenue and expenses will fall. Finally, there is an increase in total output, that is, this optimal tax policy is growth enhancing.

In this transition path there is income distribution from workers currently employed in cities and countryside to unemployed workers. The distribution of income corresponds to the fall in wages currently paid in industry and agriculture in order to make room for an increase in the working population in both sectors. Therefore, the implementation of the optimal tax leads to income distribution from employed to unemployed workers.

If the initial condition is given by an urban population below N^{**}, the transition for the market clearing wage equilibrium is quite simple. The income gap between cities and hinterland will attract people, increasing migration and urban population, decreasing rural population. All migrants will find a job in industry. So there is full employment at each point in time. Capital stock and rural wages will grow, leading to an increase in the human capital used in agriculture. This will lead to an increase in output in agriculture. In the same vein, increasing migration leads to increasing government revenue and expenditures. At the end of the process, total output will grow. In this case migration is positively related to growth.

Figure 8.2 depicts the transition path for M and W_A. If the initial condition is given by the efficiency wage equilibrium, point B, the introduction of the optimal tax shifts the locus $\dot{M} = 0[E.W.]$ to the left until it coincides with the locus

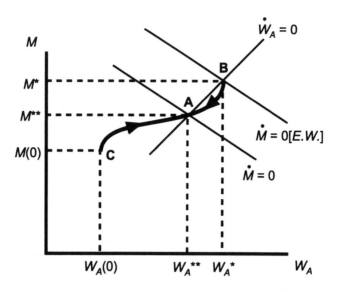

Figure 8.2   The Transition Path

$\dot{M} = 0$, where the full employment equilibrium lies. So the equilibrium shifts from point B to point A. The behaviour of migration and rural wages follow the path linking B to A, described in the figure: migration and rural wages fall. If the initial condition is below the full employment equilibrium, as point C, the transition path corresponds to an increase in migration and rural wages.

The migration path is also characterised by a fall in regional income inequality, since wages and productivity increase in the countryside matching the urban income in equilibrium. The balance is achieved by a mechanism in which both wages in industry and agriculture grow. However, rural wages grow more quickly than industrial wages.

In general, the transition path generated by the introduction of the optimal tax indicates that migration is positively related to economic growth and negatively to income inequality.[5] In this sense this is an optimal migration path since it improves income distribution and fosters growth, providing a negative correlation between growth and income inequality.[6]

8.6   CONCLUDING REMARKS

Rural–urban migration is blamed as one of the main causes of urban unemployment and poverty in less developed countries. Migration is generally related to economic motives such as the existence of income differentials between cities and the countryside. If unemployment and other negative externalities do not decrease migration, this makes room for public intervention.

This chapter tackles this problem in a simple framework. On the one hand, migration from rural sectors to urban sectors decreased rural population and pushes up wages in agriculture. After some critical level of wages it pays to substitute labour for capital. This leads to adoption of new technologies, increasing the returns to human capital, productivity and wages in agriculture.

On the other hand, the growth in urban population puts pressure on urban labour markets. Two possible scenarios are studied here. The first is full employment, in which all migrating workers are absorbed by the urban sector and find a job because industries are paying market-clearing wages. In the second scenario there is urban unemployment, which may be a result of industries paying market non-clearing wages, such as efficiency wages. In this case migration is associated with rising unemployment.

It has been shown that the government can find an optimal tax that corrects the distortions caused by market non-clearing wages in the urban sector, leading to a fall in the urban unemployment and a decrease in the rural–urban migration rate. In addition, this optimal tax leads to an optimal migration path where migration is growth enhancing. Income distribution was also analysed and depending on initial conditions, there is income distribution from employed to unemployed workers. In equilibrium regional imbalances disappear.

NOTES

1   See the review of this literature in Borjas (1996), and Barro and Sala-I-Martin (1995) for migration in neoclassical models
2   Lundborg and Segerstrom (2000) considering international migration found that differences in public policy can be growth-retarding.
3   On rural wage subsidy see Beladi and Chao (2000).
4   The formulation in equation (8.7) is consistent with jumps in the production function, see Ni and Wang (1996).
5   See Basu (2000) for similar results.
6   For the relationship between growth and inequality see Atkinson (1997), and Aghion et al. (1999).

REFERENCES

Aghion, P., E. Caroli, and C. García-Peñalosa (1999), 'Inequality and Economic Growth: The Perspective of the New Growth Theories', *Journal of Economic Literature*, **37**, 1615–60.

Akerlof, G. and J. Yellen (1986), *Efficiency Wage Models of the Labor Market*, Cambridge: Cambridge University Press.

Atkinson, A.B. (1997), 'Bringing Income Distribution in from the Cold', *Economic Journal*, **107**, 297–321.

Barro, R.J. and X. Sala-I-Martin (1995), *Economic Growth*, New York: McGraw-Hill.

Basu, B. (2000), 'Rural-Urban Migration, Urban Unemployment and the Structural Transformation of a Dual Economy', *Journal of International Trade and Economic Development*, **9**, 137–49.

Batabyal, A.A. (1998), 'Environmental Policy in Developing Countries: A Dynamic Analysis', *Review of Development Economics*, **2**, 293–304.

Beladi, H. and C.-C. Chao (2000), 'Urban Unemployment, Rural Labor Monopsony, and Optimal Policies', *Japan and the World Economy*, **12**, 1–9.

Borjas, G.J. (1996), *Labor Economics*, New York: McGraw-Hill.

Faria, J.R. and A.V. Mollick (1996), 'Urbanization, Economic Growth, and Welfare', *Economics Letters*, **52**, 109–15.

Galor, O. and D.N. Weil (2000), 'Population, Technology, and Growth: From Malthusian Stagnation to the Demographic Transition and Beyond', *American Economic Review*, **90**, 806–28.

Lundborg, P. and P.S. Segerstrom (2000), 'International Migration and Growth in Developed Countries: A Theoretical Analysis', *Economica*, **67**, 579–604.

Ni, S. and X. Wang (1996), 'A Model of Structural Breaks in Economic Growth', *Structural Change and Economic Dynamics*, **7**, 223–41.

Schultz, T.W. (1964), *Transforming Traditional Agriculture*, New Haven: Yale University Press.

Todaro, M. (1969), 'A Model of Labor, Migration and Urban Unemployment in Less Developed Countries', *American Economic Review*, **59**, 138–48.

9 Supply, Demand and Disequilibrium in the Market of Immigrants

Amnon Levy

This study presents a broad conceptual approach to the analysis of immigration by combining aspects of both supply of immigrants and demand for immigrants. Immigration is assumed to be motivated by lack of economic and noneconomic opportunities; and, correspondingly, immigrants are classified as early immigrants, late immigrants and refugees. An optimal immigration quota policy, which is based on a linear feedback rule and aimed at stabilising the host country's unemployment level, is developed. The optimal feedback coefficient is found to be dependent upon the correlations of the number of legal immigrants in the previous period with the current numbers of illegal immigrants and vacant jobs, and upon the variances of these variables. The consequences of the feedback policy on the numbers of early immigrants, late immigrants, and illegal immigrants are discussed under the assumption that early immigrants and late immigrants generate rational expectations about incomes in the host country.

9.1 INTRODUCTION

The traditional economic literature on migration is focused on the supply of immigrants and explains incidences of migration by combining two well-known ideas. One of these ideas is the location choice hypothesis raised by Schultz (1962) and Sjaastad (1962) which suggests that a difference in the discounted net present value of pecuniary and non-pecuniary income streams between two places precipitates migration. The other hypothesis introduced by Kuznets and Thomas (1958) proposes that special human capital characteristics enhance migration. That is, the migrants come from selective groups endowed with a high capacity to adapt themselves to unfamiliar environments and are dynamic and risk-taking beings. Both hypotheses are concerned with the migrants' perspective and regard migration as permanent. In contrast, an interesting more recent approach, which emphasises the demand for immigrants, has been suggested by Ethier (1985, 1986). This approach focuses on the host country's perspective, views the migration as temporary, and takes the supply of migrant labour as unlimited at predetermined terms. It treats migration symmetrically with international labour mobility into a standard factor-endowment model of international trade. At the centre of this model are factors such as the elasticity of demand for host-country exports, and the correlation between conditions in the export market and in the migrant labour market. These factors, it is suggested, imply that native labour fluctuations can be moderated by a combination of commodity dumping and migrant dumping.

Whether labour migration can be viewed as temporary or permanent, and whether the host-country welfare considerations should be confined to the native population or expanded to take into account the well-being of migrant workers and their accompanying families are open issues for debate. The rate of return of the international labour force varies significantly with regard to the migrants' countries of origin and destination. On the one hand, we find that the majority of workers migrating from the Asian and Pacific countries to the oil-producing Middle-East countries go on contract for a specified period of time and return at the end of the contract. On the other hand, guest workers in West European countries, who arrived following the labour shortage created by the economic boom of the late 1950s and the early 1960s, tended to remain despite the recession of the 1970s. Moreover, it appears that these guest workers have become a permanent part of the population and the labour supply of the West European countries. This development is due to several factors:

1.   needs that cannot be satisfied in the countries of origin have been developed in the host countries;
2.   labour surpluses in the source countries have been increased by the repercussion effects during the 1970s; and
3.   there is a growing awareness of the migrant workers' civil rights in the host countries.

Consequently, the economic gains to the West European countries have been replaced by severe social problems of unemployment and tension between natives and immigrants. Whether these problems can be resolved by dumping migrant workers is a controversial issue that involves fundamental ethical and moral arguments. This issue is beyond the scope of the present chapter. The chapter provides a conceptual analysis of the optimal management of immigration by the host country which takes into account aspects of both the supply of immigrants and the demand for immigrants. The analysis presents strong lines of similarity to the macroeconomic analyses of stabilisation policy of the rational expectations school, and assumes that for moral and ethical reasons migrants should not be dumped. The supply of migrants to the host country is classified in Section 9.2 into three distinct groups: early immigrants and late immigrants who are motivated by economic reasons, and refugees. All immigrants are assumed to be endowed with identical stocks of human capital, but facing different opportunities in their country of origin. Early immigrants are discriminated against in their homeland's labour market, and refugees are persecuted on political, ethnic, or religious grounds. The demand for immigrants is derived in Section 9.3 by minimising the expected loss from an increase in the unemployment level subject to a linear feedback rule. The extent of early immigration, late immigration and excess supply of immigrants (that is, illegal immigration) is analysed in Section 9.4 under the assumption that early immigrants and late immigrants generate their expectations about incomes in the host country rationally. Possible trajectories of immigration to the host country are described in Section 9.5. The article is concluded in Section 9.6 with a brief summary.

9.2   SUPPLY OF IMMIGRANTS

The supply of immigrants to the host country at period t is assumed to be from a single source and comprising three distinct groups. The members of the first group are those who at the end of the period $t-1$ perceived their expected income in the host country to exceed their income in the country of origin, and hence migrated at the beginning of period t. We refer to them as 'early migrants' (*EM*) and present them in our model by the linear equation:

$$EM_t = \alpha({}_{t-1}W_t^h - W_t^o) \qquad (9.1)$$

where ${}_{t-1}W_t^h$ is the expectation taken at the end of period $t-1$ of the income in the host country at t, W_t^o is the income at t in the country of origin which is assumed to be known at $t-1$, and α is a positive parameter denoting the propensity to migrate of the first group of potential migrants.

The second group of immigrants includes those individuals who at the end of period $t-1$ believed that their income in the country of destination will not exceed that in the country of origin, and hence did not immigrate immediately. These are individuals who enjoy higher incomes in the country of origin than their early immigrant counterparts. However, once realising that their expectations about incomes in the country of destination were underestimated, they migrate during the t-th period. We refer to them as late migrants (*LM*), and assume that their number increases with the expectations error as described by the following equation:

$$LM_t = \beta(W_t^h -_{t-1} W_t^h) \qquad (9.2)$$

where W_t^h is the average income in the country of destination at t, and β is the propensity to migrate of the second group of potential migrants.

The third group of immigrants consists of individuals who are motivated by nonpecuniary reasons, such as persecution on religious, ethnic and political grounds. We call them refugees. Since persecution in the country of origin might continue for more than one period, a positive correlation (θ) between immigrations of refugees in two successive periods is very likely. Thus, we describe the stream of refugees (R) to the host country by a first-order autoregressive process

$$R_t = \theta R_{t-1} + \varepsilon_{1t} \qquad (9.3)$$

where ε_1 is a white noise having zero mean and finite variance.

Summing up, the supply of migrants to the host country is given by

$$M_t^s = EM_t + LM_t + R_t \qquad (9.4)$$

9.3   DEMAND FOR IMMIGRANTS

The distinction between the various groups of immigrants, and in particular between early and late immigrants, might have important implications for the host country's level of unemployment, output and income distribution and hence for its demand for immigrants. For instance, if earning opportunities were equally distributed in the country of origin and income were directly related to possession of human capital, one could deduce from the supply equations (9.1) and (9.2) that early immigrants are endowed with less human capital than late immigrants. The host country may realise that a substantial share of the immigrant quota could be first exploited by less talented and able people, unless a screening policy is implemented. Nevertheless, a screening policy should take into account that, in contrast to late immigrants who are endowed with more human capital, early immigrants do not necessarily compete with the native population in the labour market, but are rather engaged in occupations perceived to have low status. Thus, the greater the share of early immigrants in the total immigrant population, the lower the tension between the host country's native population and immigrants.

The host country's demand for immigrants will be derived under the alternative assumptions that human capital is distributed equally in the country of origin and that income inequality is predominantly due to unequal distribution of opportunities. These assumptions imply, in terms of the supply equations specified above, that early immigrants are more severely discriminated against in their homeland's labour market than late immigrants. Since all immigrants are assumed to be identical with regard to potential performance in production, the host country is indifferent between early immigrants and late immigrants, and apply a nondiscriminating immigration policy against early immigrants. In this case, the host country is only concerned with the effect of immigration on the domestic level of unemployment.

Immigration increases the host country's supply of labour. Hence, we postulate that the host country's demand for migrants is found by minimising the expected loss from an increase in unemployment above a desired level. The increase in host country unemployment (U) at period t is given by:

$$U_t = M_t - J_t + V_t \qquad (9.5)$$

where M is the number of migrants who legally entered the host country at t, J is the number of vacant jobs at t, and V is the number of illegal immigrants who successfully enter the host country at t.

Successful illegal immigration at one period might encourage further illegal immigration in the following period. Hence, V is specified as a stochastic first-order autoregressive process:

$$V_t = \phi V_{t-1} + \varepsilon_{2t} \qquad (9.6)$$

where ϕ is the correlation coefficient between illegal immigrations in two successive periods, and ε_2 is a white noise having zero mean and finite variance σ_2^2.

It is assumed that the host-country immigration authorities are aware of the adverse effect of immigration on the domestic level of unemployment as presented in equation (9.5), and hence admit a certain number (M) of immigrants, which minimises the expected loss from an increase in the unemployment level. The optimality of the widely practiced 'lean against the wind' immigration strategy is investigated by considering the linear feedback rule:

$$M_t = g_0 - g_1 M_{t-1} \geq 0 \qquad (9.7)$$

where the parameters g_0 and g_1 indicate the maximum periodical number of immigrants admitted and the immigration feedback coefficient, respectively; and are chosen to minimise the expected loss function.

As is frequently practiced in stabilisation macroeconomic studies (for example, Chow 1970; Poole 1970; Sargent and Wallace 1976), the expected loss function is specified to be quadratic in its argument, and the stationary mean of the increase in the level of unemployment set to be equal to the desired level. Therefore, the host country's decision problem can be rendered equivalently as minimising the stationary variance of the increase in the unemployment level by an appropriate choice of g_1. By substituting (9.7) in (9.5) for M_t, the stationary variance of the increase in the unemployment level is given by:

$$var(U) = g_1^2 \, var(M) + 2g_1[cov(M_{-1}, J) - cov(M_{-1}, V)] +$$
$$2cov(J, V) + var(J) + var(V) \qquad (9.8)$$

Hence, the necessary condition for minimum var(U) implies that the optimal feedback coefficient is

$$g_1 = \frac{cov(M_{-1}, V) - cov(M_{-1}, J)}{var(M)}. \qquad (9.9)$$

Given that var(M) > 0, the second-order condition for minimum var(U) is satisfied.

Equation (9.9) indicates that the optimality of an immigration policy based on a feedback rule depends crucially on the existence of a difference between the stationary covariances of the lagged number of legal migrants with the current numbers of vacant jobs and illegal immigrants. It is reasonable to assume that the more restrictive the immigration quota in the past, the larger the illegal immigration in the present, that is, negative correlation between M_{-1} and V. It also is reasonable to assume that the more restrictive the immigration quota in the past, the greater the number of vacant jobs in the host country in the present, that is, negative correlation between M_{-1} and J. Thus, the 'lean against the wind' setting of immigration quotas (that is, $g_1 > 0$) is optimal if $cov(M_{-1}, J)$ is greater than $cov(M_{-1}, V)$ in absolute value, or equivalently if

$$|cor(M_{-1}, J) \, sd(J)| \; > \; |cor(M_{-1}, V) \, sd(V)| \qquad (9.10)$$

That is, the likelihood that a 'lean against the wind' strategy of immigration visa allocation is optimal:

1. increases with the standard deviation (sd) of the number of vacant jobs in the host country;
2. increases with the correlation (cor) between one-period lagged number of legal immigrants and current number of vacant jobs in absolute value;
3. decreases with the standard deviation of the number of illegal immigrants; and
4. decreases with the correlation between one-period lagged number of legal immigrants and current number of illegal immigrants in absolute value.

Equation (9.9) also indicates that the immigration feedback coefficient should be inversely related to the variance of the number of legal immigrants. When $cov(M_{-1}, V)$ and $cov(M_{-1}, J)$ are equal, the maximum quota, g_o, is optimal. In order to find g_o, let us compute the stationary expectation of U from equation (9.5) and (9.6), and set it to be equal to the desired increase in the level of unemployment U^*:

$$E(U) = g_0 - g_1 E(M) - E(J) + \phi V_{t-1} = U^* \qquad (9.11)$$

By substituting (9.9) for g_1 in (9.11)

$$g_o = U^* + \left[\frac{cov(M_{-1}, V) - cov(M_{-1}, J)}{var(M)} \right] E(M) + E(J) - \phi V_{t-1} \quad (9.12)$$

The host country's demand for legal new immigrants (M^d) can now be found by substituting equations (9.9) and (9.12) for g_1 and g_o, respectively, in the feedback rule (9.7):

$$M_t^d = U^* + E(J) - \phi V_{t-1}$$
$$- \left[\frac{cov(M_{-1}, V) - cov(M_{-1}, J)}{var(M)} \right] [M_{-1} - E(M)] \qquad (9.13)$$

provided that the right-hand side (r.h.s.) of this equation is non-negative. That is, the host country's demand for immigrants is equal to its desired increase in the level of unemployment and the number of vacant jobs minus the expected number of illegal immigrants and the product of the optimal feedback coefficient and the deviation of the number of immigrants admitted in the previous period from the stationary number. Note, however, that when the r.h.s. of equation (9.13) is negative, M_t^d is set to be zero because of the condition that migrants should not be dumped. In the following sections it is assumed that the r.h.s. of equation (9.13) is nonnegative.

9.4   DISEQUILIBRIUM AND THE NUMBER OF IMMIGRANTS UNDER RATIONAL EXPECTATIONS

Many of the preferred countries of destination, the West European and North American countries in particular, suffer from the problem of illegal immigration. This problem is a reflection of a permanent excess supply of immigrants. Recalling equations (9.1) to (9.4), which specify the supply of immigrants, and equation (9.13), which specifies the host country's demand for immigrants, the extent of the illegal immigration at any point of time t is given by

$$
V_t = \alpha({}_{t-1}W_t^h - W_t^o) + \beta(W_t^h - {}_{t-1}W_t^h) + R_t
$$
$$
- U^* - E(J) + \phi V_{t-1} +
$$
$$
+ \left[\frac{\mathrm{cov}(M_{-1},V) - \mathrm{cov}(M_{-1},J)}{\mathrm{var}(M)} \right] [M_{t-1} - E(M)]
$$

(9.14)

Rearranging equation (9.14) and recalling equation (9.6), the income in the host country at t can be expressed as

$$
W_t^h = \frac{1}{\beta} \{ U^* + E(J)
$$
$$
- \left[\frac{\mathrm{cov}(M_{-1},V) - \mathrm{cov}(M_{-1},J)}{\mathrm{var}(M)} \right] [M_{t-1} - E(M)]
$$
$$
- \alpha({}_{t-1}W_t^h - W_t^o) + \varepsilon_{2t} - R_t \} + {}_{t-1}W_t^h
$$

(9.15)

It is assumed that the expectations of the immigrants who are motivated by economic reasons (that is, early and late immigrants) about their income in the host country are rational. Considering Muth's (1961) definition of rational expectations, it is required that

$$
{}_{t-1}W_t^h = E_{t-1}(W_t^h)
$$

(9.16)

Taking the expectations of the r.h.s. of equation (9.15) and recalling equation (9.3) and that in steady state $E(M_t)$ is equal to $E(M_{t-1})$:

$$
{}_{t-1}W_t^h = W_t^o + \frac{1}{\alpha} [U^* + E(J) - \theta R_{t-1}]
$$

(9.17)

Under the assumption of rational expectations, the early immigrants and the late immigrants perceive the expected income differential between the countries of destination and origin to rise with the increase in the desired level of unemployment and with the number of vacant jobs in the host country, and to decrease with the expected number of refugees. The effects of these factors on the perceived income differential are moderated by the early migrants' propensity to migrate α. The underlying reason is that, *ceteris paribus*, the greater is α, the larger the number of early immigrants and hence the supply of labour at the beginning of period t.

By substituting the r.h.s. of equation (9.17) into equation (9.1), the number of early immigrants can be expressed as

$$EM_t = U^* + E(J) - \theta R_{t-1} \tag{9.18}$$

That is, if the host country applied a linear feedback immigration policy in order to reduce the expected loss from an increase in the unemployment level, and if immigrants' expectations about their income in the host country were rational, then the number of early immigrants would be equal to the sum of vacant jobs and the desired increase in the number of unemployed minus the expected number of refugees.

The substitution of the r.h.s. of equation (9.17) into equation (9.15) and the consideration of equation (9.3) imply that the income expectations error can be presented as

$$
W_t^h - {}_{t-1}W_t^h =
$$

$$
\frac{1}{\beta}\left\{\left[\frac{\text{cov}(M_{-1},J) - \text{cov}(M_{-1},V)}{\text{var}(M)}\right][M_{t-1} - E(M)]\right.
$$

$$
\left. - \varepsilon_{1t} + \varepsilon_{2t}\right\}
$$

$$\tag{9.19}$$

and recalling equation (9.2), the number of late immigrants, that is, whose prior expectations about the income differential between the countries of destination and origin were underestimated, can be rendered as

$$
LM_t = \left[\frac{\text{cov}(M_{-1},J) - \text{cov}(M_{-1},V)}{\text{var}(M)}\right][M_{t-1} - E(M)] + \varepsilon_{2t} \tag{9.20}
$$

Under a linear feedback immigration policy and rational expectations, the number of late immigrants is equal to the product of the optimal feedback coefficient and the difference between the stationary number and previous period's number of immigrants, plus the difference between the random shocks in the current number of illegal immigrants and in the current number of refugees.

Substituting equations (9.18) and (9.20) into equation (9.4) and recalling the autoregressive process described in equation (9.3), the total number of immigrants to the host country at t, that is, early immigrants plus late immigrants plus refugees, is given by

$$M_t = U* + E(J) + \left[\frac{\text{cov}(M_{-1}, J) - \text{cov}(M_{-1}, V)}{\text{var}(M)} \right] [M_{t-1} - E(M)] + \varepsilon_{2t} \quad (9.21)$$

As mentioned above, the excess supply of immigrants reflects the extent of illegal migration into the host country. Equation (9.6) describes this illegal migration as a stochastic first-order autoregressive process where the autoregression coefficient ϕ can be interpreted as indicating for the potential illegal migrants the prospects of entering the country of destination successfully. Thus, the host country's effort in deterring illegal immigration should be aimed at lowering the correlation (ϕ) between illegal immigrations in successive periods. This can be achieved by irregular and surprising investment of effort in border patrols, inspections of possible employment places and so on. Note further that the decrease in ϕ also moderates the variance of the number of illegal immigrants, as can be seen from the following equation:

$$\text{var}(V_t) = \frac{\sigma_2^2}{1 - \phi} \quad (9.22)$$

9.5   IMMIGRATION TRAJECTORIES

Equation (9.21) shows that under a linear feedback immigration policy and rational expectations the immigration into the host country follows a stochastic first-order difference equation. The solution to the deterministic part of this equation gives the instantaneous mean of the total number of immigrants entering the host country:

$$E(M_t) = U* + E(J) + [E(M_o) - U* - E(J)] \left[\frac{\text{cov}(M_{-1}, J) - \text{cov}(M_{-1}, V)}{\text{var}(M)} \right]^t \quad (9.23)$$

where $U*$ plus $E(J)$ (that is, the sum of the increase in the desired unemployment level and the stationary mean of vacant jobs in the host country) is the stationary mean of immigrants, and $E(Mo)$ is the initial mean of immigrants. This stationary mean of immigrants is asymptotically stable if

$$\left| \frac{\text{cov}(M_{-1}, J) - \text{cov}(M_{-1}, V)}{\text{var}(M)} \right| < 1 \quad (9.24)$$

That is, the smaller the difference between the covariances of the one-period lagged number of legal immigrants with the current numbers of vacant jobs and illegal immigrants and the larger the variance of the number of legal immigrants, the greater the prospects of asymptotic stability.

It was argued earlier that the covariances of the number of immigrants admitted a period ago with the current numbers of vacant jobs and illegal immigrants are likely to be negative. Thus, if $cov(M_{-1}, V)$ is greater than $cov(M_{-1}, J)$ in absolute value, $[cov(M_{-1}, J) - cov(M_{-1}, V)]$ is positive; and given that condition (9.24) holds, the instantaneous mean number of immigrants converges gradually to the stationary level from above or below as the initial mean number of immigrants is greater or smaller than the stationary level, respectively. However, in the opposite case where $cov(M_{-1}, J)$ is greater than $cov(M_{-1}, V)$ in absolute value, the trajectory of the instantaneous mean number of immigrants displays dampened, or explosive, oscillations around the stationary number provided that condition (9.24) is satisfied or not, respectively.

9.6   SUMMARY AND CONCLUSIONS

This chapter presented a broad approach to immigration analysis by combining aspects on both the supply and the demand sides of the immigration phenomenon. Immigrants were assumed to be motivated by lack of economic and noneconomic opportunities in the country of origin relative to those in the country of destination, and were classified as early immigrants, late immigrants and refugees. The chapter developed an immigration quota policy which is based on a linear feedback rule and aimed at stabilising the host country's unemployment level. The optimal feedback coefficient was found to be increasing in the correlation between the previous period's number of legal immigrants and the current number of vacant jobs in absolute value and in the standard deviation of the number of vacant jobs. The optimal feedback coefficient decreases with the correlation between the previous period's number of legal immigrants and the current number of illegal immigrants, with the standard deviation of the number of illegal immigrants, and with the variance of the number of legal immigrants.

The implications of a feedback policy for the number of immigrants and the classification of the immigrant population to early immigrants, late immigrants, and refugees were investigated by taking into account the possibility of excess supply, which was reflected by illegal immigration. The implications were based on the assumption that the expectations of early immigrants and late immigrants about their income in the country of destination are rational. The number of early immigrants was shown to be equal to the sum of the mean number of vacant jobs and the desired increase in the number of the unemployed minus the expected number of refugees. The number of late immigrants was found to be equal to the product of the immigration feedback coefficient and the difference between the stationary number of immigrants and the previous period's number of immigrants, plus the difference between the random shocks in the current numbers of illegal migrants and refugees. It was argued that the correlation between illegal immigrations in two successive periods can be interpreted as indicating the prospects of entering the country uncaught. Hence, measures of deterring illegal migration should be based on the element of surprise in order to moderate this correlation. Such measures may also reduce the variance of the number of illegal immigrants.

The chapter also described possible trajectories of immigration, and demonstrated that asymptotic stability relies on the covariances of the previous period's number of immigrants with the numbers of current illegal immigrants and vacant jobs, and on the variance of the illegal immigrants' number.

REFERENCES

Chow, G.C. (1970), 'Optimal Stochastic Control of Linear Economic System', *Journal of Money, Credit and Banking*, **2**, 291–302.

Ethier, W.J. (1985), 'International Trade and Labor Migration', *American Economic Review*, **75**, 691–707.

Ethier, W.J. (1986), 'Illegal Immigration: The Host-Country Problem', *American Economic Review*, **76**, 56–71.

Kuznets, S. and D. Thomas (1958), 'Internal Migration and Economic Growth', in *Selected Studies of Migration Since World War II*, New York: Milbank Memorial Fund, 196–211.

Muth, J.F. (1961), 'Rational Expectations and the Theory of Price Movements', *Econometrica*, **29**, 315–35.

Poole, W. (1970), 'Optimal Choice of Monetary Policy Instruments in a Simple Stochastic Macro Model', *Quarterly Journal of Economics*, **84**, 197–216.

Sargent, T.J. and N. Wallace (1976), 'Rational Expectations and the Theory of Economic Policy', *Journal of Monetary Economics*, 169–84.

Schultz, T.W. (1962), 'Reflections on Investment in Man', *Journal of Political Economy*, **70**, 1–9.

Sjaastad, L.A. (1962), 'The Costs and Returns of Human Migration', *Journal of Political Economy*, **70**, 80–93.

10 Migration Timing: Expected Returns, Risk Aversion and Assimilation Costs

Amnon Levy and Yacov Tsur

10.1 INTRODUCTION

In his seminal article on labour migration and urban unemployment in less developed countries, Todaro (1969) argues that rural–urban migration is triggered by the discounted stream of expected real income differential over the lifespan between the place of destination and the place of origin. This hypothesis is tested in numerous empirical studies including Greenwood's (1971, 1978) simultaneous equation analyses for India and Mexico, and the multinomial-logit analyses on Columbia (Fields 1982) and Venezuela (Schultz 1982), to mention a few prototype, seminal works. In all these studies the analysis is restricted to the individual's decision on migration at a given date and the timing of migration is disregarded. Given that there is a sufficient incentive for migration, it is still worth assessing the timing of migration and the gains, or losses, from migrating at one point of time rather than another.

Immediate migration or no migration during the entire lifespan (that is, corner solutions) are not the only possible solutions to the migration-timing decision problem. There are cases in which people prefer to postpone migration to a future date in their planning horizon (that is, interior solution). Disregarding the interior solutions might lead to undesired properties in the findings of empirical analyses. In particular, the possibility of an interior solution to the migration-timing problem raises severe doubts about the consistency of the estimated parameters of multinomial-logit analysis of *current* place-to-place migration since these analyses are based on the assumption that the individual's migration-timing problem can only have corner solutions. Moreover, optimal timing of migration is an important factor for a successful migration. Sub-optimal timing might lead to an unsuccessful migration and, perhaps, to a return to the place of origin. The purpose of this study is to analyse this neglected issue of migration timing.

The analysis utilises the concept of discounted stream of expected real income differential suggested by Todaro (1969) as well as the important notions of risk differential between the origin and destination (Stark and Levhari 1982) and costs of assimilation (Chiswick 1978) as building blocks of a switch model that yields the individual's optimal timing of migration. This model suggests that corner solutions to the migration timing problem, that is, immediate migration or no migration during the lifetime, occur when the individual is either risk-neutral, perceives no income-variance differential, or has no time preference. In other circumstances, people may postpone migration to a future date within their planning horizon. The switch model is developed in Section 10.2. The interior and corner solutions to the migration timing problem are presented and discussed in Sections 10.3 and 10.4, respectively.

The analysis of the optimal timing of migration also leads to the distinction between various types of migrant. Three general types of immigrant are defined, and the characters of their migration timing decisions are discussed in Section 10.5. Moreover, the population of immigrants might be of diverse ethnic background. The relative size of, and solidarity within, ethnic groups may affect individuals' migration decisions and assimilation process in the place of destination. Ethnic neighborhoods, clubs and federations may help reduce the social and economic costs of assimilation for members. In migrant societies the distribution of immigration dates and the population ethnic structure have important welfare implications. The relationships among immigration dates, ethnic composition, and income and wealth inequality are analysed and discussed in Sections 10.6 and 10.7.

10.2   A SWITCH MODEL OF THE MIGRATION TIME PROBLEM

There is a disagreement in the economic literature on whether migration should be viewed by social planners as permanent and irreversible (for example, Marr 1985) or temporary and reversible (for example, Ethier 1985). The switch model is developed under the assumption that migration is irreversible. In support of this assumption one may recall that guest workers in West European countries, who arrived following the labour shortage created by the economic boom of the late 1950s and the early 1960s, remained despite the recession of the 1970s. For many immigrants a return to the place of origin might be rejected by spouses and second generation family members and associated with an admission of failure (which they may prefer to avoid).

Under the assumption of irreversibility, the present value (PV) of the individual's stream of real income over his (or her) lifespan can be presented as

$$PV(t) = \int_0^t e^{-\rho\tau} y_o(\tau) d\tau + \int_t^T e^{-\rho\tau} y_d(\tau) d\tau \qquad (10.1)$$

where y_o and y_d are random variables denoting the potential immigrant's real incomes in the place of origin and in the place of destination, respectively, ρ his rate of time preferences, t his time of migration and $\tau \in (0,T)$ a time index.

The potential immigrant is considered to be an expected-utility maximiser. Assuming for tractability that PV is a Gaussian variate and that the potential individual's preferences over the feasible set $\{PV(t) \in \Re | 0 \leq t \leq T\}$ are presented by a negative-exponential utility function (reflecting constant absolute risk aversion), the migration date (t) can be found by maximising the mean of $PV(t)$ net of the costs of risk-bearing, which are equal to the variance of $PV(t)$ times the individual's degree of absolute risk aversion (R):

$$\max_t \{E(PV(t)) - 0.5R \operatorname{var}(PV(t))\} \qquad (10.2)$$

(See Freund (1956) for a rigorous development of the mean-variance expected utility function, and Hammond (1974) and Meyer (1987) for a discussion of the generality of this framework.)

With regard to the stochastic nature of the potential immigrant's incomes we assume that his incomes in the places of origin and destination are independently and normally distributed with finite and constant variances σ_o^2 and σ_d^2, respectively. But while the mean income in the place of origin (μ_o) is taken as time invariant, the mean income of the migrant in the place of destination converges gradually to the mean income enjoyed by the native population (μ_d).

The difference between the mean incomes of native workers and migrant workers reflects the skill differential and the migrants' disadvantage with regard to location-specific knowledge such as language, culture, prejudices, and understanding of local processes of job search. We refer to this difference as costs of assimilation and let them take the mathematically convenient form

$$C(\tau) = ce^{-\beta(\tau-t)} \qquad (10.3)$$

where $\tau - t$ is the time passed since migration, c indicates the initial costs of assimilation (that is, $c = C(\tau = t)$), and β is a positive scalar indicating the speed of assimilation.

The initial costs of assimilation and the speed of assimilation depend upon the migrant's suitability to the host-place socioeconomic conditions. The underlying rationale is that newcomers are initially disadvantaged, but as time elapses they acquire location-specific skills and their wages converge to those

accruable to natives. This rationale is supported by Chiswick's (1978) study on
the effects of Americanisation on the earnings of foreign-born people, and by
Chiswick and Miller's (1985) findings on immigrant–native wage differentials
in Australia that 'at the end of the first year of residence the overseas-born
person's income is about 10.5 per cent less than that of the native-born, and the
gap narrows by 0.2 percentage point per year' (p. 545). Applying Borjas's (1985)
technique of controlling between cohorts effects to two sets of cross-section
data on Australian native and immigrant earnings in 1973 and 1981, and
distinguishing between immigrants from English-speaking countries and
immigrants from non-English speaking countries, Beggs and Chapman (1988)
show that skills acquired overseas are easily transferred between like countries
but imperfectly transferrable to dissimilar countries. In terms of the assimilation
cost function specified above, these findings indicate that c is small and β is
significantly large for immigrants whose country of origin and destination have
similar culture and language.

Under these assumptions and specifications the distribution of the potential
immigrant's income is

$$y_o \sim N(\mu_o, \sigma_o^2) \qquad \text{for } 0 \le \tau < t \qquad (10.4a)$$

and

$$y_d \sim N(\mu_d - ce^{-\beta(\tau-t)}, \sigma_d^2) \qquad \text{for } t \le \tau \le T \qquad (10.4b)$$

Hence,

$$E[PV(t)] = \int_0^t \mu_o e^{-\rho\tau} d\tau + \int_t^T [\mu_d - ce^{-\beta(\tau-t)}] e^{-\rho\tau} d\tau \qquad (10.5)$$

and

$$\text{var}(PV(t)) = \int_0^t \sigma_o^2 e^{-2\rho\tau} d\tau + \int_t^T \sigma_d^2 e^{-2\rho\tau} d\tau \qquad (10.6)$$

Substituting equations (10.5) and (10.6) in equation (10.2) implies that the
optimal time of migration is that which maximises

$$J(t) = \int_0^t (\mu_o - 0.5 \text{Re}^{-\rho\tau} \sigma_o^2) e^{-\rho\tau} d\tau$$

$$+ \int_t^T [\mu_d - ce^{-\beta(\tau-t)} - 0.5 \text{Re}^{-\rho\tau} \sigma_d^2] e^{-\rho\tau} d\tau \qquad (10.7)$$

The interior and corner solutions to this problem are presented and discussed in the next two sections.

10.3 INTERIOR SOLUTION TO THE MIGRATION TIMING PROBLEM

The necessary conditions for maximum expected utility is

$$\frac{\partial J(t)}{\partial t} = \mu_o - (\mu_d - c) - 0.5 \mathrm{Re}^{-\rho t^*}(\sigma_o^2 - \sigma_d^2)$$

$$- \frac{c\beta}{\rho + \beta}[1 - e^{-(\rho + \beta)(T - t^*)}] = 0 \tag{10.8}$$

Given that condition (10.8) holds, the sufficient condition is given by

$$0.5 \rho R(\sigma_o^2 - \sigma_d^2) e^{-\rho t^*} + c\beta e^{(\rho + \beta)(t^* - T)} < 0 \tag{10.9}$$

The necessary condition for maximum can be equivalently rendered as

$$[(\mu_d - c) - \mu_o] + \frac{c\beta}{\rho + \beta}[1 - e^{-(\rho + \beta)(T - t^*)}]$$

$$= 0.5 \mathrm{Re}^{-\rho t^*}(\sigma_d^2 - \sigma_o^2) \tag{10.10}$$

Since the second term on the left-hand side (LHS) of inequality (10.9) is positive, the sufficient condition for maximum expected utility requires that the income in the place of destination should be less certain than the income in the place of origin (that is, $\sigma_d^2 - \sigma_o^2 > 0$). Moreover, the discounted increase in the assimilation costs from an infinitesimal delay of the migration time from the optimal date should be smaller than the decrease in the costs of risk bearing. Given that the sufficient condition is satisfied, there exists an interior solution to the individual's migration-timing problem. In this case, the necessary condition (10.10) indicates that at the optimum, the gains from an infinitesimal delay of the migration date in terms of the risk bearing differential (the term on the right-hand side) are offset by the foregone expected income differential (the first term on the l.h.s.) and the foregone benefits from not starting the assimilation process earlier (the second term on the l.h.s.).

As can be intuitively expected, the necessary condition indicates that a higher degree of absolute risk aversion postpones migration, whereas a longer life expectancy (T), that is, being young, encourages earlier migration. The former effect is due to the excess income variance in the place of destination as compared to the place of origin. The latter effect stems from the fact that longer life expectancy allows for a longer assimilation period and hence provides the migrant with the ability to enjoy a higher income in the place of destination over a longer period. Moreover, this effect is intensified when the initial assimilation costs (c) are positively related to age and the assimilation speed (β) is inversely related to age.

From the necessary condition (10.10) it is difficult to assess the effects of time preferences and assimilation speed on the date of migration. However, the effects of these factors can be found for the special case where the potential migrants are concerned with the well-being of their descendants. In this case, the planning horizon (T) is infinite and hence a closed-form solution to the optimal timing of migration is obtained:

$$t^* = \frac{1}{\rho} \ln\left[\frac{0.5R(\sigma_d^2 - \sigma_o^2)}{\mu_o - (\mu_d - c) - \dfrac{c\beta}{\rho + \beta}} \right] \tag{10.11}$$

Since the sufficient condition required that $\sigma_d^2 - \sigma_o^2 > 0$, the interior solution to the migration-timing problem presented in equation (10.11) indicates that for these far-sighted, altruistic migrants $[\mu_o - (\mu_d - c)]$ is positive. That is, these people are willing to migrate at some future point of time within their planning horizon despite the lower expected income and higher risk in place of destination in the short run. This conclusion is compatible with Todaro's (1969) assertion that 'even if expected urban real income is less than rural income for a certain period following migration, it may still be economically rational from a longer-run point of view for the individual to migrate and swell the ranks of the urban traditional sector' (p. 140). But in contrast to Todaro's (1969) suggestion, potential migrants do not have to 'balance the probabilities and risks of being unemployed or sporadically employed in the city for a certain period of time against a favorable urban (modern sector) wage differential' (p. 140). In our framework, migration is also justified by lower assimilation costs for descendants. In this respect, equation (10.11) reveals that the smaller the risk differential and the greater the initial expected income differential between the place of origin and the place of destination, the earlier the migration date. Equation (10.11) also indicates that a strong time preference (ρ), a high assimilation speed (β) and low initial assimilation costs (c) encourage earlier migration.

10.4   CORNER SOLUTIONS TO THE MIGRATION TIMING PROBLEM

The sufficient condition for maximum expected utility also indicates that an interior solution to the migration timing problem might not exist. In this case, a corner solution is adopted: immediate migration or remaining at the place of origin indefinitely. These corner solutions are adopted when people perceive the risk-differential between the place of destination and the place of origin to be non-positive, and/or when they have no time preference. In any of these cases, the decision as to whether to migrate immediately ($t^* = 0$) or to stay indefinitely in the place of origin ($t^* = T$) is reached by comparing the expected utility under these two alternatives. If $[J(0) - J(T)]$ is positive (negative), t^* is equal to zero (T).

In the case where the individual perceives no risk-differential between the place of destination and the place of origin

$$J(0) - J(T) = \int_0^T (\mu_d - ce^{-\beta\tau})e^{-\rho\tau}\,d\tau$$

$$-\int_0^T \mu_o e^{-\rho\tau}\,d\tau = \mu_d - \mu_o - \frac{\rho c[1 - e^{-(\beta+\rho)^T}]}{(\beta+\rho)(1 - e^{-\rho T})} \qquad (10.12)$$

which implies that the individual migrates immediately if the sum of the expected discounted income differential between the place of destination and the place of origin exceeds the sum of the discounted assimilation costs. Note that when people are myopic (that is, $\rho \to \infty$) and have no capacity to adapt to a new environment (that is, $\beta = 0$), immediate migration is conditioned on a positive expected instantaneous income differential between place of destination and place of origin. Otherwise, they prefer staying in their place of origin to migrating. Equation (10.12) indicates further that the prospects of immediate migration increase with the capacity to adapt to a new environment and life expectancy, and decrease with time preference and the initial assimilation costs. Of course, in the special case where people perceive that $\sigma_d^2 - \sigma_o^2 < 0$, the likelihood of immediate migration is enhanced further by the lower costs of risk bearing in the place of destination.

In the case where people have no time preference ($\rho = 0$),

$$J(0) - J(T) = \int_0^T (\mu_d - ce^{-\beta\tau} - 0.5R\sigma_d^2)d\tau - (\mu_o - 0.5R\sigma_o^2)T$$

$$= (\mu_d - \mu_o)T - 0.5R(\sigma_d^2 - \sigma_o^2)T - \frac{c}{\beta}(1 - e^{-\beta T}) \qquad (10.13)$$

Note that when people attach a higher level of uncertainty to future incomes in the place of destination than in the place of origin, they require μ_d to be significantly higher than μ_o in order to immigrate immediately. The difference between μ_d and μ_o is necessary for compensating for the excessive costs of risk bearing (the second term on the right-hand side) and for the assimilation costs (the third term on the right-hand side) in the place of destination.

10.5   TYPES OF MIGRANT

While the mathematical presentation of the switch model assumes for tractability that the individual's expected income in the place of origin is time-invariant, the discussion in this section relaxes this assumption in order to describe different types of migrant. The following discussion considers the life-cycle hypothesis that due to rising opportunity costs of investment in human capital and because of deterioration of the stock of human capital, life-cycle earnings of individuals rise with the individual's age and then decline near the retirement age and conform roughly to an inverted U-shaped curve (Modigliani and Ando 1960; and Ben-Porath 1967).

In accordance with the life-cycle hypothesis, the following discussion distinguishes between three general types of migrant: pre–prime age migrants, prime-age migrants, and post–prime age migrants. The position of each type of migrant is described in terms of expected returns, risk, and costs of assimilation. Subsequently, the more likely solution to the migration timing problem of each type is argued.

Pre–prime age migrants: Since their employment career is not established, the income in the country of origin of pre–prime age individuals is relatively low and is characterised by a relatively high degree of uncertainty. Furthermore, the assimilation costs for members of this group in a host country are relatively low due to: their incompletely shaped personality which helps them conform to new customs and modes of behaviour, and their young age which enables them to mingle and associate with their native counterparts through schooling, military service and marriage. Because of low forgone income in the country of origin, small risk differential between destination and origin, and low assimilation costs in the country of destination, pre–prime age individuals are endowed with a relatively high propensity to migrate. For many members of this group the solution to the migration timing problem is interior. That is, many of them delay migration in order to acquire minimal training necessary for being admitted to the country of destination. Notable examples of pre–prime age migrants are foreign students, semi-skilled guest workers and, in contrast, unskilled adventurers.

Prime-age migrants: For individuals who are at their prime, migration is associated with giving up an established career in the place of origin that provides a relatively high income with a low level of uncertainty. Moreover, due to their advanced age, they are less open to experience and adopt new customs and modes of behaviour and are likely to have dependents. Hence, they are liable to have high assimilation costs in the new location. Because of high levels of income and certainty in the country of origin and high assimilation costs in the country of destination, people in their prime have a relatively low inclination to migrate and, in general, tend to chose a corner solution to the migration timing problem. That is, they prefer staying in their homeland indefinitely. But if offered a very attractive position abroad or faced with persecution and calamity at home, they are likely to migrate immediately. Prime-age migration is, on the one hand, the migration of very skilful workers whose knowledge is highly rewarded abroad. On the other hand, it might be the migration of the miserable – refugees.

Post–prime age migrants: Members of this group are at the final stage of their employment career. They enjoy a relatively certain income in their homeland and assess the prospects of better employment abroad to be very low and the assimilation costs to be very high. Therefore, their inclination to migrate is very low. At this stage of life, migration is motivated by non-pecuniary reasons such as living in a better natural environment, reunion with family members, and fulfilling of cultural and spiritual aspirations. The solution to the migration timing problem is interior: migration to the desired place is delayed to the retirement period and is conditioned upon the transferability of wealth and pension rights accumulated in the place of origin to their ability to support an adequate standard of living in the place of destination.

10.6   ETHNIC AFFILIATION, IMMIGRATION DATE AND INCOME

An interesting phenomenon associated with migration is the solidification of distinct ethnic groups in the place of destination. An extreme outcome of this process is an ethnically segregated exclusive neighbourhoods and ghettos. In countries having ethnically diverse population, individuals affiliated to a larger and more veteran ethnic group, *ceteris paribus*, are likely to be equipped with better country-specific skills and to enjoy access to better employment opportunities.

Suppose that the host country's society comprises ethnic groups whose shares of the total population are $p_1, \ldots, p_N$. It is assumed that the initial costs of adaptation (c) for the n-th ethnic group decline with p_n, and the absorption speed (β) increases with p_n. Thus, the income of a member is affected by the ethnic group's relative size. Recalling equations (10.4a) and (10.4b), the mean income anticipated by the m-th individual of the n-th ethnic group who, or whose ancestors, immigrated at t_{nm} is given by

$$y_{nm}(\tau) = \bar{y}_d - c(p_n(\tau)) \exp\{-\beta(p_n(\tau))(\tau - t_{nm})\} \qquad (10.14)$$

Correspondingly, the mean income in the n-th ethnic group at τ is

$$\mu_n(\tau) = \bar{y}_d - c(p_n(\tau)) E[\exp\{-\beta(p_n(\tau))(\tau - t_{nm})\}] \qquad (10.15)$$

Equation (10.15) can also be depicted as

$$\mu_n(\tau) = \bar{y}_d - c(p_n(\tau)) M(-\beta(p_n(\tau))) \qquad (10.16)$$

where $M(\bullet)$ is the moment-generating function associated with the distribution of the time passed from the immigration date (that is, $\tau - t_{nm}$) among the members of the n-th ethnic group. Since $\tau - t_{nm}$ is a non-negative variate, $M(\bullet)$ increases with its argument and hence declines with β. Recalling the assumption about β and c, an increase in the n-th ethnic group's relative size (p_n) increases the mean income (μ_n).

The magnitude of the effect of p_n on μ_n depends further on the moments of $\tau - t_{nm}$ according to the distribution of t_{nm} – the immigration dates of the n-th ethnic group's members. As indicated by the solution of the individual's decision problem described in Sections 10.3 and 10.4, the distribution of $\tau - t_{nm}$ depends upon the joint distribution of personal characteristics, such as risk and time preferences and age and adaptive capacity, and also upon the distribution of potential gains within the population of the country of origin and its evolution. It can be affected further by the relative size of the n-th ethnic community at previous periods, which has positive external effects on the adaptation of the individual member.

In view of these arguments, and since the potential migrants' numbers from the n-th source are finite and the host-country's absorption capacity is limited, the cumulative distribution of the immigration date (t_{nm}) can be roughly approximated by an S-shaped curve at the termination of the immigration process from that source. Correspondingly, two alternative specifications of the distribution of the time that passed from immigration within the n-th ethnic group's immigrants are considered – a Gaussian and an exponential. The first provides an appropriate description of an immigration process which reaches its final stage. The second describes an immigration process which is still in its take-off stage.

When $\tau - t_{nm}$ is Gaussian, the mean income in the n-th ethnic group is given by

$$\mu_n(\tau) = \bar{y}_d - c(p_n(\tau))\exp\{-\beta(p_n(\tau))(\tau - E(t_{nm}))$$
$$+ 0.5\beta(p_n(\tau))^2 VAR(t_{nm})\}$$

(10.17)

This implies that the earlier the mean of immigration date (that is, the smaller the $E(t_{nm})$) and the more concentrated the distribution of the immigration date (that is, the smaller the $VAR(t_{nm})$) within the n-th ethnic group, the greater the effect of this group's relative size (p_n) on its mean income.

Alternatively, when $\tau - t_{nm}$ has an exponential distribution, the mean income in the n-th ethnic group is

$$\mu_n(\tau) = \bar{y}_d - \frac{c(p_n(\tau))}{1 + \beta(p_n(\tau))[VAR(t_{nm})]^{0.5}}$$

(10.18)

which leads to the opposite conclusion, namely the greater the variance of the immigration date, the greater the effect of an increase in p_n on μ_n. This is due to the fact that in the exponential case the mean of the immigration date is inversely related to the variance. Hence, the greater the $VAR(t_{nm})$ the earlier the mean immigration date, which in turn increases μ_n.

10.7 INCOME INEQUALITY BETWEEN ETHNIC GROUPS

It was argued in the previous section that an increase in the relative size of an ethnic group increases its mean income through the reduction of the adaptation costs. It should be noted further that an increment in the relative size of one ethnic group is accompanied by a comparable decline in the overall relative size of the others, which in turn affects their mean incomes. This externality should be taken into account when the change in the level of income inequality within the society is assessed.

A link between the level of income inequality and the ethnic composition of a society is provided by Theil's index of income inequality, which is based on the notion of entropy in information theory (Theil 1967). The entropy of income shares between ethnic groups is defined as

$$I = \sum_{n=1}^{N} S_n \log \frac{S_n}{p_n}$$

(10.19)

where S_n denotes the income share of the n-th ethnic group.

Let μ denote the mean income in the society as a whole, then the income share of the n-th ethnic group can be expressed as

$$S_n = p_n \frac{\mu_n}{\mu}. \tag{10.20}$$

Subsequently, Theil's index can be rendered, at any point of time τ, as

$$I(\tau) = \sum_{n=1}^{N} p_n(\tau) \frac{\mu_n}{\mu} \log \frac{\mu_n}{\mu} \tag{10.21}$$

where μ_n is related to the population share of the ethnic group and the moments of the distribution of the migration date as discussed in the previous section. Similarly to Sen's (1973), Pyatt's (1976) and Yitzhaki's (1979) interpretations of the Gini index, it can be argued that $p_n(\mu_n/\mu)\log(\mu_n/\mu)$ measures the contribution of the n-th ethnic group to the level of deprivation (or depression) within the rest of the society. This contribution is positive, zero, or negative as the n-th ethnic group's mean income is greater than, equal to, or smaller than the mean income of the society as a whole; and is amplified by the n-th ethnic group's relative size. Thus, we may argue that Theil's index of income inequality indicates the total level of relative deprivation within the society.

Immigration and differences in natural growth rates can change a country's ethnic composition $(p_1, \dots, p_N)$ and, by virtue of equations (10.16) and (10.21), the overall levels of income inequality and relative deprivation. For instance, suppose that the population of the host country is divided into two ethnic groups $(n = 1,2)$ and that initially $\mu_1 > \mu_2$. In this case, a hike in p_1, which by identity is followed by a comparable decline of p_2, increases the mean income in group 1 and reduces the mean income in group 2 and hence raises the level of income inequality and intensifies the feeling of relative deprivation within the society. In contrast, an increase in p_2 moderates the levels of income inequality and relative deprivation within the society. The magnitude of the change in these social indices depends on the shape and moments of the immigration date distributions within the two ethnic groups as indicated by equations (10.17) and (10.18).

In view of the above analysis, policy measures aimed at affecting these social indices are of two types. The first includes measures that affect the population shares $p_1, \dots, p_N$. The second includes measures which directly affect the adaptation and absorption process parameters c and β (for example, easing or toughening the procedure of obtaining residency and citizenship, anti-discrimination legislation, and social integration in the education system). Note further that since c and β depend also on the population ethnic composition, they are indirectly affected by the first-type measures. This, in turn, necessitates careful coordination in the application of the various measures.

10.8 CONCLUDING REMARKS

A switch model that determines the optimal time of migration was developed. Expected returns and risk differential between the origin and destination, time preferences, risk aversion, and life expectancy served as building blocks of the switch model. The novelty of the model is in its assumption that the decision on the migration date takes into account an assimilation process which is represented by a cost function defined on the time elapsed since migration. The existence of such an assimilation process implies that the solution to the individual's problems of migration timing is not necessarily a corner one. The model suggests that corner solutions to the migration timing problem occur only in the cases where the individual perceives no risk differential between the place of destination and the place of origin, and/or has no time preference. In any other case the individual delays migration to a future date within his/her lifespan. In accordance with the life-cycle hypothesis, three general types of migrant were defined: pre–prime age migrants, prime-age migrants, and post–prime age migrants. The solutions to the migration timing decision problem of migrants of the first and third types are likely to be interior, whereas that of the second-type migrants is likely to be a corner solution.

In empirical studies on migration decisions, disregarding any of the possible solutions to the migration-timing problem might lead to undesired properties of the findings. In particular, the possibility of interior solution to the migration timing problem raises severe doubts about the consistency of the estimated parameters of multinomial-logit analyses of current place-to-place migration. This is due, in terms of the switch model, to the fact that multinomial-logit models are based on the assumption that the individual's migration timing problem can have only corner solutions. Since multinomial-logit analyses of current place-to-place migration disregarded the possibility that some people delay migration to future dates, these analyses understate the true number of migrants, especially when between-cohort effects are controlled through the inclusion of age as an explanatory variable. And if we believe that destination–origin expected-income differential encourages migration and that destination–origin risk differential and costs of assimilation deter migration, then multinomial-logit analyses tend to understate the effect of destination–origin expected-income differential and to overstate the effect of destination–origin risk-bearing differential and the effect of the costs of assimilation on place-to-place migration. These biases can be reduced by observing the individual's behaviour during a sufficiently long period which allows an interior solution to materialise.

The incorporation of assimilation costs that decline with the time elapsed since migration can also provide an explanation to three interesting phenomena associated with migration. The first phenomenon is that people migrate even though, in the short run, they may undergo a considerable reduction in their income and face a higher risk in the new location.

The second phenomenon concerns the structure of the migrant population. The first wave of migrants consists of relatively young individuals endowed with high capacity to adapt to a new environment, whereas the subsequent migration waves are larger and more heterogeneous with regard to age. This phenomenon emerges from the high costs of assimilation for early migrants which can only be paid by individuals endowed with long life expectancy and high capacity to adapt. Kin relationship and ethnic bonds with veteran migrants moderate the costs of assimilation for later migrants and hence also enable the migration of older and less adaptable people.

The third phenomenon associated with migration is the solidification of distinct ethnic groups in the place of destination. It is expressed in the forms of segregated neighbourhoods and countrywide ethnic federations which primarily serve to reduce the costs of assimilation. In migrant societies the distribution of immigration dates and the population ethnic structure may have important welfare implications, one of which is the relationships among immigration dates, ethnic composition, and income and wealth inequality.

REFERENCES

Beggs, J.J. and B.J. Chapman (1988), 'Immigrant Wage Adjustment in Australia: Cross-Section and Time-Series Estimates', *The Economic Record*, **64**, 161–8.

Ben-Porath, Y. (1967), 'The Production of Human Capital and the Life Cycle of Earnings', *Journal of Political Economy*, **75**, 352–65.

Borjas, G.J. (1985), 'Assimilation, Changes in Cohort Quality, and the Earnings of Immigrants,' *Journal of Labor Economics*, **3**, 463–89.

Chiswick, B.R. (1978), 'The Effects of Americanization on the Earnings of Foreign-Born Men', *Journal of Political Economy*, **86**, 897–921.

Chiswick, B.R. and P.W. Miller (1985), 'Immigrant Generation and Income in Australia', *The Economic Record*, **61**, 540–53.

Ethier, W.J. (1985), 'International Trade and Labor Migration,' *American Economic Review*, 75:691–707.

Fields, G.S. (1982), 'Place-to-Place Migration in Colombia', *Economic Development and Cultural Change*, **30**, 539–58.

Freund, R.J. (1956), 'An Introduction of Risk into a Risk-Programming Model', *Econometrica*, **24**, 253–63.

Greenwood, M.J. (1971), 'A Regression Analysis of Migration to Urban Areas of a Less-Developed Country: the Case of India', *Journal of Regional Science*, **11**, 253–62.

Greenwood, M.J. (1978), 'An Econometric Model of Internal Migration and Regional Economic Growth in Mexico', *Journal of Regional Science*, **18**, 17–31.

Hammond, S. (1974), 'Simplification of Choice Under Certainty', *Management Science*, **20**, 1047–72.

Marr, W. (1985), 'The Canadian Temporary Visa Programme as an Alternative to the European Guest Worker Scheme', *International Migration*, **23**, 381–94.

Meyer, J. (1987), 'Two-Moment Decision Models and Expected Utility Maximization', *American Economic Review*, **77**, 421–29.

Modigliani, F. and A. Ando (1960), 'The Permanent Life Cycle Hypotheses of Saving Behaviour: Comparisons and Tests', in *Proceedings of the Conference on Consumption and Saving*, **2**, 49–174, Philadelphia: University of Pennsylvania.

Pyatt, G. (1976), 'On the Interpretation and Disaggregation of Gini Coefficients', *Economic Journal*, **86**, 243–55.

Schultz, T.P. (1982), 'Lifetime Migration within Educational Strata in Venezuela: Estimates of a Logistic Model', *Economic Development and Cultural Change*, **30**, 559–93.

Sen, A.K. (1973), *On Economic Inequality*, Oxford: Clarendon Press.

Stark, O. and D. Levhari (1982), 'On Migration and Risk in LDCs', *Economic Development and Cultural Change*, **31**, 191–6.

Theil, H. (1967), *Economics and Information Theory*, Amsterdam: North Holland.

Todaro, M.P. (1969), 'A Model of Labor Migration and Urban Unemployment in Less Developed Countries', *American Economic Review*, **59**, 138–48.

Yitzhaki, S. (1979), 'Relative Deprivation and the Gini Coefficient,' *Quarterly Journal of Economics*, **93**, 321–4.

11 The Effects of Income Disparities on Inter-Regional Migration in a Technologically Developed Country: Evidence from Australia

Joan R. Rodgers and John L. Rodgers

11.1 INTRODUCTION

Approximately 43 per cent of Australians change their usual residential address within a given five-year period.[1] On average, Australians move 11 times in a lifetime (Bell 1996a: 147). Many changes of residence entail short distances[2] and undoubtedly are made for a host of reasons. But other moves involve quite long distances and have labour-market implications. A geographically mobile workforce is better able to respond to changing labour-market conditions than an immobile one and, as the Australian economy restructures in response to competitive international market forces, the conditions of the Australian labour market are changing.

Demographers have long been active in researching Australia's inter-regional migration,[3] economists less so. The demographic patterns and characteristics of movers identified in the demography literature are of interest but there is still much to be learned. The economic benefits and costs of migration to the mover, and others, have not been estimated. The cause-and-effect linkages between internal migration and economic conditions have received little attention in the Australian context. Little is known about the efficacy of internal migration as a mechanism for reducing wage and unemployment-rate disparities across regions of Australia. According to Lewis and Ross (1995, p. 84): 'In the area of labour mobility considerable scope for further work exists, especially on ... the role of regional mobility in facilitating (or hindering) labour market adjustment.'

This study attempts to fill part of the gap in our knowledge. Our objective is to examine the economic forces that affect an individual's decision to migrate within Australia and to measure the strength of the relationships. The theoretical framework is the theory of mobility advanced by labour economists: the human-capital model. This study is the first to use Australian data to test the human-capital model of inter-regional migration by relating the individual's propensity to move to the present value of his or her predicted, lifetime, net-income gain from moving and the direct costs of inter-regional migration. Empirical research using North American micro-data has found that much internal migration is generally consistent with the human-capital hypothesis in that it is a response to spatial differences in economic conditions. This suggests that the theory may also explain inter-regional migration in Australia, whose economy is at a similar level of development. Other disciplines stress the influence of social and cultural factors, rather than economic factors, on migration decisions. So the outcome of a test of the human-capital hypothesis using Australian data is by no means a foregone conclusion.

11.2   PREVIOUS STUDIES OF MIGRATION IN THE HUMAN-CAPITAL FRAMEWORK

Human capital consists of skills and knowledge that are embodied in the individual. The individual can increase his or her stock of human capital by investing in additional amounts of education, training and so on. The acquisition of human capital is an *investment* in the sense that (a) human capital contributes to utility only indirectly through its ability to generate income and (b) most of the costs of acquiring human capital are incurred in the present while the resulting increase in productivity, which is reflected in lifetime earnings, occurs in the future. The human-capital model of migration dates back to the work of Sjaastad (1962). Migration, like education and training, is an investment in human capital because the individual incurs current costs, the costs of relocating and the income foregone while the move takes place, in the expectation of receiving a higher income as a consequence of the move. The human-capital model admits that psychic costs and benefits, such as proximity to family and friends and the physical and cultural environment, influence the decision to move but would not include them in a cost-benefit analysis of migration if they involve no allocation of resources.

The human-capital model hypothesises that an individual will move from his or her current location to the best alternative location if the present value of his or her predicted, lifetime, net-income gain from moving exceeds the direct cost of moving. The net income gain in any future time period is the income earned if the move takes place, minus the income that would have been earned if the move had not occurred (the opportunity cost of inter-regional migration). The current costs of moving are the income foregone while the move takes place and the cost of transporting oneself, one's family and one's belongings from the origin to the destination location. Moving costs depend upon such factors as the distance covered by the move and the number and ages of the people in the migrating family unit.

The human-capital model has been tested with aggregate-level data and with individual-level data. The earliest empirical applications used aggregate data. (See Greenwood 1975 and 1985, for surveys.) The migration flow (gross or net) between regions was regressed on regional differences in variables such as the average unemployment rate and the mean wage level, and on the distance between regions. The results of some of these studies supported the theory: better economic conditions in the destination (origin) region were associated with an increased (decreased) migration flow, other things equal. Other studies found no evidence in support of the theory. However, as Robinson and Tomes (1982: 475) point out there are problems in interpreting the results of aggregate migration regressions as tests of what is in fact a theory of migration based on individual behaviour. The theory proposes that the individual is motivated to move by the net income gain that he or she can expect in the destination region, not by mean income in the destination region. The major deficiency of the aggregate approach is its inability to explain the commonly observed, large, simultaneous in-flows and out-flows of people to and from the same region.

Two-way migration flows can be explained using individual-level data that recognise heterogeneity in the population. For example, a highly educated individual may derive a net income gain by moving into a 'high-tech' location, while another individual with little education may find relocation in the opposite direction advantageous. An individual's income is determined by his or her earning capacity, and this varies among people according to personal characteristics such as occupation, education and experience. The value placed on these personal attributes differs among locations according to local supply and demand conditions for different types of labour. The heterogeneity of earnings-related characteristics among individuals and the different values placed on these attributes in different locations can explain why some people move into a particular locality at the same time as other people move out. An individual's *expected* income depends on both earning capacity and on the probability of having a job. The latter depends on many of the same individual characteristics that determine earning capacity but also by general employment conditions in the region (Todaro 1969; Harris and Todaro 1970).

Previous tests of the human-capital model using individual-level data have met with considerable success. Nakosteen's and Zimmer's (1980) study of United States internal migration supports the human-capital model, as do later studies by Hunt and Kau (1985), Borjas et al. (1992) and Rodgers and Rodgers (1997 and 2000). Robinson and Tomes (1982) find the human-capital model to be consistent with Canadian data. However, certain groups of migrants in North America, such as single women (Enchautegui 1997) and Hispanic men (Tienda and Wilson 1992) do not appear to behave in accordance with human-capital theory.

Two studies of internal migration in Australia that have used micro-data are Flood et al. (1991) and Bell and Maher (1995). These studies use data from the 1986 and 1991 Censuses, respectively. Bell and Maher find high rates of migration among the unemployed. However, the Census records employment status after (not before) migration, so it is unclear whether unemployment is the cause or consequence of moving. Age, sex, length of time in the country, ethnicity, English proficiency, occupation, industry, education level, marital status, and presence of dependent children are also identified as factors that influence the individual's probability of moving. These results are consistent with the human-capital model although neither study is an explicit test of the theory. However, Flood et al. (1991, p. 17) cite 'counter-urbanisation' (substantial population movements from metropolitan to non-metropolitan areas, which often have low wage levels and high unemployment levels) as a counter-example to human-capital theory. The same authors also argue that in an affluent society with an extensive 'safety net', economic considerations exert little influence on decisions about where to live and work. For those at the top end of the income distribution this phenomenon is explained by a supposed low utility attached to extra income. For those at the bottom of the income distribution the explanation lies in the existence of nation-wide social policies, such as long-term unemployment benefits that do not vary with location. Such policies reduce the need to seek employment elsewhere and provide no incentive to migrate in pursuit of higher welfare benefits in other states. Finally, it is argued that Australia's centralised wage-fixing procedures have tended to suppress inter-regional wage differentials thereby creating few opportunities for migration to result in economic gain. The general conclusion of these two important studies is that Australians' moving behaviour is very diverse and much of it is not motivated by a desire to improve one's economic well-being.

11.3   THE ECONOMETRIC MIGRATION MODEL

We address internal migration using an econometric model that is estimated using a cross section of individual-level data. The first equation models an individual's income in a given region as a function of the individual's work experience, education, ability to speak English, race and occupation:

$$E(Y^k_i) = \alpha_{k0} + \alpha_{k1}X_i + u_i \qquad (11.1)$$

where

- $E(Y^k_i)$ is the expected income of person i in region k;

- X_i is a vector of income-related characteristics of person i;
- α_{k0} and α_{k1} are parameters that vary according to the region in which the individual is located; and
- u_i is a stochastic error term that is assumed to be independently and identically distributed, with mean zero and constant variance.

The individual's stream of future incomes in a particular region is predicted by substituting the individual's personal characteristics into the right hand side of the estimated version of equation (11.1) that applies to the region. Work experience is one such characteristic and as it increases with each time period until the age of retirement, predicted income varies over the remainder of the individual's working life. The present value of an individual's predicted lifetime income in a given region is the discounted sum of his or her predicted income stream in that region:

$$PV_i^k = \sum_{t=1}^{T_i} \frac{(\hat{Y}_{t,i}^k)}{(1+r)^t} \tag{11.2}$$

where

- PV_i^k is the present value of life-time income of individual i in region k;
- $\hat{Y}_{t,i}^k$ is predicted income of individual i, in period t, in region k;
- r is the rate of time preference; and
- T_i is the number of periods until individual i retires at age 65.

The final equation of the model is a probit equation. The probability of moving is a function of the differential present value of the individual's predicted income streams in the origin and destination regions:

$$P(m_i) = \beta_0 + \beta_1(PV_i^d - PV_i^o) + \beta_2 C_i + \varepsilon_i \tag{11.3}$$

where:

- $P(m_i)$ is the probability that individual i will move from origin, o, to destination, d;
- PV_i^d is both the present value of predicted life-time income of a mover in the destination region and the present value of predicted life-time income of a stayer, had he or she migrated to the destination region;
- PV_i^o is both the present value of predicted life-time income of a

stayer in the origin region and the present value of predicted lifetime income of a mover, had he or she not migrated from the origin
region;

- C_i is a vector of variables that reflect the ith person's direct cost of
  moving; and

- e_i is a stochastic error term that is assumed to be independently and
  identically distributed, with mean zero and constant variance.

The econometric model described above is different to those employed in
previous cross-section studies of inter-regional migration in that equation (11.3)
relates the probability of moving to the present value of the predicted gain in
lifetime income associated with inter-regional migration rather than to the
predicted gain in income in a single time period.[4] A large, positive, statistically
significant value for β_1 and large, statistically significant values for β_3 of the
appropriate sign constitute evidence in support of the human-capital hypothesis.

11.4   DATA, DEFINITIONS AND MEASUREMENT

The best data set currently available with which to study individuals' decisions
to move within Australia is the Census of Population and Housing, which is
conducted every five years by the Australian Bureau of Statistics. Each person
who spent the night of 6 August 1996 in an Australian household is asked:
'What is (your) usual address?' and 'What was (your) usual address one year
ago (6 August 1995)?' and 'What was (your) usual address five years ago
(6 August 1991)?'. A person's 'usual' address is the address at which he or she
has lived or intends to live for a total of six months or more in the relevant year.
Data from the 1996 Household Sample File (HSF), which is a one-per cent
simple random sample of 1996 Census data (ABS 1998), was used to estimate
the econometric model described in the previous section. A major advantage of
the HSF is that it provides unit-record data on a large random sample of people
and thereby allows the examination of moving behaviour throughout the entire
country. The major disadvantage of the HSF is that the data are cross-section,
rather than panel, and consequently there is only one observation per person on
(virtually) all variables. In particular, there are no observations on movers prior
to migration and only one observation after a move. This makes it difficult to
identify the causes and effects of migration. To determine whether people move
in response to particular conditions, we would like to observe the presence, or
absence, of those conditions both before and after moving. To determine the
economic consequences of migration, we would like to observe people's earnings
in a number of years both before and after moves occur.

Despite the limitations of cross-section data, econometric studies based on them have been used to understand migration behaviour in other countries. The approach is to estimate a mover's income, *if he or she had not moved*, by the income of people who have the same income-related characteristics as the mover and who live in the mover's origin location. Similarly, a stayer's income, *if he or she had moved*, is estimated by the income of people who have the same income-related characteristics as the stayer and who moved out of the stayer's location. This is the methodology employed in this study.

To test the human-capital hypothesis for Australia we select individuals with strong attachments to the labour force, namely male labour-force participants. These are the people to whom the theory applies. We do not include females because their labour-market behaviour and experiences tend to be different from, and more complex than those of males. In particular, larger proportions of females than males are not full-time participants in the labour market and therefore are likely to be 'tied' to their partner's migration decision. Therefore, females should be analysed separately. Specifically, we focus on the migration behaviour of males in the HSF who:

1.   were resident in an occupied private dwelling, rather than an institution, on Census night 1996;[5]
2.   were resident in Australia on Census night 1991;[6]
3.   were aged between 24 and 65 years on Census night 1996;[7]
4.   were in the labour force in the week prior to Census night 1996; and
5.   report valid data on internal migration, income and other variables used in the econometric analysis described in Sections 11.5, 11.6 and 11.7.

The HSF contains three variables with which to identify migration: the region of usual residence on census night, the region of usual residence one year prior to census night, and the region of usual residence five years prior to census night. Coded in the HSF are 41 mutually exclusive and collectively exhaustive geographical regions (see Table 11.1). In this study a 'stayer' is defined as someone with the same region of usual residence on Census night, one year earlier and five years earlier. Of the 29 774 men who meet our selection criteria, 23 389 are stayers. The remaining 6 385 (approximately 21 per cent) changed region during the five-year period from August 1991 to August 1996. The 41 regions vary considerably both in geographical area and in the size of their populations. The non-metropolitan regions cover large areas and a move between them would almost certainly necessitate a change of job.[8] The metropolitan regions are much smaller geographically and a move between metropolitan regions of Sydney, Melbourne, Brisbane, Adelaide or Perth would not necessarily require a change of job. As this study deals with only those moves that have labour-market implications, the 41 regions were aggregated into 21 districts, five of which are the metropolitan areas of Sydney, Melbourne, Brisbane, Adelaide and Perth, and the other 16 are the regions in non-metropolitan areas

Table 11.1
The 41 Regions Identified in the Household Sample File

Metropolitan Sydney

1. Inner Sydney or Eastern Suburbs
2. St George–Sutherland
3. Canterbury–Bankstown or Fairfield–Liverpool
4. Outer South Western or Outer Western Sydney
5. Inner Western Sydney or Central Western Sydney
6. Blacktown-Baulkham Hills
7. Lower Northern Sydney or Northern Beaches
8. Hornsby–Ku-ring-gai or Gosford–Wyong

Non-Metropolitan NSW

9. Hunter
10. Illawarra or South Eastern NSW
11. Richmond–Tweed or Mid-North NSW
12. Northern or Far West–North Western NSW
13. Central West NSW or Murray–Murrumbidgee

Metropolitan Melbourne

14. North Eastern Melbourne
15. Inner Eastern Melbourne
16. Southern Melbourne
17. Outer Eastern Melbourne
18. Outer Western Melbourne
19. North Western or Inner Melbourne
20. South Eastern Melbourne or Mornington Peninsula

Non-Metropolitan Victoria

21. Barwon–Western District, Vic
22. Central Highland–Wimmera or Loddon–Mallee, Vic

23. Goulburn–Ovens–Murray or Gippsland, Vic

Metropolitan Brisbane

24. Brisbane Inner City Ring
25. Brisbane Outer City Ring
26. South or East BSD Balance
27. North or West BSD Balance

Non-Metropolitan Queensland

28. Moreton, Qld
29. Wide Bay–Burnett, Darling Downs or Sth West Qld
30. Mackay–Fitzroy–Central West Queensland
31. Northern North West or Far North Queensland

Metropolitan Adelaide

32. Northern Adelaide
33. Western or Eastern Adelaide
34. Southern Adelaide

Non-Metropolitan South Australia

35. Other SA

Metropolitan Perth

37. Central or East Metropolitan Perth
36. North Metropolitan Perth
38. South Metropolitan Perth

Non-Metropolitan Western Australia

39. Other WA

Other

40. Tasmania
41. ACT–NT

listed in Table 11.1. A mover is defined as someone who resided in different districts on the nights of 6 August 1991 and 6 August 1996. Of the 6 385 men who changed region between 1991 and 1996, 3 618 are movers according to our definition. The other 2 767 men were excluded from the study.

Our definitions of stayers and movers are necessarily far from perfect. First, the HSF provides no information with which to identify people who moved prior to August 1991. Therefore, some of those defined as stayers may be people who moved *more than* five years prior to Census night 1996, in which case their incomes reflect the long-term effect of moving, not staying. Secondly, the HSF provides no information about whether a move was accompanied by a change of job or occupation, and no explicit information about the distance covered by a move. Therefore, even after combining regions into districts, some moves to adjacent districts may have involved short distances and may well have had no labour-market implications. Some intra-district changes of address may have involved long distances and may have had labour-market implications, yet we excluded them from the study. Finally, the HSF provides no information on residence at dates between August 1991 and August 1995. It is possible, therefore, that some of our stayers may have moved out of, then returned to, the same region between 1991 and 1995.

The Census data also have some eccentricities that are relevant to the estimation of the model.

1   The HSF records the individual's gross weekly income 'usually received from all sources'. We would prefer to concentrate on the types of income that are likely to be related to migration decisions, in particular, wages, salaries and self-employment income.

2   The HSF records gross weekly income in intervals, the smallest and largest of which are open-ended. Consequently, weekly income cannot be converted into an hourly wage by dividing by hours worked. Furthermore, the calculation of average income requires some assumptions. The mean incomes reported in this study have been calculated using the midpoint of each class interval to represent all incomes in a given category. The open-ended category 'more than $1 500 per week' is represented by $2 250; 'less than $40 per week' is represented by $20.

3   The Census records the individual's labour-force status and the number of hours worked in the week prior to Census night rather than in a typical week. Therefore, a person who reports that he was 'unemployed' or worked zero hours can report validly that he usually earned a positive income, even from wages or salary.

4   A related problem exists in recording the individual's occupation and industry. The Census asks what the individual's occupation and industry were in the main job held in the week prior to Census night, rather than in the individual's usual type of employment. People who were unemployed

in the week prior to Census night are placed in a separate category, 'not applicable', so that their usual occupation and industry are not known.

We decided to remove unemployed men from our data set because their incomes were small enough to suggest that many of them did not report the income that they 'usually received' when in paid employment. (The unemployed earned $202 per week on average, compared with an average of $747 per week for employed men.) The employed men retained in our data set are likely to receive the bulk of their income in the form of wages and salaries. We also removed men who reported that they usually received non-positive gross weekly income. In summary, the analysis reported below is based upon 21 381 men who form our sample. All of them satisfy the basic selection criteria (a) through (e) stated at the beginning of this section. All were employed in the week prior to Census night 1996 and usually earned positive income. The number of stayers is 18 628. The number of movers, all of whom are inter-district movers, is 2 753.

11.5   DESCRIPTIVE STATISTICS

Table 11.2 summarises the moving behaviour of the 2 753 inter-regional migrants in our sample between the 21 districts that were constructed from the 41 regions in Table 11.1: metropolitan Sydney, 5 districts in non-metropolitan NSW, Melbourne, 3 districts in non-metropolitan Victoria, Brisbane, 4 districts in non-metropolitan Queensland, Adelaide, non-metropolitan South Australia, Perth, non-metropolitan Western Australia, Tasmania and the ACT–NT. Each cell of Table 11.2 records the number movers from the district stated in the row heading to the district stated in the column heading. For example, there were 414 men who moved out of one of the eight regions that comprise the Sydney metropolitan area, of whom 183 moved to one of the five regions in non-metropolitan NSW, 30 moved to Melbourne and so on. There were 324 men who moved into one of the eight regions that comprise the Sydney metropolitan area, of whom 132 came from one of the five regions in non-metropolitan NSW, 47 came from Melbourne and so on. The numbers of stayers in the 21 districts appear in the last row of Table 11.2.

Table 11.2 (a) and 11.2 (b) reveals that 1 310 of the 2 753 movers in our sample (47.6 per cent) moved within the same state. The largest net population in-flows occurred in Brisbane (300–233 = 67) and non-metropolitan South-East Queensland (222–99 = 123). The largest net population out-flows were experienced by Sydney (324–414 = –90), Melbourne (256–332 = –76) and Adelaide (100–160 = –60). All districts in Victoria had net population outflows. Western Australia and the coastal regions of NSW and Queensland had net population inflows. The predominance of intra-state moves, population

Table 11.2 (a)
Number of Movers and Stayers

From (in 1991)		Syd ney	1	2	Non-metro NSW 3	4	5	Mel- bourne	1	Non-metro Vic 2	3	Bris- bane
Sydney		0	43	61	31	17	31	30	4	3	4	60
Non-metro	1	35	0	4	5	4	4	4	0	0	1	5
NSW	2	44	3	0	4	1	6	3	0	0	1	5
	3	18	8	3	0	3	6	3	0	0	0	8
	4	21	10	6	17	0	2	3	0	5	0	4
	5	14	4	11	4	6	0	5	1	3	11	7
Melbourne		47	8	5	5	2	10	0	23	39	49	38
Non-metro	1	5	0	1	1	1	0	20	0	6	8	2
Vic	2	3	0	0	1	1	5	31	10	0	9	2
	3	6	3	1	22	0	11	56	3	10	0	3
Brisbane		38	2	2	55	1	4	20	1	3	3	0
Non-metro	1	10	2	1	6	1	1	6	0	0	0	30
Qld	2	1	0	2	1	2	3	3	0	1	0	32
	3	0	0	1	3	1	1	2	0	0	0	18
	4	14	1	1	1	1	0	8	0	2	1	39
Adelaide		22	2	0	2	1	5	17	1	3	2	14
Non-metro	SA	3	0	0	0	0	1	5	0	2	1	1
Perth		10	0	1	0	2	0	9	0	2	2	9
Non-metro	WA	1	0	1	2	1	2	4	0	0	0	5
Tasmania		9	1	3	2	0	2	11	1	2	2	2
NT&ACT		23	3	22	3	2	4	16	0	0	1	16
Total		324	90	126	95	47	98	256	44	81	95	300
Stayers		3808	620	636	405	339	455	3260	365	453	600	1442

Total (in 1996):

movements from the South East to the North and West, and out of Sydney to nearby coastal regions are consistent with those documented in the demography literature (see Flood et al. 1991: 2). They indicate that the moving behaviour of the men in our sample is not atypical.

Table 11.3 gives the characteristics of stayers and movers. The mean income of the movers in our sample is $760 per week; stayers earn on average $745. The difference is likely explained by the following factors:

Table 11.2 (b)
Number of Movers and Stayers

From (in 1991)		Total (in 1996):										
		Non-metro Qld				Ade-laide	Non-metro SA	Perth	Non-metro WA	Tas-man	NT& ACT	Total
		1	2	3	4							
Sydney		31	3	1	17	11	0	29	4	6	28	414
Non-metro NSW	1	3	5	1	1	1	0	1	1	1	5	81
	2	5	0	1	2	0	0	3	0	1	21	100
	3	12	2	0	1	0	1	0	2	0	4	71
	4	3	4	2	2	2	0	2	0	1	2	86
	5	5	2	0	0	1	0	1	2	0	10	87
Melbourne		26	4	5	9	9	1	20	0	8	24	332
Non-metro Vic	1	2	1	2	2	3	1	1	1	6	0	63
	2	6	0	1	4	3	3	1	1	1	6	88
	3	11	6	4	2	5	2	5	3	1	5	139
Brisbane		67	21	11	20	10	1	10	1	3	10	233
Non-metro Qld	1	0	19	7	7	0	1	1	3	2	2	99
	2	11	0	22	12	0	0	3	3	0	4	100
	3	6	6	0	6	1	0	3	0	0	4	52
	4	8	8	18	0	1	1	1	1	2	6	114
Adelaide		6	3	1	4	0	49	9	1	2	16	160
Non-metro SA	SA	3	2	0	1	37	0	2	4	1	4	67
Perth		4	0	1	2	2	2	0	90	1	11	148
Non-metro WA	WA	1	1	4	2	3	0	76	0	1	3	107
Tasmania		5	1	2	2	2	0	5	2	0	6	60
NT&ACT		7	6	3	8	9	5	8	9	7	0	152
Total		222	94	86	104	100	67	181	128	44	171	2 753
Stayers		511	458	331	491	1165	459	1263	518	572	477	18 628

1. Movers are better educated than stayers. For example, 24.2 per cent of movers have a university degree, postgraduate diploma or higher degree compared to 15.7 per cent of stayers. At the other extreme, 30.7 per cent of stayers but only 24.1 per cent of movers left school before age 16 and have no other qualification.

2. A larger percentage (51.3) of movers than stayers (43.3 per cent) are managers or professionals, which are high-paying occupations with national, rather than local, labour markets.

Table 11.3
Characteristics of Stayers and Movers

		Stayers (1)	Movers (2)
Income per Week			
MDINCP	(mean) in $	744.90	759.99
Age			
DAGEP0	24 – 29 years, 0 otherwise	0.1198	0.2735 ***
DAGEP1	30 – 34 years, 0 otherwise	0.1366	0.2096 ***
DAGEP2	35 – 39 years, 0 otherwise	0.1666	0.1969 ***
DAGEP3	40 – 44 years, 0 otherwise	0.1671	0.1275 ***
DAGEP4	45 – 49 years, 0 otherwise	0.1625	0.0919 ***
DAGEP5	50 – 54 years, 0 otherwise	0.1213	0.0585 ***
DAGEP6	55 – 59 years, 0 otherwise	0.0841	0.0298 ***
DAGEP7	60 – 64 years, 0 otherwise	0.0421	0.0124 ***
Work Experience			
EXPER1	experience = age – age left school – yrs in higher education	24.5754	18.4348 ***
Marital Status			
DMARL1	1 if in a registered marriage; 0 otherwise	0.7362	0.5648 ***
FamilyType			
DKIDS0	1 if an independent adult; 0 otherwise	0.1664	0.2928 ***
DKIDS1	1 if couple without children; 0 otherwise	0.2242	0.2525 ***
DKIDS2	1 if family with children <15 years only; 0 otherwise	0.3669	0.3661
DKIDS3	1 if family with children <15 yrs & dep students 15–24 yrs; 0 otherwise	0.0702	0.0316 ***
DKIDS4	1 if family with dependent students 15–24 years only; 0 otherwise	0.0736	0.0225 ***
DKIDS5	1 if family with nondependent children only; 0 otherwise	0.0891	0.0222 ***
Immigrant Status			
DYARP0	1 if Australian born; 0 otherwise	0.7456	0.8071 ***
DYARP1	1 if arrived in Australia before 1981; 0 otherwise	0.1914	0.1359 ***
DYARP2	1 if arrived in Australia 1981–85; 0 otherwise	0.0280	0.0200
DYARP3	1 if arrived in Australia 1986–90; 0 otherwise	0.0350	0.0371

		Stayers (1)	Movers (2)
Education			
DEDUC0	1 if left school before 16 & no other qualification; 0 otherwise	0.3069	0.2408 ***
DEDUC1	1 if left school after 16 & no other qualification; 0 otherwise	0.1547	0.1616
DEDUC2	1 if has a basic vocational qualification; 0 otherwise	0.0282	0.0280
DEDUC3	1 if has a skilled vocational qualification; 0 otherwise	0.2773	0.2499 ***
DEDUC4	1 if has an associate diploma; 0 otherwise	0.0412	0.0436
DEDUC5	1 if has an undergraduate diploma; 0 otherwise	0.0352	0.0345
DEDUC6	1 if has a bachelor degree; 0 otherwise	0.1094	0.1747 ***
DEDUC7	1 if has a postgraduate diploma; 0 otherwise	0.0194	0.0309 ***
DEDUC8	1 if has a higher degree; 0 otherwise	0.0277	0.0360 **
Occupation			
DOCCP1	1 if a specialist manager; 0 otherwise	0.0594	0.0777 ***
DOCCP2	1 if other manager; 0 otherwise	0.0847	0.0570 ***
DOCCP3	1 if a professional; 0 otherwise	0.1591	0.2085 ***
DOCCP4	1 if an associate professional; 0 otherwise	0.1295	0.1700 ***
DOCCP5	1 if a trades-person; 0 otherwise	0.2076	0.1802 ***
DOCCP6	1 if a clerical or service worker; 0 otherwise	0.0965	0.0963
DOCCP7	1 if a production or transport worker; 0 otherwise	0.1421	0.0973 ***
DOCCP8	1 if an unskilled worker; 0 otherwise	0.1211	0.1130
Race			
DRACE	1 if indigenous; 0 otherwise	0.0086	0.0094
English Proficiency			
DNENGP0	1 if English is first language; 0 otherwise	0.8816	0.9513 ***
DNENGP1	1 if speaks English very well; 0 otherwise	0.0668	0.0356 ***
DNENGP2	1 if speaks English but not very well; 0 otherwise	0.0515	0.0131 ***
No. of Obs		18 628	2 753

Note: *, ** and *** indicate a statistically significant difference on a two-tailed test at the 10%, 5% and 1% levels, respectively.

3.   Movers are more likely to speak English as their first language (95.1 per cent) than stayers (88.2 per cent). Stayers are slightly more likely to speak English poorly (5.2 per cent) than movers (1.3 per cent).

Other attributes that affect a person's earning capacity or reflect his cost of moving are as follows.

4.   Movers are younger than stayers. 27.4 per cent of movers are younger than 30 years, compared to 12 per cent of stayers; 24.8 per cent of stayers are older than 50 years, compared with 10.1 per cent of movers. This is consistent with the fact that the young have a long working life over which to recoup the economic costs of moving.
5.   Being younger, movers have less work experience (18.4 years) than stayers (24.6 years).
6.   Movers are less likely to be married (56.5 per cent) than stayers (73.6 per cent) and are more likely to be childless (54.5 per cent) than stayers (39.1 per cent). Marital status and type of family are both determinants of the direct cost of moving.
7.   Movers are more likely to be Australian born (80.7 per cent) than stayers (74.6 per cent). Movers are less likely to have immigrated to Australia before 1981 (13.6 per cent) than stayers (19.1 per cent).

11.6   ECONOMETRIC ANALYSIS OF PREDICTED LIFETIME INCOMES

According to human-capital theory the probability of moving (equation (11.3)) is a function of the present value of predicted life-time income in both the origin and destination locations. For a mover, the destination location is the district of usual residence on Census night. The origin – where the mover would have lived *if* he had not moved – is the district of usual residence five years prior to Census night. For a stayer, the origin location is the district of usual residence five years prior to Census night. The destination – where the stayer would have lived *if* he had moved – is unknown. Our approach is to allow that the stayer could have moved to any of the 21 districts with the probability of moving to a particular district set equal to the proportion of movers from the stayer's origin district who moved to that particular district between 1991 and 1996. Thus, each stayer's present value of predicted life-time income in the destination location is a weighted average of the present values of his predicted life-time income streams in all 21 districts. The weights are the proportions of movers from the stayer's origin district who moved to the 21 districts between 1991 and 1996.

Predicted weekly income in each of the 21 districts was obtained from a regression of 'usual weekly income' on personal earnings-related characteristics (equation (11.1)) using all men in our sample who were resident in the given district on Census night 1996. The 21 separate income regressions allow income-related personal characteristics to be valued differently in the various districts. We have not controlled for migration selectivity, nor for labour-force selectivity, because the HSF is insufficiently rich to enable these processes to be modeled.[9] Thus, we assume that each man's weekly income is determined only by his observable personal attributes. By substituting each man's personal characteristics into the right-hand-side of each income regression we obtained a prediction of that person's usual weekly income if he were to reside in each of the 21 districts. Weekly income is projected into the future by increasing the individual's level of work experience by one for each year of his remaining working life. We multiplied weekly income predictions by 52 to obtain annual income predictions. Finally, the individual's stream of predicted annual incomes in each district was discounted back to its present value using a 10 per cent rate of discount (equation (11.2)).

The 21 income equations were estimated using LIMDEP (Greene 1998) and appear in Table 11.4. The explanatory variables (education, potential experience, potential experience squared, English proficiency, race and occupation) are those typically used in the labour-economics literature. In general, the coefficients in the income equations have the expected sign and many are statistically significant. Higher levels of education have a positive impact on earnings, other things equal, particularly in the state capitals and to a lesser extent in non-metropolitan districts. In every district, a man with a university degree has a significantly higher income than a man who left school before age 16 and acquired no further qualifications. The premium for a university degree ranges from $178.19 per week in Northern North West or Far North Queensland to $413.21 per week in Illawarra or South Eastern NSW. The education dummies are positive and significant (as expected) in 91 out of 168 cases; non-significant in 76 cases; and (unexpectedly) negative and significant in one case. Experience displays the typical non-linear effect on income in every district and the effect is significantly different from zero in 17 of the 21 districts. In all districts except the ACT-NT, income is maximised after at least 23 and at most 33 years of experience, that is, between age 47 and 57 years. Compared with those whose first language is English, income is significantly lower according to the level of English proficiency, *ceteris paribus*, in more than half the districts, including all the capital cities. The largest language differential occurs in the ACT–NT, where a man who does not speak English very well earns $343.45 per week less than a man whose first language is English. People of indigenous origin earn less than non-indigenous Australians, *ceteris paribus*, in 15 of the 21 districts; significantly less in nine districts. The largest effect of race is in Melbourne where the indigenous earn $359.75 per week less

Table 11.4
(Log)Income Equations

Variable	Sydney	Hunter	Illawarra, SE NSW	Richm'd-Tweed, mid North NSW	Northern & Far NW Western NSW	Central NW NSW, Murray-Murrumbidgee	Melbourne
ONE	301.47 ***	179.03 **	314.51 ***	344.02 ***	162.45	280.55 ***	226.89 ***
DEDUC1	101.33 ***	37.19	-15.45	-9.90	137.67 *	19.52	102.89 ***
DEDUC2	158.06 ***	-16.78	153.05 ***	-188.65 ***	32.25	41.91	68.17
DEDUC3	27.69	94.51 **	42.94	-45.62	84.09	38.66	27.74
DEDUC4	86.98 **	228.90 **	221.21 ***	-16.78	296.00	157.50 **	137.36 ***
DEDUC5	176.82 ***	100.58	28.41	-69.15	148.65	153.90	150.08 ***
DEDUC6	344.98 ***	318.37 ***	413.21 ***	229.96 **	215.93 *	334.28 ***	372.46 ***
DEDUC7	285.26 ***	50.06	366.83 ***	-161.60	286.57 **	209.87 *	178.17 ***
DEDUC8	545.31 ***	545.04 **	492.86 ***	330.54	436.95 **	410.01 **	704.55 ***
EXPER1	23.61 ***	23.81 ***	13.85 ***	8.77	25.81 ***	14.87 **	20.73 ***
EXP1SQ	-0.42 ***	-0.40 ***	-0.24 **	-0.17	-0.51 ***	-0.26 **	-0.35 ***
DNENGP1	-104.00 ***	-164.22 ***	-20.13	-146.57 **	-304.11 ***	302.46	-146.68 ***
DNENGP2	-221.38 ***	-240.80 ***	-0.10	-233.10	-248.05 **	-16.15	-173.33 ***
DRACE	-18.04	-167.19 ***	-147.58 *	-59.00	-168.55 **	-133.56	-359.75 ***
DOCCP1	535.26 ***	419.91 ***	436.63 ***	286.68 ***	503.57 ***	468.63 ***	557.07 ***
DOCCP2	392.45 ***	391.57 ***	143.48 **	177.83 ***	98.86	114.80 *	402.67 ***
DOCCP3	283.33 ***	332.16 ***	281.69 ***	330.78 ***	249.79 ***	203.67 ***	317.80 ***
DOCCP4	248.37 ***	278.22 ***	149.95 ***	149.41 ***	266.56 **	193.88 ***	274.17 ***
DOCCP5	71.09 ***	149.06 ***	75.79 *	78.46 **	66.30	106.48 **	114.72 ***
DOCCP6	99.12 ***	157.13 ***	128.90 **	81.79 **	72.33	78.24 *	158.89 ***
DOCCP7	11.63	293.51 ***	121.97 ***	101.69 **	189.13 ***	71.75 *	106.03 ***
Wald's χ^2	1 423.49 ***	242.03 ***	266.06 ***	94.57 ***	120.91 ***	133.59 ***	1 364.33 ***
Sample size	4132	710	762	500	386	553	3516
av. income	851.99	784.32	710.43	568.92	648.34	640.00	796.00

(continued)

Table 11.4 (continued)
Log(Income) Equations

Variable	Barwon-Western District, Vic.	Central-Highland-Wimmera Loddon-Mallee, Vic	Goulburn-Ovens-Murray, Gippsl'd, Vic	Brisbane	Moreton, Qld	Wide Bay-Burnett, Darling Downs, SW Qld	Mackay-Fitzroy-Central West Qld
ONE	283.69 ***	215.26 ***	348.89 ***	242.08 ***	267.86 ***	387.07 ***	295.93 **
DEDUC1	108.77 *	77.68 *	83.05 **	54.75 *	126.32 ***	27.07	2.12
DEDUC2	190.87 ***	-23.56	132.23 *	143.24 **	180.73	236.93 *	5.79
DEDUC3	142.55 ***	56.82	39.35	2.32	64.14 **	28.81	12.39
DEDUC4	138.01 *	182.03 ***	94.21	85.16 **	103.55	15.27	245.93
DEDUC5	49.83	256.83 **	82.96	112.36 *	90.60	-21.42	136.86
DEDUC6	217.83 **	231.55 **	330.99 ***	228.73 ***	229.09 **	262.08 **	217.73
DEDUC7	289.36 ***	363.63 *	177.94 **	212.27 **	124.01	209.53 **	342.26
DEDUC8	557.42 ***	272.27 **	379.63 **	310.41 ***	681.45 ***	719.07 ***	256.56
EXPER1	8.41	21.09 ***	7.44 *	23.26 ***	10.56 *	5.04	25.07 **
EXP1SQ	-0.16	-0.42 ***	-0.15 *	-0.44 ***	-0.20 *	-0.11	-0.48 **
DNENGP1	-12.91	-26.83	-24.84	-92.02 **	-57.12	-271.50 **	-48.49
DNENGP2	7.40	59.77	-76.35	-112.44 **	-270.01 ***	10.34	-224.36
DRACE	-20.92	80.05	272.53 ***	44.72	189.47	-47.80	61.87
DOCCP1	477.30 ***	377.53 ***	489.52 ***	486.47 ***	363.71 ***	456.34 ***	365.12 ***
DOCCP2	153.31 **	94.24 *	52.14	338.33 ***	320.23 ***	82.74	119.84
DOCCP3	267.32 ***	251.56 ***	183.98 ***	338.07 ***	400.92 ***	250.64 ***	289.40 **
DOCCP4	234.02 ***	198.48 ***	170.97 ***	249.00 ***	259.84 ***	197.51 ***	255.18 ***
DOCCP5	92.84 **	70.25 *	100.29 ***	85.12 ***	124.22 ***	68.82 **	179.64 **
DOCCP6	146.69 ***	57.04 *	105.71 ***	116.97 ***	144.98 ***	122.15 ***	7.39
DOCCP7	159.04 ***	26.28	62.96 *	69.93 ***	104.65 ***	40.62	482.71 ***
Wald's χ^2	288.10 ***	161.97 ***	574.84 ***	485.65 ***	197.15 ***	143.08 ***	89.15 ***
Sample size	409	534	695	1742	733	552	417
av. income	647.48	607.36	598.20	736.03	632.74	577.68	836.74

(continued)

Table 11.4 (continued)
Log(Income) Equations

Variable	Northern NW, Far North Qld	Adelaide	Other SA	Perth	Other WA	Tasmania	ACT-NT
ONE	333.58 ***	238.49 ***	351.93 ***	254.12 ***	196.31 **	270.79 ***	381.58 ***
DEDUC1	118.26 **	130.44 ***	13.60	138.49 ***	24.15	12.49	-3.54
DEDUC2	-54.26	111.80 *	48.76	58.74	121.91	82.93	-29.07
DEDUC3	27.49	95.87 ***	73.33 **	43.56	88.66 **	35.39	39.56
DEDUC4	146.77	190.44 ***	224.98 **	35.40	64.73	94.69	-24.74
DEDUC5	5.18	184.17 **	61.57	62.79	-59.98	159.09 **	194.20
DEDUC6	178.19 **	413.21 ***	315.05 **	349.16 ***	271.60 ***	376.08 ***	189.62 ***
DEDUC7	62.50	375.07 ***	94.24	336.77 ***	-35.16	137.99	203.02 *
DEDUC8	454.65 *	579.65 ***	244.73	632.35 ***	188.95	604.15 ***	401.09 ***
EXPER1	13.99 **	15.95 ***	8.20	20.25 ***	25.87 ***	10.68 *	20.11 ***
EXP1SQ	-0.25 *	-0.24 ***	-0.15	-0.35 ***	-0.56 ***	-0.18	-0.23
DNENGP1	-84.30	-139.05 ***	144.31	-53.76	87.88	89.21	-54.22
DNENGP2	347.98 *	-185.80 ***	-149.36 ***	-187.03 ***	258.42	-1.38	-343.45 ***
DRACE	-259.96 ***	45.34	-294.47 ***	-108.00	-314.24 ***	-78.87 *	-269.58 ***
DOCCP1	474.66 ***	379.98 ***	389.84 ***	460.26 ***	667.18 ***	533.26 ***	368.21 ***
DOCCP2	209.24 ***	368.61 ***	23.06	370.58 ***	127.52 **	165.41 ***	342.90 ***
DOCCP3	378.92 ***	212.34 ***	238.70 ***	291.69 ***	422.60 ***	224.27 ***	217.82 ***
DOCCP4	150.89 ***	163.08 ***	140.61 ***	303.80 ***	308.15 ***	229.03 ***	173.01 ***
DOCCP5	150.31 ***	48.77 *	101.31 ***	145.09 ***	263.13 ***	107.59 ***	-16.86
DOCCP6	97.92 **	113.03 ***	117.80 ***	165.70 ***	199.79 ***	153.47 ***	73.91
DOCCP7	108.44 **	53.00 *	128.81 ***	138.57 ***	278.34 ***	175.92 ***	-45.34
Wald's χ2	168.77 ***	381.30 ***	115.51 ***	406.62 ***	230.03 ***	189.35 ***	288.26 ***
Sample size	595	1265	526	1444	646	616	648
av. income	705.55	706.40	592.72	815.62	725.19	647.53	884.77

Notes: (a) Standard errors were corrected for heteroscedasticity using White's consistent estimator of the covariance matrix. (b) *, ** and *** indicate statistical significance on a two-tailed test at the 10%, 5% and 1% levels, respectively. (c) The joint significance of the slope coefficients is tested using a Wald test (see Greene 2000, p. 507).

than the non-indigenous. Finally, people in all occupational categories earn significantly more than the unskilled, *ceteris paribus*, the most lucrative occupations being Professionals, Specialist Managers, Other Managers and Associate Professionals.

11.7   ECONOMETRIC ANALYSIS OF THE PROBABILITY OF MOVING

The probit equation that explains the probability of moving (equation (11.3)) was estimated using LIMDEP's univariate probit routine (Greene 1998, p. 444). The equation's estimated coefficients appear in Table 11.5. Column 1 lists the coefficient on the differential present value of lifetime income in the origin and destination regions followed by the coefficients of variables that proxy the cost of moving. The version of the probit model in Column 2 includes only variables that proxy the cost of moving. Column 3 contains a version of the probit model that includes only the differential present value of lifetime income in the origin and destination regions. The joint significance of all coefficients (except the constant) is tested using a chi-square statistic (Greene 1998, p. 444), the value of which appears at the bottom of Table 11.5 and is statistically significant at the 1-per-cent level. The coefficients are very similar in magnitude from one version of the model to another.

The coefficient of DIFF-NPV in Column 1 and Column 3 is small (0.0006) but different from zero at the 1-per-cent level of statistical significance. The stability of the coefficients across the three versions of the probit equation presented in Table 11.5 considerably simplifies the computation and interpretation of the marginal effect of DIFF-NPV.[10] The marginal effect of DIFF–NPV, is 0.0001. This means that a \$1 000 increase in the present value of the lifetime-annual-income differential results in a 0.01-per-cent increase in the probability of moving. A \$100 000 increase in the present value of the lifetime-annual-income differential is required to increase in the probability of moving by one per cent. This very small, although statistically significant, effect constitutes weak evidence in support of the human-capital model.

The following *ceteris-paribus* results are observed in relation to the variables that reflect the costs of moving. Consistent with the human-capital model of migration, the coefficients of marital status and type of family have the expected signs and are statistically significant. Men who are in a registered marriage are less likely to move than other men. Men with spouses but no children and men in families with children less than 15 years old have approximately the same propensity to move as independent males. Men in families with children older than 15 years are less likely to move than independent males. Immigrants who arrived in Australia prior to 1981 and between 1981 and 1985 are less likely to

Table 11.5
Probability of Moving

Variable	Coefficient (1)	Coefficient (2)	Coefficient (3)
Constant	−0.9311 ***	−0.9241 ***	−1 .1299 ***
DIFF-NPV	0.0006 ***		0.0006 ***
DMARL1	−0.3181 ***	−0.3174 ***	
DKIDS1	0.0206	0.0192	
DKIDS2	−0.0135	−0.0170	
DKIDS3	−0.3962 ***	−0.4017 ***	
DKIDS4	−0.5737 ***	−0.5811 ***	
DKIDS5	−0.6276 ***	−0.6325 ***	
DYARP1	−0.1458 ***	−0.1509 ***	
DYARP2	−0.2161 ***	−0.2186 ***	
DYARP3	−0.0450	−0.0495	
DEDUC1	0.1243 ***	0.1160 ***	
DEDUC2	0.1292 *	0.1237 *	
DEDUC3	0.0700 **	0.0657 **	
DEDUC4	0.1652 ***	0.1540 ***	
DEDUC5	0.1495 **	0.1355 **	
DEDUC6	0.3730 ***	0.3582 ***	
DEDUC7	0.4029 ***	0.3929 ***	
DEDUC8	0.3474 ***	0.3192 ***	
R2	0.3278	0.3283	0.2832
chi-sq stat	776.72 ***	794.06 ***	16.02 ***
N	21 381	21 381	21 381

Note: *, ** and *** indicate a statistically significant difference on a two-tailed test at the 10%, 5% and 1% levels, respectively.

move than the Australian born. Those who arrived between 1986 and 1990 are indistinguishable from the Australian born in their propensity to move. Educated men are more likely to move than men who left school before age 16 and acquired no other educational qualifications. Education at the tertiary level has a large positive impact on the propensity to move; those with a bachelor's degree (only), a postgraduate diploma or a post-graduate degree are the most likely to move.

11.8 CONCLUSION

Our test of the human-capital model of internal migration, using Australian unit-record data finds weak evidence that Australian men move in response to potential gains in lifetime income. Certainly, our results suggest that Australian male labour-force participants are less likely to move in response to individual monetary incentives than their North American counterparts. This raises a whole range of questions:

- Is it due to lack of labour-market information about specific job opportunities? Most Australian newspapers and other sources of job information are State based and have a State-based circulation, which makes it difficult to obtain information about job opportunities in other States (Flood et al. 1991, p. 5).
- Is it related to labour-market demand characteristics, such as more intra-firm geographical transfer with promotion in North America than in Australia? Flood et al. (1991, p. 5) make the point that in Australia, firms are generally organised into State branches, and within-branch transfers are more common than inter-state transfers.
- Is it due to institutional differences? Only since the mid 1990s has centralised wage-fixing been replaced by enterprise bargaining in Australia. This suggests that during the time period of our study, 1991 through 1996, wage premiums may have been difficult for potential movers to find, at least within the same occupation. Unemployment benefits in Australia are generous by North American standards and, in general, have no time limit. Employment benefits such as long-service leave and immobile superannuation schemes may explain immobility of employment and thereby a lack of geographic mobility related to economic incentives.
- Is it something about the culture or the geography of the country? Although a large country in terms of land area, Australia has only a few large cities capable of being magnets for those seeking more remunerative jobs and cultural amenities. Australians' apparent fondness for living near 'the beach' may mean that lifestyle considerations outweigh potential income gains in decisions about whether or not to move.

Finally, perhaps we may be permitted to 'blame the data'. Cross-section surveys, although much better than aggregate flow data, are nevertheless ill equipped to analyse the causes and effects of migration. Our inability to distinguish people who are 'truly' stayers from people who moved more than five years ago may explain the small effect of the expected income differential on the propensity to move. Our inability to observe the income profiles of the men in our data set over a series of years, particularly those of inter-regional migrants before and after moving, may obfuscate the effect of lifetime income differentials on the propensity to move. Movers may experience a decrease in income immediately after moving only to recover in the longer term. These issues require longitudinal data, spanning not just a few years but a decade or more. Longitudinal data are available in other countries but not in Australia. Until such data are available and are used in more definitive studies of migration behaviour, we cautiously conclude that economic incentives play a smaller role in the internal migration decisions of Australian men than of their North American counterparts.

NOTES

1. The percentage of all Australians who changed their usual address has been high for several decades: 43 per cent in both 1991–96 and 1986–91 (computations by the authors using ABS 1998 and ABS 1988, respectively); 43 per cent in 1981–86 (Bell 1996a, p. 149); 41 per cent in both 1976–81 and 1971–76 and 39 per cent in 1966–71 (Department of Immigration and Ethnic Affairs 1986: 4–5).
2. Bell (1996b, p. 9) found that about 50 per cent of address changes involve distances of 25 kilometres or less. Two-thirds involve distances of 50 kilometres or less. Moves of 500 kilometres or more account for less than 13 per cent of internal migration.
3. See, for example, Newton and Bell (1996); Bell (1991) and (1995); Flood et al. (1991; Department of Immigration and Ethnic Affairs (1986); Rowland (1979), all of which contain extensive bibliographies.
4. The authors wish to thank an anonymous referee of an earlier report of this study for this suggestion.
5. People living in institutions such as prisons and hospitals are excluded because they are unlikely to report incomes that reflect participation in the labour market. On the other hand, visitors to households are included in the analysis because the same data are collected on them as are collected on people living at home on Census night.
6. Only those overseas immigrants who became Australian residents prior to 1991 have the necessary data with which to identify moves, namely, a valid Region of Usual Residence five years prior to Census night 1996.
7. The age criterion ensures that the young men in our sample were old enough to participate in the labour market, and the old men in our sample were unlikely to have retired in the interval 1991 through 1995, over which moves are observed.
8. A major problem for studies of migration is the aggregation of the Australian Capital Territory (ACT) and Northern Territory (NT), which are not contiguous, into one region.
9. This part of our analysis is similar to that of Enchautegui (1997: 537).

10. The marginal effect of an exogenous variable in a probit model is nonlinear and is typically computed at the mean values of the remaining variables in the model. However, if the probit model contains dummy exogenous variables it no longer makes sense to compute the marginal effects at the means; rather they should be computed at specific combinations of the dummy variables.

REFERENCES

Australian Bureau of Statistics (1988), *1991 Census of Population and Housing: Household Sample File. User's Guide*, data provided on electronic medium through the Social Science Data Archives, ANU, Canberra.

Australian Bureau of Statistics (1998), *1996 Census of Population and Housing: Household Sample File. Technical Documentation*, Catalogue No. 2037.0 [plus data provided on electronic medium], Canberra: The Australian Government Publishing Service.

Bell, Martin (1991), *Internal Migration in Australia 1981–86*, Canberra: The Australian Government Publishing Service.

Bell, Martin (1995), *Internal Migration in Australia 1986–91: Overview Report*, Canberra: The Australian Government Publishing Service.

Bell, Martin (1996a), 'Repeat and Return Migration', in P.W. Newton and M. Bell (eds), *Population Shift, Mobility and Change in Australia*, Canberra: The Australian Government Publishing Service.

Bell, Martin (1996b), *Understanding Internal Migration*, Canberra: Bureau of Immigration, Multicultural and Population Research.

Bell, M. and C. Maher (1995), *Internal Migration in Australia 1986–91: The Labour Force*, Canberra: The Australian Government Publishing Service.

Borjas, George J., Stephen G. Bronars and Stephen J. Trejo (1992), 'Self-Selection and Internal Migration in the United States', *Journal of Urban Economics*, **32**, 159–85.

Department of Immigration and Ethnic Affairs (1986), *Adult Migrant Education Program, 1984–85 Research Program: Internal Migration,* [Researched and written by Neilson Associates Pty Ltd.], Canberra: The Australian Government Publishing Service.

Enchautegui, Maria E. (1997), 'Welfare Payments and Other Economic Determinants of Female Migration', *Journal of Labor Economics*, **15** (3), pt 1: 529–54.

Flood, J., C.A. Maher, P.J. Newton and J.R. Roy (1991), *Determinants of Internal Migration in Australia*, Canberra: DITAC.

Greene, William H. (1998), *LIMDEP, Version 7.0, User's Manual*, revised edition, Castle Hill, NSW: Econometric Software, Inc.

Greene, William H. (2000), *Econometric Analysis*, (4th edition), Upper Saddle River, New Jersey: Prentice-Hall International.

Greenwood, Michael (1975), 'Research on Internal Migration in the United States', *Journal of Economic Literature*, **13** (June), 397–433.

Greenwood, Michael (1985), 'Human Migration: Theory, Models, and Empirical Studies', *Journal of Regional Science*, **25** (4), 521–44.

Groenewold, Nicolaas (1993), 'The Interaction of Regional Unemployment Rates, Regional Wages and Inter-Regional Migration in Australia', Centre for Regional Economic Analysis, University of Tasmania. Paper – No. TS–04.

Harris, John R. and Michael Todaro (1970), 'Migration, Unemployment and Development: A Two-Sector Analysis', *American Economic Review*, **60** (1), 126–42.

Hunt, Janet C., and James B. Kau (1985), 'Migration and Wage Growth: A Human Capital Approach', *Southern Economic Journal*, **51** (3), 697–710.

Lewis, Phillip and Russell Ross (1995), 'Do Labour Markets Adjust?', in Keith Norris and Mark Wooden (eds), *The Changing Australian Labour Market*, Commission Paper No. 11, Economic Planning Advisory Commission, Canberra: The Australian Government Publishing Service.

Newton, P.W. and M. Bell (eds) (1996*), Population Shift. Mobility and Change in Australia*, Canberra: The Australian Government Publishing Service.

Nakosteen, Robert A. and Michael Zimmer (1980), 'Migration and Income: The Question of Self-Selection', *Southern Economic Journal*, **46** (3), 840–51.

Robinson, Chris and Nigel Tomes (1982), 'Self-Selection and Interprovincial Migration in Canada', *Canadian Journal of Economics*, **15** (3), 474–502.

Rodgers, John L. and Joan R. Rodgers (1997), 'The Economic Impact of Rural-to-Urban Migration in the United States: Evidence for Male Labor-Force Participants', *Social Science Quarterly*, **78** (4), 937–54.

Rodgers, Joan R. and John L. Rodgers (2000), 'The Effect of Geographic Mobility on Labor-Force Participants in the United States', *Journal of Labor Research*, **21** (1), 117–32.

Rowland, D.T. (1979), *Internal Migration in Australia*, Canberra: The Australian Government Publishing Service.

Sjaastad, Larry A. (1962), 'The Costs and Returns of Human Migration', *Journal of Political Economy*, **70** (5), 80–93.

Tienda, Marta and F.D. Wilson (1991), 'Migration and the Earnings of Hispanic Men.' *American Sociological Review*, **57** (October), 661–78.

Todaro, Michael (1969), 'A Model of Labor Migration and Urban Development in Less Developed Countries', *American Economic Review*, **59** (1), 138–48.

12 Populate or Perish: Scale, Growth and Australia's Post-War Immigration

John S. Landon-Lane and Peter E. Robertson

12.1 POST-WAR IMMIGRATION IN AUSTRALIA

What was the economic effect of Australia's high levels of post-war immigration? The answer to this question is important in the light of recent changes in immigration policy in Australia. There has been a significantly lower intake of migrants during the 1990s compared to the post-war average and, following the Fitzgerald Report (CAAIP 1988) an increased emphasis on the skill content of immigrants. This chapter reviews the long-term growth effects of Australia's post-war migration policy. We construct a model of economic growth in a small open economy, calibrated to Australian data. The model is used to determine how much capital accumulation and growth might have occurred in the absence of immigration. The model therefore provides quantitative estimates of the impact of post-war immigration on growth and income levels.[1]

The rate of net migration in Australia is shown in Figure 12.1. The post-war era kicked off with historically high rates of immigration from 1947–51, when net migration was around 3–4 per cent of the labour force. The subsequent rate of net migration is shown to be about 2 per cent of the labour force from 1950 to 1970. After this it falls slightly, mainly due to the rising size of the labour force, with a roughly constant flow of immigrants of just under 90 000 per year. This was roughly in accordance with government policy, which aimed for a rate of 1–2 per cent per year (Pope 1982).

Given such a large and sustained flow of migrants, it is difficult to imagine that it did not have a profound effect on the national economy. The motives for immigration, however, were not based on economic objectives. This is evident in Arthur Calwell's 'twenty million' speech:[2]

> Twenty million Australians in our time? ... to develop our country, to make its defense more secure, to gain added riches from the soil and machines ... and a higher standard of living for all.

Arndt (1968) interprets the political climate, arguing that impetus to populate Australia with immigrants was due to:

> the sudden awareness of herself as a small nation in possession of a large continent, far from her allies, close to powerful and potentially eruptive forces to her North.

Despite this initial political impetus for migration, according to Arndt (1968), economic arguments became more important over subsequent decades. In particular the main benefits of immigration were thought to be from economies of scale. These are argued to exist, first, in the provision of social overhead capital such as roads, electricity distribution, education and health. Second, a larger population also provides a larger domestic market for industry, which is important for the non-traded sector.

Nevertheless by the mid-1970s, there was substantial questioning of the existing immigration policy (Douglas 1982). Lloyd (1982) argued first, that there was a lack of convincing empirical evidence that economies of scale are significant. Second, he argued that the high rates of protection, designed to attract migrants to Australia's manufacturing industry, resulted in restricting the competitive process that would otherwise cause industry to exploit available economies of scale. According to Mitchell (1969), economies of scale were exhausted by 1960. The view that economies of scale and other external effects of immigration are small, if at all positive, is now generally accepted (Foster 1996; Castles et al. 1998).

To see this orthodox argument suppose aggregate output is produced with an aggregate production function, $Y = F(K, L)$, where K is inputs of capital services and L is inputs of labour services and that $F(K, L)$ exhibits constant returns to scale. Then the production function can be written as $y = f(k)$, where $y = Y/L$ and $k = K/L$. If K is constant, then an inflow of immigrants will result in a reduction of GDP per worker, y, since an increase in L causes a reduction in k. This consequence of immigration in a constant returns to scale world, and fixed capital, is expressed starkly by Withers:

> [T]he situation of the 1890s, where Australia had the highest standard of living in the world, no longer exists because Australia, as it were, chose to share that high standard of living with the large number of people that came after that period. (Withers, as cited in Douglas, 1982)

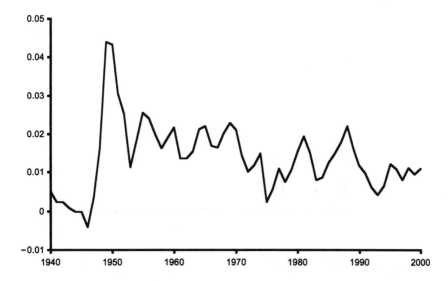

Source: Australian Historical Statistics

Figure 12.1   Net Migration as a Fraction of the Labour Force, 1940–2000

This decline in GDP per worker is a consequence of the implicit assumption that, since immigrants do not own capital, they are poor relative to domestic residents. Hence average GDP per person falls, even though, in fact, everyone may be better off than they were prior to the arrival of immigrants. The decline in GDP per worker is real, but it is also a consequence of averaging across the income of the original population, and the less wealthy migrant population.

However in the medium to long term, the capital stock is not fixed. If, for example, physical capital can substitute for natural resources then immigration will also generate a positive effect on growth rates. To clarify this point consider a small economy, that can borrow as much as it wishes at a constant interest rate, r. Given a steady state level of capital $k^*=K/L$, an increase in L to, say, L', will induce borrowing so that the steady state level of capital per worker is maintained. Hence K increases to K' such that $K' = k^*L'$. If capital is costly to install, the adjustment will not be instantaneous. The economy converges to restore the steady state ratio $k^* = K/L$. Immigration therefore induces growth.

This response is illustrated in Figure 12.2, which illustrates the logarithm of GDP per worker. When the economy grows at a constant rate, the log of GDP per worker has a constant positive slope. At a time, t_0, when immigration occurs, output per worker declines since capital per worker has declined. As discussed above, this can be thought of as the cost of immigration to a representative incumbent resident, if she was required to share her income with new residents.

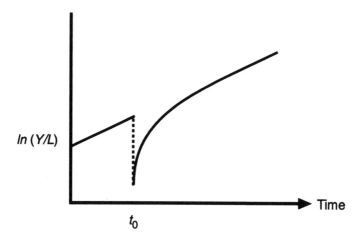

Figure 12.2   GDP per Worker

In this way it overstates the actual cost to incumbents, since actual transfers to immigrants were not designed to bring immigrants up to the Australian average income. Similarly, the increase in growth can be thought of as the catch-up of the less wealthy immigrant group, and need not imply any real income gains to the original inhabitants.

Thus, in a constant-returns-to-scale framework, immigration reduces output per worker in the short term, and has no real effect on average welfare in the long term. In addition, however, immigration policies came with significant economic costs. First, the policy was supported with high rates of assistance for immigrants. Further, as discussed above, a high tariff rate was also a cost of Australia's immigration policy (Lloyd 1982). Moreover, there is an increasing concern over negative environmental externalities associated with population size. Hence, the failure to adopt suitable policies in the past may have resulted in unnecessary costs of immigration (Clarke and Ng 1994). Thus, the current orthodox view is supportive of reductions in immigration rates and, moreover, questions the wisdom of the high rates of immigration during the post-war era.

12.2   SCALE, IMMIGRATION AND NEW GROWTH THEORY

The revival in growth theory over the last 15 years provides an opportunity to review the orthodox view of post-war immigration. A central tenet of endogenous growth models is that the size of a country may have important consequences for wealth accumulation. A number of empirical studies have tried to identify such consequences, with only limited success. Little attention has been paid to the effects of immigration in this respect.

The effect of an increased flow of labour on the growth rate depends on the underlying causes of growth. There is substantial debate on this issue, but there are two orthodox views. In the neoclassical growth framework, growth in output per worker can be described by technical progress (output per unit of input), which is independent of the accumulation of inputs. The second view – endogenous growth theory – is that the accumulation of factors is critical in determining the rate of technical progress, and hence the rate of growth.

The effect of immigration in a neoclassical model was discussed in the previous section. Some endogenous growth models, such as that of Romer (1990), based on production functions that exhibit some form of scale economies in the generation of knowledge. Romer's model emphasises that – since knowledge is non-rivalrous – a higher population size does not depreciate the knowledge stock per worker, in the same way it reduces the size of the physical capital stock per worker. In this type of model, therefore, it may first appear that immigration has significant benefits by increasing the scale of the economy. This hypothesis can be criticised for two reasons. First, Jones (1999) and Young (1998) argue that the prediction – that higher population levels result in faster growth rates of GDP per worker – conflicts with evidence of twentieth-century growth. Second, for small open economies, such as Australia, the relevant scale effect is not the size of the domestic economy but the international economy, since knowledge can readily be imported.

Nevertheless, immigration may have aided the process of learning and assimilation of existing knowledge into the workforce by increasing the domestic market size and so allowing domestic firms to achieve economies of scale due to fixed costs. Although market size can be expanded through trade, the size of the domestic market is clearly still important for the non-exportable sector, such as services and public utilities as well as a protected manufacturing sector.[3]

The evidence on the existence of economies of scale in Australia is fairly scant. Jolley (1971) looked for evidence of economies of scale in post-war Australian non-primary production. He finds mixed evidence, with estimates of the elasticity of scale ranging from –0.08 to 0.3, over the period 1948–49 to 1965–66. Tran Van Hoa (1969) also finds evidence of economies of scale in Australian manufacturing during the post-war era, 1949–50 to 1959–60.[4] Further anecdotal evidence is presented by Forster (1970). He finds that there was a growing degree of specialisation and significant agglomeration effects in manufacturing in the post-war era. Forster also suggests that small industry size resulted in restrictive shortages of suitably trained labour, possibly reflecting the high costs of training small numbers of people.

This evidence, however, is supported by a recent a revival in empirical research on external economies of scale and other types of spillover between firms. In particular, Caballero and Lyons (1990, 1992) and Lindström (2000) find evidence of large external effects in European and US manufacturing value added data. Lindström (2000), for example, finds elasticities of around 0.3. That is, a 1-per-cent increase in aggregate value added, results in a 0.3-per-cent increase in each firm's output. Similarly, Oulton (1996) reports values of 0.20 to 0.24 in British manufacturing data.

The interpretation of these results is not uncontroversial. However, the preferred interpretation of Oulton (1996) and Caballero and Lyons (1990) is that their results represent positive spillovers within manufacturing industries.[5] The authors consider that these may be a result of knowledge spillovers, and improved matching between agents within larger industries. Nevertheless, they do not rule out traditional sources such as the availability of skilled labour, shared workforce experience within industries and the provision of public infrastructure. Moreover, the values obtained are in a similar range to the earlier Australian studies. Hence, from the perspective of the immigration debate, the most important contribution of new growth theory is the revival of empirical interest in scale effects and spillovers at the industry level. The remainder of this chapter re-considers the role of immigration on Australia's post-war experience in the light of this recent empirical literature.

12.3   SIMULATION ANALYSIS

If economies of scale exist in industry, what effect does immigration have on growth rates and income levels? Suppose there are economies associated with the size of the capital stock. Immigration increases the labour force, but reduces capital per worker. It will also raise the return to capital and so induce capital accumulation. With more labour and more capital, increasing returns to scale imply greater output per unit input. Thus, immigration results in a real productivity gain, because it allows a greater scale of operation. The resulting time path for an economy that exhibits economies of scale, is illustrated in Figure 12.3.

From this figure, it can be seen that the GDP per worker still falls initially. Eventually, however, GDP rises due to accumulation.[6] As before, the fall in GDP per worker need not imply that welfare declines, and is consistent with a Pareto improvement in welfare. Due to accumulation of capital and the economies of scale, GDP eventually exceeds the level that would have been attained in the absence of immigration, as indicated by the dashed line. The constant difference between the dashed and solid line at the end of the transitional period is a measure of the gains from immigration.

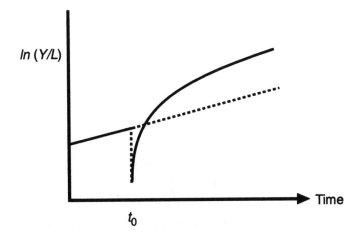

Figure 12.3   Time Path under Economies of Scale

12.3.1   Investment Decisions and GDP Growth

We consider a small open economy that faces an exogenous world cost of borrowing, $\bar{r}$ (Pitchford 1990; Obstfeld and Rogoff 1996). Hence, consumption and investment decisions are separable since debt allows investment and savings to diverge. A representative firm chooses investment to maximise

$$\sum_{t=0}^{\infty} \left(\frac{1}{1+\bar{r}}\right)^t \left[B_t F(K_t, A_t L_t) - \phi(I_t / K_t) - w_t L_t - I_t\right] \qquad (12.1)$$

subject to

$$I_t = K_{t+1} - K_t + \delta K_t \qquad (12.2)$$

$$\phi(I_t / K_t) = \chi I_t^{\beta} K_t^{1-\beta}, \beta > 1 \qquad (12.3)$$

$$F(K_t, (AL)_t) = K_t^{\alpha} (AL)^{1-\alpha}, \alpha < 1 \qquad (12.4)$$

Effective labour inputs are AL and grows at an exogenous rate, $(AL)_t = (AL)_0 (1+\lambda)^t$. Hence, if the growth rates of A and L are n and g respectively, then $\lambda = (1+n)(1+g)$.

The Lagrangian for this problem is

$$\sum_{t=0}^{\infty}\left(\frac{1}{1+\bar{r}}\right)^{t}[B_{t}F(K_{t},A_{t}L_{t})-\phi(I_{t}/K_{t})-w_{t}L_{t}-I_{t}$$
$$-q_{t}(K_{t+1}-K_{t}-I_{t}+\delta K_{t})] \tag{12.5}$$

Maximising with respect to I_{t} gives

$$q_{t}=1+\beta\chi\left(\frac{I_{t}}{K_{t}}\right)^{\beta-1} \tag{12.6}$$

This can be rearranged to give the growth rate of capital as a function of q_{t}.

$$\frac{I_{t}}{K_{t}}=\frac{K_{t+1}-K_{t}}{K_{t}}+\delta=\left(\frac{q_{t}-1}{\beta\chi}\right)^{\frac{1}{\beta-1}} \tag{12.7}$$

The first order condition with respect to K_{t+1} gives

$$q_{t+1}-q_{t}=\bar{r}q_{t}+\delta q_{t+1}-B_{t+1}F_{1}(K_{t+1},A_{t+1}L_{t+1})-$$
$$(\beta-1)\chi(I_{t+1}/K_{t+1})^{\beta} \tag{12.8}$$

We allow for the possibility of external economies of scale, through the productivity term B_{t}. Specifically we assume there is a large number of identical firms, indexed by $i \in [0,1]$. We assume each firm's capital stock provides external benefits to other firms. Specifically we assume $B_{t}=B_{0}\left(\int_{i=0}^{1} K_{it}dK\right)^{\gamma}$
$=B_{0}K_{t}^{\gamma}$, $\gamma<\alpha<1$. Aggregate output can therefore be written as $Y=K^{\alpha+\gamma}(AL)^{1-\alpha}$. In what follows we also assume $\alpha+\gamma<1$, so that the model exhibits diminishing returns to reproducible factors.

12.3.2 Balanced Path Growth

On a balanced path the growth of output and capital will be constant. We let μ be the balanced path growth rate of capital. Hence on a balanced path, $I_{t}/K_{t}=\mu+\delta$. Substituting this into (12.6) and solving for the balanced path value of q^* gives

$$q^* = 1 + (\delta + \lambda)^{\beta - 1} \beta \chi \tag{12.9}$$

Similarly on a balanced path the left-hand-side of (12.8) must be zero, since $q = q^*$. Hence it follows that the marginal product of capital, $B_{t+1} F_1(K_{s+1}, A_{t+1} L_{t+1})$, must be constant. Substituting for q^* gives

$$\alpha K_{t+1}^{\alpha + \gamma - 1} (AL)_{t+1}^{1-\alpha} = (\bar{r} + \delta)(1 + \beta \chi (\delta + \lambda)^{\beta - 1}) -$$

$$(\beta - 1)\chi(\delta + n)^{\beta} \equiv M \tag{12.10}$$

For this to be constant over time requires

$$(1 + \mu) = (1 + \lambda)^{\frac{\alpha - 1}{\alpha + \gamma - 1}} \tag{12.11}$$

Although the marginal product is constant when capital grows at rate μ, the capital labour ratio is continually rising. This is consistent with the Australian growth experience where the capital–labour ratio has risen for long periods. From (12.10) note that this constant value of M implicitly defines a level of capital that is consistent with a balanced path. That is

$$K_t^* = \left(\frac{M}{\alpha(AL)_t^{1-\alpha}} \right)^{\frac{1}{\alpha + \gamma - 1}} \tag{12.12}$$

Thus, given the parameters of the production function and the exogenous values of labour, L_t, and labour augmenting technology, A_t, we can determine K_t^*. Finally by linearising around the steady state, we obtain an expression for the growth rate of capital (Landon-Lane and Robertson 2001).

$$\ln K_t = \ln K_0^* + \ln(1 + \mu)t + e^{-\varepsilon t}(\ln K_0 - \ln K_0^*) \tag{12.13}$$

where the convergence rate, ε, is a function of the parameters of the model. This is a closed form expression that describes the evolution of capital given the current level of capital and knowledge about the balanced path level of capital.

12.4   CALIBRATION AND SIMULATION METHOD

12.4.1   Calibration

There are six structural parameters that need to be determined. They are the real interest rate, $\bar{r}$, capital's share of income, α, the shift parameter of the investment adjustment cost function, χ, the elasticity of adjustment costs to investment, β, the depreciation rate of capital, δ, and the effect of the externality of production, γ. The calibrated values for the parameters used can be found in Table 12.1, and are standard for this type of simulation (Kydland and Prescott 1982; Hansen 1985). The real interest rate is assumed to be 5 per cent, which equates to a time discount rate of approximately 0.95. This value is certainly in the middle of the range of values used in the literature for the time discount rate of a model where one period equates to a calendar year. Capital's share of income is calibrated to be 36 per cent of total income of the economy. The values for the parameters that define the investment adjustment cost function, (12.3), are chosen so that the adjustment cost of installing new capital is between 10 per cent and 14 per cent of the total investment cost, in line with adjustment costs of capital in Barnett and Sakellaris (1999). The depreciation rate was chosen to be 5 per cent per year.

A critical parameter is the size of the scale effect, γ. To obtain an upper bound for our experiments, we use equation (12.11) and the trend rates of growth. Figure 12.4 shows that that there is a change in slope in output per worker around the year 1971. Values for μ are calculated for the two periods, by estimating a regression of the log of real gross domestic product (GDP) on a time trend for pre- and post-1971 periods. Similarly the growth rate of labour, n, is obtained by estimating a regression of the log of total workforce on the time trends.[7] Then from (12.11), for each period, we have two unknowns, γ and $\lambda = (1+n)(1+g)$.

Table 12.1
Calibrated Values of the Structural Parameters

Parameter	Value
$\bar{r}$	0.05
α	0.36
χ	1.4
β	2
δ	0.05

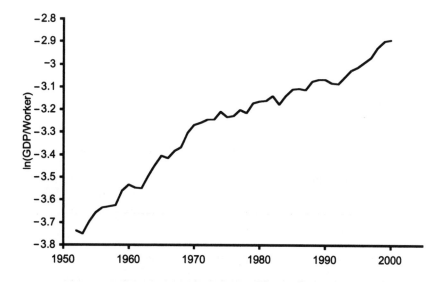

Figure 12.4 Output per Worker in Australia, 1952–2000

Setting $g = 0$ provides us with the upper bound on γ, of approximately 0.25.[8] This compares favourably with other empirical evidence. For example, Lindstrom's (2000) estimate of the output elasticity of scale in the manufacturing sector is 0.3. Given a manufacturing share of GDP of approximately 20 per cent, this implies an elasticity for aggregate output of 0.06. In terms of our model, where the scale effect works through the capital stock, this implies an upper estimate of $\gamma = 0.06/\alpha = 0.16$. In view of this, we regard a more modest elasticity of around 0.05 to 0.1 as reasonable for Australia in the immediate post-war period. In the experiments below, however, we report results for a value of γ equal 0.2, 0.1 and 0. The implied values of n, g and γ are given in Table 12.2, for each period.

12.4.2 Counterfactual Scenario

The counterfactual experiment that is carried out looks at the outcomes that would have occurred, according to the calibrated model, if the migration that occurred in Australia from 1947 to 1952 had not materialised. That is, a counterfactual workforce series, L', that excludes the effect of the observed net migration to Australia from 1947 until 1952 is constructed according to the following formula,

Table 12.2
Growth Rates for Australia, 1952–2000

1952–1971			
γ	0.2	0.1	0
μ	0.0488		
n	0.0223		
g	0.0107	0.0182	0.0258
1972–2000			
γ	0.2	0.1	0
μ	0.0311		
n	0.0196		
g	0.0019	0.0068	0.0117

$$L'_t = L'_{t-1} \frac{L_t - 0.47M_t}{L_{t-1}} \tag{12.14}$$

where M_t refers to net migration. It is assumed that 47 per cent of all migrants are immediately available to work (see Table 12.3 in Withers 1989). Note that the workforce growth rate used in (12.14) is exactly the growth rate in workforce that would give $L'_t = L_t - 0.47M_t$ if $L'_{t-1} = L_{t-1}$. Hence, the counterfactual workforce series, L', includes the cumulative effect on the workforce of not having migration for the preceding periods. In particular, the counterfactual workforce after 1952 has exactly the same growth rate as the observed data. Thus the counterfactual experiment looks at the effect on the economy if expected net migration, equal to those who came to Australia in the proceeding years, failed to materialise.[9] The counterfactual and actual labour data are shown in Figure 12.5.

Given either the observed (base case) values of L, or counterfactual values of L, (12.14) can be used to calculate the implied value of K^* for each period. The evolution of the capital stock, K_t, is governed by (12.13). If L_t does not equal L_t^*, the balanced growth path value for L_t, then $K_t \neq K_t^*$ in period t and the value of K_{t+1} will be determined by (12.13). Once a capital stock series has been constructed for both the baseline and counterfactual case it is possible to use the production function, (12.4), to construct an output series for each case,

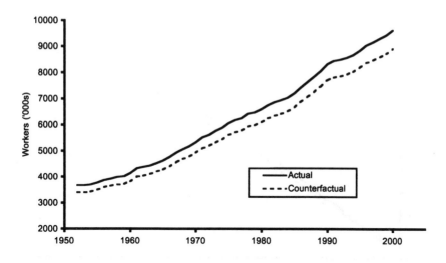

Figure 12.5   Actual and Counterfactual Workforce, 1952–2000

and thus to construct an output per worker series for both the baseline and counterfactual case.

12.5   RESULTS

The initial impact of the non-arrival of the migrants in 1952 is for each worker present in Australia in 1952 to be better off in an output per worker sense. This is due to the fact that capital is slow to change which results in the fall in output being smaller in magnitude than the fall in workforce. Figure 12.6 below depicts the long-run effects under the assumptions used in this experiment for different values of γ, the value of the production externality. In the long run, when there are production externalities, the output per worker in the counterfactual series eventually falls below the output per worker in the baseline series. Hence, when there are production externalities, the long-run welfare, as measured by output per worker, of those workers present in 1952 is greater in the presence of migration.

Under the assumptions of the model, and given that population growth rates have not changed, the long-run growth rate of output per worker does not change. The initial slowing of growth in output per worker in the counterfactual example is due to the slower growth rate in the capital stock, required to maintain the balanced path marginal product of capital.

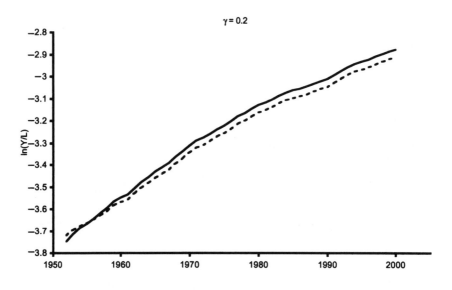

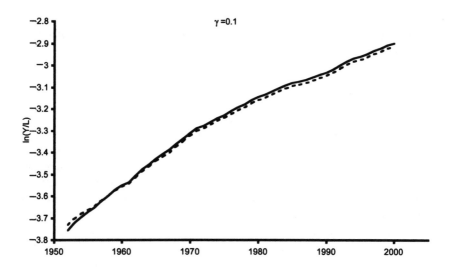

Figure 12.6   Baseline and Counterfactual Output per Worker Series for Australia

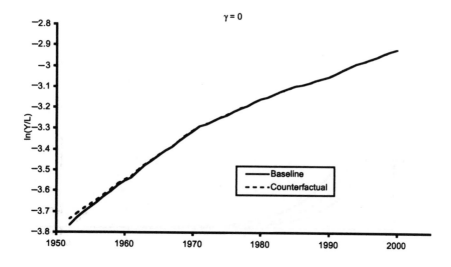

Figure 12.6   Baseline and Counterfactual Output per Worker Series for Australia (continued)

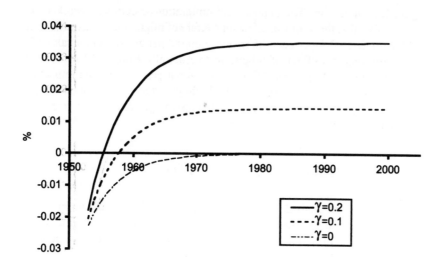

Figure 12.7   Difference in Output per Worker between Baseline and Counterfactual (%)

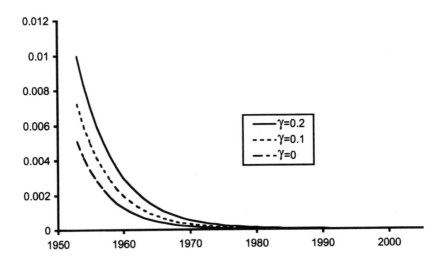

*Figure 12.8   Difference in Growth Rates in Output per Worker between
               Baseline and Counterfactual*

Figure 12.7 shows the effect of post-war immigration on output per worker. For a value of $\gamma = 0.2$, the long-run effect on welfare of migration to Australia from 1947 to 1952 is a 3.5-per-cent difference in output per worker. For a value of $\gamma = 0.1$, the long-run effect of migration to Australia from 1947 to 1952 is approximately a 1.4-per-cent difference in output per worker. The impact on growth rates is shown in Figure 12.8. This highlights that these fairly substantial welfare gains, only imply very slight differences in growth rates over the 15-year transition period.

12.6   SUMMARY AND CONCLUSION

'Populate-or-perish': this slogan sums up the motives of Australia's immigration policies. Economic arguments were never a dominant consideration until the end of the twentieth century. When the economics of immigration was debated in the 1970s and 1980s, the emergent orthodox view was that, with constant-returns-to-scale, immigration provided no real income growth in the long run, and may impose negative environmental externalities.

In expressing the current orthodox view that immigration might actually reduce average levels of GDP per capita, Lloyd (1982) reflected '… it is difficult to believe that governments make monumental errors of this kind and sustain them for 30 years.[10] Recent research on the causes of growth suggests the possibility that, indeed, the government's policy was not a monumental error. The view that country size is important has become popular through various endogenous growth models. Although the evidence is not strong, a number of studies have argued that there may be significant external economies of scale in modern manufacturing sectors.

We present a growth model that allows for production externalities and reconsiders the effect that this externality would have on the overall impact of migration to Australia's economy. We therefore restrict attention to the immediate post-war immigration period, 1947–52, where the conventional wisdom suggests that such economies of scale were likely to have been more significant, and look at the long-run effects of this immediate wave of immigrants.

We find that with modest economies of scale around the 1950s and 1960s, post-war immigration would have resulted in substantial economic gains. For a moderate-sized externality ($\gamma = 0.1$) it was found that the long-run effect on welfare, in terms of output per worker, was around 1.4 per cent. This is not an insignificant welfare gain. If the modest scale effects were indeed present in post-war Australia, the cost of attaining Australia's cultural diversity may not be as high as the orthodox view suggests.

NOTES

1   In what follows we ignore many aspects of immigration such as the effect on the age of the workforce, the effect on population support ratios. These aspects of immigration can be controlled by variation in the immigration policy, and do not bear on the fundamental issue of the effect of an increased labour supply on national wealth.

2   See Pope (1982). Borrie (1963) discusses the traditional motive for immigration prior to the Second World War.

3   Immigration may also interact with productivity growth by accelerating the adoption of technology or new vintages of capital. This possibility is discussed by Nevile (1990).

4   His results also show a smaller scale effect in this period compared to the first half of the century.

5   Basu and Fernald (1995) argue that these results are so large that it is puzzling that the sources of the externality are not more obvious. They therefore reject this explanation for the large estimated coefficients.

6   Robertson (forthcoming) shows that immigration may result in a slow growth of human capital during this transitional phase.

7   The two time periods used are 1952–71 and 1972–2000.

8   If we considered the first period only, a higher value of *g* is possible. We imposed a restriction that *g* must be constant across the two periods, however, so restricted attention to values less than 0.25.

9   In this sense the assumption is that the migrants never made it to Australia. This is treated as an unanticipated shock. That is, decisions before the realisation of this shock would have been made under the assumption that these migrants were going to arrive. Therefore, the capital stock brought into the beginning of the period in 1952 will be the same for both the baseline case and the counterfactual case.

10   Lloyd is cited in Chapter 10 of Douglas (1982). Nevertheless, current orthodoxy suggests that governments have made such errors with regard to tariff policy.

REFERENCES

Arndt H.W. (1968), *A Small Rich Industrial Country. Studies in Australian Development Aid and Trade*, Melbourne: F.W. Chelshire.

Barnett, S.A. and P. Sakellaris (1999), 'A New Look at Firm Market Value, Investment, and Adjustment Costs', *Review of Economics and Statistics*, **81** (2), 250–60.

Basu, S. and John G. Fernald (1997), 'Returns to Scale in US Production: Estimates and Implications', *Journal of Political Economy*, **105** (2), 249–83.

Borrie, W.D. (1963), 'The Peopling of Australia', in H.W. Arndt and W.M. Corden (eds), *The Australian Economy*, Melbourne: F.W. Cheshire.

CAAIP [Fitzgerald Report] (1988), *Immigration: A Commitment to Australia. The Report of the Committee to Advise on Australia's Immigration Policies*, Canberra: AGPS.

Caballero, R. and R.K. Lyons (1990), 'Internal vs External Economies in European Industry', *European Economic Review*, **34**, 805–26.

Caballero, R. and R.K. Lyons (1992), 'External Effects in US Procyclical Productivity', *Journal of Monetary Economics*, **29**, 209–25.

Castles, S., W. Foster, R. Ireland and G. Withers (1998), *Immigration and Australia: Myths and Realities*, Sydney: Allen and Unwin.

Clarke, H.R. and Y.K. Ng (1994), 'Population Growth and the Benefits from Optimally Priced Externalities', *Australian Economic Papers*, June, 113–9.

Douglas, D. (ed.) (1982), *The Economics of Australian Immigration: Proceedings of the Conference on the Economics of Immigration*, Sydney: Sydney University Extension Programme.

Forster. C. (1970), 'Economies of Scale and Australian Manufacturing', in C. Forster (ed.), *Australian Economic Development in the Twentieth Century*, Sydney: Allen and Unwin, pp. 123–68.

Foster, W. (1994), *The Macroeconomic Effects of Change in the Size and Composition of Australia's Migrant Intake: Results from the Extended Access Economics Murphy Model*, Canberra: AGPS.

Foster, W. (1996), *Immigration and the Australian Economy*, Department of Immigration and Multicultural Affairs, Canberra: AGPS.

Hansen, G. (1985), 'Indivisible Labor and the Business Cycle', *Journal of Monetary Economics*, **16**.

Jolley, A.N.E. (1971), 'Immigration and Australia's Post-War Economic Growth', *Economic Record*, **47**, 47–59.

Jones, Charles I. (1999), 'Growth: With or Without Scale Effects?', *American Economic Review*, **89** (2), 139–144.

Kydland, F. and E. Prescott (1982), 'Time to Build and Aggregate Fluctuations', *Econometrica*, **50**.

Landon-Lane, John S. and Peter E. Robertson (2001), 'Calibrating Growth Models', mimeo, UNSW.

Lindström, Tomas (2000), 'External Economies in Procyclical Productivity: How Important Are They?', *Journal of Economic Growth*, **5** (2), 163–84.

Lloyd, P.J. (1982), 'The Effects of Immigration on Economic Growth via Technological Change and Economies of Scale', in D. Douglas (ed.), *The Economics of Australian Immigration: Proceedings of the Conference on the Economics of Immigration*, Sydney: Sydney University Extension Programme.

Mitchell, C. (1969), 'A Herd of Sacred Cows: The Economic Case Against Immigration', *Nation*, **18**, 13–16.

Nevile, John (1990), *The Effect of Immigration on Australian Living Standards*, Canberra: AGPS.

Obstfeld, M. and K. Rogoff (1996), *International Macroeconomics*, Cambridge, Massachusetts: MIT Press.

Oulton, N. (1996), 'Increasing Returns and Externalities in UK Manufacturing: Myth or Reality', *Journal of Industrial Economics*, **44**, 99–113.

Pitchford, J.D. (1990), 'Investment and Immigration', EPAC Background Paper 4, Canberra: AGPS.

Pope, David (1982), 'Immigration and Government Policy: Role and Effects', in D. Douglas (ed.), *The Economics of Australian Immigration: Proceedings of the Conference on the Economics of Immigration*, Sydney: Sydney University Extension Programme.

Robertson, Peter E. (forthcoming), 'Demographic Shocks and Human Capital Accumulation in the Uzawa-Lucas Model', *Economics Letters*.

Romer, Paul (1990), 'Endogenous Technical Change', *Journal of Political Economy*, **98** (5), S71-S102.

Tran van Hoa (1969), 'Market Imperfections and Increasing Returns to Scale in Australian Manufacturing Industry', *Economic Record*, **45**, 243–50.

Vamplew, Wray (ed.) (1987), *Australian. Historical Statistics*, Sydney: Fairfax, Syme & Weldon.

Withers, Glenn (1989), 'The Immigration Contribution to Human Capital Labour', in David Pope and Lee J. Alston (eds), *Australia's Greatest Asset: Human Resources in the Nineteenth and Twentieth Centuries*, Annandale, Australia: The Federation Press.

Young, Alwyn (1998), 'Growth Without Scale Effects', *Journal of Political Economy*, **106** (1), 41–63.

APPENDIX

Table 12.3
Summary of Notation

Y	Gross Domestic Product
K	Aggregate capital services
L	Labour- number of workers
A	Productivity of labour services
I	Gross Investment
q	Shadow price of capital (Tobin's q)
γ	Spillover elasticity from capital
μ	Balanced path growth rate of capital
n	Growth rate of Labour
g	Growth rate of Labour efficiency units
λ	Growth rate of effective Labour
$\bar{r}$	Exogenous world cost of borrowing
α	Capital share of GDP
χ	Adjustment cost shift parameter
β	Adjustment cost function elasticity
w	Return to Labour
δ	Depreciation of capital

13 Demographic Change, Foreign Borrowing and Intergenerational Equity

Ross S. Guest and Ian M. McDonald

13.1 INTRODUCTION

Australia has traditionally been a borrower, running current account deficits and accumulating net foreign liabilities. Since the early 1980s the rate of foreign borrowing has increased, causing the level of net foreign liabilities as a percentage of GDP to increase (see Figure 13.1). This increase is due to private sector borrowing and thus private decision making – indeed, as Figure 13.1 shows, the share of public sector borrowing in net foreign liabilities fell to almost zero by 2000. Also, from the early 1980s an increasing share of net foreign liabilities were equity rather than debt, which levelled off during the 1990s, although it increased in the late 1990s (see Figure 13.1).

The growth in net foreign liabilities has led to many expressions of alarm and claims of excessive borrowing by economic commentators. This alarm was greatest in the 1980s and appears to have receded somewhat in the 1990s, perhaps as it became clear that the historically high levels of borrowing were not causing a crisis for the Australian capital market in that foreign funds had by no means dried up. Furthermore, the arguments of academic economists, led by John Pitchford (see, for example, Pitchford 1990), may have played a role in the change in general views. However, expressions of concern about Australia's levels of net foreign liabilities are still frequently made and perhaps became a little louder in the very late 1990s as foreign borrowing ticked up quite sharply again (see Figure 13.1).

High and/or increasing levels of foreign borrowing raise the spectre of servicing and repayment problems that are feared to precipitate capital flight, bankruptcy for a significant number of businesses, both in the financial sector and other sectors, savage macroeconomic adjustment, a prolonged interruption

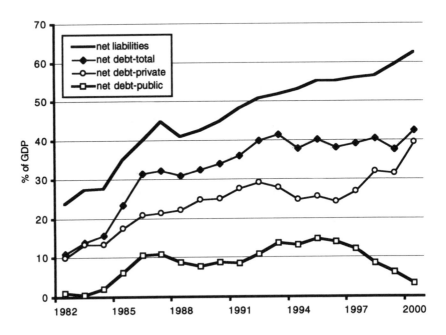

Figure 13.1   Australia's Foreign Liabilities (% of GDP)

to economic growth and, most importantly, cuts in living standards. There is however another perspective on foreign borrowing. Foreign borrowing can lead to improved outcomes for living standards. Foreign borrowing can help to finance investment expenditures, thereby facilitating a high rate of economic growth without the need to constrain domestic consumption. Furthermore, periods of foreign borrowing can allow a country to smooth consumption over time, thereby achieving better outcomes for living standards in the face of, for example, demographic change.

In evaluating a country's level of foreign borrowing, both of the two perspectives in the previous paragraph should be considered. However, the traditional emphasis has been to focus on the first, that is, on avoiding the dangers of payments crises. This emphasis has led to the use of the concept of sustainability as a criterion to evaluate the soundness of a country's debt position. To assess sustainability a quantitative target that is often used is the ratio of foreign debt to GDP. This ratio recognises the fact that as debt rises relative to GDP the costs of serving that debt also rise, thereby tending to increase debt. A vicious spiral of ever-increasing debt leading to insolvency is envisaged. To end this spiral may require, if left too late, a savage macroeconomic adjustment with the attendant adverse impact on living standards referred to above. Other ratios, such as foreign debt servicing costs to exports and current account deficit to exports, are also put forward as indicators of the vicious circle. The trigger points for these ratios vary somewhat.[1]

In this chapter, to evaluate the criticisms that Australia has accumulated excessive foreign borrowing and should, through government policy, force a reduction in the level of foreign borrowing, we use a different approach from the sustainability approach. We consider paths of foreign borrowing associated with paths of investment, saving and consumption that maximise the economic well-being of Australian residents calculated over a long period of time, effectively infinite, into the future. That is, we apply the economic theory of optimising consumption to the foreign borrowing issue. We also consider paths in which, compared to the optimal paths, foreign borrowing is forced to lower levels. From this analysis, we draw inferences about the wisdom of targeting foreign borrowing. We conclude that, for the Australian economy, targeting foreign borrowing is likely to cause a loss in living standards and therefore is not a good objective for economic policy.

In principle, our optimising approach nests the sustainability approach in that our optimal paths are constrained such that foreign borrowing is sustainable. From the set of sustainable foreign borrowing paths, our optimality approach selects the path that maximises social welfare. Thus our approach incorporates the two perspectives. However, there are some caveats that should be born in mind in interpreting our results. In our view, as will be seen below, the caveats are not so important for Australia and so our conclusion from this analysis that foreign borrowing should not be targeted holds for Australia. However, for other countries it may not be so clear cut. The caveats we have in mind are as follows.

First, for countries with high levels of government foreign debt, either actual or expected, the assumptions of our optimising approach may yield misleading results. In our optimising approach, foreign borrowing is contracted because the benefits outweigh the costs, evaluated over a long time horizon, with the costs including the loss of consumption required to finance repayment. Private lenders and borrowers have the incentive to avoid borrowing contracts for which the costs outweigh the benefits. This includes avoiding those loans where there is not a reasonable expectation of repayment. Governments may not be so well motivated. Their time horizons may be shorter. They may be inadequately monitored. These characteristics can make governments adopt excessive levels of foreign debt for short-term political advantage.[2]

Secondly, equity owned by foreign residents is thought to be less of a problem than debt to foreign residents. This is because with equity the risk is held by the foreign resident while with debt the domestic borrower bears the risk. As noted above, for Australia the growth of equity has been the major contributor to the increase in Australia's foreign borrowing. However, equity is not without risk for the domestic economy. A substantial liquidation of equity by foreign owners and repatriation of their wealth will put substantial downward pressure on the exchange rate leading to the attendant problems therein.[3]

Thirdly, poorly regulated capital markets can lead to problems even for private contracts to borrow. The East Asian currency crisis has led to a significant re-evaluation of the factors that render a currency vulnerable to speculative attacks. In this re-evaluation the role of the level of foreign borrowing has been de-emphasised. Instead poor regulation of capital markets and financial institutions are thought to be of greater importance (see, for example, Radelet and Sachs 1999; and Loayza, Schmidt-Hebbel and Serven 2000). Related to poor regulation is excessive borrowing in short-term assets.

Fourthly, the exchange rate regime can encourage borrowing contracts with unfortunate externalities. In particular fixed exchange rate regimes coupled with attempts to fix the exchange rate above free market rates tends to encourage borrowing in foreign-currency denominated assets. This type of borrowing can cause a crisis if the country is subjected to an adverse shock that raises the real burden of borrowing should the exchange rate be forced to devalue.

Fifthly, even with a flexible exchange rate, economies can experience difficulty in adjusting to adverse shocks, such as a deterioration in the terms of trade. For example, as explained in McDonald (1996, pp. 470–1), a downwardly sticky real wage can inhibit the adjustment process following an adverse terms of trade shock, and cause a high level of unemployment.

These caveats do not have force for Australia. Government borrowing from foreign residents is low. Equity is the major form of foreign borrowing. Financial markets are well regulated. The exchange rate regime is flexible. The level of foreign borrowing in foreign currencies is not a problem.[4] And in recent years the Australian economy appears to be able to cope well with the very large adverse shock of the Asian currency crisis.[5]

In the analysis in this chapter we use our optimal path as the benchmark. Some may object to this on the grounds that distortions in the actual economy cause saving to fall short of the level implied by optimal decision-making. Fitzgerald (1996, p. 3) argues that Australia's tax and social security system biases decisions 'away from saving and towards present consumption'. However there are other distortions that bias decision making the other way. In particular, the lack of risk-sharing instruments (see, for example, Loayza, Schmidt-Hebbel and Serven 2000) leads to excessive saving. So, on balance, the net effect on saving of distortions is, in theory, ambiguous.

Turning to empirical experience, the improvement in living standards enjoyed over a long period of time in industrialised countries suggests very strongly that there has been no lack of provision for future generations. That is, saving does not appear to have been too low. To us it is not ethically acceptable to argue that the living standards of people alive in the past should have been lower so that those alive today and in the future should be even better off. Increasing the gap in living standards between people alive at different points in time is inequitable. So we do not regard our optimal simulations, in which living standards grow steadily through the twenty-first century, as open to the criticism that they imply saving rates that are too low and levels of borrowing that are too high.

In our investigation of prospective paths of foreign borrowing for the Australian economy, we consider two scenarios of particular topical interest. These scenarios are driven by low immigration and low fertility respectively. We show that the future path of foreign borrowing associated with the optimal path of living standards is very sensitive to the demographic scenario.

The fact that the level of foreign borrowing associated with the optimal path of living standards depends on the demographic future of the economy suggests that attempts to achieve a target level of foreign borrowing which is not influenced by prospective demographic trends may cause a decline in living standards. To illustrate this point, we report simulations in which foreign borrowing is reduced to a level below the level associated with the path of optimal living standards. These simulations show that such programmes of forced reduction in foreign borrowing would reduce living standards throughout the twenty-first century. They also show that programmes of forced reduction in foreign borrowing have implications for intergenerational equity that may be questioned. In particular people living in the near future are disadvantaged relative to people living in the more distant future. The inequity implied by this redistribution is that those living in the more distant future will have higher living standards. Thus the reduction in living standards implied by the programmes of forced reduction in foreign borrowing that we consider fall more heavily on those who are less well off. This is an outcome that is usually considered inequitable.

The chapter proceeds as follows: in Section 13.2, the small open economy model of economic growth and foreign borrowing used to produce our simulations is described. Section 13.3 describes the demographic projections. In Section 13.4 the paths of foreign borrowing implied by the maximisation of a social welfare function are discussed. Section 13.5 considers the cost to living standards of implementing a forced reduction in foreign borrowing instead of following the optimal paths of foreign borrowing described in Section 13.4. Section 13.6 concludes the chapter.

13.2   THE SMALL OPEN ECONOMY MODEL OF ECONOMIC GROWTH AND FOREIGN BORROWING

The simulations in this chapter are based on a small open economy Ramsey model of optimal saving with heterogeneous consumers, a vintage production function and a positive rate of technical progress. The level of foreign borrowing evolves through the interaction of the growing economy with a perfect world capital market (PWCM). In a PWCM agents in the domestic economy can borrow or lend any amounts at an exogenously set rate of interest. In this section we give a brief, non-technical account of the model, emphasising the role of foreign borrowing. See Appendix A for a technical account of the model and the empirical specification of the parameters.

For a country facing a PWCM, the socially optimal rate of investment is the level of investment at which the marginal product of investment adjusted for depreciation is equal to the world rate of interest. This implies that through the projection period the capital stock grows with employment growth and total factor productivity growth. The latter are assumed exogenous in our model. Employment growth is determined by the demographic projection on which a particular simulation is based. Thus demographic projections with high employment growth cause high levels of investment. The accumulation of capital, the growth of employment and the rate of growth of total factor productivity determine the path of output over the projection period.

The path of net output – that is, output minus investment – is available to finance a path of consumption over the projection period and to service and make repayments on any foreign borrowing. The ability to accumulate or decumulate foreign borrowing allows the path of consumption to differ from the path of net output. Foreign borrowing allows consumption to exceed net output. But the terminal wealth constraint in the model, where wealth equals the capital stock minus foreign borrowing, prevents the economy from accumulating foreign borrowing without limit.[6] The paths of consumption generated by our model follow the usual pattern thought desirable by economists in that consumption grows smoothly. In consequence, any fluctuations in output due to demographic fluctuations over the projection period are not carried through to consumption. Instead foreign borrowing or lending in the PWCM allows agents in the economy to smooth the path of consumption. Thus foreign borrowing can improve the intertemporal distribution of living standards.

An important characteristic of our model that deserves emphasis is that the paths of living standards we derive do not violate the terminal wealth constraint. Thus, along these paths of living standards, foreign borrowing is serviced. There is no reneging on the obligations due to foreign borrowing. Thus, the paths of foreign borrowing are sustainable. This implies that the paths of foreign borrowing are no reason for foreign lenders to fear that they will lose their assets because they cannot be repaid. It is sometimes argued that high levels of foreign borrowing will cause a risk premium to be demanded by foreign lenders. This would make the interest paid on foreign borrowing a positive function of the level of foreign borrowing. But because the paths of foreign borrowing produced from our simulations are serviced and repaid, if the level of foreign borrowing at points in a simulation appears high this is no reason for thinking that the foreign borrowing cannot be repaid. It can, due to the specification of the model.[7]

It will be seen that the levels of foreign borrowing implied by optimal paths of living standards are influenced by demographic change. That there is such a relation shows the limitations of using the historical record of levels of foreign borrowing to make judgements on whether current levels of foreign borrowing are excessive. The excessiveness or not of current levels of foreign borrowing is influenced by, among other things, the demographic future. This may be, indeed is for Australia, very different from the demographic past. Thus, simple historical comparisons can be misleading.

13.3   THE DEMOGRAPHIC PROJECTIONS

To simulate paths of living standards and the associated paths of foreign borrowing, we use three demographic projections. Each projection runs from 1999 to 2168. In the Base case, for the entire projection period the total fertility rate is set at 1.75 and the rate of immigration is set at 0.54 per cent of the population. The mortality rate is set such that life expectancy increases by 0.4 years every five years. The Base case can be thought of as roughly a continuation of the current demographic situation. To assess the effect of reduced immigration the ZIMM (zero immigration) projection sets the rate of immigration at zero throughout the projection period. Fertility and mortality are as in the Base case. To assess the effect of reduced fertility, the 'TFR1.3' projection sets the TFR (total fertility rate)[8] to fall from 1.75 to 1.3 by 2009, at which rate it remains for the remainder of the projection period. The immigration rate and mortality are as in the Base case. The assumptions for each demographic projection are summarised in Table 13.1.

To project paths of employment from the demographic projections, we assume that the employment/population ratios by age group are constant at their 1999 levels for the entire projection period. Thus the growth of aggregate employment is influenced by changes in the age structure of the population. For example an ageing demographic structure tends to reduce the rate of growth of aggregate employment because of the increasing proportion of people in the older age groups. These people have lower employment/population ratios.

We also weight workers of different ages by efficiency factors that reflect their relative productivity. These weights, based on wages earned by different age groups, tend to be lower for young workers. Incorporating these efficiency factors is an additional mechanism through which changes in the demographic structure affect the rate of growth of employment. For example, an ageing population tends to increase the rate of growth of employment, measured in efficiency units, because of the shift in the workforce to adults who have higher efficiency factors than young people.

The net effect of ageing on the rate of growth of aggregate employment is in

Table 13.1
Demographic Scenarios

Scenario name	Description
Base case	TFR=1.75; annual net immigration=0.54% of population; mortality assumption: increase in life expectancy of 0.4 years every 5 years.
TFR1.3 (low fertility)	TFR falls from 1.75 in 1997 to 1.30 in 2009. This is the lowest likely fertility rate.
Zero immigration (ZIMM)	Annual net immigration = 0; TFR=1.75.
Homogeneous Population (Homo)	Base case population projection. Constant aggregate employment to population ratio. Hence, aggregate employment grows (or declines) at the same rate as total population from 1997.

Notes: TFR is total fertility rate. The base case rate of 1.75 is close to the number observed in Australia in the last two years. Base case immigration rate of 0.54% of the population is close to the actual rate of immigration in recent years.

general ambiguous, depending on the relative strength of changing employment population ratios and changing average labour productivity. For our simulations of Australia, the former outweighs the latter and thus ageing tends to reduce the rate of growth of aggregate employment.

To allow for the relatively high consumption demands of old people, due to the high levels of medical expenditure on old people, our definition of living standards is consumption per consumption unit. This is aggregate consumption divided by aggregate population measured in consumption units. Consumption units are people weighted by their relative demands for consumption. According to our calculations, people over 75 years old consume 19 per cent more than younger adults. So a person age 75 years or more equals 1.19 consumption units, while a younger adult equals one consumption unit. The weighting of people by their consumption demands implies that a given amount of aggregate consumption yields a lower living standard if the proportion of old people in the population increases. Thus, an ageing population tends to have a negative effect on the living standards obtained from a given path of aggregate consumption.

The support ratio, that is the ratio of employment to population, summarises for a population projection dependency characteristics that have important implications for saving and living standards. A decrease in the support ratio implies a pressure on resources in that there is a greater number of people per worker to 'support'. See Guest and McDonald (2001) for discussion of the support ratios. In Figure 13.2, the support ratios for the three population projections are shown. In calculating these support ratios, employment is measured in efficiency units and population is measured in consumption units, as described above. For each of the population projections the support ratio follows a downward trend over the twenty-first century with a tendency to decrease at a slower rate in the second half of that century. Furthermore, by 2100 both low fertility and zero immigration would lead to a lower support ratio than for the Base case. So both low fertility and zero immigration increase the pressure of providing living standards to the population. However while the path of the support ratio for the zero immigration projection is uniformly below the support ratio for the Base case, this is not so for the path of the support ratio for the low fertility projection. The later actually increases at impact, that is in the first decade of the twenty-first century, and then decreases, cutting the path of the support ratio for the Base case in the late 2040s. The initial rise of the support ratio in the low fertility case reflects the reduction in the number of children caused by an immediate reduction in fertility. The implications of these demographic scenarios for living standards is calculated and discussed Guest and McDonald (2001). In this chapter the focus is on the implications for foreign borrowing.

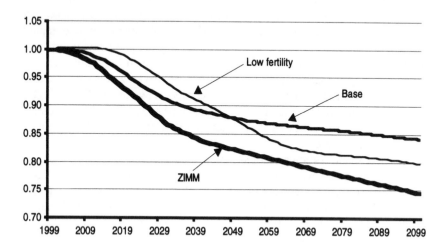

Figure 13.2   Support Ratios, Australia, 1999 to 2100

13.4   PATHS OF FOREIGN BORROWING WHEN LIVING STANDARDS ARE OPTIMISED

In the Base case, for the period 1999 to 2100, the optimal path of living standards grows at the annual rate of 1.27 per cent. (In reporting the results of our simulations we focus on the period 1999 to 2100.) This is less than the annual rate of growth of output per worker for this period, which is 1.46 per cent. The shortfall of growth in living standards reflects in part the ageing of the Australian population. The projected rate of growth of living standards is also less than the rate enjoyed over the past 30 years, which was 1.9 per cent per year. This reflects in part the change from a 'younging' population structure to an ageing structure.

Paths of foreign borrowing for the simulations are shown in Figure 13.3. For the Base case, foreign borrowing as a percentage of GDP has two peaks: the first in 2006 at 64.6 per cent and the second in 2072 at 64.3 per cent. By 2100 the level of foreign borrowing is at 49.5 per cent. Thus for most of the twenty-first century, foreign borrowing is at similar levels to the level in 1999. Underlying this is an annual rate of growth of employment of 0.54 per cent.

To give an idea of the effect of the ageing demographic structure on the levels of foreign borrowing implied by choosing an optimal path for living standards, we simulated the Base case population projection assuming that the age structure of the population remained unchanged at its 1999 structure throughout the projection period. Thus in this simulation, labeled Homo (for homogenous population), the aggregate employment–population ratio remains constant at its 1999 value. The annual growth rate of employment is 0.68 per cent, 0.14 percentage points higher than for the Base case. This higher rate shows that the decrease in the aggregate employment–population ratio implied by ageing more than offsets the beneficial effect to labour productivity, discussed above. The implied path for foreign borrowing is shown in Figure 13.3. It is uniformly higher than the path for the Base case, peaking at 90.0 per cent in 2015. The higher level of foreign borrowing reflects two forces. First, a higher growth rate of employment and thus higher investment. Secondly a support ratio that does not decline over the projection period, and thus a reduced demand to save for the future.

An immediate cessation of immigration into Australia, sustained throughout the future, yields a lower growth rate of population and employment. By 2100, the ZIMM projection yields a population level of 16.5 million people, 44.1 per cent of the population in the Base case for 2100. The annual growth rate of employment is negative, at –0.34 per cent, reflecting the decrease in the aggregate population under this projection. Without immigration, the negative rate of natural increase, due to the total fertility rate being below replacement, dominates the aggregate population outcome. This demographic future would have a slight negative effect on living standards, yielding an annual growth rate of 1.21 per

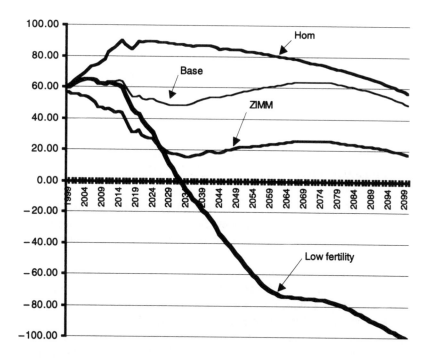

Figure 13.3   Foreign Debt, Australia, 1999 to 2100

cent, 0.06 percentage points less than for the Base case. This implies by 2100 a level of living standards 5.6 per cent less than the Base case. The optimal path of living standards for the economy with zero immigration implies a smaller level of foreign borrowing. Figure 13.3 shows that foreign borrowing peaks at 26.2 per cent in 2072.

An immediate and substantial drop in fertility in Australia to a total fertility rate of 1.3 yields a significantly lower growth rate of population and employment. By 2100, the TFR1.3 projection yields a population level of 22.6 million, 60.4 per cent of the 2100 population yielded in the Base case. The annual growth rate of employment would be 0.01 per cent. This demographic future would have a positive effect on living standards, yielding an annual growth rate of living standards of 1.31 per cent, 0.04 percentage points higher than for the Base case. This implies a level of living standards by 2100 4.6 per cent higher than for the Base case. The optimal path of living standards for the economy with a TFR of 1.3 implies a very different pattern of foreign borrowing over the 21st century, compared with the previous two cases. Foreign borrowing trends down almost immediately to be –100.6 per cent of GDP by 2100. That is, the optimal path is associated with a considerable buildup of foreign assets. There are two forces driving this pattern. First, the initial rise in the support ratio in the TFR1.3 projection provides people with the opportunity to initially save at high levels in preparation for the impending pressure on resources to be caused by the future fall in the support ratio. Secondly, the slow growth of employment, relative to the Base case, implies that the optimal disposition of saving is in foreign assets rather than the domestic capital stock.

13.5   THE COST TO LIVING STANDARDS OF FORCED REDUCTIONS IN FOREIGN BORROWING

The levels of foreign borrowing in our Base case simulation may strike some people as large. One can infer this view from the fact that some people have expressed concern in the past with foreign borrowing levels that are, as a percentage of GDP, less than the levels in our Base case. In this section, to get some idea of the problems that may be caused by governments setting economic policy to reduce the level of foreign borrowing, we consider the impact on living standards of aiming for lower levels of foreign borrowing than in our Base case simulation. We use the Base case demographic projection.

Foreign borrowing can be reduced by cutting back investment or cutting back consumption. To reduce investment below the optimal level would impose a loss of output on the economy. That is a clear loss. Furthermore, the advocates of reducing the level of foreign borrowing, at least those from the right wing, do not argue that investment is too high. So to assess the impact of reducing the level of foreign borrowing, we assume that investment follows the optimal path. It is the path of consumption that is chosen in our simulations to achieve the target of reduced foreign borrowing. We do this in the following way. We set a target level for foreign borrowing, for example 40 per cent of GDP, and a year by which this target is to be reached, for example 2020. Then we calculate the annual rate of growth in living standards that will achieve the foreign borrowing target by the target date. After the target date we assume that living standards in each year are at the level that maintains foreign borrowing at the target level, for example at 40 per cent of GDP.

Note that we do not specify the government policy that would achieve the path of living standards required to achieve the foreign borrowing target. To influence the path of living standards, there are two policy instruments open to the government. These are higher tax rates and lower government consumption expenditures. (Remember that our measure of consumption is private plus public). It should be borne in mind that higher taxes or lower government expenditures are likely, in the real world, to reduce output. Higher taxes have a disincentive effect. Lower government consumption expenditures, if focussed on education or health, would reduce labour productivity. Our model has not been extended to allow for these adverse effects. In consequence, the actual outcomes from the foreign borrowing reduction scenarios could be worse than our calculations suggest.

The results of our modeling of two foreign borrowing reduction programmes are in Figures 13.4 and 13.5. Consider the case alluded to above of reducing foreign borrowing to 40 per cent of GDP by 2020, the 40/20 programme. The annual growth of living standards from 1999 to 2040 that would achieve this aim is 1.1 per cent, 0.17 percentage points less than the annual growth rate for the optimal simulation. The path of foreign borrowing is shown in Figure 13.4. Note that there is a small initial increase such that foreign borrowing peaks at 63.7 per cent of GDP in 2004.[9] After 2004 the level of foreign borrowing decreases smoothly to reach 40 per cent of GDP by 2020.

Figure 13.5 shows that reducing foreign borrowing to 40 per cent of GDP by 2020 would make those people alive between 1999 and 2020 worse off relative to the Base case. It can be seen from Figure 13.5 that the ratio of the living standard implied by the 40/20 programme relative to the optimal path for living standards, that is, the Base case, is less than one throughout 1999 to 2020. The shortfall in living standards, or belt-tightening, increases up to the year 2020, at which time living standards would be 1.8 per cent less than under the optimal path. Thereafter living standards are generally higher than the Base case, being on average for the period 2021 to 2100, 0.8 per cent higher than for the Base case.

The results of a more draconian foreign borrowing reduction programme, that is reducing foreign borrowing to zero by 2020, is also reported in Figures 13.4 and 13.5. It can be seen in Figure 13.5 that this programme magnifies the effect on living standards of the 40/20 plan. The cost to people living in the period 1999 to 2020 is greater, with the greatest cost in 2020 when living standards would be 5.4 per cent below the outcome for the optimal case. Thereafter, living standards are higher than the Base case, being on average for the period 2021 to 2100, 2.9 per cent higher than for the Base case.

So for either the 40/20 or the 0/20 programme there is a redistribution of living standards away from people alive in the near future towards people alive in the distant future. Without this redistribution, that is, under the optimal plan, the latter would be better off. So the redistribution increases the intertemporal inequity by redistributing from the less well off to the better off.

Setting a constant numerical target for foreign borrowing imposes a loss of living standards relative to the optimal path for people alive after 2020. However, for those alive before 2020 the 20/60 programme has no effect on living standards. Thus, although over the century the 20/60 simulation and the Base case have similar levels of foreign borrowing on average, the living standards implied by targeting foreign borrowing at 60 per cent of GDP is on average lower. The average loss per year in living standards is 0.2 per cent.

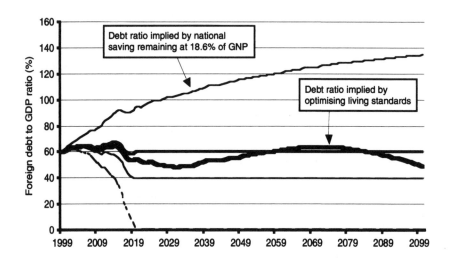

Figure 13.4   Foreign Debt Under Alternative Debt Stabilisation Scenarios,
Base Case Population Projection, Australia, 1999 to 2100

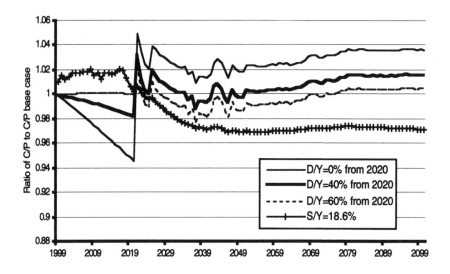

Note: D/Y refers to net foreign liabilities to GDP

Figure 13.5   Effect on Living Standards Under Alternative Stability
Scenarios, Australia, 1999 to 2100

Finally, to round out our investigation of foreign borrowing, we consider the effect on foreign borrowing of maintaining the rate of saving in Australia at its current level of 18.6 per cent of GDP. The simulations reported so far imply some increase in saving as a percentage of GDP in the early part of the projection period, see Guest and McDonald (2001). However, some people may question our simulations on the basis that the increase in national saving and the associated reduction in the current account deficit will not eventuate for Australia. There is a degree of pessimism in some quarters about increasing saving and reducing the current account deficit. While we would counter with the point that along our projected paths the increase in national saving does not require a reduction in living standards, it is of interest to consider what would happen if the ratio of national saving to GDP stays at its 1999 level.[10] Would this be a problem? Would foreign borrowing spiral under this scenario? Would living standards suffer significantly?

To answer these questions, we consider the impact on foreign borrowing and living standards of a failure of national saving to increase as a share of GDP above its present level, and thus a failure of the current account deficit to fall below its current level. We do this by assuming that investment is determined optimally as in the base case above but that the rate of national saving is constrained to be equal to the actual rate of national saving in 1999, that is 18.6 per cent of GDP. This projection yields a path of foreign borrowing shown in Figure 13.4. The path of foreign borrowing as a percentage of GDP is above the paths of the previous simulations. However it does not spiral. Instead it tends to asymptote to a level somewhere in excess of 130 per cent of GDP. As shown in Figure 13.5, the effect on living standards, relative to the Base case, is positive up to 2022 and then negative. Thus, those people living in the near future gain at the expense of those in the distant future. The average loss to living standards over the twenty-first century is 1.6 per cent per year. The smallness of this average loss, the fact that it falls on people who will be better off and the lack of a tendency of foreign borrowing to spiral suggests that if the rate of national saving in Australia fails to increase from its 1999 level it would not be a matter for concern.

13.7   CONCLUSION

This chapter has shown that the levels of foreign borrowing that support an optimal path of living standards through time depend on the demographic structure of the economy. Optimising living standards under the assumption that the current rates of fertility and immigration continue implies a level of foreign borrowing that fluctuates around 60 per cent of GDP, its current level, throughout the twenty-first century. The average level of foreign borrowing over the twenty-first century implied by this simulation is 58.1 per cent of GDP. As shown by our calculation of the support ratio – the ratio of employment to population – these current demographic trends embody a significant ageing of the population. This is reflected in a significant decline in the support ratio from 1999 onwards. Were this change in the demographic structure not to occur, then optimising living standards would imply higher levels of foreign borrowing. The actual number, according to our calculations, is 77.9 per cent of GDP.

We consider two alternative demographic projections designed to highlight the impact on foreign borrowing of factors currently thought to potentially impinge on Australia's demographic future. The first is a lower level of immigration. As noted in the introduction, groups in favour of reduced or even zero immigration have been vocal in the last decade in Australia. Furthermore, there are concerns that the supply of immigrants to Australia may decrease in future years. We considered a demographic projection in which the level of immigration is zero for the entire projection period, that is, the next 170 years. Optimising living standards in that extreme case yields a lower level of foreign borrowing, averaging 27.3 per cent of GDP. Secondly, there is good reason to believe that fertility in Australia may fall in the near future. This would continue the trend of the last decade and be in line with a number of industrialised countries that have significantly lower rates of fertility than does Australia. To consider this possibility, we analysed a population projection we call TFR1.3 in which the total fertility rate falls from its current rate of 1.75 to 1.3 by 2009, at which rate it remains for the rest of the projection period. This projection has a very large impact on foreign borrowing. Optimising living standards for this low fertility case yields a much lower level of foreign borrowing, compared with the Base case. By 2033 the foreign borrowing level becomes negative – that is, optimising living standards requires lending to overseas rather than borrowing from overseas. By 2100 the level of foreign assets in this case is 100.6 per cent of GDP.

It is clear from our simulations that the level of foreign borrowing implied by optimising living standards is very sensitive to prospective demographic patterns. This sensitivity casts doubt on the wisdom of setting macroeconomic policy to target foreign borrowing because it shows how difficult it would be to evaluate a particular borrowing outcome. Given the uncertainty of the actual demographic future, there can be no tightly defined yardstick against which the actual outcome can be compared.

We also considered the impact on living standards of forced reductions in foreign borrowing. That is instead of allowing foreign borrowing to be determined by the optimal path of living standards, as in the simulations summarised in the previous two paragraphs, we allowed living standards to be determined by a target for foreign borrowing. These simulations showed that targeting foreign borrowing can cause a reduction in living standards that falls on people who are less well off. For example, in one of our borrowing stabilisation programmes, we set the borrowing target at 40 per cent of GDP to be achieved by the year 2020. This reduces living standards for those alive in the period 1999 to 2020 by 0.8 per cent relative to the Base case. After 2020 people gain on average by 0.8 per cent for 2021 to 2100.

Thus, a forced decrease in foreign borrowing increases the inter-temporal inequity in living standards. For example, a borrowing target of 40 per cent of GDP to be achieved by the year 2020 increases the levels of living standards in 2100 relative to 2020 from 279 per cent to 288 per cent. The inequity of this intertemporal redistribution is that the living standards of the people who suffer will be about one-third of the living standards of people alive in 2100, who gain.

There is even a cost, albeit small, of lower living standards from the policy of the Base case population projection, preventing foreign borrowing from following the rather small fluctuations implied by optimising the path of living standards. Forcing foreign borrowing to be equal to 60 per cent of GDP from 2020 onwards reduces living standards by 0.2 per cent per year on average for the twenty-first century.

Our simulations cast doubt on the wisdom of setting macroeconomic policy to target foreign borrowing because they show that falls in living standards can result from picking the wrong target. Furthermore, for the borrowing-reduction targets we consider, the burden of these losses tends to be spread inequitably.

It has been argued by some that the current level of saving in Australia implies a 'spiraling' growth of foreign borrowing, if investment is to be at desirable levels (see Fitzgerald 1996). To analyse this prospect within our framework we considered a simulation in which the rate of national saving was fixed for the entire projection period at its 1999 level of 18.6 per cent of GNP. The level of investment was set optimally. This simulation revealed that current saving rates will not cause borrowing to spiral. Instead foreign borrowing asymptotes to a level somewhere in excess of 130 per cent of GDP.

Thus, spiraling foreign borrowing does not seem to us to be a significant problem.

The basic message of our simulations is that setting macroeconomic policy to target foreign borrowing is a poor idea.[11] Such a target, being very sensitive to demographic outcomes, is hard to define. It would vary over time. Selecting the wrong target imposes significant losses in living standards, losses that tend to be inequitably distributed, falling more heavily on those with a lower standard of living. Furthermore, the dangers of spiraling foreign borrowing are slight. However this message is based on our model of economic growth of a small open economy. Some reasons people have put forward for concern about Australia's borrowing bring in factors that are, strictly speaking, outside our model. It is argued that a high level of foreign borrowing makes the economy vulnerable to speculative attacks and adverse shocks. Furthermore a high level of foreign borrowing may increase the risk premium on overseas borrowing and thus the cost of borrowing. Although our model does not allow for uncertainty, the thrust of our analysis can shed some light on these arguments.

APPENDIX A

Description of the Model of Optimal Saving

The model is a Ramsey model with heterogeneous consumers and workers, a reference level of consumption, and a putty-clay vintage production function. We adopt the small open economy assumption of an exogenous interest rate, which is reasonable for Australia.[12] The interest rate is held constant. This model is based on the standard one-good, small open economy model with many periods – see for example Obstfeld and Rogoff (1996, pp. 60–2) – modified to include a positive rate of technical progress and to allow for a changing demographic structure.[13]

The future living standards we calculate are based on the decisions of a social planner to maximise a social welfare function, given by

$$
V = \sum_{j=1}^{h} \left\{ N_j \left(\frac{C_j}{P_j} - \chi \frac{C_{j-1}}{P_{j-1}} \right)^{1-\beta} \frac{(1-\rho)^{1-j}}{(1-\beta)} \right\}
$$

$$
+ N_h \omega \left(\frac{W_h}{N_h} \right)^{1-\psi} \frac{(1-\rho)^{1-h}}{(1-\psi)}
$$

(A13.1)

(Symbols are defined in Table 13.1.) The social welfare function is the sum of the utility levels generated from consumption running up to h periods in the future and of the level of wealth at the end of the h periods. As implied by the use in the social welfare function of consumption per consumption unit ($= C/P$ with C = aggregate consumption and P = total population measured in consumption units), aggregate consumption is assumed to be allocated to people according to their consumption demand weights discussed in Section 13.3. Wealth at the end of the period is allocated equally between people defined in natural units. The utility function includes a reference level of consumption, specified as the level of consumption per consumption unit in the previous period. Thus the utility function allows for habit formation in consumption. In all the simulations in this chapter we set $\chi = 1$. The rate of time preference is assumed constant over the planning horizon. It is determined by

$$\rho = (1-r)(1+a)^{\frac{-\beta}{1-\alpha}} - 1 \qquad \text{(A13.2)}$$

This choice of ρ implies that a period of balanced growth in the exogenous variables of the model will imply that the ratio of consumption to output will approach a constant value.[14] Our chosen form of the social welfare function is discussed further in Section 13.4.

The social planner faces the following constraints. First domestic expenditure, foreign borrowing/lending and output (GDP) are related by an international budget constraint for each period

$$Y_j = I_j + C_j + D_{j-1}(1+r) - D_j \qquad \text{for } j = 1,...h \qquad \text{(A13.3)}$$

The world rate of interest, at which the economy can lend or borrow unlimited amounts, is assumed constant over the projection period. Secondly, output is related to the inputs of labour and capital by a vintage Cobb Douglas production function

$$Y_j = \sum_{k=1}^{T} \left[(1-\delta)^{k-1} A_{j-k} I_{j-k}^{\alpha} 1_{j-(k-1)}^{1-\alpha} \right] \qquad \text{for } j = 2,...h. \text{(A13.4)}$$

Output in period 1 is exogenous.[15] The production function is a putty-clay vintage production function with constant returns to scale.[16] The constant rate of total factor productivity increases the efficiency parameter, A, of new capital goods at the rate a. The substitution possibilities at the time that the capital goods are constructed follows the Cobb Douglas form. There is a one period gestation from construction to operation for capital goods. Once installed capital goods have a fixed capital–labour ratio. During their operating life, capital goods depreciate in that their labour requirement and the output they produce decrease at a constant rate d over time. After T periods of operation capital goods are scrapped. The socially efficient age of scrapping for a capital good is determined as the age when its average product of labour is equal to the marginal product of labour on new capital goods. Under this rule, T is determined by the world interest rate.[17] Units of labour are measured in efficiency units that allow for differences in productivity by age and gender. Thirdly, in any period the total amount of labour allocated to vintages of capital is constrained by the exogenously determined aggregate level of employment according to

$$L_j = \sum_{k=1}^{T_j} (1-\delta)^{k-1} 1_{j+1-k} \qquad \text{for } j = 2,...h \qquad \text{(A13.5)}$$

Fourthly, terminal wealth is determined by the sum of capital stock and foreign assets at the end of period h according to

$$W_h = \left[\sum_{k=h-T+1}^{T_h-1} (1-\delta)^k I_{h-k} \right] - D_h \qquad (A13.6)$$

The solution to the model is derived from the first order conditions for maximising (A13.1) subject to (A13.3) to (A13.6). The simulations use these equations. The model has the well-known properties of the small open economy model. In particular, Fisher separation holds, that is, investment levels and thus output levels are determined independently of the allocation of consumption across time periods. Consumption smoothing generated by maximising the social welfare function causes consumption per person[18] to grow at a fairly constant rate. However, the growth of output per person varies with changes in the employment/population ratio. Thus, to bridge the gap between consumption and output, the optimal proportion of GDP saved is influenced by changes in the demographic structure.

The first order conditions determine investment in the following way. The condition that the marginal product of investment equals the cost of capital determines the capital/labour ratio on the new vintage of capital by[19]

$$K_j \equiv \frac{I_j}{1_{j+1}} = \left[\frac{\alpha A_j}{E_j} \right]^{\frac{1}{1-\alpha}} \qquad \text{for } j = 1-T,\ldots h-1 \qquad (A13.7)$$

where E_j, the cost of capital in period j, is determined by

$$E_j = \frac{1}{\sum_{k=1}^{T}(1+r)^{-k}(1-\delta)^{k-1}} \qquad \text{for } j = 1-T,\ldots h-T \qquad (A13.8)$$

and

$$E_j = \frac{1-(1+r)^{j-h}(1-\delta)^{h-j}}{\sum_{k=1}^{h-j}(1+r)^{-k}(1-\delta)^{k-1}} \qquad \text{for } j = h-T+1,\ldots h-1 \qquad (A13.9)$$

The cost of capital is lower in the last $T-1$ years of the projection period because investment in those years contributes to terminal wealth. The age of the oldest capital good used in period j is determined by the equality of the average product of labour on the oldest capital good with the marginal product of labour on the new capital. This gives

$$T = \frac{-(1-\alpha) \ln(1-\alpha)}{\ln(1+a)} \qquad (A13.10)$$

The number to be employed on the newest vintage is equal to aggregate employment growth plus labour released from old vintages because either their capacity contracts due to depreciation or they are scrapped. This gives

$$1_{j+1} = L_{j+1} - (1-\delta)L_j + (1-\delta)^T 1_{j+1-T} \quad \text{for } j = 1-T,\ldots h \quad \text{(A13.11)}$$

Employment on the newest vintage determines the level of investment according to

$$I_j = K_j 1_{j+1} \quad \text{for } j = 1,\ldots h-1 \quad \text{(A13.12)}$$

With investment and employment determined, output is determined by the production function, (13.4).

For consumption, the condition that the marginal rate of substitution between consumption in adjacent periods equal the world rate of interest implies that the path of consumption per consumption unit satisfies

$$\frac{(N_j/P_j)}{(N_h/P_h)}\left(\frac{c_h}{c_j}\right)^\beta + \chi \frac{(N_{j+1}/P_j)}{(N_h/P_h)}\left(\frac{c_h}{c_{j+1}}\right)^\beta (1+\rho)^{-1} = \frac{(1-r)^{h-j}}{(1+\rho)^{h-j}} \quad \text{(A13.13)}$$

$$\text{for } j = 1,\ldots h-1$$

where

$$c_j \equiv \frac{C_j}{P_j} - \chi \frac{C_{j-1}}{P_{j-1}} \quad \text{for } j = 1,\ldots h \quad \text{(A13.14)}$$

The inclusion of terminal wealth in the social welfare function implies for optimality that terminal wealth satisfy

$$W_h = \omega^{1/\beta} (P_h/N_h)^{(1-\beta)/\beta} C_h \quad \text{(A13.15)}$$

Equations (A13.2) to (A13.15) determine the optimal path of living standards for the projection period.

Table A13.1
Definition of Variables

Subscript	time period
C	aggregate consumption
W	wealth=capital stock plus overseas assets
I	aggregate investment
D	overseas borrowing
r	world interest rate
δ	rate of depreciation
L	aggregate employment in relative efficiency units
l	employment in relative efficiency units on a vintage of capital in its first period of use
T	age of oldest capital good in use
h	terminal period of the maximisation problem
N	population in natural units
P	population in consumption units

Table A13.2
Employment/Population Ratios
(hours per week per person)

Age group	15–19	20–24	25–29	30–34	35–39	40–44	45–49	50–54	55–59	60–64	65–69
Males	11.0	26.6	34.1	34.1	35.9	35.9	34.4	34.4	26.7	15.4	8.6
Females	8.7	20.9	19.5	19.5	18.4	18.4	19.1	19.1	11.3	4.2	2.2

Table A13.3
Labour Productivity Weights

Age group	15–19	20–24	25–29	30–34	35–39	40–44	45–49	50–54	55–59	60–64	65–69
Males	0.469	0.772	1.097	1.097	1.234	1.234	1.226	1.226	1.211	0.991	0.991
Females	0.500	0.838	1.096	1.096	1.110	1.110	1.407	1.407	1.092	0.957	0.957

Table A13.4
Consumption Weights

Age group	0–15	16–24	25–39	40–49	50–59	60–64	65–69	70–74	75+
Consumption weight	0.68	0.89	1.00	0.98	1.00	1.05	0.87	0.95	1.19

257

Table A13.5
Values of Parameters and Exogenous Variables

α	δ	a	r	β	ω	ρ	h
0.3	0.05	0.01	0.06	2	6.788	0.03122	170 years

NOTES

1 Moore (1990, p. 28) reports that these trigger ratios typically include debt to exports of 160 per cent, CAD of 20 per cent of exports and debt servicing costs of 15 per cent of exports. As an example of different levels, Markkula (1996) quotes the ratios used by Merita Bank as debt to exports of 200 per cent, debt servicing costs of 25 per cent of exports and debt to GDP of 100 per cent. Econometric tests of solvency for particular countries have been conducted by Ahmed and Rogers (1996), Ghosh and Ostry (1995) and Milbourne and Otto (1992).

2 The opposite can be true. Governments, influenced by political pressure for low levels of foreign borrowing, may adopt policies that are too conservative. This possibility may be real for Australia. The fact that the level of foreign borrowing is easily publicised, partly because it is a quantitative measure, increases the possibility of deficit fetishism.

3 Our model, by not including risk, does not offer a distinction between equity and debt. However, as argued below, for Australia we do not see this as an important omission.

4 It now appears to be the case that a depreciation of the Australian dollar causes the ratio of net foreign liabilities to decrease rather than increase, see Adams, Dixon, McDonald and Rimmer (2000).

5 Whether this is due to the inflation target approach to monetary policy or the decentralisation of wage determination or some other reason is not settled. Mishkin and Schmidt-Hebbel (2001) argue that cross country evidence suggests that inflation targeting has been tested favourably by adverse shocks in that there was little exchange rate pass through and so the real wage resistance mechanism referred to in the text did not eventuate. Instead nominal devaluation led to a real devaluation.

6 We assume a finite horizon of 170 years for our simulations. This length of time is effectively infinite for the purposes of this chapter.

7 Fitzgerald (1996) argues that high foreign borrowing makes the economy more vulnerable to adverse external shocks. Because our model is a

certainty model, it does not address this issue explicitly. However we discuss this in the conclusion.

8   The total fertility rate is the number of children a woman would have if she were to bear children through her reproductive years at each age at the rates observed in a particular year.

9   To avoid this initial increase, an even lower growth rate of consumption would have to have been chosen for the period 1999 to 2020.

10   In so far as the actual rate of saving for Australia is influenced by our specification of optimality considerations, our results can be interpreted as a forecast of the pattern of actual saving, thereby suggesting that the sceptics will be wrong. Note that along the optimal paths, the hump in saving does not imply a drop in living standards at any time.

11   Ian Harper (1996) comes to a similar conclusion but for a different reason. He argues against targeting the current account, and thus foreign borrowing, on the grounds that it may cause the government to impose macroeconomic restraint on the economy. Such restraint would tend to reduce national saving, as it did in the early 1990s, an outcome Harper regards as bad. While we are not so concerned with reductions in the level of national saving, we concur with Harper that targeting foreign borrowing can lead to macroeconomic restraint. This is bad in our view simply because of the high rate of unemployment that would be caused. Relating this argument to the analysis in this chapter, our approach is a long-run approach. The risk of macroeconomic restraint is an additional problem of targeting foreign borrowing, derived from an analysis of short-run macroeconomic stabilisation policy.

12   The particular paths produced by the simulations are checked to ensure that they do not call into question the assumption of a perfect world capital market. For example, the 'best' path could require a current account deficit at some point of such a large size as to strain the credibility of assuming continued access to the world capital market at an unchanged interest rate.

13   In the Obstfeld and Rogoff (1996) description of the model, some of output, called government spending, is assumed not to add to consumption, investment or the accumulation of overseas assets. Our model does not include such a category of expenditure.

14   The combination of our demographic projections and our assumption of an unchanging retirement age do not yield a balanced growth path, in that the aggregate employment/population ratio tends to a decreasing path. However, experimentation shows that, given the length of the projection period in the simulations this violation of balanced growth does not have a significant impact on the behaviour of variables such as consumption and saving in the first fifty years of the projection.

15   In the simulations in this chapter output in year 1 is set equal to actual
     GDP for Australia in 1999.
16   With substantial decreases in population, the net effect on returns to scale
     is the result of a race between decreasing congestion costs and the loss of
     economies of scale. The constant returns to scale assumption presumes
     that this race is a dead heat.
17   This rule presumes that new capital goods are constructed. In the
     Doomsday case there are periods in which no capital goods are constructed
     and then T is determined differently. This is explained in the section on
     the Doomsday case.
18   Strictly speaking, consumption per consumption unit.
19   Investment is assumed to have a one period gestation lag from construction
     to first use date.

REFERENCES

Adams, P., P. Dixon, D. McDonald and M. Rimmer (2000), 'The Exchange
    Rate Puzzle and Forecasts for the Australian Economy from 2000–01 to
    2004–05', *The Australian Bulletin of Labour*, **26** (4), 257–78.

Ahmed, S. and J.H. Rogers (1996), 'Government Budget Deficits and Trade
    Deficits: Are Present Value Constraints Satisfied in Long-term Data?',
    Journal of Monetary Economics, **36**, 351–74.

Cutler, D.M., J.M. Poterba, L.M. Sheiner and L.H. Summers (1990), 'An Aging
    Society: Opportunity or Challenge?', *Brookings Papers on Economic
    Activity*, (1), 1–74.

Fitzgerald, V. (1996), 'Public Policy and National Saving', *Agenda*, **3** (1), 3–
    30.

Ghosh, A. and J.D. Ostry (1995), 'The Current Account in Developing Countries:
    A Perspective from the Consumption Smoothing Approach', *World Bank
    Economic Review*, **9**, 305–33.

Guest, R.S. and I.M. McDonald (2001), 'Ageing, Optimal National Saving and
    Future Living Standards in Australia', *Economic Record*, **77** (237), 117–34.

Harper, I.R. (1996), 'Public Policy and National Saving: Comment', *Agenda*, **3**
    (1), 21–24

Howard, D.H. (1989), 'Implications of the US Current Account Deficit', *Journal
    of Economic Perspectives*, **4** (Fall), 153–65.

Loayza, N., K. Schmidt-Hebbel and L. Serven (2000), 'Saving in Developing
    Countries: An Overview', *The World Bank Economic Review*, **14** (3), 393–
    414.

Markkula, K. (1996), *Unitas*, **3**, 22–3.

McDonald, I.M. (1996), *Macroeconomics*, second edition, Brisbane: John Wiley
    and Sons.

Milbourne, R. and G. Otto (1992), 'Consumption Smoothing and the Current Account', *Australian Economic Papers*, December, 369–84.

Mishkin, F.S., and K. Schmidt-Hebbel (2001), 'One Decade of Inflation Targeting in the World: What Do We Know and What Do We Need to Know?', NBER Working Paper 8397.

Moore, D. (1990), 'Debt – Is it Still a Problem ?', *Australian Economic Review*, 4, 17–32.

Obstfeld, M. and K. Obstfeld (1996), *Foundations of International Macroeconomics*, Cambridge: MIT Press.

Pitchford, J.D. (1990), *Australia's Foreign Debt: Myths and Realities*, Sydney: Allen and Unwin.

Radelet, S. and J.D. Sachs (1998), 'The East Asian Financial Crisis: Diagnosis, Remedies, Prospects', *Brookings Papers on Economic Activity*, 1, 1–90.

PART THREE

Growth: Trade, Capital Accumulation
and Debts

14 Trade Liberalisation and Labour Markets in Developing Countries: Theory and Evidence

Jorge Saba Arbache

14.1 INTRODUCTION

The increase in wage inequality in several countries in the last two decades has stimulated the search for explanations of the phenomenon in the economic literature. There is consensus among economists that one of the causes of the growth of wage inequality is the change in the structure of labour demand in favour of skilled workers, reflected in the increase of returns to education, and in some countries in the rise of unemployment among individuals with fewerqualifications (Freeman 1995; Gottschalk and Smeeding 1997). However, there is no consensus about the underlying causes of the change in the structure of labour demand. On the one hand, empirical evidence shows a relationship between an increase in international trade, wage distribution and level of employment, which led several economists to conclude that recent internationalisation of economies no doubt contributed to the increase in the dispersion of wages and unemployment. This proposition is sustained by the theorems of Heckscher and Ohlin and Stolper and Samuelson. On the other hand, other economists argue that the recent wave of technological innovations has had a strong impact on the structure of labour demand, since it is labour saving, especially of less skilled labour.[1] Disentangling these two explanations is, however, not an easy task because they may be potentially associated.

I would like to thank Miguel León-Ledesma, Francis Green, Fábio Veras, Sarquis J.B. Sarquis, Steve de Castro and Carlos Henrique Corseuil for their comments and suggestions on an early version of this paper. The usual disclaimer applies. I gratefully acknowledge financial support from the Institute for Applied Economics Research (IPEA), Brazilian Research Council (CNPq), and the UK Economic and Social Research Council, grant number R000223184.

The literature on trade liberalisation and distribution of wages has at least two characteristics. The first is that it aims at explaining the experience of developed countries, especially the OECD countries. The second is that there was very little theoretical progress on the issue, and the theorems of Heckscher and Ohlin and Stolper and Samuelson continued to be the main analytic tool to explain the relationship between international trade and distribution of income. The case of developing countries has received less attention. It is assumed that the impact of trade liberalisation in these countries is the opposite of that in developed countries. That is to say, if there is a worsening of the income distribution in developed countries, there will be an improvement of income distribution in developing countries, just as the standard theory of international trade predicts.

The experience of trade liberalisation in developing countries is quite varied, but understanding the effects of openness on their labour markets can be a complex task due to a number of reasons. In the first place, many of these countries have recently gone through structural changes and adjustments. Following on the instability of the international economy at the end of the 1970s and in the beginning of the 1980s, several developing countries adopted programmes of structural adjustment to solve imbalances of the balance of payments and to control high inflation rates. Starting from the middle of the 1980s, many of these countries adopted unprecedented economic reforms involving trade liberalisation, privatisation of state companies, deregulation of the financial and capital markets, as well as product and labour markets, besides wide reform of the state, which have caused fast and deep changes in their economies. Such changes demand that the analysis of the experience of developing countries be more elaborated.

In the second place, many developing countries followed import substitution industrialisation strategies until immediately before the trade liberalisation. The structure of protection built over decades determined the direction of the allocation of resources. As a consequence, the remuneration of productive factors and, consequently, the rate of investment, was influenced directly by the orientation of industrial and trade policies, and the allocation of resources was quite sensitive to the structure of protection and to the exchange rate. Krueger (1998) argues that such policy distorted relative prices, moving resources away from activities in which the country has comparative advantages and leading to the production of goods of worse quality at a higher price. As a result, the allocation and the rate of return of factors of production differ from those that would prevail in an open economy. Such effects can have serious implications for the distribution of income after openness.

In the third place, since technological innovations originate in developed countries where incentives exist for application, diffusion and propagation (Lucas 1990; Stokey 1991; Young 1991), the literature normally takes for granted that the hypothesis of technological innovations is more appropriate to explain the worsening of the income distribution in developed countries. Although some developing countries have been receiving enormous amounts of foreign direct investment and have been experiencing fast technological modernisation with significant productivity increases (for example, Brazil, China, India and South Korea), they tend to import rather than to create technologies. Therefore, if technology affects the labour markets of developing countries, it may follow a different pattern from that of developed countries.

A feel for the complexity of the effects of openness on the labour markets of developing countries can be given by recent empirical studies which show that trade liberalisation in some of these countries is associated with an increase of the returns to human capital and the worsening of wage distribution, as in the developed countries. To the extent that developing countries have abundant unskilled labour, this result is puzzling. In accordance with the standard theory of international trade, developing countries should specialise in the production of goods intensive in unskilled labour, thus increasing the relative demand for this factor and reducing the wage differential. These results put in doubt the importance of the standard theory of international trade to explain, at least in the short term, the rise of wage inequality in developing countries.

Hypotheses trying to explain the unexpected worsening of wage distribution in developing countries have only appeared recently. The explanations are still partial and preliminary, but they suggest that the opening to trade unchains a simultaneous – not a sequential, as in developed countries – process of technological modernisation and increase of capital stock, provoking a positive impact in the demand for skilled labour, thus increasing the returns to human capital and the dispersion of wages. Discussing these hypotheses in light of the empirical evidence is the main task of this chapter.

The aim of this text is to present a theoretical and empirical review of the recent literature about the effects of trade liberalisation on the labour markets of developing countries. The chapter is organised as follows. Section 14.2 presents the standard theory of international trade and income distribution. Section 14.3 presents a selection of empirical results on openness and labour markets in developed and developing countries. Section 14.4 discusses theories that seek to explain the rising wage inequality following trade liberalisation in developing countries. The last section brings the final remarks.

14.2 THEORY OF INTERNATIONAL TRADE AND INCOME DISTRIBUTION

The basic precept of free trade theory is that it is more efficient for each country to produce the goods it is best able to produce, due to supply conditions of human resources, natural and physical capital, in comparison to its trade partners.

This occurs due to the derived gains from specialisation of production. The principle of comparative advantage established by David Ricardo suggests that a country should concentrate on producing goods that have the smallest relative cost of production, and not the smallest absolute cost of production. In Ricardo's formulation, labour is the only production factor. What is unclear in that theory is the effects of free trade on income distribution, since the theory is based on only one factor of production.

The theorem of Heckscher and Ohlin (HO) extends Ricardo's model to two production factors, capital and labour. The model establishes that a country has comparative advantage in the production of goods which are intensive in the factor of production that is relatively more abundant, since this factor is relatively cheaper when compared to the price of the other factor, which is relatively scarce. Thus, countries in which capital supply is relatively large should concentrate on the production of capital intensive goods, and vice versa for countries whose labour supply is relatively large.

Starting from the picture proposed by HO, the theorem of Stolper and Samuelson (SS) was the first theoretical formulation to explain the effects of free trade on income distribution among production factors. The basic result of SS is that protectionism increases the returns of the scarce production factor – labour in developed countries, and capital in developing countries. For a simple illustration, suppose the case of a developing country with abundant supply of labour. Suppose that country can produce two goods, A and B, A being intensive in labour and B in capital. Suppose that the government imposes an import tariff for the good B of X per cent. As a consequence of the price increase of the imported good of X per cent, resources are now shifted to the production of good B. As a result, there is an increase in the demand for capital, which is the intensive factor in the production of good B. The larger demand for that factor forces the rise of its price relative to the price of labour, changing the relative prices of production factors in favour of capital. Notice that the return to capital increases more than proportionately to the increase of the price of good B due to the 'magnification effect' (Jones 1965). If, on the contrary, the country faces a policy of trade liberalisation, inverse results would be observed. The return to capital falls by a larger proportion than the price reduction of the imported good, at the same time that the return to labour increases, since the country specialises in the production of good A. The message is that developing countries which introduce programmes of trade liberalisation should have an improvement of the income inequality indicators, since they are abundant in labour. The opposite should happen for developed countries, since they are abundant in capital.

The factor-price equalisation theorem (FPE) (Samuelson 1948; 1949) extends the analysis of SS to show that, under certain hypotheses, international trade homogenises the absolute return of production factors among economies. Thus, the real wage in developed and developing countries tends to converge to an intermediate point, reducing, therefore, the wages of workers in developed countries and increasing the wages in developing countries. The main assumptions used for the formulation of the theory are: the production factors are qualitatively the same between economies; the production functions are also the same among economies; free movement of goods among economies; there are no transport costs or import taxes; and production factors do not move among economies. Starting from these conditions, Samuelson shows that, in equilibrium, the real prices of factors will be the same among economies.[2]

Starting from the theoretical structure of HO, Rybczynski (1955) examines the effects of an increase on the supply of one of the production factors, keeping constant the supply of the other factor. He shows that the increase in the supply of a factor results in an absolute increase of the production of the good that uses this factor intensively, and in an absolute decrease in production of the other good. The result is the worsening of the terms of trade between the goods, with a price reduction of the good that uses the now more abundant productive factor. An important implication of this theorem is that it helps to show how the entrance of countries with supply of such different factors in the international economy affects the returns of factors. According to the theorem, the entrance of developing countries in international trade is sufficient to expand the absolute supply of the labour factor in the international market, affecting its returns (for example, China and India). Notice that this effect will be observed with the entrance of developing countries in international trade, not requiring changes in the structure of protection. Rybczynski shows that the predictions of SS are applied without the need of reduction or elimination of protection. What matters are the effects of the absolute increase in the supply of production factors on their international prices.

The crucial point of the standard theory of international trade is the correspondence between prices of products and prices of factors, which implies that an increase of the relative price of a good results in an increase of the relative return of the factor used intensively to produce that good. The result is that trade liberalisation changes the relative prices of the factors of production in an economy in accordance with the changes in the demand of goods determined by the entrance of the country in the international economy.

The recent literature on trade and income distribution elaborates the above analysis by considering capital, skilled and unskilled labour as the relevant factors of production. The theoretical justification is the assumption of complementarity of capital and skilled labour, as originally proposed by Rosen (1968) and Griliches (1969), and recently explored by Goldin and Katz (1998), Krusell et al. (1997) among others. Thus, contrary to the traditional theory which treats labour as a homogenous factor of production, labour is divided into skilled and unskilled labour, the returns of which can be differently affected by international trade. It is always assumed that developed countries are abundant in skilled labour, while developing countries are abundant in unskilled labour.

The main predictions of the standard theory of international trade for the distribution of wages are summarised in Table 14.1.

Many of the assumptions required for the SS and FPE are obviously unrealistic, as Samuelson recognised, especially those concerning the homogeneity of goods, factors and production functions among economies. Therefore, the predictions of the theorems may not be directly applied but instead should be interpreted as long term trends.[3]

Table 14.1
Predicted Effects of the Standard Theory of International Trade on the Distribution of Wages

Developed countries	Developing countries
The opening affects the prices of factors through the change of relative prices of goods. Openness provokes reduction of the relative prices of products intensive in unskilled labour and increases the relative prices of products intensive in skilled labour. As a consequence, the relative wage of skilled labour should increase, while that of unskilled labour should decrease	The opening affects the prices of factors through the change of relative prices of goods. Openness provokes reduction of relative prices of products intensive in skilled labour and increased the relative prices of products intensive in unskilled labour. As a consequence, the relative wage of skilled labour should decrease, while that of unskilled labour should increase
After liberalisation, unskilled labour should suffer a reduction of the relative wage more than proportional to the reduction of the prices of goods intensive in that factor	After liberalisation, skilled labour should suffer a reduction of the relative wage more than proportional to the reduction of the prices of goods intensive in that factor
Convergence of the absolute prices of factors of production among countries as liberalisation intensifies, the trade barriers are removed, and the imperfections and frictions of market mechanisms disappear	Convergence of the absolute prices of factors of production among countries as liberalisation intensifies, the trade barriers are removed, and the imperfections and frictions of market mechanisms disappear
Wage inequality should increase	Wage inequality should decrease

14.3   EMPIRICAL EVIDENCE

Since the early 1970s in the USA, the 1980s in some other OECD countries, and late 1980s and 1990s in several developing countries, it has been observed that earnings have become more unequal between more and less skilled workers.[4] This phenomenon has coincided with periods of trade liberalisation which drove economists to search for a causal relation between the two facts. In this section we present a selection of empirical studies on international trade and wage inequality in developed and developing countries.

Two approaches have been widely employed to investigate the empirical relationship between shifts in international trade and changes in the wage dispersion: the factor content of trade analysis used by labour economists, and the trade framework used by trade economists. Slaughter (1999) shows that these two approaches are distinguished by how they model the national labour demand schedule. While trade economists are concerned with the effects of an increase of trade on the production structure and price changes across industries and therefore on the income of the production factors, labour economists concentrate their attention on the effects of trade on the income of factors through the content of production factors in the exported and imported goods which are added to the domestic supplies, and thus determine the effective supply of the factors. Succinctly, while the trade approach assumes multiple sectors, the labour approach assumes a single sector. Consequently, they imply different empirical strategies for analysing rising wage inequality.

In order to assess the HO and SS predictions, trade economists investigate the impacts of international trade on wages through changes in product prices. When price increases are concentrated in skill intensive sectors, relative wages of skilled workers adjust in response to demand shifts for these workers, while demand for unskilled workers tends to decrease, causing a reduction in their relative wages. Thus, sector bias matters in the explanation for wage changes. In the case where openness alters technology either through trade or inflow of innovations, knowledge, capital and foreign competition, wages tend to rise for workers employed intensively in industries experiencing relatively large technology gains, and vice versa for workers in other sectors.

To test the factor content of trade, one calculates how much skilled and unskilled labour is contained in the production of goods exported by a country and compares them with the required amount of these workers if the imported goods were produced internally. The difference between the amount of factors used in exports and imports is interpreted as the net impact of trade in the demand for skilled and unskilled labour, which is then compared with the demand that would be observed in the absence of international trade. If, for example, the exported goods require more unskilled labour than the imported goods, then the increase of trade would increase the demand for this production factor and consequently its relative earnings. A developed country imports goods from developing countries with high content of unskilled labour, but exports goods with high content of skilled labour, which increases the 'relative supply' of unskilled labour within the country, and vice versa for skilled labour. The balance between factors that 'come in' and 'come out' in the economy through trade determines the impact on relative earnings.

A great deal of work has investigated the role of technological innovations in demand for skilled workers, that is, the skill-biased technological change (SBTC) hypothesis. It is claimed that labour demand in many advanced economies has shifted away from unskilled workers toward skilled workers as a consequence of technologies that require less workers but more qualifications (Berman et al. 1994; Berman et al. 1998). The SBTC hypothesis has no *direct* link with trade, at least in the case of developed countries, although the same seems not to be true of developing countries, as will be discussed later. The SBTC hypothesis is seen as the main theoretical alternative to the view that trade is the key cause of rising wage inequality.

14.3.1 Evidence for Developed Countries

In general, empirical research shows that the impact of international trade on wage inequality is modest. This can be partly explained by the small proportion of products imported from developing countries (Krugman 1995; Desjonqueres et al. 1999). In the USA, for example, only about 30 per cent of total imports come from developing countries, which represents less than 4 per cent of GNP. Most of the trade flow of the OECD countries is limited to trade among themselves, leaving little room for the labour market to be affected by imports from developing countries. Additionally, in the last 30 years, developing countries have opened up relatively more than advanced countries. Although the average degree of openness of advanced economies is twice as great as that of developing economies, between 1970 and 1992 the growth rate of the degree of openness of developing countries was higher than that of developed countries.[5]

Empirical work which looks for an association between trade, prices and rising skill premium has mixed results. On the one hand, Sachs and Shatz (1994) and Haskel and Slaughter (2001) investigate the cases of the USA and the UK, respectively, and find a relative increase in prices of products intensive in skilled labour as a result of international trade. Leamer (1994; 1996) also finds an increase in relative prices of products intensive in skilled labour and a fall in relative prices of sectors intensive in unskilled labour (textile, clothes, footwear) for the USA, but only in the 1970s, when there was a large increase in American imports. Haskel and Slaughter (2000) find effects of changes in the US trade barriers on wage inequality through sector-biased changes in prices. Greenhalgh, Gregory and Zissimos (1998) find that international trade has a negative effect on the wages of less skilled workers in the UK. On the other hand, Lawrence and Slaughter (1993) and Bhagwati (1991) do not find a clear trend in relative prices of goods in the USA during the 1980s. Revenga (1992) measures the impact of changes in imports on wages in the USA and finds that the prices of imported goods have small effects on wages. Krugman (1995) shows that American trade with developing countries had only a small impact on prices and wages. Grossman (1987) observes only minor sensitivity of wages to tariff changes and prices of imports in the USA, although he finds that the impact on employment levels is significant in a few industries. Freeman and Katz (1991) and Gaston and Tefler (1995) show that international trade has a significant effect on inter-industry structure of employment in the USA in the short term, but only a small impact on wages.

Many studies have addressed the impact of technology on wages in the HO framework, such as Baldwin and Cain (2000), Berman et al. (1998) and Leamer (1998). Studies assessing the sector bias of technological change find evidence that total factor productivity (TFP) raised skill differentials in the USA (Leamer 1998). Haskel and Slaughter (2001) find evidence on TFP changes and foreign competition in the UK. Feenstra and Hanson (1999) decompose the US TFP and find that computerisation (and outsourcing) have affected wage inequality.

The literature which uses factor content of trade analysis to test the effects of trade on wages finds favourable evidence for the predictions of the HO. Borjas et al. (1992) show that the increase in the relative supply of unskilled labour derived from trade is responsible for the increase of 15 per cent in income inequality in the USA. Sachs and Shatz (1994) find for the USA that the increase in international trade reduces the demand for employment in sectors that produce goods intensive in unskilled labour due to the reduction of production of those goods. Katz and Murphy (1992) find that changes in the labour content of US imports have had only a very small effect on wages. Wood (1994) analyses the case of several developed countries and shows that 20 per cent of the decline in the demand for unskilled labour is a result of international trade. Feenstra and Hanson (2000) employ a more appropriate calculation and industry level disaggregation and find that trade has only a small impact on the relative supply of unskilled workers in the USA.[6]

Outsourcing of goods to developing countries has also been seen as a source of wage inequality in developed countries. Slaughter (1995) and Feenstra and Hanson (1996) examine whether the outsourcing of American companies in developing countries contributes to the explanation of the increase of wage inequality in the USA and find only a modest contribution as a cause of the decline of wages of unskilled workers. Anderton and Brenton (1998), however, find that outsourcing contributes significantly to explain the decline of relative wages and employment of unskilled workers in the UK. Such an effect is found to be especially important in industries that require little capital stock and technology, such as textiles and footwear.

Using the SBTC hypothesis, Berman et al. (1994) decompose the increase in the demand for skilled labour in the US manufacturing sector and find that 70 per cent of the variation can be explained by changes within industries, and that only 30 per cent is due to changes across industries. Such a result is interpreted to indicate that most of the change in the structure of labour demand in favour of skilled workers occurs due to technological innovations, and not to changes associated with international competition. Machin (1996) uses the same decomposition to investigate the case of the UK and finds that 83 per cent of changes in labour demand can be explained by intra-industrial variations. Machin also shows that research and development, technological innovations and, above all, the use of computers, are important factors in the rise in the relative demand for skilled labour. Desjonqueres et al. (1999) and Berman et al. (1998) show that the increase in relative demand for skilled labour in several OECD countries is associated with the introduction of new technologies. Berman et al. also find that the main changes in the structure of labour demand in several developed countries are restricted to the same industries. They interpret this result as evidence that innovations and technological diffusion are concentrated in some industries, independent of whether the sectors are tradables or non-tradables. They also show that the share of skilled workers increased in all sectors of the economy, and not just limited to tradables, suggesting that there was an upgrade of technology which cut across the economy.

Overall, the empirical research shows that the increasing wage dispersion in developed countries cannot be unequivocally credited to trade with developing countries. Although there is no consensus on the causes of rising wage inequality, it is agreed that, whatever the reason behind the phenomenon, the change in the structure of labour demand in favour of skilled workers is a common feature.

14.3.2 Evidence for Developing Countries

This section presents a selection of empirical results on the effects of trade liberalisation on the labour markets of developing countries. Although the findings are mixed, there is growing empirical evidence showing that trade is being associated with an increase, not a decrease, in the relative demand for skilled workers and rising wage inequality, thus rejecting the predictions of the HO and SS. It seems that while Latin American and other countries have experienced an increase of wage dispersion after trade liberalisation, East Asian countries had an improvement in income inequality indicators after openness with a strong orientation towards exports was introduced in the 1960s and 1970s. Accordingly, Wood (1994; 1999) finds rising demand for unskilled labour and decline in wage inequality in South Korea, Taiwan and Singapore following trade liberalisation. These cases are consistent with the hypothesis that the integration of developing countries in the international economy is accompanied by a reduction of income inequality and greater employment (Krueger 1983; 1990).

The above optimistic hypothesis, however, is challenged by a large number of papers on countries that opened up to trade later. The evidence is increasingly supporting the view that the debate is no longer about the causal effects of openness on inequality, but rather the magnitude of the growth of inequality. Robbins (1995) examines the changes of wage differentials in Colombia in response to the increase of exports due to exchange rate devaluations and to the increase of the proportion of imports of capital goods in relation to GDP. He finds an increase in wage differentials, which was attributed to changes in the composition of demand induced by exports, and a positive correlation between the increase of imports of machines, equipment and introduction of new technologies, and the rising demand for skilled labour. Robbins and Gindling (1999) investigate the changes in relative wages and in supply and demand for skilled labour in Costa Rica before and after trade liberalisation and find that the skill premium rose after liberalisation as a result of the changes in the structure of labour demand. Robbins (1994a) examines the changes in the structure of wages after trade liberalisation in Chile and finds that although the content of skilled labour in imports exceeds the content in exports, the returns to skilled labour grew following liberalisation. Robbins concludes that the most plausible explanation for the result is the increasing imports of capital goods that are complementary to skilled labour. Beyer et al. (1999) use a time series approach and find a long term correlation between openness and wage inequality in Chile.

Hanson and Harrison (1999) examine the changes in wages and employment of skilled and unskilled workers after trade liberalisation in Mexico. They find little variation in employment levels, but a significant increase in skilled workers' relative wages. However, no correlation was found between the intensity of skilled labour and changes in relative prices, as suggested by the SS model. They also show that foreign companies and the ones linked with exports pay higher wages to skilled labour. Feliciano (1993) and Cragg and Epelbaum (1996) find that the increase in the returns to education in Mexico contributed to the rise of relative wages of skilled workers. Green et al. (2001) find a substantial rise in the returns to college education in Brazil following trade liberalisation, which was shown to be due to rising relative demand for college educated workers. However, contrary to what was found for other developing countries, there was no change in overall wage inequality. They show that the small proportion of college educated workers and the rise of wages of illiterate workers contributed to the result. Barros et al. (2001) use a computable general equilibrium analysis to assess the effects of trade liberalisation on the Brazilian labour market and also find no significant impact of openness on income inequality.

Feenstra and Hanson (1997) show that the American '*maquiladoras*' in the north of Mexico caused a significant increase in the relative demand for skilled workers in the border region with the USA, where there is a large concentration of foreign direct investment. They decompose the increase in demand for skilled labour and find that, as in developed countries, most of the change in the structure of demand is explained by intra-industry variations, that is to say, it is associated with the introduction of technologies that require skilled labour. Menezes-Filho and Rodrigues (2001) also employ the same decomposition analysis and observe similar results for Brazilian manufacturing after liberalisation. Arbache and Corseuil (2000) find that employment shares in Brazilian manufacturing are negatively associated with import penetration, and this effect is stronger for industries intensive in unskilled labour. They also show that the inter-industry wage premium is positively associated with import penetration. Arbache and Menezes-Filho (2000) also find a positive relationship between the inter-industry wage premium and tariff reductions in Brazil. They show that product market rents are strongly affected by trade liberalisation, and that part of the rents are distributed to the labour market in the form of a higher wage premium through increasing productivity.

Another strand of research looks for the effects of trade on employment. If developing countries are full of unskilled workers, openness will lead to an expansion of employment of unskilled labour intensive sectors, which are supposed to dominate their economies, thus increasing employment. Márquez and Pagés (1997) estimate labour demand models with panel data for 18 Latin American countries and find that trade reforms had a negative effect on employment growth. Maia (2001) uses input-output analysis to investigate the impact of trade and technology on skilled and unskilled labour in Brazil before and after openness. She finds that trade destroyed more unskilled than skilled jobs and that technology was responsible for the creation of a very large proportion of the skilled jobs, while it destroyed millions of unskilled jobs. Currie and Harrison (1997) and Revenga (1997) find for Morocco and Mexico, respectively, a modest impact of reductions in tariff levels and import quotas on employment, which was due partly to firms cutting margins and raising productivity.

Overall, empirical evidence suggests a relationship between trade liberalisation, wage inequality and employment which goes in the opposite direction to the predictions of the standard theory of international trade. Whatever the explanation for the phenomena, it requires a more sophisticated theoretical treatment than the available models. A tentative summary of empirical evidence would show a common feature of the impact of trade liberalisation on labour markets in developed and developing countries, that is, a change in the structure of labour demand in favour of skilled workers. This does not imply, however, that the causes of the shift of labour demand are also common to the two groups of countries. In the next section we present and discuss hypotheses and models that try to explain the rising wage inequality in developing countries following trade openness.

14.4   TRADE LIBERALISATION AND WAGE INEQUALITY IN DEVELOPING COUNTRIES: NEW EXPLANATIONS

14.4.1   Capital, Technology and Skilled Labour

The new growth theory argues that trade liberalisation expands markets, induces the increase of research and development, reallocates employment to more innovative activities that require more human capital, and increases the knowledge flow among countries. This view is shared by many authors who have contributed to the new growth theories, such as Aghion and Howitt (1992), Grossman and Helpman (1991), Parente and Prescott (1994) and Romer (1990). Accordingly, Sarquis and Arbache (2001) argue and show empirically that an economy may benefit from being more open through enhancing the external effects of human capital, and Edwards (1998) and Cameron et al. (1998) present empirical evidence that more open economies grow more quickly and have larger TFP growth rates. While an integrated theoretical body (see a survey of the theory in Aghion and Howitt 1998), the new growth theory suggests that there exists a positive correlation between openness, growth and human capital, or alternative factors related to education and knowledge such as research and development and innovations. In this context, more liberal policies on trade, investment, and financial and capital markets tend to create better prospects for growth and should attract foreign direct investment.

The process of economic openness tends to be accompanied by the introduction of new technologies, new practices of human resource administration, more efficient production processes, and the incorporation of new and more advanced machines and equipment. Additionally, the greater access to international markets of goods and capital reduces the costs of investment and imported machines and technologies, making possible higher growth rates for investment and productivity.

To see how the new growth theory can be employed to explain the relation between trade liberalisation and labour markets in developing countries, suppose the following hypothetical – and quite simple – scenario: (i) two countries, one of which is technologically advanced and the other is less advanced; (ii) capital and skilled labour are complementary production factors; and (iii) the advanced technology is built into machines and equipment produced in the more advanced country. If the less advanced country introduces a trade liberalisation policy, the import price of capital goods should drop. As long as the capital goods have incorporated new technologies, the increase of imports of machines and equipment should cause a diffusion of technical innovations, changing the technological level of the less advanced country.

The key questions for our purpose are: 'How does greater capital and technology imports affect the labour market of the less advanced country?' and 'Will there be an increase in the relative demand for skilled labour as a result of the complementarity of capital, technology and skilled labour?'. Provided that the capital goods and technologies transferred to developing countries through trade with the more advanced country are biased in favour of skilled labour, since they were developed in the country where this factor is abundant, the structure of labour demand tends to move in favour of skilled labour, and there should be an increase in the returns to human capital. This hypothesis was described by Robbins (1996) as 'skill-enhancing trade'. In fact, Berthélemy et al. (1997) use a cross-country analysis and find evidence of a positive correlation between the increase of returns to schooling and economic openness. The intensity of the increase of relative demand for skilled labour will depend, however, on the growth rate of capital per worker (Johnson 1997). Therefore, the greater the amount of foreign direct investment and the increase of imports of machines and equipments, the greater the effects on the structure of labour demand.

Ceteris paribus, the growing demand for skilled labour may have, as a consequence, an increase, and not a decrease, in wage dispersion of developing countries, which is the opposite of what the standard theory of international trade predicts. The change in the distribution of wages will depend (i) on the technological gap between the new and the old technology – the more intensive in skilled labour the new technology, the larger the changes in the wage distribution (O'Connor and Lunati 1999); and (ii) on how intense the imports of capital are.

Although the complementarity of capital and skilled labour and the complementarity of technology and skilled labour are linked, since technology is built into machines and equipment, conceptually these effects are different, since the first refers to the elasticity of substitution between production factors for a given technology, while the second refers to a bias in the technology towards a production factor. Recent studies examine the statistical relationship between technology and demand for labour in developed countries using research and development proxies (Berman et al. 1994) and use of computers (Author et al. 1998; Green et al. 2001) and find a strong positive correlation between them. Other studies investigate the relation between stock of physical capital and demand for skilled labour (Bartel and Lichtenberg 1987; Berndt et al. 1995; Dunne and Schmitz 1995; Wolff 1996) and find a strong positive correlation as well.

The effects of openness on wage distribution in the short term will, however, be the result of the supply and demand conditions of skilled and unskilled labour and of the nature of the economic transformations provoked by openness. Given an autonomous increase in the demand for skilled labour, the increase in this factor's supply can grow since developing countries usually have a low enrolment rate in school (in relation to developed countries). That is to say, there is room for increasing the human capital stock. The profile of the distribution of schooling is important in determining the economy's capacity to supply skilled labour in the face of an autonomous increase in that factor's demand. The higher the proportion of the population in high school, the greater is the capacity for faster adjustment in the labour market, since with a little investment it can increase the supply of people with higher education. In the case where that proportion is small and most of the population has just primary education, the responsiveness will be slower, which can have adverse effects on income distribution, even in a middle term. The analysis becomes more complex when the schooling distribution for age cohorts and the profile of the age distribution of the population are considered. A young population with a high rate of school attendance provides an ideal and dynamic supply, in the medium and long term, to face the process of economic growth. Lucas (1988) stresses that the quality of education is as important as its quantity. Thus, analyses of skilled labour supply should consider not only the schooling of the population, but also the quality of the education.[7]

The relative increase in demand for skilled labour can have more intense effects on developing than on developed countries due to the high shortage of skilled labour. But these effects will depend on the elasticity of substitution between skilled and unskilled labour and on the supply of skilled labour in the short term. The smaller the substitutability of skilled for unskilled labour, and the more inelastic the supply of skilled labour, the larger the dispersion of wages will be. Thus, supposing that there is an autonomous and proportional increase in the demand for skilled and unskilled labour, the new wage equilibrium should show a relative increase in skilled workers' wages, since the supply of unskilled labour is more elastic. This suggests that the mean elasticity of substitution of skilled labour for unskilled labour is larger in developed than in developing countries, since the supply of skilled labour is greater in those countries.

These considerations imply that (i) the introduction of capital and new technologies can increase inequality more quickly in developing countries than in developed countries due to the greater shortage of skilled labour, and that (ii) any spurt in economic growth caused by openness will not have a neutral effect on relative wages, even if the growth is neutral in relation to the factor inputs and if the supply of these inputs grows at the same rate as GDP. On the other hand, the HO and SS would predict that the reduction of wage inequality in developing countries which have experienced openness should be modest due to the excess of unskilled labour.

In spite of the elegance of the above arguments which try to explain the increasing wage inequality in developing countries following openness, it may happen that (i) trade liberalisation may not have any impact on the accumulation of human capital and on the attraction of foreign direct investments, or that (ii) the worsening of wage inequality indicators in developing countries is a transitory, and not a permanent, effect. In that case, the effects mentioned above may not happen, or the change of the structure of labour demand in favor of skilled labour can be transitory, if it occurs at all.

Lucas (1990) argues that the low or non-existent supply of skilled labour in developing countries can reduce foreign direct investment, since financial capital tends to migrate to areas in which human capital is abundant. Based on his 1988 model which shows a dynamic relation between schooling and physical capital – where human capital is measured both as the level of individual schooling (internal effect), and as an average level of education which also has a positive effect on the production function (external effect) – Lucas argues that unlike what is suggested by the neoclassical theory, capital does not necessarily migrate from rich to poor countries. The reason is that in poor countries the stock of internal and external human capital is low and this has an adverse effect on the marginal productivity of physical capital which is higher where there are larger amounts of internal and external human capital. Thus, the availability of human capital would work as an incentive to foreign direct investment. Benhabib and Spiegel (1994) use cross-country analysis to find a positive relationship between the stock of human capital and investment in physical capital, which suggests that the return on investment is a positive function of the supply of human capital. Thus, it may be that economic openness is a necessary but not a sufficient condition to attract capital and advanced technologies to developing countries.

Nelson (1994) argues that human capital is not *per se* enough to guarantee the attraction of capital and new technologies. The institutional framework can be a decisive factor in the development of new technologies. Romer (1993) also highlights the importance of the institutional framework as a factor to explain economic growth. Other factors may also contribute to growth such as low transaction and transport costs, a well defined regulatory and legal framework, good social infrastructure, political stability, among other things. Knowing that not all developing countries enjoy these conditions, it can be said that economic openness is a factor that contributes but does not determine investment in physical capital and technology. In light of these caveats, openness should not be seen as a panacea for growth, nor as a cause of the increase in wage inequality in developing countries.

Pissarides (1997) presents a model that shows that the increase in wage inequality in developing countries may only be a transitory, and not a permanent, effect. The idea is that openness favours faster transfers of new technologies to developing countries which require skilled labour, increasing the returns to human capital. However, Pissarides suggests that technology transfer is neutral after the effects of a learning period for assimilation and implementation of the new production processes wears off. As soon as workers learn the new technologies, there is a reduction of the effects of openness on the structure of labour demand for skilled labour, since the economy reaches a new technological steady state level. Therefore, the effect of the increase on the returns to human capital is temporary, and the skilled workers benefit only during the transition period to the new technological level. Furthermore, the supply of skilled labour can increase in the long term as a response to the initial increase in the demand for this factor, resulting in the disappearance in the long term of the wage differential gain for the skilled workers. Goldin and Katz (1998) reach a similar conclusion. They argue that the demand for skilled workers can follow a technological cycle. The demand rises when new technologies and machinery are introduced, but it declines with the learning of their use by workers.

Therefore, the transfer of technologies does not guarantee that the wage inequality observed in the initial stages of openness prevails in the long term. It is necessary to differentiate the process of innovation, which requires cognitive human capital, from the process of productive implementation, which requires learning-by-doing. The imports of capital goods and of new technologies of developed countries is connected to the second case, which does not guarantee dynamic change in the technological level.

14.4.2 Other Possible Explanations

Davis (1996) presents a model in which the main hypothesis is that the availability of a country's production factors is taken in relation to a group of countries with similar endowments, not in relation to the international economy. Davis proposes a simplified model with only two cones of production diversification, one for developed and another for developing countries. The countries of one cone produce goods that are not produced in the countries of the other cone. Inside each cone are countries with relatively similar, but not the same, supply of factors, which gives each country different comparative advantages inside its cone, leading it to a specialisation of production. Thus, the availability of factors should be taken from the relative, and not from the absolute perspective. In another way, a country may not be abundant in skilled labour on a global scale, but it can be abundant in skilled labour inside its cone. In the same way, a country that is abundant in skilled labour in a global level may not be abundant in skilled labour inside its cone. What matters in the model is the relative position of the country in its own cone, and not in relation to all countries.

In this framework, trade liberalisation can raise the demand for skilled labour in a developing country as long as it is among the countries of its cone which has a relatively high supply of skilled labour. On the other hand, a country from a cone where there is a greater supply of unskilled labour can experience a reduction in wage inequality. The reduction of the prices of products produced in the other cone (products of developed countries) does not have any effect on the prices of the factors of production in developing countries, since they do not produce the same goods.

Wood (1999) argues that the entry of countries like China, India, Bangladesh, Pakistan and Indonesia in the world market for goods with a high content of unskilled labour in the mid-1980s had an important impact on the explanation of the increased income inequality of medium-income countries, particularly those in Latin America. His argument is that the increased supply of unskilled labour-intensive goods changed the structure of supply of goods in the world market, reducing their prices and the return to factors involved in the production of such goods. This harmed the countries which had some comparative advantage in their production. As a consequence, these countries would have been pressured to change their production techniques in a search for comparative advantage in the production of goods which use semi-skilled labour, resulting in an increase in the demand for this type of worker and therefore causing a rise of the wage dispersion.

Feenstra and Hanson (1995) develops a model that shows that the increase of wage inequality in developed and developing countries is consistent with capital flow from advanced to developing countries in an era of globalisation. The idea is that the flow of foreign direct investment changes the structure of production and increases the stock of capital of developing countries, which can have significant effects on the level and profile of investment and in the technologies available locally. The model assumes the production of a simple final good that requires a continuum of intermediary goods with varying proportions of skilled and unskilled labour. Developing countries have a smaller cost of production for some phases of the final good, and vice versa for developed countries. As soon as the economies open up, and assuming that capital returns are higher in developing countries, there will be a transfer of capital from developed to developing countries. In an intuitive way, the model suggests that the stages of production which demand less skilled labour (by the measure of the advanced country) will be transferred to the less developed countries where unskilled labour is relatively cheaper. However, the kind of labour that is actually demanded is skilled when judged from the perspective of the developing countries. The specialisation of production increases the average requirements of labour in both sets of countries, since the average input will be more intensive in skilled labour. As a result, the relative demand for skilled labour increases in both regions and thus causes rising wage inequality in both groups of countries.

Although the Davis (1996), Wood (1999), and Hanson and Harrison (1995) models are quite interesting, they are, strictly speaking, derived from the HO and SS approach, since they borrow the central idea that the returns to factors of production are conditional on their relative distribution among countries. Thus, it seems that there would exist two main classes of models to explain the effects of trade liberalisation on the labour market of developing countries: those associated with the HO and SS theory, and those that argue that technological changes coming through trade are the root of the problem. The great difference between the experiences of developed and developing countries is perhaps the timing, since in the former group the liberalisation process and technological transformations were sequential, while among the latter it was a simultaneous process.

14.5   FINAL REMARKS

In this chapter, we saw that the impact of trade liberalisation on labour markets of developing countries is ambiguous. While the Asian tiger countries experienced a reduction in wage inequality – which is in agreement with the standard theory of international trade – the Latin American and other countries experienced a rise in wage inequality following openness. Several models and hypotheses have tried to explain this phenomenon, but none of them can be taken as a general theory. Although quite interesting, the skill enhancing trade hypothesis can be criticised on the grounds that trade liberalisation is a necessary, but not a sufficient condition to explain technological modernisation and the increase in the stock of capital per capita, which are supposed to shift labour demand in favour of skilled workers thus causing wage inequality. Many developing countries have high degrees of economic openness (for example, African countries) which, however, does not guarantee incorporation of new technologies, increase in TFP and attraction of foreign direct investment. Human capital, the institutional framework and political stability, for example, all seem to contribute significantly in attracting capital and new technologies. Therefore, openness is a factor that contributes but does not completely determine investment in capital and new technologies. Whatever the reason behind the phenomenon, new technologies seem to play a role in the explanation of the shift in labour demand.

Finally, it may be that the available empirical evidence shows only a transitory rather than a permanent picture. In this case, the standard theory of international trade would still keep its status as the key analytical tool for understanding the relationship between trade and wages.

NOTES

1   Some other causes have been proposed to explain the increasing income inequality, such as changes in industrial structure, decline of institutions, especially the decreasing union density and bargaining power (Gosling and Machin 1995), decline of minimum wages (Fortin and Lemieux 1997), and migration of less skilled workers (Borjas et al. 1992).

2   The predictions of this theory irritated politicians and labour unions of developed countries because of the fear that globalisation (and especially NAFTA, in the American case) is a threat to employment and wages (see discussion in Slaughter 1999).

3   There are alternative theories that differ from the SS results, for example, the factor intensity reversal, the Metzler paradox, and the specific factor model, associated with Ricardo and Viner. The study of these theories goes beyond the scope of this text.

4   For a detailed survey of the theoretical and empirical literature, see for example, Cline (1997).

5   Calculated with data from Penn World Table 5.6 for medium and low income developing countries and OECD countries. The concept of economic openness used is (exports + imports)/GNP.

6   Leamer (1998) severely criticises the factor content of trade approach arguing that exogenous output prices, not endogenous factor quantities, determine relative wages.

7   Wood (1994) and Robbins (1994b) show that the rise in the supply of formal education is a fundamental factor in explaining the fall of wage inequality verified in the Asian tigers and in Malaysia.

BIBLIOGRAPHY

Aghion, P. and P. Howitt (1992), 'A Model of Growth Through Creative Destruction', *Econometrica*, **60**, 323–51.

Aghion, P. and P. Howitt (1998), *Endogenous Growth Theory*, Cambridge, MS: The MIT Press.

Anderton, B. and P. Brenton (1998), 'Outsourcing and Low-Skilled Workers in the UK', GSGR Working Paper No.12/98, University of Warwick.

Arbache, J.S. and C.H. Corseuil (2000), 'Trade Liberalization and Structures of Wage and Employment' [*Liberalização comercial e estrutura de emprego e salários*], Campinas: Anais do XXVIII Encontro Nacional de Economia.

Arbache, J.S. and N. Menezes-Filho (2000), 'Rent-Sharing in Brazil: Using Trade Liberalization as a Natural Experiment', Rio de Janeiro: Annals of the V Annual Meeting of the Latin American and Caribbean Economic Association.

Author, D., L. Katz and A. Krueger (1998), 'Computing Inequality: Have Computers Changed the Labor Market?', *Quarterly Journal of Economics*, **113**, 1169–213.

Baldwin, R.E. and G.C. Cain (2000), 'Shifts in US Relative Wages: The Role of Trade, Technology, and Factor Endowments', *Review of Economics and Statistics*, **82**, 580–95.

Barros, R.P., C.H. Corseuil, S. Cury and P.G. Leite (2001), 'Openness and Income Distribution in Brazil' [*Abertura econômica e distribuição de renda no Brasil*], Proceedings of the Workshop on Trade Liberalization and the Labor Market in Brazil, Brasília, UnB/IPEA.

Bartel, A.P. and R. Lichtenberg (1987), 'The Comparative Advantage of Educated Workers in Implementing New Technology', *Review of Economics and Statistics*, **69**, 1–11.

Benhabib, J. and M.M. Spiegel (1994), 'The Role of Human Capital in Economic Development: Evidence from Aggregate Cross-Country Data', *Journal of Monetary Economics*, **34**, 143–73.

Berman, E.J., J. Bound and Z. Griliches (1994), 'Changes in the Demand for Skilled Labor within US Manufacturing: Evidence from the Annual Survey of Manufacturers', *Quarterly Journal of Economics*, **109**, 367–98.

Berman, E., J. Bound and S. Machin (1998), 'Implications of Skill Biased Technological Change: International Evidence', *Quarterly Journal of Economics*, **113**, 1245–79.

Berndt, E., C.J. Morisson and L.S. Rosenblum (1992), 'High-Tech Capital Formation and Economic Performance in US Manufacturing Industries: An Exploratory Analysis', *Journal of Econometrics*, **65**, 9–73.

Berthélemy, J.C., S. Dessus and A. Varaudakis (1997), 'Human Capital and Growth: The Role of the Trade Regime', mimeo, OECD Development Center.

Beyer, H., P. Rojas and R. Vergara (1999), 'Trade Liberalization and Wage Inequality', *Journal of Development Economics*, **59**, 103–23.

Bhagwati, J. (1991), 'Free Traders and Free Immigrationists: Strangers or Friends?', Russell Sage Foundation Working Paper.

Borjas, G., R. Freeman and L. Katz (1992), 'On the Labor Market Effects of Immigration and Trade', in G. Borjas and R. Freeman (eds), *Immigration and the Work Force: Economic Consequences for the United States and Source Areas*, Chicago: University of Chicago Press and NBER.

Cameron, G., J. Proudman and S. Redding (1998), 'Productivity Convergence and International Openness', in J. Proudman and S. Redding (orgs), *Openness and Growth*, London: Bank of England.

Cline, W.R. (1997), *Trade and Income Distribution*, Washington, DC: Institute for International Economics.

Cragg, M.I. and M. Epelbaum (1996), 'Why Has Wage Dispersion Grown in Mexico? Is it Incidence of Reforms or Growing Demand for Skills?', *Journal of Development Economics*, **51**, 99–116.

Currie, J. and A. Harrison (1997), 'Sharing Costs: The Impact of Trade Reform on Capital and Labor in Marroco', *Journal of Labor Economics*, **15**, s44–s71.

Davis, D.R. (1996), 'Trade Liberalization and Income Distribution', NBER Working Papers #5693.

Desjonqueres, T., S. Machin and J. Van Reenen (1999), 'Another Nail in the Coffin? Or Can the Trade Based Explanation of Changing Skill Structures be Resurrected?', *Scandinavian Journal of Economics*, **101**, 533–54.

Dunne, T. and J.A. Schmitz (1995), 'Wages, Employer Size-Wage Premia and Employment Structure: Their Relationship to Advanced-Technology Usage in US Manufacturing Establishments', *Economica*, **62**, 89–107.

Edwards, S. (1998), 'Openness, Productivity and Growth: What Do We Really Know?', *Economic Journal*, **108**, 383–98.

Feenstra, R.C. and G. Hanson (1995), 'Foreign Investment, Outsourcing and Relative Wages', in R.C. Feenstra and G.M. Grossman (eds), *Political Economy of Trade Policy: Essays in Honor of Jagdish Bhagwati*, Cambridge, MS: The MIT Press.

Feenstra, R.C. and G.H. Hanson (1996), 'Globalization, Outsourcing, and Wage Inequality', *American Economic Review*, **86**, 240–45.

Feenstra, R.C. and G.H. Hanson (1997), 'Foreign Direct Investments and Relative Wages: Evidence from Mexico's Maquiladoras', *Journal of International Economics*, **42**, 371–94.

Feenstra, R.C. and G.H. Hanson (1999), 'The Impact of Outsourcing and High-Technology Capital on Wages: Estimates for the United States, 1979–1990', *Quarterly Journal of Economics*, **114**, 907–40.

Feenstra, R.C. and G.H. Hanson (2000), 'Aggregation Bias in the Factor of Content of Trade: Evidence from US Manufacturing', *American Economic Review*, Papers and Proceedings, **90**, 155–60.

Feliciano, Z. (1993), 'Workers and Trade Liberalization: The Impact of Trade Reforms in Mexico on Wages and Employment', mimeo, Harvard University.

Fortin, N.M. and T. Lemieux (1997), 'Institutional Changes and Rising Wage Inequality: Is There a Linkage?', *Journal of Economic Perspectives*, **11**, 75–96.

Freeman, R.B. (1995), 'Are Your Wages Set in Beijing?', *Journal of Economic Perspectives*, **9**, 15–32.

Freeman, R.B. and L.F. Katz (1991), 'Industrial Wage and Employment Determination in an Open Economy', in J.M. Abowd and R.B. Freeman (eds), *Immigration, Trade, and the Labor Market*, Chicago: University of Chicago Press.

Gaston, N. and D. Tefler (1995), 'Union Wage Sensitivity to Trade and Protection: Theory and Evidence', *Journal of International Economics*, **39**, 1–25.

Goldin, C and L.F. Katz (1998), 'The Origins of Technology-Skill Complementarity', *Quarterly Journal of Economics*, **113**, 693–732.

Gosling, A. and S. Machin (1995), 'Trade Unions and the Dispersion of Earnings in British Establishments, 1980–90', *Oxford Bulletin of Economics and Statistics*, **57**, 167–84.

Gottschalk, P. and T.M. Smeeding (1997), 'Cross-national Comparisons of Earnings and Income Inequality', *Journal of Economic Literature*, **35**, 633–87.

Green, F., A. Dickerson and J.S. Arbache (2001), 'A Picture of Wage Inequality and the Allocation of Labor Through a Period of Trade Liberalization: The Case of Brazil', *World Development*, **29**, 1923–39.

Green, F., A. Felstead and D. Gallie (forthcoming), 'Computers Are Even More Important Than You Thought: An Analysis of the Changing Skill-intensity of Jobs', *Applied Economics*.

Greenhalgh, C., M. Gregory and B. Zissimos (1998), 'The Labor Market Consequences of Technical and Structural Changes', Discussion Paper No. 29, Centre for Economic Performance LSE/University of Oxford.

Griliches, Z. (1969), 'Capital–Skill Complementarity', *Review of Economics and Statistics*, **51**, 465–8.

Grossman, G. (1987), 'The Employment and Wage Effects on Import Competition in the United States', *Journal of International Economic Integration*, **2**, 1–23.

Grossman, G.M. and E. Helpman (1991), *Innovation and Growth in the Global Economy*, Cambridge Mass.: The MIT Press.

Hanson, G.H. and A. Harrison (1995), 'Trade, Technology, and Wage Inequality', NBER Working Paper #5110.

Hanson, G.H. and A. Harrison (1999), 'Trade Liberalization and Wage Inequality in Mexico', *Industrial and Labor Relations Review*, **52**, 271–88.

Haskel, J. and M.J. Slaughter (1998), 'Does the Sector Bias of Skill-biased Technical Change Explain Changing Skill Differentials?', NBER Working Paper #6565.

Haskel, J. and M.J. Slaughter (2000), 'Have Falling Tariffs and Transportation Costs Raised US Wage Inequality?', mimeo, Queen Mary and Westfield College.

Haskel, J. and M.J. Slaughter (2001), 'Trade, Technology and UK Wage Inequality', *Economic Journal*, **111**, 163–87.

Johnson, G.E. (1997), 'Changes in Earnings Inequality: the Role of Demand Shifts', *Journal of Economic Perspectives*, **11**, 41–54.

Jones, R.W. (1965), 'The Structure of Simple General Equilibrium Models', *Journal of Political Economy*, **73**, 557–72.

Katz, L.F. and K.M. Murphy (1992), 'Changes in Relative Wages, 1963–1987: Supply and Demand Factors', *Quarterly Journal of Economics*, **107**, 35–78.

Krueger, A.O. (1983), *Trade and Employment in Developing Countries*, Chicago: Chicago University Press.

Krueger, A.O. (1990), 'The Relationship Between Trade, Employment, and Development', in G. Ranis and T. Schultz (eds), *The State of Development*

Economics: Progress and Perspectives, Cambridge, UK: Basil Blackwell.

Krueger, A.O. (1998), 'Why Trade Liberalization is Good for Growth', *Economic Journal,* **108**, 1513–22.

Krugman, P. (1995), 'Technology, Trade, and Factor Prices', NBER Working Paper #5355.

Krusell, P., L.E. Ohanian, J.V. Ríos-Rull and G.L. Violante (1997), 'Capital–Skill Complementarity and Inequality: A Macroeconomic Analysis', Staff Report 239, Federal Reserve Bank of Minneapolis.

Lawrence, R.Z. and M.J. Slaughter (1993), 'International Trade and American Wages in the 1980s: Giant Sucking Sound or Small Hiccup', *Brooking Papers on Economic Activity,* **2**, 161–226.

Leamer, E.E. (1994), 'Trade, Wages and Revolving-Door Ideas', NBER Working Paper #4716.

Leamer, E.E. (1996), 'Wage Inequality from International Competition and Technological Change: Theory and Country Experience', *American Economic Review,* **86**, 309–314.

Leamer, E.E. (1998), 'In Search of Stolper-Samuelson Effects on U.S. Wages', in Susan Collins (ed.), *Exports, Imports, and the American Worker,* Washington, DC: The Brookings Institution.

Lucas, R.E. (1988), 'On the Mechanics of Economic Development', *Journal of Monetary Economics,* **22**, 3–42.

Lucas, R.E. (1990), 'Why Doesn't Capital Flow from Rich to Poor Countries?', *American Economic Review. Papers and Proceedings,* **80**, 92–6.

Machin, S. (1996), 'Changes in Relative Demand for Skills', in A.L. Booth and D.J. Snower (eds), *Acquiring Skills: Market Failures, their Symptoms and Policy Responses,* Cambridge: Cambridge University Press.

Maia, K. (2001), 'The Impact of Trade, Technology and Final Demand on the Structure of Employment in Brazil, 1985–1995' [*O impacto do comércio, da mudança tecnológica e da demanda final na estrutura de emprego do Brasil, 1985–1995*], Proceedings of the Workshop on Trade Liberalization and the Labor Market in Brazil, Brasília, UnB/IPEA.

Márquez, G. and C. Pagés (1997), 'Trade and Employment: Evidence from Latin America and Caribbean', mimeo, Inter-American Development Bank.

Menezes-Filho, N.A. and M. Rodrigues Jr. (2001), 'Openness, Technology and Skills: Evidence from the Brazilian Manufacturing' [*Abertura, tecnologia e qualificação: evidências para a manufatura brasileira*], Proceedings of the Workshop on Trade Liberalization and the Labor Market in Brazil, Brasília, UnB/IPEA.

Nelson, R.R. (1994), 'What Has Been the Matter with Neo-Classical Growth Theory?', in G. Silverberg and M. Soete (eds), *The Economics of Growth and Technical Change: Technologies, Nations, Agents,* Cheltenham, UK and Northampton, MA: Edward Elgar.

O'Connor, D. and M.R. Lunati (1999), 'Economic Opening and Demand for Skills in Developing Countries: A Review of Theory and Evidence', Technical Papers, No. 149, OECD Development Centre.

Parente, S.L. and E.C. Prescott (1994), 'Barriers to Technology Adoption and Development', *Journal of Political Economy*, **102**, 298–321.

Pissarides, C.A. (1997), 'Learning by Trading and Returns to Human Capital in Developing Countries', *World Bank Economic Review*, **11**, 17–32.

Revenga, A. (1992), 'Exporting Jobs? The Impact of Import Competition on Employment and Wages in US Manufacturing', *Quarterly Journal of Economics*, **107**, 255–84.

Revenga, A. (1997), 'Employment and Wage Effects of Trade Liberalization: The case of Mexican Manufacturing', *Journal of Labor Economics*, **15**, s20–s43.

Robbins, D.J. (1994a), 'Worsening Relative Wage Dispersion in Chile During Trade Liberalization, and its Causes: Is Supply at Fault?', Development Discussion Papers No. 484, Harvard Institute for International Development, Harvard University.

Robbins, D.J. (1994b), 'Malaysian Wage Structure and its Causes', mimeo, Harvard Institute for International Development, Harvard University.

Robbins, D.J. (1995), 'Wage Dispersion and Trade in Colombia: An Analysis of Greater Bogota: 1876–1989', mimeo, Harvard Institute for International Development, Harvard University.

Robbins, D.J. (1996), 'HOS Hits Facts: Facts Win; Evidence on Trade and Wages in the Developing Countries', Development Discussion Paper No. 557, Harvard Institute for International Development.

Robbins, D.J. and T.H. Gindling (1999), 'Trade Liberalization and the Relative Wages for More-skilled Workers in Costa Rica', *Review of Development Economics*, **3**, 140–54.

Romer, P.M. (1990), 'Human Capital and Growth: Theory and Evidence', *Carnegie-Rochester Conference Series on Public Policy*, **32**, 251–86.

Romer, P.M. (1993), 'Idea Gaps and Object Gaps in Economic Development', *Journal of Monetary Economics*, **32**, 513–42.

Rosen, S. (1968), 'Short-Run Employment Variation on Class-I Railroads in the US, 1947–63', *Econometrica*, **36**, 511–29.

Rybczynski, T.M. (1955), 'Factor Endowment and Relative Commodity Prices', *Economica*, **22**, 336–41.

Sachs, J.D. and H.J. Shatz (1994), 'Trade and Jobs in US Manufacturing', *Brooking Papers on Economic Activity*, **1**, 1–84.

Samuelson, P.A. (1948), 'International Trade and the Equalization of Factor Prices', *Economic Journal*, **58**, 163–84.

Samuelson, P.A. (1949), International Factor Price Equalization Once Again', *Economic Journal*, **59**, 181–97.

Sarquis, S.J. and J.S. Arbache (2001), 'Openness and External Effects of Human Capital', mimeo, London School of Economics.

Slaughter, M.J. (1995), 'Multinational Corporations, Outsourcing, and American Wage Divergence', NBER Working Paper #5253.

Slaughter, M.J. (1999), 'Globalisation and Wages: The Tale of Two Perspectives', *World Economy*, **22**, 609–29.

Stokey, N.L. (1991), 'Human Capital, Product Quality and Growth', *Quarterly Journal of Economics*, **106**, 587–616.

Wolff, E.N. (1996), 'Technology and Demand for Skills', STI Review – OECD, **18**, 95–123.

Wood, A. (1994), *North-South Trade, Employment and Inequality. Changing Fortunes in Skill-Driven World*, Oxford, UK: Clarendon Press.

Wood, A. (1999), 'Openness and Wage Inequality in Developing Countries: The Latin American Challenge to East Asian Conventional Wisdom', in R.E. Baldwin, D. Cohen, A. Sapir and A. Venables (eds), *Market Integration, Regionalism and Global the Economy*, Cambridge: Cambridge University Press.

Young, A. (1991), 'Learning by Doing and Dynamic Effects of International Trade', *Quarterly Journal of Economics*, **106**, 369–405.

15 Relative Wages and Trade in a Growing Small Open Economy: Mexico, 1987–95

André Varella Mollick

15.1 INTRODUCTION

Studies of wage inequality across manufacturing industries rely on explanations based on technology and trade. The former directs labour demand towards more specialized workers, increasing the relative demand for skilled workers and their wages (Berman et al. 1994; 1998). Increasing trade with low-wage countries, on the other hand, induces in countries such as the United States a shift in resources towards industries that use skilled labour more intensively, thereby raising wage differentials. Borjas and Ramey (1995) provide (surprising) plots of common trends between the US trade deficit in durable goods and the average log wage differential between college graduates and less educated workers.

Empirical evidence for countries other than the USA has grown lately. For less developed countries (LDCs), Levinsohn (1999) uncovers the role of plant size in employment changes during openness in Chile, but does not discuss wage differentials. An LDC country in which there is plenty of evidence is Mexico. That is perhaps because Mexico opened to trade and slashed tariffs and quotas across all sectors of activity in 1985. Towards the end of the 1980s, Mexico was much more open to foreign trade, with obvious effects on costs and microeconomic efficiency.[1] After a long period of reduction in the relative wage (skilled workers/unskilled workers) from 1965 to 1980, relative wages in Mexico started to grow exactly after 1985 (Feenstra and Hanson 1997).

The author would like to thank, without implicating, João Faria (the editor), Miguel León-Ledesma and José de Jesús Salazar for very helpful comments on an earlier version of this chapter.

Has openness to trade in Mexico played any role in the upward reversal in wage differentials? In Mexico, the widening of the wage gap came together with little change in the relative employment of skilled labour. One explanation for this, consistent with the Stolper–Samuelson theorem, is that trade increased the relative price of skill-intensive products. Hanson and Harrison (1999) report regressions of the log change in output prices on the log ratio of white to blue collar employment over the 1984–90 period in Mexico and do not find a significant correlation. Feenstra and Hanson (1997) argue that the rise in wage inequality across dissimilar countries is consistent with an explanation based on more outsourcing by Northern multinationals contributing to a worldwide increase in the relative demand for skilled labour. They show that the economic effect of FDI on relative wages is as expected in Mexico, although the overall fit of their regressions is very poor.

Other than trade, several studies (for example, Murphy and Welch 1992; and Katz and Murphy 1992) have investigated declines in the relative wages of less–skilled workers and in their employment in US manufacturing. A synthesis of this body of work is that the labour market of less-skilled workers has worsened in the developed world (not only in the USA) in the last two decades, despite their increasing scarcity relative to the rapidly expanding supply of skilled labour (Berman et al. 1998).

Labour economists focus on skill-biased technological change (SBTC) for various reasons. First, as documented in Berman et al. 1994), employment shifts to skill-intensive sectors seem too small, contrary to explanations based on product demand shifts (trade, sector-biased technological change, Hicks-neutral technical progress). Secondly, most US industries have increased the ratio of skilled to unskilled labour, despite the increase in the relative price of skilled labour (Katz and Murphy 1992). Thirdly, there exist strong within-sector correlations between indicators of technological change and increased demand for skills (Berman et al. 1994; and Machin and Van Reenen 1998).

Skill upgrading and SBTC complement the explanation based on openness for the rising trend in relative wages. Lacking reliable data on computer usage and R&D intensity in Mexico, however, the present paper adds to the literature from at least two perspectives. First, we use data for Mexico from 1987 to 1995 and confirm the increasing wage inequality in Mexican manufacturing as measured by wages of skilled relative to unskilled workers. The sample period is not arbitrary: it coincides with the start of Mexican economic reforms towards a more open economy. The data come from Mexico's INEGI and includes national and sector-based data. Secondly, we estimate a model that explains relative wages as a function of import penetration, export intensity, and sales as control variable. This chapter thus moves away from openness only (tariffs and quotas) and delves into a combination of growing trade and growth in explaining the wage gap.

Our major results can be stated simply. Ordinary least squares (OLS) estimates uncover negative and significant import penetration coefficients, while export intensity has no effect. A higher degree of imports contributes to a reduction in the wage gap as expected. However, under exchange rates as instrumental variables, estimation by the generalized method of moments (GMM) suggests that import penetration and export penetration ratios are not significant. Our results are also robust to sector based estimates. Overall, we do not find supportive evidence for the trade-based mechanism in Mexico, despite the considerable increase in external trade in our sample.

This chapter is composed of five sections. Section 15.2 introduces the specifications on trade and the wage gap widening in Mexico. In Section 15.3 we explain the data that come from Mexico's INEGI and Section 15.4 presents the estimations. Section 15.5 reviews the main conclusions of the study and presents extensions for further work.

15.2   HYPOTHESIS AND FRAMEWORK

In a partial equilibrium context, let the wage (w^*) be given to a firm, although the firm may pay a premium to compensate workers for loyalty, firm-specific skills and so on. Firms face two types of worker (skilled and unskilled workers) and may pay a different premium ($> w^*$) to each type of worker. Assume a firm in the manufacturing industry will face an upward sloping curve for labour supply of either type. Assume the demand curve of the industry for each type of labour to be downward sloping. This must be true as long as skilled and unskilled labour are not perfect substitutes for each other. Changes in the volume of trade, created outside the industry, are shocks to the demand for labour.[2]

If countries are different (North and South), it is reasonable to conceive Northern countries as forming an integrated equilibrium, while Southern factor returns differ from those in the North. Trade among Northern countries involves 'horizontal' two-way trade in intermediate goods and North–South trade involves 'vertical' trade of skill-intensive intermediates for labour intensive manufactures.

Under some assumptions, for a given country, changes in the value of the wage gap between skilled and unskilled labour ($\Delta W/W$) will be determined by changes in the relative demand of skilled to unskilled workers ($\Delta D/D$) and relative supply of skilled to unskilled workers ($\Delta S/S$). The whole effect on relative wages is adjusted by a parameter reflecting the degree of substitution between the two types of labour (σ), estimated at around 1.5 in the literature (Johnson 1997):

$$\Delta W/W = (1/\sigma) [\Delta D/D - \Delta S/S] \tag{15.1}$$

In the USA, imports from Mexico are assumed to substitute for labour intensive activities. An increase in Southern imports in the US is a negative shock to the demand for unskilled labour. Given an upward sloping supply curve to the industry, the shock would result in a reduced premium for unskilled workers. Holding shipments constant, increased imports from Mexico imply a shift within the domestic industry toward skill-intensive activities. A higher premium for skilled workers should follow.

More than 80 per cent of Mexican foreign trade is with the USA. Our empirical analysis below employs Mexican data. In Mexico, more imports from the USA should reduce the relative demand for skilled workers. An increase in imports from the North is thus a negative shock to the demand for skilled labour. Given an upward sloping supply curve to the industry, the shock would result in a reduced premium for skilled workers. Holding shipments constant, increased imports from the USA imply a shift within the domestic industry toward less skill-intensive activities. It should be associated with a lower wage premium for skilled workers. More imports from the USA should thus bring about a lower wage gap in Mexico.

On the other hand, to the extent that tradable activities in Mexico employ largely unskilled workers, more exports should raise the relative demand for unskilled workers. That would contribute to a shortened wage gap in favour of skilled workers. When an economy such as Mexico opens to trade, one would expect a higher demand for its products. Mexico produces goods relatively more abundant in the labour factor and a rise in the price of goods abundant in labour should prevail. The effect of more export intensity on the wage gap can be positive only if exports create greater proportional demand for skilled workers, which may happen under SBTC and dynamic externalities. Ignoring this possibility, higher export-intensity should move higher labour demand for unskilled workers, thereby moving down relative demand for labour. The wage gap must fall with higher export intensity.

This reasoning provides us with a simple, 'textbook-like' view of relative wages and trade.[3] Following Pizer (2000), Gaston and Trefler (1994), Revenga (1992), and Freeman and Katz (1991), the following model captures the essence of the demand and supply framework. It is estimated for aggregate Mexican manufacturing as follows:

$$W_{it} = c + \beta_1 \text{Imp}_{it} + \beta_2 \text{Exp}_{it} + \beta_3 S_{it} + \varepsilon_{it} \qquad (15.2)$$

where:

W_{it} = relative wage (wage differential) between skilled and unskilled workers in industry i and month t. In the empirical tests in Section 15.4, W_{it} is measured in three different forms;

Imp_{it} = ratio of import penetration for industry i at month t, defined as the ratio of imports to domestic sales in each industry;

Exp_{it} = ratio of export intensity for industry i at month t, defined as the ratio of exports to domestic sales in each industry;

S_{it} = real sales in industry i and month t.

Contrary to Pizer (2000) and Gaston and Trefler (1994), however, we do not estimate a two–step procedure for the dependent variable since we do not control for workers-specific characteristics (age, sex, education, race, and so on).[4]

Since data on imports for each industry from 1987 to 1995 are not available in Mexico, import penetration ratios can not be calculated for the INEGI's 9-industry decomposition. Export intensity ratios by industry, however, can be calculated and we can estimate a subset of equation (15.2) for the aggregate and for each industry ($i = 1,2, ..., 9$) as follows:

$$W_{it} = c + \beta_1 \text{Exp}_{it} + \beta_2 S_{it} + \varepsilon_{it} \qquad (15.3)$$

We estimate equations (15.2) and (15.3) by OLS and GMM. The latter complements the former in exploring residuals that are uncorrelated with instruments, therefore considering correlations of the instruments and residuals as close to zero as possible. In our context, OLS estimates imply serial correlation. Even though we correct the OLS estimates for serial correlation and heteroskedasticity by using the Newey-West (1987) procedure in the computation of the residuals, GMM provides further evidence on the baseline estimates. In general, GMM yields results that are robust to both serial correlation and heteroskedasticity in time series.

15.3   DATA DESCRIPTION AND MAIN FEATURES

This study examines wage, employment, shipment, and export data for a panel of nine Mexican industries during the 1987–95 period. The beginning year marks the start of Mexico's opening process to foreign trade and in the last year of the sample Mexico was suffering from the currency crisis of December 1994.

INEGI's dataset does not contain imports per sector for the 1987–95 period, which makes us focus on the export side only for analysis of each sector. All Mexican manufacturing data in this study come from Mexico's INEGI and a representative survey of Mexican manufacturing across the country. The frequency is monthly. As measures of industry employment, the number of production workers (unskilled) and non-production workers (skilled) is considered. For the wage variable the average nominal earnings in pesos ('*salarios*' for '*obreros*', blue-collar workers; '*sueldos*' for '*empleados*', white-collar workers) are taken and deflated by the Mexican aggregate consumer price index. We thus obtain the real wage *(relwage)* by type of worker and define the (real) relative wage as the real wage of skilled workers divided by unskilled workers. We also obtain the real wage adjusted for hours worked *(hrwage)* by type of worker and define the (real) relative wage as the real wage of skilled workers adjusted by hours worked, divided by unskilled workers adjusted by hours worked. Finally, our third and last measure of relative wages *(npshare)* is the share of non-production wages in the total wage bill of the manufacturing survey, which is also used in the field (for example, Feenstra and Hanson 1997; and Berman et al. 1998). Note that *npshare* would reflect the wage gap only if labour supply is totally inelastic so that demand changes translate into wage changes and not into employment changes.

The following definitions are useful:

Employment: persons employed during a month in a given establishment or outside it (under the establishment's control), under regular compensation schemes. Employment includes regular workers under temporary leave and excludes workers that provide temporary work through '*honorarios*'. It also excludes retired workers.

Hours Worked: Number of hours, regular and extra, worked during a given month, minus suspended time due to stops, strikes, vacation, illness, or to natural factors.

Non-Production Workers ('Empleados'): workers engaged in planning and supervision, performing accounting, sales, research, advertising, and related functions. It includes the owner of the firm.

Production Workers ('Obreros'): workers engaged in manual work, operating machines and equipment, and also personnel involved in support tasks (cleaning, repair, storing, packing, and so on.)

Wages paid to Non-Production Workers ('Empleados'): the cash amount, before any deduction, paid in a given month to workers. It includes productivity bonuses, incentives, vacational pay, an extra month's pay at the end of the year ('*aguinaldos*'), commissions on sales and temporary leave under payment. It excludes pensions to retired workers, payment of '*honorarios*' to workers not under the payroll and pay for termination of contract.

Wages paid to Production Workers ('Obreros'): the cash amount, before any deduction, paid in a given month to workers. It includes productivity bonuses, incentives, vacational pay, an extra month's pay at the end of the year ('*aguinaldos*'), and temporary leave under payment. It excludes pensions to retired workers and pay for termination of contract.

Exports by industry are in US dollars and shipments (or sales) by industry are in pesos. In order to define the *export intensity ratio* (xint), we divide the exports of each industry by shipments, employing the nominal exchange rate to convert the denominator from pesos into US dollars. The nominal exchange rate also comes from INEGI's data set and is the interbank bid rate. For the whole of the Mexican manufacturing sector, we also define the *import penetration ratio* (*mpen*), defined as the amount of imports divided by shipments, the former also converted into US dollars by the nominal exchange rate.[5]

Figure 15.1 shows for the aggregate of Mexican manufacturing relative wages and non-production employment shares. Real relative wages (*relwage*) moved from about 0.90 to 1.40 in the nine years studied. Real relative wages corrected for hours-worked (*hrwage*) move from about two to three in the period, a higher proportional increase. The share of nonproduction wages in the total wage bill (*npshare*) rises from 0.48 to 0.58. The figure confirms the upward trend of relative wages, whose explanation has been a source of controversy in the literature.

Figure 15.1 also plots two important measures of trade for the aggregate of Mexican manufacturing in our sample. Both export-intensity and import-penetration ratios tripled in the nine years. As expected, after the peso devaluation of December 1994, exports surged and imports fell. Note that the end of 1994 had the peak in the import penetration ratio for Mexico, consistent with studies of currency crisis (for example, Kaminsky and Reinhart 1999) that document rising imports as one indicator of coming currency crisis.

The relative participation of non-production workers in the total workforce has remained stable, at around 0.30, in our sample. Therefore, in contrast to industrial economies such as the USA and the UK that share a trend increase in the share of skilled workers in employment (Berman et al. 1998), Mexican manufacturing has not hired relatively more skilled workers.

Other figures contain relative wages, relative employment, and export intensity ratios for each sector and are available upon request. Common features across the nine sectors of Mexican manufacturing are: (i) rising real relative wages (skilled/unskilled) in all sectors; (ii) flat skilled labour shares in employment in all industries, with the exception of Machinery Equipment (sector 8) that had the ratio fall from about 0.30 to 0.23 in the sample; and (iii) initially flat and then rising export intensity ratios in all sectors.

Some sectors display substantial increases in export intensity levels. Textiles (sector 2), wood (sector 3), and machinery equipment (sector 8) had export intensity ratios of about 0.50 that surged to 2.50 or higher at the end of the sample. Sector 9 (other industries) moved up by many times at the end of the sample, although the sector contributes less than 1 per cent of total employment to Mexican manufacturing.

Across sectors, there has not been much variation in employment shares during the period. Perhaps the only change in the composition was food and

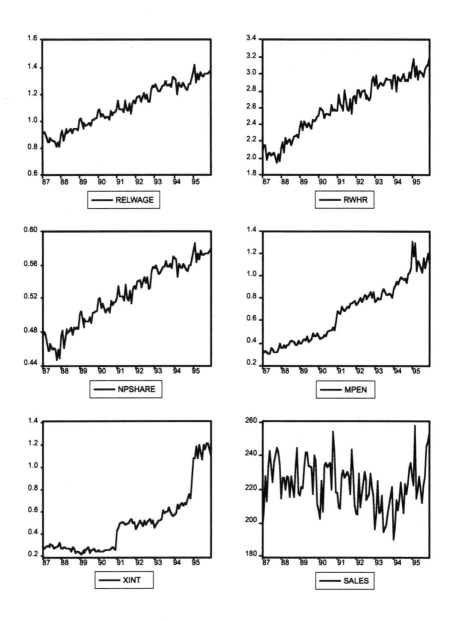

*Figure 15.1   Aggregate Mexican Manufacturing: Real Wage Measures,
            Export-Intensity and Import Penetration Ratios and Real Sales*

beverages that increased its share of total employment from 19 per cent in early 1987 to 23 per cent at the end of 1995, while textiles reduced its share from 13 per cent to 11 per cent. Machinery equipment was the largest employer at the beginning of the sample (29 per cent) and remained at the top at the end (28 per cent).

Table 15.1 reports the variation between 1987 and 1995 of non-production employment shares, non-production wage bill shares, and export intensity ratios. At the aggregate level, while the non-production employment share stays flat

Table 15.1
Mexican Manufacturing: Descriptive Statistics, 1987–95

Sector	Non-production employment shares		Non-production wage bill shares		Export intensity ratios	
	Jan. 87	Dec. 95	Jan. 87	Dec. 95	Jan. 87	Dec. 95
Aggregate Mexican manufacturing	0.3041	0.3038	0.4745	0.5780	0.2911	1.1028
1. Food, beverages, and tobacco	0.3115	0.3359	0.4613	0.5793	0.1519	0.1723
2. Textiles, footwear, and clothing	0.2015	0.2011	0.3177	0.3800	0.3440	3.0895
3. Wood and furniture	0.2311	0.2255	0.3813	0.4481	0.5954	2.8533
4. Paper, printing, and publishing	0.2728	0.2802	0.3966	0.5299	0.1258	0.3323
5. Chemicals, petroleum, and coal products	0.3982	0.4221	0.5788	0.6532	0.2551	0.5188
6. Mineral products	0.2832	0.2892	0.4599	0.6481	0.1996	0.4740
7. Basic metals	0.2825	0.2993	0.4294	0.5511	0.2579	0.5781
8. Machinery and electronic equipment	0.3047	0.2479	0.4863	0.5410	0.4944	2.1201
9. Other industries	0.3525	0.3328	0.5712	0.6773	0.5973	9.3702

Notes: Original data are from Mexico's INEGI. Figures in the table are from author's calculations. The first two columns measure the extent of employment and wages on non-production workers in the total of employment and wages of each industry. The last column has the export-intensity figures for the aggregate and each of the nine sectors, calculated as the ratio of exports to sales, the latter converted into US$ for comparison with exports. See Section 15.3 for detailed explanation.

between the start (0.3041) and the end of our sample (0.3038), there is a substantial increase in the relative participation of non-production wages in total wages (up from 0.4745 to 0.5780). The latter is consistent with what studies for industrial economies (Berman et al. 1998) report but the former is at odds. Our data sample suggests Mexican manufacturing has paid relatively more to non-production workers while keeping the same relative levels of employment.

At the sectoral level, consider first column 1 in Table 15.1. Sector 1 (food, beverages, and tobacco) increases the share of skilled workers in total employment from 31 per cent to almost 34 per cent, while chemicals, petroleum and coal products (sector 5) increases the ratio from 40 per cent to 42 per cent, the highest share across all industries. There is a significant reduction in the skilled labour share of machinery equipment (sector 8) from 30 per cent to 25 per cent. The sector with the lowest share (textiles, sector 2) remained at the same 20 per cent levels of early 1987.

Column 2 in Table 15.1 has the summary of the non-production wage bill shares calculations. It can be seen that there was an overall increase in the ratio at the aggregate (from 0.475 to 0.578) and at each sector. At the end of our sample, only sectors 2 (textiles) and 3 (wood) had non-production shares of less than 50 per cent. Finally, column 3 in Table 15.1 reports the overall rise in export-intensity ratios at both the aggregate and by sector in these years. Aggregate manufacturing has exports to shipments varying more than threefold from 0.2911 in January of 1987 to 1.1028 in December 1995. Some sectors responded differently, however, to more foreign trade: sector 1 (food, beverages, and tobacco) had only minimal gains (from 0.15 to 0.17). All others responded more positively, ranging from sixteen times in other industries, to tenfold in textiles, and twofold in chemicals.

15.4   RESULTS

The correlation coefficients in Table 15.2 for trade and wages match our priors: the relative wage rate is positively correlated to export intensity (0.83), to import penetration (0.94) and is negatively related to real sales (−0.26). Also, the relative wage rate corrected for hours worked is positively correlated to export intensity (0.78), to import penetration (0.92) and is negatively related to real sales (−0.22). The non-production workers' share in the wage bill is also positively correlated to export intensity (0.80), to import penetration (0.93) and is negatively related to real sales (−0.27). The correlation with sales, which is just a control variable, is much weaker. And the correlation coefficients for each pair of the dependent variables (*relwage*, *hrwage*, and *npshare*) are close to one.

Unit root tests in Table 15.3, under the methodology of Dickey-Fuller, document non-stationarity for most of the series in levels and stationarity in

Table 15.2
Correlation Matrix: Aggregate Mexican Manufacturing

	RELWAGE	SALES	MPEN	XINT	NPSHARE	HRWAGE
RELWAGE	1					
SALES	–0.25985	1				
MPEN	0.94314	–0.09338	1			
XINT	0.82791	0.03898	0.91890	1		
NPSHARE	0.99751	–0.26978	0.93283	0.79962	1	
HRWAGE	0.98806	–0.22361	0.92352	0.77988	0.99251	1

Notes: Data are of monthly frequency from 1987:01 to 1995:12. The variables are defined as follows: *Relwage* stands for the relative wage between white-collar (non-production or *empleados*) and blue-collar (production or *obreros*) in Mexican manufacturing. *Hrwage* stands for the relative wage between white-collar (non-production or *empleados*) and blue-collar (production or *obreros*) corrected for hours worked. *NPshare* means the share of non-production workers in the total wage bill in Mexican manufacturing. *Xint* stands for the export intensity in overall manufacturing, defined as: exports/sales. *Mpen* represents the import penetration in manufacturing, defined as: imports/sales. Alternative definitions of *xint* and *mpen* (for example, exports/ (imports + sales – exports) and imports/(imports + sales – exports)) do not alter the results. *Sales* represent real sales of the industry: nominal sales in pesos deflated by the Mexican general consumer price index (1994 = 100). See Section 15.3 for further details on the data construction.

differences. We cannot reject, at the 5-per-cent significance levels, the null hypothesis that there is a unit root in each of the time series when expressed in levels, while we are always able to reject the null in first differences. Under our ADF tests, the series can be classified as integrated of order 1: I(1). The lag selection criterion of the lags in the ADF regressions is based on a data dependent procedure, which usually has more power than an information criterion as showed by Ng and Perron (1995). See notes to Table 15.3 for a detailed explanation.

Table 15.4 reproduces the OLS estimates of specifications (15.2) and (15.3) in Section 15.2 for the aggregate of Mexican industry. For specification (15.2) with three parameters, negative and significant import penetration coefficients are found. A higher degree of imports contributes to a reduction in the wage gap, in agreement with theoretical conjectures. However, export intensity coefficients are never significant. Real sales are control variables and are estimated negative, although not much attention should be paid to their signs given their endogeneity with wages in general equilibrium.

It is interesting to compare these results to some in the literature. For the manufacturing sector in the USA, a similar framework in Revenga (1992) finds sizable significant effects of import competition on employment and wages.

Table 15.3
Unit Root Tests: Aggregate Mexican Manufacturing

Series	Trend included?	ADF (k)	
		Series in levels	Series in first diffs.
Aggregate manufacturing			
Relwage	YES	−2.252 (12)	−7.415 (10) ***
NPshare	YES	−1.984 (12)	−7.989 (10) ***
Hrwage	YES	−1.796 (11)	−7.167 (10) ***
Xint	YES	−1.332 (1)	−3.733 (10) **
Mpen	YES	−3.222 (12) *	−6.171 (5) ***
Sales	NO	−1.082 (12)	−3.002 (12) **

Notes: See notes to Table 15.2. Data are of monthly frequency from 1987:01 to 1995:12. We include the trend or not depending on what is suggested by the plots. ADF(k) refers to the Augmented Dickey-Fuller t-tests for unit roots. The lag length (k) is chosen by the Campbell-Perron data dependent procedure, whose method is usually superior to a fixed k chosen a priori and to k chosen by the information criterion. See Ng and Perron (1995). The method starts with an upper bound, k_{max}=12, on k. If the last included lag is significant, choose k = k_{max}. If not, reduce k by one until the last lag becomes significant (we use the 5 per cent value of the asymptotic normal distribution to assess significance of the last lag). If no lags are significant, then set k = 0. Next to the ADF critical t-value, in parentheses is the selected lag length. The symbols * [**] (***) attached to the figure indicate rejection of the null of no-stationarity at the 10 per cent, 5 per cent, and 1 per cent levels, respectively.

The plant-level study in Bernard and Jensen (1997) argues that increases in employment at exporting plants contribute heavily to the increase in relative demand for skilled labour. Freeman and Katz (1991) find, for the USA, a positive relationship between wage premiums and imports and a negative relationship between wage premiums and imports. Also, Pizer (2000) and Gaston and Trefler (1994) find for the USA a negative association between import penetration and the wage premium, while export intensity is positively associated with wage premiums.

The overall fit of the OLS regressions in Table 15.4, with sales and the trade series explaining from 9 per cent to 16 per cent of the overall movements in relative wages, is relatively good comparing to previous work on Mexico (for example, Feenstra and Hanson (1997) and Hanson and Harrison (1999). Conceptually, our results are more directly comparable to those in Revenga (1992) and Freeman and Katz (1991), given that our definitions of the left-hand

Table 15.4
OLS Estimations: Aggregate Mexican Manufacturing

Variables	Dependent var.: ΔRelwage$_t$		Dependent var.: ΔNPshare$_t$		Dependent var.: ΔHrwage$_t$	
Constant	0.0056 **	0.0047 ***	0.0027 **	0.0027 **	0.0060 ***	0.0051 ***
	(0.0020)	(0.0017)	(0.0010)	(0.0009)	(0.0020)	(0.0017)
δmpen$_t$	−0.1478 **		−0.0720 **		−0.1505 **	
	(0.0601)		(0.0316)		(0.0554)	
δxint$_t$	0.0402	−0.0221	0.0164	−0.0139	0.0103	−0.0530
	(0.0510)	(0.0518)	(0.0242)	(0.0253)	(0.0477)	(0.0461)
δsales$_t$	−0.2144 **	−0.2136 ***	−0.0981 ***	−0.0977 ***	−0.1596 **	−0.1588 **
	(0.0652)	(0.0676)	(0.0309)	(0.0316)	(0.0643)	(0.0660)
N	106	107	106	107	106	107
F stat.	7.5574 ***	8.2538 ***	7.0677 ***	7.5677 ***	6.5915 ***	6.5582 ***
Adj. R^2	0.1565	0.1204	0.1466	0.1103	0.1366	0.0949

Notes: Data are of monthly frequency from 1987:01 to 1995:12. The standard errors below the coefficients are computed by the Newey–West (1987) correction of the variance–covariance matrix for heteroskedasticity and autocorrelation. In the OLS estimations, all series are in logarithms. Analysis of both the Akaike and Schwarz–Bayes information criteria does not support the inclusion of any lags of the independent variables in any specification. The symbols * [**] (***) attached to the figure indicate rejection of the null of non-stationarity at the 10 per cent, 5 per cent, and 1 per cent levels, respectively.

Table 15.5
GMM Estimations: Aggregate Mexican Manufacturing

Variables	Dependent var.: ΔRelwage$_t$		Dependent var.: ΔNPshare$_t$		Dependent var.: ΔHrwage$_t$	
Constant	0.0041 (0.0023)	0.0033 (0.0026)	0.0016 (0.0013)	0.0021 (0.0016)	0.0041 (0.0023)	0.0044 (0.0033)
$\Delta mpen_t$		−0.3254 (0.7424)		−0.1779 (0.3859)		−0.2862 (0.7213)
$\Delta xint_t$	0.1300 (0.2220)	0.2856 (0.4137)	0.0613 (0.1091)	0.1385 (0.2079)	0.0505 (0.2228)	0.2282 (0.4146)
$\Delta sales_t$	−0.4452 (0.6969)	−0.1305 (0.8027)	−0.2130 (0.3470)	−0.0109 (0.4380)	−0.2639 (0.6874)	−0.1401 (0.7048)
N	107	106	107	106	107	106
Hausman	0.4259 **	0.6079 **	0.6134 **	0.4653 **	0.2491 **	0.3163

Notes: Data are of monthly frequency from 1987:01 to 1995:12. All series are in logarithms. The standard errors below the coefficients are computed by the Newey-West (1987) correction of the variance-covariance matrix for heteroskedasticity and autocorrelation. Method of estimation is generalized method of moments (GMM), with Bartlett kernel, Andrews bandwidth and instrument set to $\{s_t, s_{t-1}, s_{t-2}\}$ or $\{s_t, s_{t-1}\}$ depending on the model, where s is the nominal spot MXN/USD exchange rate. The models are thus exactly identified (3 parameters and 3 instruments or 2 parameters and 2 instruments) and we do not report the J-statistic on overidentified restrictions. 'Hausman' means the statistic defined by $(b_{ols} - b_{gmm})' (var(b_{ols}) - var(b_{gmm}))^{-1} (b_{ols} - b_{gmm})$, distributed with a chi-square with g degrees of freedom, where g is the number of potential endogenous regressors. If 'Hausman' is large, we reject the adequacy of OLS. The symbols * [**] (***) attached to the figure indicate rejection of the null of at the 10 per cent, 5 per cent, and 1 per cent levels, respectively.

side variables are closer to theirs. Pizer (2000) and Gaston and Trefler (1994), for example, introduce a two-step procedure to measure relative wages and Bernard and Jensen (1997) use plant-level data, a dimension not captured in the present paper.

Possible endogeneity of the right-hand side of the specifications refers to the political economy of wages and openness. Trade can affect wages in principle under the framework in Section 15.2, but lobbying and protection on wages can affect the volume of trade, as well. Revenga (1992), for example, reports two-stage least squares (2SLS) estimates very different from OLS. She obtains a (nearly significant) positive effect of import prices on employment and a positive and significant effect of import prices on wages.

In order to address this issue and check the robustness of our estimates, we perform in Table 15.5 GMM estimations on (15.2) and (15.3) above. We use current and lagged values of the exchange rate as instruments, since exchange rates are correlated with the right-hand side variables, while there is no motive for exchange rates to be correlated with the residuals.[6]

Our empirical models in Table 15.5 are exactly identified (the same number of instruments and the same number of parameters) and we do not report the J–statistic associated with overidentified restrictions. We perform several estimations of overidentified models, however. For both models, estimating with additional lags of exchange rates as instruments, the J-statistic times N shows invariably that the null (overidentified restrictions are satisfied) is rejected at standard significance levels. The additional instruments thus do not help in explaining the model and we keep the exactly identified model.

The GMM results in Table 15.5 differ notably from the OLS results in Table 15.4. Under GMM, import penetration and export penetration ratios are never significant. A positive coefficient on the export intensity ratio in Mexico would suggest that a higher ratio yields a higher wage gap, contributing to a widening in the wage differentials. In our 1987–95 sample period, Mexican manufacturing shows a positive association between wage differentials and export activity that is never statistically significant. Export intensity correlating positively with relative wages is the feeling one gets from Figure 15.1 and the message one receives from plant-level work by Bernard and Jensen (1997).

In order to evaluate whether the GMM technique is necessary, Hausman tests on the difference between the coefficients reported in Tables 15.4 and 15.5 are reproduced in the last row of Table 15.5 ('Hausman'.) The test follows a chi-square distribution with g degrees of freedom, where g is the number of potential endogenous regressors [3 in model (15.2) in Section 15.2 and 2 in model specification (15.3)]. Assuming the GMM estimates in Table 15.5 are unbiased, large differences between GMM coefficients and OLS ones from Table 15.4 can be interpreted as evidence that GMM is important and that the omission results in bias. For all cases except one, Hausman tests reject the adequacy of OLS.[7] In general, we can thus conclude that GMM is necessary in this context.

Evidence at the sectoral level, though not explored in detail in this chapter but available upon request, does not make much difference. For OLS estimates not reported, only in sectors 5 (chemicals), 7 (base metals), and 9 (others), is the export-intensity coefficient significant statistically: a negative coefficient is found in all cases, matching the theoretical priors. The sales coefficients are different from zero and enter with a negative sign in explaining the wage gap. Evidence of trade effects on wages at the sectoral level is even weaker under GMM estimations, since they do not find statistically significant effects in any specification.

15.5   FINAL REMARKS

This chapter explores the trade-based hypothesis (Freeman and Katz 1991; Revenga 1992) in explaining rising wage differentials in Mexican manufacturing after opening to foreign trade in the late 1980s. Although the graphs suggest a positive relationship between both trade measures (import penetration and export intensity) and wage differentials, econometric evidence is not supportive of the hypothesis.

Theoretically, more trade with the USA will affect relative wages in Mexico through a negative shock to the demand for skilled labour. Under reasonable conditions, increased imports from the USA would imply a domestic shift toward less skilled intensive activities: a lower wage gap is thus expected in Mexico. Previous studies have used outsourcing (Feenstra and Hanson 1997) or Stolper-Samuelson arguments (Hanson and Harrison 1999) as driving forces. This paper employs relative demand shifts, motivated by the tripling of Mexican foreign trade during 1987–1995.

Estimates by OLS are not confirmed by GMM estimates. In only one valid OLS specification does import penetration impact relative wages negatively as expected. Our best inference is to cast doubt on widespread strong import penetration effects found for the whole of manufacturing under OLS. Evidence thus seems fragile for the trade-based hypothesis. More detailed work at the sectoral level also does not support a different from zero effect on relative wages in any specification.

Left aside in this study is SBTC, which would require data of high frequency on research and development expenditures and computer usage. The complementary route to the present study is to explore skill upgrading and technology, following Machin and Van Reenen (1998), which is left for further work.

NOTES

1   See Tybout and Westbrook (1995) for cost function estimates of various manufacturing sectors in Mexico between 1984 and 1990.
2   See Johnson (1997), Lovely and Richardson (1998), and Abrego and Whalley (2000) for theoretical constructions.
3   A more elaborate theoretical framework might lead to a different specification, of course. For example, the framework in Pizer (2000) contends that the wage premium must decline in quantity competing industries (Cournot-type) when domestic trade barriers are reduced, with the result reversed under (Bertrand) price-competition.
4   Cragg and Epelbaum (1996) find that, despite the magnitude and pace of the reforms in Mexico, industry-specific effects explain little of the rising wage dispersion, while occupation-specific effects can explain almost half of the growing wage dispersion. We do not pursue this route in this paper.
5   Alternative definitions of *xint* (for example, exports/(imports + sales − exports) and *mpen* (imports/(imports + sales − exports) do not alter the results.
6   In the model $y = \alpha + x_1\beta_1 + \varepsilon$, we suspect that $E(x_1\text{'}\varepsilon) \neq 0$, which would make OLS estimators inconsistent. The instrumental variables proposal finds Z such that $E(Z\text{'}\varepsilon) = 0$. With homoscedastic errors GMM and 2SLS are the same; with heteroscedastic errors 2SLS is less efficient than GMM. The GMM method minimizes, with respect to the vector of parameters q, the quadratic form $m(y, X, \theta)\text{'}.W. m(y, X, \theta)$, where W is the weighting matrix (for example, the Newey-West covariance matrix. Regardless of W, GMM is always consistent and asymptotically unbiased. Under the correct W, GMM is also asymptotically efficient in the class of estimators defined by the orthogonality conditions (see Johnston and DiNardo 1997, cap. 10).
7   Under OLS in Table 15.4, a negative import penetration coefficient is found for relative wages corrected for hours worked as dependent variable. The export intensity coefficient is not statistically significant.

REFERENCES

Abrego, Lisandro and John Whalley (2000), 'Demand Side Considerations and the Trade and Wages Debate', NBER Working Paper # 7674, April.
Berman, Eli, John Bound and Zvi Griliches (1994), 'Changes in the Demand for Skilled Labor within US Manufacturing: Evidence from the Annual Survey of Manufactures', *Quarterly Journal of Economics*, **109** (2), 367–97.

Berman, Eli, John Bound and Stephen Machin (1998), 'Implications of Skill-Biased Technological Change: International Evidence', *Quarterly Journal of Economics*, **113** (4), 1245–79.

Bernard, Andrew and J. Bradford Jensen (1997), 'Exporters, Skill Upgrading, and the Wage Gap', *Journal of International Economics*, **42**, 3–31.

Borjas, George and Valerie Ramey (1995), 'Foreign Competition, Market Power, and Wage Inequality: Theory and Evidence', *Quarterly Journal of Economics*, **110** (4), 1075–111.

Cragg, Michael Ian and Mario Epelbaum (1996), 'Why Has Wage Dispersion Grown in Mexico? Is It the Incidence of Reforms or the Growing Demand for Skills?', *Journal of Development Economics*, **51**, 99–116.

Feenstra, Robert and Gordon Hanson (1997), 'Foreign Direct Investment and Relative Wages: Evidence from Mexico's Maquiladoras', *Journal of International Economics*, **42**, 371–93.

Freeman, Richard and Lawrence Katz (1991), 'Industrial Wage and Employment Determination in an Open Economy', in John Abowd and Richard Freeman (eds), *Immigration, Trade, and Labor Markets*, Chicago: NBER, pp. 235–59.

Gaston, Noel and Daniel Trefler (1994), 'Protection, Trade, and Wages: Evidence from US Manufacturing', *Industrial and Labor Relations Review*, **47** (4), 574–93.

Hanson, Gordon and Ann Harrison (1999), 'Trade Liberalization and Wage Inequality in Mexico', *Industrial and Labor Relations Review*, **52** (2), 271–88.

Johnson, George (1997), 'Changes in Earnings Inequality: The Role of Demand Shifts', *Journal of Economic Perspectives*, **11** (2), 41–54.

Johnston, Jack and John DiNardo (1997), *Econometric Methods*, fourth edition, New York: McGraw-Hill.

Kaminsky, Graciela and Carmen Reinhart (1999), 'The Twin Crises: The Causes of Banking and Balance-of-Payments Problems', *American Economic Review*, **89** (3), 473–500.

Katz, Lawrence and Kevin Murphy (1992), 'Changes in Relative Wages, 1963–1987: Supply and Demand Factors', *Quarterly Journal of Economics*, **107** (1), 35–78.

Levinsohn, James (1999), 'Employment Responses to International Liberalization in Chile', *Journal of International Economics*, **47**, 321–44.

Lovely, Mary and J. David Richardson (1998), 'Trade Flows and Wage Premiums: Does Who or What Matter?', NBER Working Paper # 6668, July.

Machin, Stephen and John Van Reenen (1998), 'Technology and Changes in Skill Structure: Evidence from Seven OECD Countries', *Quarterly Journal of Economics*, **113** (4), 1215–44.

Murphy, Kevin and Finis Welch (1992), 'The Structure of Wages', *Quarterly Journal of Economics*, **107** (1), 285–326.

Ng, Serena and Pierre Perron (1995), 'Unit Root Test in ARMA models with Data Dependent Methods for the Selection of the Truncation Lag', *Journal of the American Statistical Association*, **90**, 268–81.

Pizer, Steven (2000), 'Does International Competition Undermine Wage Differentials and Increase Inequality?', *Journal of International Economics*, **52**, 259–82.

Revenga, Ana (1992), 'Exporting Jobs? The Impact of Import Competition on Employment and Wages in US Manufacturing', *Quarterly Journal of Economics*, **107** (1), 255–84.

Tybout, James and Daniel Westbrook (1995), 'Trade Liberalization and the Dimensions of Efficiency Change in Mexican Manufacturing Industries', *Journal of International Economics*, **39**, 53–78.

16 R&D Spillovers and Export Performance: Evidence from the OECD Countries

Miguel León-Ledesma

16.1 INTRODUCTION

There is little doubt that exports are an important factor in explaining the long-run growth performance of countries and regions. Recent empirical evidence in Frenkel and Romer (1999) and Marin (1992) has found support for this hypothesis, as did earlier attempts by Balassa (1978) and Michaely (1977). Several explanations have been given for this phenomenon, from the externalities effect of Feder (1982) to the demand oriented model of Thirlwall (1979) and the recent endogenous growth models summarised in Grossman and Helpman (1991) and Aghion and Howitt (1998). These latter models have emphasised the effect of trade as the vehicle for a faster diffusion of knowledge from frontier to laggard countries through trade-related R&D spillovers.

On the other hand, empirical studies on technological factors affecting trade have found a strong impact of domestic innovation efforts on competitiveness (see, for instance, Fagerberg 1988, and Soete 1981). Product and process innovation seems to be a crucial factor in gaining market share in international markets at least in those involving developed countries.

In this chapter we try to combine both pieces of evidence and analyse whether trade related international R&D spillovers are an important factor determining exports. In other words, we try to answer the question of whether R&D efforts in one country affect positively the exports of its trade partners through technological diffusion. As we shall see later, this is a more accurate specification for testing the technology gap trade theory. On the other hand, if R&D spillovers are shown to be an important determinant of exports this has interesting implications for growth modelling. This is because the link between trade and growth may well not stop at the first generation effect from trade to growth.

The chapter is organised as follows. Section 16.2 discusses the theoretical motivation for this empirical exercise and its implications. Section 16.3 describes the specification and data, and discusses the panel cointegration techniques on which the estimations are based. Section 16.4 comments on the empirical results, and Section 16.5 concludes.

16.2   R&D SPILLOVERS, TRADE AND GROWTH

In their very influential paper, Coe and Helpman (1995) provide evidence on the extent and importance of R&D spillovers for explaining productivity growth. Although evidence is provided only for OECD advanced countries, Coe et al. (1997) also find a significant impact of spillovers on less developed countries arising from R&D performed in advanced countries. They use a simple framework to prove their point. Coe and Helpman (1995) estimate the total factor productivity level (TFP) as a function of domestic and foreign R&D. Foreign R&D is defined as an import share weighted average of the R&D of the trading partners of a particular country. They find evidence that both domestic and foreign R&D have a positive and significant impact on TFP. This impact is higher the higher the degree of openness of the country. Hence, if a country increases its degree of openness, its trade partners increase their R&D stock or if the country's import share from technologically advanced countries increases, the country's TFP will increase.

Their theoretical background relies on Grossman and Helpman (1991) although it can also be derived from Rivera-Batiz and Romer (1991). The argument runs as follows. In the simple case of horizontally differentiated intermediate inputs, the theory assumes that factor productivity depends on the number of intermediate inputs used in the production process. This is because of the increasing division of labour due to Smithian specialisation. Firms seeking monopoly rents will perform R&D to create new intermediate inputs. Since aggregate output will depend on a measure of the available number of inputs, TFP will depend on the cumulative past investment in R&D. In a closed economy the argument stops there. However, in the case of an open economy in which output is internationally traded, TFP will depend not on the domestic R&D capital stock but on that of the world. Trade will ensure that two economies do not produce the same intermediate inputs. That is, trade allows economies to use a wider range of production inputs and hence achieve higher levels of efficiency. In the most plausible scenario in which economies have both traded and non-traded goods, TFP will depend on both domestic and foreign R&D capital stocks. In other words, trade is a source of growth because it allows countries to enjoy inputs of production from its trading partners. Although this way of modelling R&D spillovers is probably the more fashionable, trade will also enhance productive efficiency by allowing contact with different organisational and managerial structures and the use of reverse engineering.

Evidence for these models is reviewed by Navarreti and Tarr (2000). They conclude that the import related R&D spillovers hypothesis finds strong support in the empirical literature.[1] Keller (2000) also finds strong support using micro data at the firm level. Keller's results show not only that the spillovers related to importing activities are important for boosting productivity but also that small countries tend to enjoy higher spillovers, as well as countries with a higher share of intermediate goods in total imports. Hakkura and Jaumotte (1999) also show that these spillovers are more related to trade within industries and between firms.

Although most studies have concentrated on the effects of imports on TFP, exports can also be a channel of knowledge transmission. Firms selling in the international market have access to new technologies and products and also can engage in quicker learning-by-doing by specialising in products with extensive market potential. Although the evidence on these grounds is not as strong as with imports,[2] this may be due to the micro nature of the data. Firm level studies tend to ignore the fact that at the macro level the gains can be higher because of substantial positive spillovers from exporter firms to the rest of the economy as reported by Aitken et al. (1997). Hence, exports can also be a source of knowledge spillovers and aggregate learning affecting productivity levels. Of course, from a different perspective, exports have the important role of relaxing international payments constraints allowing for higher imports without incurring balance of payments crises (Thirlwall 1979). In this sense exports are necessary to afford the foreign technology contained in intermediate input imports.

All the theory and evidence discussed above sets out a strong relation between trade and productivity growth through technological knowledge flows. In this sense, this literature provides quite useful information and serves as a starting point for our empirical exercise. This branch of the literature, however, concentrates on the effects of trade-related spillovers on growth in what seems to be a rather unidirectional relationship. This is an understandable simplification for models would otherwise be analytically intractable. However, it is our aim to look at the impact that technological flows have on trade performance itself. By doing so we open up the models to a richer set of dynamics relating trade, technology and growth. The obvious candidate to look at when we try to analyse the latter link is the technology gap trade theory.

Technology-based theories of trade have long emphasised the role of innovation and technological differences in determining the pattern of trade. The first attempt to do so is due to Posner's (1961) technology gap trade model, later extended by Hufbauer (1966). For Posner, countries at the technological frontier would enjoy export advantage of technologically advanced products. This advantage, however, is only temporary. Since knowledge is a public good, it is free to flow to less advanced countries. This flow is subject to both demand

and imitation lags. The former refers to the time it takes for the consumers to respond to the appearance of a new or cheaper product. The latter is related to the reaction capacity of foreign producers to adapt their production structure in order to produce the new goods with cheaper labor.[3] Another significant branch of models relating technological differences and trade is the product cycle model of Vernon (1966) and Hirsch (1974). Although from a different perspective, the conclusions of this model are very similar to those of the technology-gap. Innovation in leader countries generates new products that pass through different stages of maturity. Initially the new good is only produced by the innovator country. Once the good has reached a standardisation phase, the production localises in backward countries whose labour costs are lower. Foreign direct investment plays here a crucial role in the diffusion of technical knowledge. More recently, Krugman (1979 and 1986) developed formal models of technology gap trade. His conclusions are similar to those of previous models, but he also concludes that diffusion will cause an improvement in both exports and the terms of trade in laggard countries.

Although the theoretical models considered only one leader and one follower country, the picture of the world economy is considerably more complex. In reality we have a group of countries (roughly the G7) that are capable of performing most of the innovations in the world, together with a group of close catchers-up and finally those countries lagging behind. From this it is obvious that exports in one country will depend on the R&D domestically performed and on the R&D of its trade partners. Although there may be long adoption lags, the steady-state picture would be one in which exports will depend on the rate of innovation at home and that of the trading partners.

The majority of the empirical studies on the technological factors affecting trade performance find strong evidence that domestic innovation is an important variable.[4] Most of the studies on technology gap theories concentrate on the effects of innovation on a sectoral basis as opposed to the country-wide empirical approach to test endowment theories (Wakelin 1998). Examples of these studies finding positive effects of innovation on relative export performance include Soete (1981, 1987), Dosi et al. (1990), Greenhalgh et al. (1994), Magnier and Toujas-Bernate (1994) and Wakelin (1998). Cotsomitis et al. (1991) found only weak evidence on the effect of innovation. Few attempts have analysed the effect of innovation on aggregate export performance. An example of this is Fagerberg (1988) who finds that innovation and investment play a crucial role in explaining competitiveness for a set of 15 OECD countries. Although the sectoral studies give a more precise and detailed analysis of the factors driving export performance, aggregate studies are a better approach to understanding the world's changing pattern of trade by country.

A remark should be made at this point. Despite the fact that the technology gap theories of trade insist on both innovation and diffusion as determinants of trade, none of the studies mentioned take into account the effect that innovation in trading partners has on domestic exports. A close look at all the technology-based theories of trade will indicate that countries that do not perform R&D will nonetheless export goods at a lower stage of the technical ladder. That is, aggregate exports, regardless of the composition, will depend on the innovation efforts made abroad. It is the stock of past and present knowledge flowing from frontier to backward countries that allow the latter to enjoy growing exports as the frontier countries innovate. The recent advance in this area in growth theory and empirics can prove to be quite useful when analysing trade performance.

The rest of this paper will be devoted to analysing the aforementioned point. What is the importance of trade-related technology spillovers in determining export performance? As discussed earlier, previous empirical work on growth has focused on the effect of trade as the channel of R&D spillovers affecting *productivity*. The empirical work on trade only takes domestic R&D as the relevant innovation variable affecting exports. Here, we analyse whether R&D investment performed by trading partners is in fact also an important factor determining trade performance. We do so by taking a simple but informative approach adapting the Coe and Helpman methodology to estimate export functions for 21 OECD countries for the period 1970 to 1990.

16.3   SPECIFICATION, DATA AND ESTIMATION

16.3.1 Specification

The common specification of an export demand function contains basically two arguments: relative prices and world income. The former tries to capture price competitiveness while the latter is a normalisation variable accounting for other factors affecting export performance. According to this, the logarithmic version of an export demand function can be expressed as:

$$X_t = a + b \cdot RER_t + c \cdot Z_t \qquad (16.1)$$

where X is the level of real exports, RER is the real exchange rate as a proxy for relative prices and Z is the world's income. All variables are expressed in logs unless stated otherwise. In recent years, some authors have introduced innovation as another argument in the export demand function accounting for non-price competitiveness arising from research activities. This is the usual specification in empirical applications of technology-based trade theories. In our specifications, we will test the influence of both domestic R&D and that of foreign R&D. Given the nature of the data, especially for R&D, and the problems involved in estimating the equations in levels, the regressions will be run using pooled data for all 21 chosen OECD countries using recent panel cointegration techniques. We estimate four specifications of the export demand function:

$$X_{it} = a_i + b \cdot RER_{it} + c \cdot Z_{it} + d \cdot SD_{it} \tag{i}$$

$$X_{it} = a_i + b \cdot RER_{it} + c \cdot Z_{it} + d \cdot SD_{it} + e \cdot SF_{it} \tag{ii}$$

$$X_{it} = a_i + b \cdot RER_{it} + c \cdot Z_{it} + d \cdot SD_{it} + e \cdot (m_{it} \cdot SF_{it}) \tag{iii}$$

$$X_{it} = a_i + b \cdot RER_{it} + c \cdot Z_{it} + d \cdot SD_{it} + e \cdot G7 \cdot SD_{it} + f \cdot (m_{it} \cdot SF_{it}) \tag{iv}$$

where i is a country index, SD is domestic R&D capital stock, SF is foreign R&D stock, m is the fraction of imports relative to GDP (not in logs) and $G7$ is a dummy variable for the more advanced Group of Seven OECD countries. Note that each country has a different intercept term to allow for country-specific time-invariant fixed effects.

Equation (i) is the basic specification for testing the effect of domestic R&D on export performance as commented earlier. Since our estimations are in levels, we take as the relevant innovation variable the stock of accumulated R&D from Coe and Helpman. We assume, for theoretical consistency, that the level of exports depends on accumulated knowledge rather than on the flow of new innovations. Equation (ii) introduces the stock of foreign R&D to measure the extent to which technological spillovers affect a country's exports. Note that the coefficient e in equation (ii) may capture two effects. The first is the technology diffusion effect that we would expect to have a positive impact on a country's exports. The second one is a competition effect. Since most of the exports are intra-OECD, an increase in foreign R&D stock can have a negative impact insofar as the exports of two countries may be competing for market share. The net effect will determine the sign of the foreign R&D coefficient. The foreign R&D capital stock is an import share weighted average of the R&D stocks of a country's trading partners. Hence, diffusion of knowledge will depend not only on the extent to which trading partners innovate, but also on the relative importance of trading partners. That is, trade with the USA will lead to a higher degree of diffusion than with, say, Portugal or Greece. A problem with this measure of foreign R&D capital stock is that it treats closed and open economies equally. However, it is obvious that the degree of international openness will also affect the extent of knowledge spillovers. In order to account for this problem we estimate equation (iii) in which we have interacted SF_{it} with the import–GDP ratio ($m_{it} \cdot SF_{it}$). This is the preferred way of measuring the impact of foreign technology, since it accounts for the extent to which the country has contact with international markets and uses foreign intermediate inputs. Another advantage of this specification is that we can obtain country-specific time-varying foreign R&D elasticities. Finally, in equation (iv) we introduce an interaction term between domestic R&D stock and the G7 countries' dummy variable to allow for different elasticities of domestic R&D between the seven largest economies and the rest of the OECD countries considered. This is because we would expect the G7 economies to have a larger reward on their R&D because of larger markets allowing for better opportunities to innovate and higher complementarities between R&D activities.

16.3.2 Data

We estimate equations (i) to (iv) for a panel of 21 OECD countries for the period 1971 to 1990. The countries used for estimation are the United States, Japan, Germany, France, Italy, the United Kingdom, Canada, Australia, Austria, Belgium, Denmark, Finland, Greece, Ireland, Netherlands, New Zealand, Norway, Portugal, Spain, Sweden and Switzerland. We excluded Israel from the Coe and Helpman sample due to the lack of comparable data for some of the export demand function variables. The period of estimation was chosen on the basis of availability of R&D capital stock data, which are taken from Coe and Helpman. Although it would be possible to extend their calculations to more recent years, we decided not to in order to ensure consistency of the data throughout the period and comparability with the results obtained in Coe and Helpman.

All the data except for the innovation variables and the import shares matrix are taken from the OECD Statistical Compendium (1997). Exports are defined as the real value in local currency of exports of goods and services. World income is defined as the sum of the income of the 21 OECD countries in constant 1991 US PPPs, minus the income of country i:

$$Z_i = \sum_{j=1}^{21} Y_j \quad \text{with } j \neq i$$

The RER_{it} variable is the export price divided by the import price of goods and services times the effective nominal exchange rate. The import–GDP ratio is real imports of goods and services divided by real GDP at the same base year. Domestic R&D stock is taken from Coe and Helpman. It is calculated using R&D expenditures and applying the perpetual inventory method, using an estimated initial value for the R&D stock. Finally, foreign R&D is calculated multiplying the bilateral import shares matrix times the domestic R&D stock for each country. This gives us a 20 x 21 matrix with the stock of foreign R&D for each of the countries. Since Israel was taken out of the sample, we adjusted the import weights matrix given in Coe and Helpman.

Following Lichtenberg and van Pottelsberghe (1998), we do not transform the R&D variables into index numbers. Although exports are measured in local currencies and Z, SD and SF are measured in constant US PPPs, the effect of using different currencies would be captured by the country-specific fixed effects.

Transforming the R&D variables into index numbers would generate a problem. Taking equation (iii) and assuming that we index *SD* and *SF* as 1991=1, we would have (all variables in logs):

$$X_{it} = a_i + b \cdot RER_{it} + c \cdot Z_{it} + d \cdot SD_{it}/SD_{i,91} + e \cdot [m_{it} \cdot (SF_{it}/SF_{i,91})]$$

$$= a_i + b \cdot RER_{it} + c \cdot Z_{it} + d \cdot SD_{it}/SD_{i,91} + e \cdot m_{it} \cdot (SF_{it}) - e \cdot m_{it} \cdot SF_{i,91}$$

(16.2)

It is clear that the last term of (16.2) is not time invariant and thus equation (iii) would be misspecified if we estimate it using index numbers and fixed effects.

16.3.3 Estimation

In this section we review the estimation techniques used to obtain the relevant parameters of the model. We estimate the model in levels, since we are interested in the long-run determinants of exports and the impact of foreign technology is subject to diffusion lags. This fact poses some difficulties because the time series component of the panel may not be stationary, and there is the possibility of obtaining spurious relations amongst the variables. One possibility to control for this problem is to run separate regressions for each country using the different well-known cointegration techniques. There are two problems with this. First, the limited number of observations in our panel makes it difficult to make inferences about the presence of unit roots or cointegration relations of the variables. Both due to this shortage and the small sample period, all the tests developed in time series literature suffer from low power. This could lead us to accept the null of a unit root or no cointegration when the alternative is true. Secondly, estimating the model using time series data will leave us with few degrees of freedom to make inferences, especially in models like ours in which we can have five independent variables. Using recent panel cointegration techniques we can increase the power of the tests and the degrees of freedom by combining cross-section and time series information.[5] This is, of course, at the expense of not allowing for much heterogeneity between the different cross-sections of the panel but the mere fixed effects.[6] Three aspects of the estimation procedure are relevant here: testing for unit roots, testing for cointegration and estimating the long-run vector.

Several tests have been proposed to check whether or not the panel series have a unit root. Two of them – Breitung and Meyer (1994) and Levin and Lin (1993) – assume that the auto-regressive coefficient of the variable is equal across cross-sections. A third and less restrictive test is due to Im et al. (1997) in which the autorregressive parameters are allowed to differ under the alternative. The three tests are based on the ADF regression:[7]

$$\Delta x_{i,t} = \alpha_i + \rho_i x_{i,t-1} + \sum_{j=1}^{p_i} \gamma_{ij} \Delta x_{i,t-j} + \xi_{i,t} \qquad (16.3)$$

The Breitung and Meyer (1994) test assumes $\rho_i = \rho$ and $\gamma_{ij} = \gamma_j$ and test for H_o: $\rho = 0$. They show that the t-statistic for the null hypothesis is asymptotically N (0, 1) as $N \to \infty$. The validity of this test is lower the larger the time dimension T. Levin and Lin (1993) propose a panel ADF test that allows for individual specific time trends and short run dynamics. Levin and Lin (1993) allow for a higher degree of heterogeneity of the cross-sections and also for a more general correlated and heteroscedastic structure of errors. Levin and Lin (1993) derive the asymptotic distributions of the panel estimator of r under different degrees of heterogeneity.[8] They propose a transformation of the t-statistic for H_o: $\rho = 0$ against H_A: $\rho_i = \rho < 0$. As is the norm for panel unit root tests, the adjusted t-statistic $t_{\rho*}$ converges to a N (0, 1) as $T, N \to \infty$.

Finally, the Im et al. (1997) (IPS) panel unit root test is based on the null of non-stationarity $(\rho_i = 0 \forall i)$ against the alternatives H_A: $\rho_i < 0$, $i=1, 2, ..., N_I$, $\rho_i = 0$, $i= N_I + 1, N_I + 2, ..., N$. Note that the IPS test does not assume that all cross-sectional units converge towards the equilibrium value at the same speed under the alternative, that is, $\rho_1 = \rho_2 = ... = \rho_N < 0$, and thus is a less restrictive test than Levin and Lin (1993). The IPS test is based on the standardised t-bar statistic as follows:

$$\Gamma_t = \frac{\sqrt{N}[\bar{t}_{NT} - \mu]}{\sqrt{v}} \sim N(0,1) \qquad (16.4)$$

where $\bar{t}_{NT}$ is the average of the N cross-section ADF(p_i) t-statistics. μ and v are, respectively, the mean and variance of the average ADF(p_i) statistic under the null, tabulated by Im et al. (1997) for different Ts and lag orders of the ADF. Im, et al. (1997) also show that under the null of a unit root Γ_t converges to N(0,1) as $N/T \to k$ (k is any finite positive constant).

We now switch to the panel cointegration tests. We follow Kao (1999) and Pedroni (1999) who provide a set of panel cointegration tests under different assumptions about the cointegration vector. Two families of tests can be identified. The first is the family of panel tests in which we assume the same auto-regressive coefficient for the errors of the cointegration equation. These tests are only valid if the long-run cointegrating vector is assumed to be the same for the different cross-sectional units although allowing for heterogeneity in the intercepts and time trends. The second family is the group mean approach. In this case, cointegration tests are based on transformations of the average of the individual unit root tests, thus allowing for a high degree of heterogeneity in the panel. It is easy to see that, in the case of ADF tests, the first family is equivalent to the Breitung and Mayer and Levin and Lin (1993) unit root tests and the second to the IPS test. Since we are assuming equal slope coefficients in our long-run vector, we will focus on the first set of panel tests.

We will use three tests for cointegration. The first two are DF tests and the third an ADF test to allow for serial correlation in the errors of the equation, following Kao (1999).[9] The DF tests can be calculated from the estimated OLS residuals as:

$$\hat{e}_{i,t} = \gamma \hat{e}_{i,t-1} + u_{i,t} \tag{16.5}$$

The null is H_o: $\gamma = 1$ against H_A: $\gamma < 1$. Two DF type tests can be calculated from this regression:

$$DF_\gamma = \frac{\sqrt{NT} (\hat{\gamma} - 1) + s\sqrt{N}}{\sqrt{10.2}},$$

$$DF_t = \sqrt{1.25} t_\gamma + \sqrt{1.875} N.$$

Finally, the ADF test augments (16.5) with the lagged values of the first difference of the errors. Applying the transformation proposed by Kao (1999) to the t-statistic of γ in the augmented regression we can test for cointegration allowing for autocorrelated errors. The three statistics converge towards $N(0,1)$.

Regarding the estimation of the long-run cointegration vector, we rely on Kao and Chiang (1998) who discuss the properties of the OLS, Fully Modified (FM) and dynamic OLS (DOLS) estimators. Kao and Chiang (1998) find that the OLS fixed effects estimation of the panel is subject to a non-negligible bias in finite samples. For this reason, they propose two alternative estimators. The FM estimator, as in Pedroni (1996), performs better, as it is asymptotically normal with zero mean. The other proposed alternative is the DOLS estimator based on Stock and Watson (1993). It is obtained running the following regression:

$$y_{it} = \alpha_i + \beta x_{it} + \sum_{j=1}^{p} \eta_j \Delta x_{i,t-j} + \sum_{j=1}^{p} \zeta_j \Delta x_{i,t+j} + e_{it} \tag{16.6}$$

Hence, the DOLS regression adds to the OLS the leads and lags of the differences of the independent variables. This ensures asymptotically unbiased estimations and avoids the estimation of nuisance parameters. Kao and Chiang (1998) also show that the DOLS estimator is preferable to both the OLS and the FM for finite samples. We will report both the OLS and the DOLS estimations of our four specifications of the export demand function with R&D spillovers.

16.4 RESULTS

The procedure followed to obtain the elasticities of interest is similar to the Engle-Granger procedure in single time series estimations. First, we test for the existence of unit roots. If the series are I(1) we then test if they are cointegrated in the long run by applying cointegration tests on the residuals of the OLS fixed effects regression. Finally, we obtain the parameters of interest estimating the long-run vector using both OLS and DOLS.

Table 16.1 reports the three panel unit roots tests mentioned in the previous section for all the variables used in the model. Where we had to choose the number of lags of the ADF test we did so by using the general to specific procedure proposed by Hall (1990). It is easy to see that in all but one case, the tests indicate that the variables involved in the regression are non-stationary. Note that both the Levin and Lin (1993) and IPS tests have been applied to the original series minus the cross-sectional mean. This is to account for the possible existence of dependence between the cross-sectional units. The rejection of the null in the BM (Breitung and Mayer) test of Z_{it} may be due to the fact that this variable, by construction, is subject to a high degree of cross-sectional dependence.

Table 16.2 contains the three panel cointegration tests applied to the OLS residuals of equations (i) to (iv). Except for the DF_{γ} test in equations (i) and (ii), the rest of the tests show that the null of no cointegration is strongly rejected. These results indicate that there is a long-run relationship between the level of exports and the rest of independent variables included in the models.

Table 16.1
Panel Unit Roots Tests

	BM	LL-93	IPS
X	0.022	2.651	−0.881
Z	**−7.653**	1.848	0.500
RER	1.417	5.465	−0.720
SD	0.798	4.200	0.929
SF	3.002	6.546	−0.663
m·SF	1.660	5.932	3.346

Notes:
1 The BM test is based on Breitung and Meyer (1994). The LL-93 is the modified panel unit root test of Levin and Lin (1993). The IPS test is based on Im, Pesaran and Shin (1997). The number of lags and deterministic trends has been selected following Hall (1990).
2 Bold characters denote the rejection of the null of a unit root at the 5% level.

Table 16.2
Panel Cointegration Tests

	DF$_g$	DFt	ADFt
Equation 1	−0.868	**59.763**	−2.186
Equation 2	−0.975	**59.559**	−2.563
Equation 3	**−2.056**	**58.518**	−2.437
Equation 4	**−3.590**	**56.256**	−3.021

Notes:
1   All the tests were performed on the residuals of the OLS regression.
2   The DF$_g$, DF$_t$ and ADF$_t$ are from Kao (1999) and Pedroni (1999) (see text). The number of lags for the ADF test has been selected following Hall (1990)
3   Bold characters denote the rejection of the null of no cointegration at the 5% level.

The estimation results are reported in Tables 16.3 and 16.4. Although the *t*-statistics of the OLS regression are not reliable due to the aforementioned bias, we report them in order to compare the results with the DOLS estimation. A surprisingly positive result is that both methods of estimation yield very similar results. This indicates that our specifications are robust to the estimation method. Only the elasticities of domestic R&D are consistently and considerably lower in the OLS regression. The signs and sizes of the parameters on the traditional export function variables (*Z* and *RER*) are as expected. We find a low but significant relative price effect on exports, and an income elasticity in the range of one.[10] The impact of domestic R&D is clearly positive and significant in all the specifications with an elasticity of around 0.250 for the DOLS estimation. However, note that the elasticity of domestic R&D is substantially greater for the G7 group as shown in equation (iv), with an elasticity close to 0.5. This result supports previous studies finding a significant impact of innovation on trade performance.[11]

Regarding foreign R&D the results for equation (ii) show that this variable has a negligible impact on export performance in the OECD countries. This may be due to the combination of the diffusion and competition effects commented on earlier. However, when we take into account the degree of openness of the economy, foreign R&D becomes a positive and statistically significant variable. Foreign R&D, through trade-related innovation spillovers, has a long-run positive impact on the level of exports. Although this impact seems to be smaller than the domestic return to R&D, this indicates that the direction and amount of trade with technologically advanced countries is a relevant factor to explain the success of the exporting sector of an economy. We calculated foreign R&D elasticities for each country and three years (1971, 1980 and 1990) as reported in Tables 16.5 and 16.6 using the DOLS results for

Table 16.3
Export Function Estimation Using OLS

	(i)	(ii)	(iii)	(iv)
Z_{it}	1.322	1.609	1.172	0.991
	(27.844)	(11.063)	(21.042)	(17.136)
RER_{it}	−0.066	−0.065	−0.080	−0.112
	(−4.217)	(−4.160)	(−5.194)	(−7.413)
SD_{it}	0.181	0.184	0.189	0.191
	(8.427)	(8.607)	(9.031)	(9.687)
$G7 \cdot SD_{it}$				0.214
				(7.328)
SF_{it}		−0.090		
		(−0.807)		
$m \cdot SF_{it}$			0.045	0.062
			(4.844)	(6.847)
$N*T$	420	420	420	420
$\overline{R}^2$	0.998	0.998	0.998	0.998

Notes:
1　The OLS estimations are based on pooling data for the 21 countries for the period 1971–1990. T-ratios in parentheses.
2　All equations include unreported country specific fixed effects.

equation (iv). The elasticities were obtained by multiplying the coefficient on $m \cdot RF$ times the degree of openness. Overall the results show that the elasticity is higher the smaller the size of the economy due to the higher degree of openness. Another important result is that the impact of R&D spillovers has increased in recent years. Amongst the smaller economies, Belgium and Ireland seem to be the most sensitive to foreign R&D, whereas Australia and Finland seem to be the least sensitive.[12] Spain and Greece experienced the highest increase in the foreign R&D elasticity from 1971 to 1990. Although the magnitude of the impact may not seem to be important, for some countries this is as high as the effect of relative price changes, and the effect has shown an upward trend in recent years. Also, we cannot forget that the competition effect may be covering a stronger impact on export performance through technology diffusion. Nevertheless, domestic R&D still has a stronger impact on export performance.

Table 16.4
Export Function Estimation Using DOLS

	(i)	(ii)	(iii)	(iv)
Z_{it}	1.208	1.699	1.031	0.862
	(19.647)	(9.430)	(14.807)	(12.299)
RER_{it}	−0.052	−0.040	−0.060	−0.094
	(−2.970)	(−2.327)	(−3.494)	(−5.401)
SD_{it}	0.239	0.250	0.252	0.254
	(8.353)	(8.589)	(9.065)	(9.637)
$G7{\cdot}SD_{it}$				0.224
				(6.079)
SF_{it}		−0.102		
		(−1.025)		
$m{\cdot}SF_{it}$			0.050	0.070
			(4.853)	(6.987)
$N*T$	357	357	357	357
$\bar{R}^2$	0.998	0.998	0.998	0.999

Notes:
1 The DOLS estimations are based on pooling data for the 21 countries for the period 1971–1990. One lag and one lead of the differenced independent variables are used to estimate the dynamic model. T-ratios in parentheses.
2 All equations include unreported country specific fixed effects.

16.5   CONCLUDING REMARKS

In this chapter we have analysed the impact of international R&D spillovers on the export performance of 21 OECD countries. The question has important implications for both trade theory and growth theory. Technology-based trade theories emphasise the effect that catching-up has on determining the trade pattern of countries. However, empirical applications of these theories do not test directly the effect that innovation arising in frontier economies has on the follower ones. On the other hand, although growth theory and empirics has taken into account the direct effect of R&D spillovers on productivity, they have tended to ignore its possible effect on growth through improved competitiveness.

We have attempted to analyse this impact by using an approach that draws on the one in Coe and Helpman (1995) to estimate long-run export demand functions. Our results are just aggregate magnitudes and would require further

Table 16.5
Elasticity of Exports with Respect to Foreign R&D Using the OLS
Estimations of Equation (16.4)

	1971	1980	1990
United States	0.0041	0.0043	0.0063
Japan	0.0047	0.0051	0.0062
Germany	0.0114	0.0138	0.0159
France	0.0114	0.0140	0.0167
Italy	0.0080	0.0090	0.0118
United Kingdom	0.0110	0.0126	0.0166
Canada	0.0107	0.0141	0.0192
Australia	0.0079	0.0087	0.0108
Austria	0.0166	0.0226	0.0286
Belgium	0.0290	0.0365	0.0434
Denmark	0.0213	0.0208	0.0226
Finland	0.0130	0.0141	0.0151
Greece	0.0092	0.0103	0.0184
Ireland	0.0251	0.0293	0.0337
Netherlands	0.0244	0.0270	0.0305
New Zealand	0.0116	0.0139	0.0168
Norway	0.0245	0.0210	0.0210
Portugal	0.0189	0.0175	0.0258
Spain	0.0074	0.0100	0.0157
Sweden	0.0133	0.0145	0.0169
Switzerland	0.0181	0.0248	0.0294

consideration and analysis especially making use of sectoral data. In any case, clear patterns arise from our empirical exercise. First, domestic R&D is a very important factor determining exports in advanced economies. The impact of domestic innovation is considerably higher in the technologically advanced countries. Secondly, although its impact is lower than that of domestic R&D, R&D of trading partners has a positive and significant impact on export performance. That is, countries importing more from technologically advanced countries or with a higher degree of openness seem to benefit from their stock of knowledge. Finally, this impact seems to be stronger in small economies and increasingly important in recent years.

A final remark concerning income distribution is due here. Recent literature on the effects of trade on wage structure and skill premiums tends to separate

Table 16.6
Elasticity of Exports with Respect to Foreign R&D Using the DOLS
Estimation of Equation (16.4)

	1971	1980	1990
United States	0.0047	0.0049	0.0071
Japan	0.0054	0.0058	0.0070
Germany	0.0130	0.0157	0.0180
France	0.0129	0.0159	0.0190
Italy	0.0091	0.0102	0.0133
United Kingdom	0.0125	0.0143	0.0188
Canada	0.0121	0.0160	0.0218
Australia	0.0090	0.0099	0.0123
Austria	0.0188	0.0256	0.0324
Belgium	0.0329	0.0414	0.0492
Denmark	0.0241	0.0236	0.0256
Finland	0.0147	0.0160	0.0172
Greece	0.0105	0.0116	0.0208
Ireland	0.0285	0.0333	0.0382
Netherlands	0.0277	0.0306	0.0346
New Zealand	0.0132	0.0158	0.0190
Norway	0.0277	0.0239	0.0238
Portugal	0.0214	0.0198	0.0293
Spain	0.0084	0.0114	0.0178
Sweden	0.0151	0.0165	0.0192
Switzerland	0.0206	0.0281	0.0333

the 'trade' effect and the 'technical change' effect when trying to explain trends in income distribution in both developed and developing countries. Our results suggest that the foreign technology and trade variables are interdependent. The idea that foreign innovation tends to harm skilled workers at home may be ignoring the fact that spillovers can enhance the export performance of national sectors in which we enjoy a comparative advantage. Empirical work on this area could shed light on some of the puzzles about the relation technology–trade–income distribution.

NOTES

1   As mentioned earlier, the main source for aggregate level evidence is Coe and Helpman (1995). Further evidence can be found in Kao, Chiang and Chen (1999).

2   See, for instance, Pack (1993) and Bernard and Jensen (1999) and Aw, Chung and Roberts (2000).

3   Hufbauer's (1966) model focuses on learning-by-doing as the main factor determining the imitation lag, since successful production of new goods requires a certain degree of accumulated experience.

4   Regardless of whether we use input or output innovation measures.

5   See Banerjee (1999) for an overview of the literature on panel data unit roots and cointegration.

6   There is the possibility of allowing for a very high degree of heterogeneity in the panels by using the so-called mean group estimators (for example, Pesaran and Smith, 1995). Given the nature of our data we prefer to use pooled estimators although we impose stronger restrictions.

7   For simplicity we will ignore deterministic trends in the explanation of the tests.

8   We refer to Levin and Lin (1993) for details on these transformations.

9   Pedroni (1999) also provides non-parametric versions of these tests equivalent to the Phillips-Perron procedure for individual time series.

10 Usually the estimated income elasticity of exports is higher than one for the majority of OECD countries except the USA and the UK. However, when we include innovation variables its size will be reduced. This is because the export-income elasticity may capture many of the non-price competitiveness factors affecting exports, including innovation.

11 Our results are not comparable to previous studies because we make use of R&D capital stocks and use aggregate data instead of sectoral data. Nevertheless, other studies such as Wakelin (1998) report similar elasticities using pooled industry data and country dummies.

12 This may indicate that spatial distance is also a relevant variable to understand the degree of technology diffusion as found in Vamvakidis (1998).

REFERENCES

Aghion, P. and P. Howitt (1998), *Endogenous Growth Theory*, Cambridge, MA: MIT Press.

Aitken, B., G.H. Hanson and A.E. Harrison (1997), 'Spillovers, Foreign Investment, and Export Behaviour', *Journal of International Economics,* **43**, 103–32.

Aw B.Y., S. Chung and M.J. Roberts (2000), 'Productivity and Turnover in the Export Market: Micro-Level Evidence from the Republic of Korea and Taiwan (China)', *World Bank Economic Review*, **14**, 65–90.

Balassa, B. (1978), 'Exports and Economic Growth: Further Evidence', *Journal of Development Economics*, **5**, 181–9.

Banerjee, A. (1999), 'Panel Data Unit Roots and Cointegration: An Overview', *Oxford Bulletin of Economics and Statistics*, Special Issue, 607–29.

Bernard, A. and J.B. Jensen (1999), 'Exceptional Exporter Performance: Cause, Effect, or Both?', *Journal of International Economics,* **47**, 1–25.

Breitung, J. and W. Mayer (1994), 'Testing for Unit Roots in Panel Data: Are Wages at Different Bargaining Levels Cointegrated?', *Applied Economics*, **26**, 353–61.

Coe, D.T. and E. Helpman (1995), 'International R&D Spillovers', *European Economic Review*, **39**, 859–87.

Coe, D.T., E. Helpman and A.W. Hoffmaister (1997), 'North-South R&D Spillovers', *Economic Journal*, **107**, 134–49.

Cotsomitis, J., C. De Bresson and A. Kwan (1991), 'A Re-Examination of the Technology Gap Theory of Trade: Some Evidence From Time Series Data for OECD Countries', *Weltwirtschaftliches Archiv*, **127**, 792–99.

Dosi, G., K. Pavitt and L. Soete (1990), *The Economics of Technological Change and International Trade,* Brighton: Harvester Wheatsheaf Publishers.

Fagerberg, J. (1988), 'International Competitiveness', *Economic Journal*, **98**, 355–74.

Feder, G. (1982), 'On Exports and Economic Growth', *Journal of Development Economics*, **12**, 59–73.

Frenkel, J. and D. Romer (1999), 'Does Trade Cause Growth?', *American Economic Review*, **89**, 379–99.

Greenhalgh, C., P. Taylor and R. Wilson (1994), 'Innovation and Export Volumes and Prices, a Disaggregated Study', *Oxford Economic Papers*, **46**, 102–34.

Grossman, G.M. and E. Helpman (1991), *Innovation and Growth in the Global Economy*, Cambridge, MA: MIT Press.

Hakura, D. and F. Jaumotte (1999), 'The Role of Inter- and Intra-Industry Trade in Technology Diffusion', IMF Working Paper, 99/58, Washington, DC: IMF.

Hall, A. (1990), 'Testing for a Unit Root in Time Series with Pretest Data-Based Model Selection', North Carolina State University Working Paper.

Hirsch, S. (1974), 'Capital or Technology? Confronting the Neo-Factor Proportions and Neo-Technology Accounts of International Trade', *Weltwirtschafliches Archiv*, **90**, 535–63.

Hufbauer, G.C. (1966), *Synthetic Materials and the Theory of International Trade*, London: Duckworth.

Im, K.S., MH. Pesaran and Y. Shin (1997), 'Testing for Unit Roots in Heterogeneous Panels', mimeo, Department of Applied Economics, University of Cambridge.

Kao, C. (1999), 'Spurious Regression and Residual-Based Tests for Cointegration in Panel Data', *Journal of Econometrics*, **90**, 1–44.

Kao, C. and M-H. Chiang (1998), 'On the Estimation and Inference of a Cointegrated Regression in Panel Data', Working Paper, Center for Policy Research, Syracuse University.

Kao, C., M-H. Chiang and B. Chen (1999), 'International R&D Spillovers: An Application of Estimation and Inference in Panel Cointegration', *Oxford Bulletin of Economics and Statistics*, Special Issue, 691–709.

Keller, W. (2000), 'Do Trade Patterns and Technology Flows Affect Productivity Growth?', *World Bank Economic Review*, **14**, 17–47.

Krugman, P. (1979), 'A Model of Innovation, Technology Transfer, and the World Distribution of Income', *Journal of Political Economy*, **87**, 253–66.

Krugman, P. (1986), 'A "Technology Gap" Model of International Trade', in K. Jungenfelt and D. Hague (eds), *Structural Adjustment in Advanced Economies*, Macmillan.

Levin, A. and C-F. Lin (1993), 'Unit Root Tests in Panel Data: New Results', *Discussion Paper*, 93/56, Department of Economics, University of California, San Diego.

Lichtenberg, F.R. and B. van Pottelsberghe de la Potterie (1998), 'International R&D Spillovers: A Comment', *European Economic Review*, **42**, 1483–91.

Magnier, A. and Toujas-Bernate, J. (1994), 'Technology and Trade: Empirical Evidences from the Major Five Industrialised Countries', *Weltwirschaftliches Archiv*, **130**, 494–520.

Marin, D. (1992), 'Is the Export-Led Growth Hypothesis Valid for Industrialised Countries?', *Review of Economics and Statistics*, **74**, 678–88.

Michaely, M. (1977), 'Exports and Growth: An Empirical Investigation.' *Journal of Development Economics*, **4**, 49–53.

Navaretti, G.B. and D.G. Tarr (2000), 'International Knowledge Flows and Economic Performance: A Review of the Evidence', *World Bank Economic Review*, **14**, 1–15.

OECD (1997), *OECD Statistical Compendium*, Paris: OECD.

Pack, H. (1993), 'Technology Gaps Between Industrial and Developing Countries: Are There Dividends for Late Comers?', *Proceedings of the World Bank Conference on Development Economics*, Washington, DC: The World Bank.

Pedroni, P. (1996), 'Fully Modified OLS for Heterogeneous Cointegrated Panels and the Case of Purchasing Power Parity', Working Paper in Economics 96/020, Indiana University.

Pedroni, P. (1999), 'Critical Values for Cointegration Tests in Heterogeneous Panels with Multiple Regressors', *Oxford Bulletin of Economics and Statistics*, Special Issue, 653–70.

Pesaran, M.H. and R.P. Smith (1995), 'Estimating Long-Run Relationships from Dynamic Heterogeneous Panels', *Journal of Econometrics*, **68**, 79–113.

Posner, M. (1961), 'International Trade and Technical Change', *Oxford Economic Papers*, **13**, 323–41.

Rivera-Batiz, L. and P.M. Romer (1991), 'Economic Integration and Endogenous Growth', *Quarterly Journal of Economics*, **106**, 531–55.

Soete, L. (1981), 'A General Test of Technological Gap Trade Theory', *Weltwischaftliches Archiv*, **117**, 638–59.

Soete, L. (1987), 'The Impact of Technological Innovation on International Trade Patterns: the Evidence Reconsidered', *Research Policy*, **16**, 101–30.

Stock, J.H. and M.W. Watson (1993), 'A Simple Estimator of Cointegrating Vectors in Higher Order Integrated Systems', *Econometrica*, **61**, 783–820.

Thirlwall, A.P. (1979), 'The Balance of Payments Constraint as an Explanation of International Growth Rates Differences', *Banca Nazionale del Lavoro, Quarterly Review*, **128**, 45–53.

Vamvakidis, A. (1998), 'Regional Integration and Economic Growth', *World Bank Economic Review*, **12**, 251–70.

Vernon, R. (1966), 'International Investment and International Trade in the Product Cycle', *Quarterly Journal of Economics*, **80**, 190–207.

Wakelin, K. (1998), 'The Role of Innovation in Bilateral OECD Trade Performance', *Applied Economics*, **30**, 1335–46.

17 Finite Lifetimes, Economic Policies and Capital Accumulation

Marco A.C. Martins and
Jorge Thompson Araujo

17.1 INTRODUCTION

A well-established result of contemporary microeconomically based macroecomics is that the way in which individuals take into account the future affects the characterisation of an equilibrium situation as well as adjustments in relation to it. Infinite-horizon models of the Ramsey–Cass–Koopmans variety yield equivalent outcomes for both a centrally planned and a decentralised economy, which may be summarised by the modified golden rule of capital accumulation: in a Pareto-optimal steady-state equilibrium, the marginal product of capital must exceed the rate of population growth by exactly the magnitude of individuals' rate of time preference. With an AK production function, the modified golden rule is no longer the expression of long-run equilibrium: rather, it is a constant rate of balanced growth that characterises the steady state.

Jones and Manuelli (1992) argue that one-sector overlapping-generations models with convex technologies, but without an intergenerational mechanism of income transfers cannot generate a non-zero equilibrium growth rate. Using a version of Diamond's (1965) standard OLG model, they note that when 'young', that is, in the first period of their lives, individuals do not have sufficient income with which to acquire a stock of capital large enough as to sustain long-run growth. Intergenerational transfers – for example, through income redistribution from the older generation to the young financed by income taxation

This chapter is a revised and expanded version of 'Economic Growth with Finite Lifetimes', by the same authors, which appeared in *Economics Letters*, **62** (1999), 377–81. We would like to thank Elsevier Science for permission to reprint this previously published material in this book. The findings, interpretations and conclusions expressed in this chapter are entirely those of the authors. They do not necessarily coincide with the views of the Federal Senate, Brazil, or of the World Bank, its Executive Directors or the countries they represent.

– are required to produce endogenous growth without resorting to any kind of technological nonconvexity.

The introduction of a bequest motive in OLG models in an 'altruistic' manner *à la* Barro (1974) – parents' utility function now including the utility of their children – generates a finite-horizon analogue to the infinite-horizon models. Since a utility function of this nature can be solved recursively forward, the welfare of all future generations matters for currently living individuals, which therefore behave *as if* they were infinitely-lived. In this case, Jones and Manuelli point out that sustained long-run equlilibrium is possible.

Altruism in the above sense is not the sole method of introducing a bequest motive in OLG models. Parents may not directly consider the utility of their children, but rather confront their own consumption level with the absolute magnitude of the bequest to be left – the so-called warm-glow theory of giving. It is the absolute bequest which is the decision variable of direct concern to parents, not children's total welfare. Such a model is not an analogue to infinite-horizon models. And neutrality results such as the Ricardian Equivalence theorem are not to be expected to hold (see Hoover 1988; Andreoni 1989). It is a straightforward consequence of the fact that, in this case, individuals do not behave as if they were infinitely-lived.[1]

The purpose of this chapter is to study the impact of stylised fiscal and monetary policies on capital accumulation, using a version of the linear endogenous growth models of the AK family[2] within an OLG structure with warm-glow giving. Observe that previous contributions using that kind of bequest motive concentrate on individual strategic behaviour rather than on capital accumulation over time, which is the focus of our chapter. Also, rewriting the basic AK model within an 'altruistic' OLG framework would not be of much interest, as it would be a (almost perfect) finite-horizon version of the already existing infinite-horizon contributions to this literature. We show that *sustained long-run growth is possible within this class of finite-lifetime model*. Furthermore, we demonstrate that capital accumulation is influenced by macroeconomic management, in the form of government debt and fiat money – the former hampers growth because it competes with physical capital for individuals' savings, while the latter, by reducing the sacrifice of waiting for the returns to capital to come, fosters it.

Section 17.2 introduces the basic model. Section 17.3 explores the notion that, with a bequest motive of this nature, the Ricardian Equivalence Theorem does not generally hold – in particular, it is shown that the rate of growth of the capital stock is adversely affected by the presence of government debt. Section 17.4 discusses the role of money, in an analysis that reproduces the so-called 'Tobin effect' by rejecting superneutrality. Section 17.5 briefly outlines how functional distribution of income can be dealt with in the context of the model. Section 17.6 contains some concluding comments.

17.2   A SIMPLE MODEL OF CAPITAL ACCUMULATION

The present formulation is a straightforward extension of Martins (1980, 1994, 1995), which relies on Samuelson's pioneering OLG model as a framework of analysis. Population growth is absent. There is one consumption good, which may be immediately consumed or saved as capital for next period's production. The (net) production function is taken to be one of the 'AK' type (Rebelo 1991; Barro and Sala-i-Martin 1995). At each period t, generation t inherits W_t units of the good, leaving W_{t+1} as a bequest for the next generation. Positive growth is said to occur when the stock of the good increases from one generation to the following one.

At time t, a fraction $C_t(t)$ of the initial endowment of an individual born at time t is consumed, the remainder is saved so as to generate productive resources or 'capital' for the next period's production activity. K_t is the non-consumed part of the representative agent's endowment W_t at time t, so that the productive process not only recovers K_t, but also generates a net product AK_t. Gross product $AK_t + K_t$ will then form the agent's next period endowment. It goes without saying that the only reason why our representative agent cares about the endowment at $t+1$ is that he/she possesses an absolute bequest motive. We postulate a separable logarithmic utility function in order to generate a closed-form solution. Assuming perfect foresight, the representative individual takes W_t as given and maximises utility with respect to $C_t(t)$, K_t and W_{t-1}. The optimisation problem is:[3]

$$\text{Max } U(C_t(t), W_{t+1}) = \ln C_t(t) + \delta \ln W_{t+1} \qquad (17.1)$$

$$\text{s.t.} \quad C_t(t) + K_t = W_t$$
$$W_{t+1} = AK_t + K_t$$

Observe that both constraints bind.[4]

From the first-order conditions, we obtain:

$$\lambda_1 / \lambda_2 = W_{t+1} / \delta C_t(t) = 1 + A \qquad (17.2)$$

where λ_i is the Lagrange multiplier associated with the ith restriction.

Substituting the constraints into (17.2) yields:

$$W_{t+1} / W_t = [\delta / (1 + \delta)](1 + A) \qquad (17.3)$$

From (17.3), we can determine the rate of growth of the representative agent's endowment of the good, λ:

$$\lambda = \frac{K_t - K_{t-1}}{K_{t-1}} = \frac{\delta A - 1}{1 + \delta} = \frac{A - \frac{1}{\delta}}{1 + \frac{1}{\delta}} \qquad (17.4)$$

Equation (17.4) resembles the solution of infinite horizon models with an 'AK' production function, in that the endogenous rate of growth λ depends on technology (A) and preferences (δ). As in those models, constant returns to capital are sufficient to generate endogenous growth. The economy will grow irrespective of the size of the initial endowment, as long as $A > \frac{1}{\delta}$. However, δ represents the agent's preference for the future, and it is not an intertemporal discount rate. It is not necessary to discount the future in order to relate the endogenous growth rate to the representative agent's preferences. Hence, our equation (17.4) has not exactly the same interpretation as in the usual 'AK' models found in the literature, as economic agents in our formulation view the future in a different manner.

Endogenous growth is reflected in the fact that in equilibrium the endowment to be bequeathed at time $t+1$ is larger than the corresponding one for time t, that is, $W_{t+1} > W_t$. The importance of the degree of preference for the future can now be evaluated: if $\delta \to 0$, equation (17.4) tells us that $\lambda \to -1$ (or *minus* 100%), that is, the entire endowment will tend to be consumed with no concern about future generations. Therefore, there cannot be growth if individuals do not leave any bequest to their descendants. This result delivers a very simple steady-state behavioural rule for the case of positive growth: always leave to your offspring more than you have received as an initial endowment.

Another noteworthy result from the first-order conditions is the equilibrium consumption allocation:

$$C_t(t) = \frac{W_t}{1 + \delta} \qquad (17.5)$$

Equation (17.5) replicates the traditional result of some versions of the permanent-income theory that consumption is a linear function of initial wealth.

17.3 A NON-EQUIVALENCE RESULT

In this section, we start from the idea that the Ricardian Equivalence Theorem does not generally hold in an OLG economy with warm-glow giving (see Hoover 1988; Andreoni 1989). But how does the mode of financing government spending affect the *rate* of growth? We now assume that, at time t, the government makes

$E_t - T_t$ of net transfer payments to generation t, where E_t and T_t are, respectively, gross transfers and lump sum taxes at time t. The government also sells to the same generation B_t units of bonds, to be redeemed one period later, at the price of $(1 + r_t)^{-1}$, where r_t is the current real rate of interest. Taking W_t, E_t and T_t as given, the representative individual maximises utility with respect to $C_t(t)$, K_t, B_t and W_{t+1}. The problem now becomes:

$$\text{Max } \ln C_t + \delta \ln W_{t+1} \tag{17.6}$$

$$\text{s.t.} \quad C_t(t) + K_t + B_t(1 + r_t)^{-1} = W_t + E_t - T_t$$

$$W_{t+1} = (1 + A) K_t + B_t$$

Note that B_t is a flow variable (new bond issues); in this simple two-period framework, it is also the outstanding stock of bonds at the beginning of period t. From the first-order conditions with respect to capital and bonds, we immediately see that $r_t = A$ for all t. The first-order conditions also allow us to write:

$$\frac{(1 + A)K_t + B_t}{\delta\left[W_t + E_t - T_t - \dfrac{B_t}{1 + A} - K_t\right]} = 1 + A \tag{17.7}$$

Given the initial endowment W_t, we can now derive the demand functions for $C_t(t)$, K_t, B_t and W_{t+1}. However, bonds and capital are perfect substitutes in the representative individual's portfolio, so that we can only determine their *joint* demand function. We then obtain:

$$K_t + \frac{B_t}{1 + A} = \frac{\delta}{1 + \delta}[W_t + E_t - T_t] \tag{17.8}$$

$$C_t(t) = \frac{W_t + E_t - T_t}{1 + \delta} \tag{17.9}$$

$$W_{t+1} = \left(K_t + \frac{B_t}{1 + A}\right)(1 + A) = \frac{(1 + A)\delta}{1 + \delta}(W_t + E_t - T_t) \tag{17.10}$$

At time t, government spending comprises net transfers $E_t - T_t$ and B_{t-1} units of redeemed bonds (including interest payments). They are financed by the auction of B_t units of newly issued bonds at the market price of $(1 + r_t)^{-1}$ (where $r_t = A$ in equilibrium). The government's budget constraint is thus as follows:

$$E_t - T_t = \frac{B_t}{1+A} - B_{t-1} \tag{17.11}$$

Substituting the government's budget constraint into (17.8) – (17.10) yields:

$$K_t + \frac{B_t}{1+A} = \frac{\delta}{1+\delta}\left[W_t + \frac{B_t}{1+A} - B_{t-1}\right] \tag{17.12}$$

$$C_t(t) = \frac{W_t}{1+\delta} + \frac{1}{1+\delta}\left[\frac{B_t}{1+A} - B_{t-1}\right] \tag{17.13}$$

$$W_{t+1} = \frac{(1+A)\delta}{1+\delta}\left[W_t + \frac{B_t}{1+A} - B_{t-1}\right] \tag{17.14}$$

Equations (17.13) and (17.14) show that the equilibrium allocation $(C_t(t), K_t, W_{t+1})$ is not independent of national debt, so that Ricardian Equivalence is not generally valid with the kind of preferences we are considering.

An important qualification must be made at this stage. The individual's endowment, W, is no longer the appropriate variable with which to treat capital accumulation: from the second-period restriction to the problem (17.6), we see that the endowment is composed of both capital *and* government bonds. Taking into consideration the corresponding restriction to an individual born at time $t-1$ and substituting into (17.12) yields:

$$\frac{K_t - K_{t-1}}{K_{t-1}} = \frac{\delta A - 1}{1+\delta} - \frac{B_t / K_{t-1}}{(1+A)(1+\delta)} \tag{17.15}$$

Equation (17.15) gives us the endogenous rate of growth of the capital stock. Note that the resulting rate is equal to the one obtained in the previous section less a term that depends positively on the ratio of government debt at time t to capital stock at time $t-1$. The greater is that ratio, the smaller is the equilibrium rate of growth of the capital stock. This is our non-neutrality result: the flow of government debt financing as a proportion of the pre-existing stock of capital actually negatively affects the rate of capital accumulation.[5] Government debt crowds out productive investment as it competes with capital for individuals' non-consumed output.

Notice that equation (17.15) predicts that such negative effects will be smaller for larger A and/or δ, all of which are empirically testable implications of the model.

17.4   MONEY AND GROWTH

The introduction of money allows for the specification of a further link between present and future. Following Martins (1980), the model is now extended to three periods. The representative individual must carry money from period t to $t+1$ in order to provide for his/her consumption at $t+1$. That is, it is assumed that the holding period of (equity-) capital is longer (that is, three periods) than that of money (two periods). Hence, the role of money cannot be performed by the real good. For the sake of simplicity, the individual is assumed to use the first period of his/her life for portfolio allocations only, devoting the second period for consumption and the third for bequeathing activities. The optimisation problem now becomes:

$$\text{Max } U(C_t(t+1), W_{t+2}) = \ln C_t(t+1) + \delta \ln W_{t+2} \qquad (17.16)$$

$$\text{s.t.} \quad M_t(t+1) + P_t K_t = P_t W_t + E_t - T_t$$

$$P_{t+1} C_t(t+1) + M_t(t+2) = M_t(t+1)$$

$$P_{t+2} W_{t+2} = P_{t+2}(1+A)K_t + M_1(t+2)$$

$M_t(t+i)$ is the nominal amount of money held by the individual born at time t carried over his ith period of life. Taking W_t, E_t and T_t as given, the individual now optimises with respect to $C_t(t+1), M_t(t+1), K_t, M_t(t+2)$ and W_{t+2}. With a positive rate of return on capital, the representative agent will use only capital to provide for his/her bequeathing activities in period $t+2$: hence, $M_t(t+2) = 0$ (see Martins 1980). Money is held only insofar it is not dominated in the rate of return by any other asset: this is possible only in the first and second periods. Therefore, we can simplify notation so that $M_t(t+1)$ is henceforward represented by M_t. The restrictions on (17.16) now read:

$$M_t + P_t K_t = P_t W_t + E_t - T_t \qquad (17.17a)$$

$$P_{t+1} C_t(t+1) = M_t \qquad (17.17b)$$

$$W_{t+2} = (1+A)K_t \qquad (17.17c)$$

Restriction (17.17c) clearly shows that money is not a part of the individual's endowment. So, the analysis teaches us that the concept of *wealth* should be derived from it. Observe also that the government's budget constraint is simply given by $E_t - T_t = M_t - M_{t-1}$, that is, the primary deficit is financed by monetary expansion.

From the first-order conditions with respect to $C_t(t+1)$, W_{t+2}, M_t and K_t, we obtain:

$$P_{t+1}C_t(t+1) = P_tW_{t+2}/\delta(1+A) = M_t \qquad (17.18)$$

Substituting (17.18), the definition of the government's budget constraint, and the third constraint into the second one in (17.16) gives us an expression for P_t:

$$P_t = (\delta M_t + M_{t-1})/W_t \qquad (17.19)$$

Inserting (17.19) in (17.18) yields:

$$W_{t+2}/W_t = [\delta(1+A)(1+\pi_t)]/[1+\delta(1+\pi_t)] \qquad (17.20)$$

where $\pi_t = (M_t - M_{t+1})/M_{t-1}$, the rate of monetary expansion.

From (17.20), the endogenous growth rate of capital accumulation can then be determined:

$$\frac{K_t - K_{t-1}}{K_{t-1}} = \frac{\delta A(1+\pi_t) - 1}{1 + \delta(1+\pi_t)} \qquad (17.21)$$

The outcome is that the equilibrium growth rate now depends positively on π_t. (Note that if $\pi_t = 0$, we rescue equation (17.4) of the moneyless model.) It is interesting to note that this result is in direct opposition to the notion of 'superneutrality' in monetary growth models. Our result is a version of the so-called 'Tobin effect', according to which faster money growth leads to higher capital holdings. Monetary expansion fosters capital accumulation here because the sacrifice of waiting for the returns to capital to come is diminished, as fiat money enables agents to consume in the second period of their lives. Note that this is a model-specific and purely theoretical result and it should be clear that a cheap-money policy is not being advocated.[6] In a model with constant returns with respect to capital, the Tobin effect not only permits greater capital accumulation, but also generates a higher rate of growth.

17.5 ADDRESSING FUNCTIONAL DISTRIBUTION OF INCOME

The model, as it stands, does not lend itself immediately to income distribution analysis, a central concern of this volume, for a simple reason: it has only one factor of production, 'broadly-defined' capital K. At any given time, payments to capital as a factor of production fully exhaust output, that is, $Y(t) = AK(t)$ for all t. Therefore, income distribution is simply not an issue in this model and this, as such, is not a problem. It just means that, in order to be used as an instrument with which to make sense of stylised facts involving the growth–distribution nexus – a major issue in modern-time global and national policymaking – the model needs to be modified accordingly. In this section, we outline two ways in which this can be accomplished, without presenting the mathematical details.

The first is to modify the presentation of the model's technology. This approach retains the idea that what ultimately governs factor income distribution is the contribution of each factor of production to the output-generating process. The 'AK' model can be easily reinterpreted in that 'broadly-defined' capital K can be taken to be a composite index of different reproducible means of production – or, to put it simply, different kinds of capital. For example, it can be decomposed into physical capital – accumulated by putting aside some portion of physical output in the form of savings – and human capital (accumulated by putting aside some portion of the individual's time for knowledge-enhancing activities that can be used to increase his or her productivity at work). This is the approach followed, for example, by Lucas (1988), and it allows for the maintenance of the mathematical property according to which the output equilibrium growth rate is endogenously determined in the model.

From the point of view of our basic model, a different presentation of its technological assumptions entails also new ways of displaying how intertemporal allocative decisions are made. This is not a straightforward subject. On the one hand, individuals not only have to decide on how to allocate physical output – between consumption and bequests – but also on how to allocate their time – between 'work', leisure, and knowledge-enhancing activities. This implies that the intertemporal structure of the model has to be revised accordingly. On the other hand, since human capital is now part of total accumulated wealth, it has to be somehow incorporated into the bequeathing process. Can human capital be inter-generationally transmitted in the same way as physical wealth? Certainly many assumptions can be made concerning individuals' preferences once total wealth is broadened to encompass human capital as well.

The second approach is to eschew altogether technological considerations and to focus entirely on differentiated savings behaviour on the part of distinct income groups. This is, of course, the approach followed in the so-called 'Kaldorian' models (see, for example, Kaldor 1955–56). Baranzini (1982; 1991) takes one step further within this tradition by framing the distinct classes' savings behaviour in an intertemporal framework very similar to ours – that is, by means of an overlapping-generations model in which at least one of the classes has a utility function with an absolute bequest motive. Baranzini's analysis distinguishes between a 'capitalist' class, whose utility function contains a bequest to be set aside to each subsequent generation, and a 'workers' class, which lives off wages alone and does not engage in bequeathing. The key purpose of this formulation is to endogenously generate, using a life-cycle framework, the savings propensities for each class, which are usually taken as given in more traditional versions of the 'Kaldorian' approach. The functional distribution of income – understood here as dividing the pie between 'capitalists' and 'workers' – is thus derived from these model-generated propensities to save.

These two approaches can be combined[7] by assigning factors of production to each class: physical capital to 'capitalists' and labour to 'workers'. (Assigning human capital to 'workers' would not only make them behave in 'capitalistic' ways but would also create the same modelling problems raised in our discussion of the 'technological' approach.) Once this assignment is made, equilibrium would be defined along the lines of Diamond's (1965) model, in which each factor would be paid in accordance with its marginal productivity, irrespective of the intertemporal structure. The main drawback of this option, however, is that the capital–labour combination in a production function would generate diminishing returns to physical capital and would thus eliminate endogenous growth: the equilibrium growth rate would be determined by the (exogenously given) rate of growth of the labour force.

Therefore, it is possible to extend our model in ways in which income distribution could be meaningfully handled. However, each one of these individual alternatives would generate its own modelling trade-offs, and many of the clear-cut and 'well-behaved' properties of our model would be lost in the process.

17.6   CONCLUDING REMARKS

The model presented in this chapter demonstrates that sustained growth is possible in a one-sector overlapping-generations framework with convex technologies (represented here by a relevant particular case: the AK production function) without income redistribution from the old to the young supported by income taxation and without 'pure' altruism of the Barro (1974) kind. The critical assumption is that agents' utility function embodies warm-glow giving.

This representation of the bequest motive allows us to derive clear policy implications from the model: government debt crowds out investment in physical capital, while fiat money expansion stimulates it, due to the liquidity services provided by currency. The reason for these non-neutrality results is straightforward: differently from Barro's (1974) formalisation of intergenerational altruism – which also permits sustained growth in the present framework – warm-glow giving precludes finitely-lived individuals behaving as if they were infinitely-lived.

NOTES

1   Andreoni's (1989) warm-glow theory of giving is not the only approach to insert the absolute amount of the bequest in the consumer's utility function. For Andreoni, this is due to a form of 'impure altruism', in which people selfishly enjoy giving, experiencing a 'warm glow' from leaving a bequest. In Hoover (1988) and Baranzini (1982, 1991) this absolute bequest motive can also be interpreted as a limited form of altruism. Merton (1969) (see also Samuelson, 1969) includes in the utility function of a representative individual a 'bequest valuation function' which resembles the 'scrap functions' in production growth models. Martins (1995) interprets this formulation as a primary demand for capital: capital accumulation is the expression of an individual's concern for the future, which he/she values positively. It is interesting to note that this literature is very little interconnected; that is, we seldom see cross references among the contributors.

2   Our choice is fundamentally due to the simplicity of this model, and the results can be easily extended to more general functions within the class of convex technologies. See Sala-i-Martin (1990, 4) for a defense of the AK model and Solow (1994, 51) for a criticism.

3   The formulation in (17.1) collapses the individual's and the firms' problem into a single one. It is straightforward to rewrite the maximisation problem for individuals and firms separately, as in Diamond's (1965) model.

4   Given the definition of the endowment in the second-period restriction, the first-period restriction can be re-expressed as:

$$C_t(t) + (K_t - K_{t-1}) = AK_{t-1},$$

that is, the national income identity.

5   This model actually replicates within a much simpler structure a conclusion previously reached by Saint-Paul (1992) with Blanchard's (1985) 'perpetual youth' model modified only to include an AK production function.

6   A negative long-run effect of inflation on growth is shown by the available evidence to be a more plausible outcome for moderate-to-high inflation episodes (see, for example, Bruno and Easterly 1994), although it is recognised that there may be a positive relationship between the two for relatively low inflation rates. The Tobin effect obtained here is a logical consequence of the way we modelled the production side of the economy. If we treat firms and families separately, and incorporate transaction costs to investment due to the presence of inflation, the negative relationship between the two variables may be replicated in our framework.

7   For an example of an early attempt to combine older, non-intertemporal variations of the 'technological' and the 'Kaldorian' approaches see Samuelson and Modigliani (1966).

REFERENCES

Andreoni, J. (1989), 'Giving with Impure Altruism: Applications to Charity and Ricardian Equivalence', *Journal of Political Economy,* **97**, 1447–58.

Araujo, J.T. and M.A.C. Martins (1999), 'Economic Growth with Finite Lifetimes', *Economic Letters,* **62**, 377–81.

Baranzini, M. (1982), 'Can the Life-Cycle Theory Help in Explaining Income Distribution and Capital Accumulation?', in M. Baranzini (ed.), *Advances in Economic Theory,* Oxford: Blackwell; New York: St. Martin's Press.

Baranzini, M. (1991), *A Theory of Wealth Distribution and Accumulation,* Oxford: Clarendon Press.

Barro, R.J. (1974). 'Are Government Bonds Net Wealth?', *Journal of Political Economy,* **91**, 1095–117.

Barro, R.J. and X. Sala-i-Martin (1995), *Economic Growth,* McGraw-Hill.

Blanchard, O.J. (1985), 'Debt, Deficits and Finite Horizons', *Journal of Political Economy,* **93** (6) (December) 1045–1076.

Blanchard, O. J. and S. Fischer (1989), *Lectures on Macroeconomics,* Cambridge (Mass.): The MIT Press.

Bruno M.and W. Easterly (1994), 'Inflation Crises and Long-run Growth', mimeo, The World Bank.

Diamond, P.A. (1965), 'National Debt in a Neoclassical Growth Model', *American Economic Review,* **55**, 1126–50.

Hoover, K.D. (1988), *The New Classical Macroeconomics,* Cambridge, Mass.: Basil Blackwell.

Jones, L.E. and R.E. Manuelli (1992), 'Finite Lifetimes and Growth', *Journal of Economic Theory,* **58**, 171–97.

Kaldor, N. (1955–56), 'Alternative Theories of Distribution', *Review of Economic Studies,* 83–100.

Lucas, R. (1988), 'On the Mechanics of Economic Development', *Journal of Monetary Economics,* pp. 3–42.

Martins, M.A.C. (1980), 'A Nominal Theory of the Nominal Rate of Interest and the Price Level', *Journal of Political Economy,* **88**, 174–85.

Martins, M.A.C. (1994), 'Interests, Prices and the Barsky and Summers' Resolution of the Gibson Paradox under the Gold Standard System', *Revista Brasileira de Economia,* **48**, 3–28.

Martins, M.A.C. (1995). 'Bonds, Interests and Capital Accumulation', *Revista Brasileira de Economia,* **49**, 557–82.

Merton, R.C. (1969), 'Lifetime Portfolio Selection under Uncertainty: The Continuous-Time Model', *Review of Economics and Statistics,* 247–57.

Rebelo, S. (1991), 'Long-run Policy Analysis and Long-Run Growth', *Journal of Political Economy,* **99** (3), 500–21.

Sala-i-Martin, X. (1990), 'Lecture Notes on Economic Growth (II): Five Prototype Models of Endogenous Growth', NBER Working Paper No. 3564, December.

Saint-Paul, G. (1992), 'Fiscal Policy in an Endogenous Growth Model', *Quarterly Journal of Economics*, **107** (November), 1243–60.

Samuelson, P.A. (1958), 'An Exact Consumption-Loan Model of Interest with or without the Social Contrivance of Money', *Journal of Political Economy*, **66**, 467–82.

Samuelson, P.A. (1969), 'Lifetime Portfolio Selection by Dynamic Stochastic Programming', *Review of Economics and Statistics*, 239–46.

Samuelson, P.A. and F. Modigliani (1966), 'The Pasinetti Paradox in Neo-Classical and More General Models', *Review of Economic Studies*, 321–30.

Solow, R.M. (1994), 'Perspectives on Growth Theory', *Journal of Economic Perspectives*, **8** (1) (Winter), 45–54.

18 Optimal Capital Accumulation with Trade, Sovereign Debt and Trustworthy Reputation

Amnon Levy

18.1 INTRODUCTION

This chapter analyses the optimal accumulation of capital stock, external debt and reputation by incorporating explicitly the inclination of a sovereign country to service its external liabilities and the adverse effects of not meeting foreign loan commitments on the country's trustworthy reputation. Repudiation and loss of reputation might limit the country's access to international markets of credit, consumer and capital goods; and subsequently might result in a higher average cost of servicing the country's future external liabilities, less favourable terms of trade with the rest of the world and accelerated depreciation of capital stock.

Since 1973, the external debts of the developing countries have been growing at unprecedented rates, and this has led to a heightened concern about these countries' ability and commitment to service and repay their liabilities. This concern is rooted in the fact that a country's external debt is a sovereign debt and unlike a private debt it is not subject to laws regarding bankruptcy and enforcement of collateral. Thus, when the potential penalties on default are insufficient, a rise in the country's degree of indebtedness increases its inclination to repudiate some, or all, of its external liabilities (Krugman 1988, 1989). As has been suggested by Eaton and Gersovitz (1981) and Kletzer (1984), it is possible that the extent of repudiation may be limited by the country's concerns about the adverse effect of a default on its trustworthy reputation and, subsequently, on its access to foreign loans. The role of reputation, in conjunction with the desire for continued access to external loans, as a deterrent against repudiation has been analysed by Grossman and Van Huyck (1988), who distinguished between justifiable and excusable defaults and unjustifiable and inexcusable defaults and derived a reputation equilibrium in which the lenders' expectations about contingent debt servicing are validated. By assuming that small countries face competitive foreign investors, Bulow and Rogoff (1989) have disputed the role of the 'reputation for repayment' as a support for extending loans to small countries and have argued that lending to these countries should be supported by direct sanctions.

The present chapter incorporates both the reputational argument and the possibility of an implementation of trade sanctions against a defaulting country into the analysis of external debt and capital accumulation within an intertemporal utility maximisation framework. In this framework, the indebted country chooses the paths of consumption, import, export and repudiation of external liabilities so as to maximise the sum of the discounted utilities from consumption over an infinite planning horizon while taking into account the evolution of its production capacity, external debt and reputation. In addition to the potentially adverse effect of a deterioration in its trustworthy reputation on access to foreign loans, the motion equations of the indebted country's capital stock and external debt incorporate the possibility of lenders' retaliation by limiting the country's access to international markets. Trade sanctions against the defaulting country are likely to reduce the revenues from exports, increase the price of imports and accelerate the depreciation of capital items whose maintenance depends on foreign spare parts and skills.

The details of this analysis are presented in the following sections. Section 18.2 displays the indebted country's intertemporal utility maximisation as an optimal control problem in which the control variables are consumption, import, export and rate of repudiation; and the state variables are capital, external debt and reputation. It also derives the necessary conditions for maximisation. Section 18.3 analyses the characteristics of the optimal trajectories of the control and state variables. Section 18.4 describes the steady-state levels of repudiation, reputation, import, capital, output and external debt.

18.2   DYNAMIC MODEL OF OPTIMAL DEBT ACCUMULATION AND REPUDIATION WITH CONSIDERATION FOR RETALIATION

The analysis of capital, external debt and reputation accumulation is based on the assumption that the indebted country chooses the paths of consumption, import, export and the rate of repudiation of external liabilities so as to maximise the sum of the discounted utilities from consumption within an infinite horizon while taking into account the effects of repudiation and retaliatory sanctions on the country's capital stock, external debt and reputation. The choice of infinite time interval is to enable the assessment of long-run (steady state) effects.

In mathematical notation the sovereign's decision problem is portrayed as

$$\underset{(c,m,x,v)}{\text{maximising}} \int_0^\infty e^{-\rho t} u(c_t)\,dt \qquad (18.1)$$

subject to the state-transition equations:

$$\dot{K}_t = f(K_t, m_t) - c_t - x_t - \delta(R_t)K_t \qquad (18.2)$$

$$\dot{D}_t = q(R_t)m_t - p(R_t)x_t + r(R_t)(1 - v_t)D_t \qquad (18.3)$$

$$\dot{R}_t = -\beta(v_t - v^*). \qquad (18.4)$$

Here,

u = the sovereign's instantaneous utility,

ρ = the sovereign's rate of time preference, $\rho \geq 0$,

K = the country's capital stock in physical units,

D = the country's amount of external debt in dollars,

R = the sovereign's trustworthy reputation $-R \geq 0$ and larger values of R indicate a higher reputation,

c = the country's consumption level in physical units,

m = the country's import level in physical units,

x = the country's export level in physical units,

v = the rate of repudiation of external liabilities, $0 \leq v \leq 1$,

v^* = the excusable rate of repudiation,

β = the reputational loss parameter, $\beta > 0$,

δ = the rate of capital depreciation,

f = the aggregate production function (aggregate production is measured in physical units),

q = the aggregate price of imported goods in dollars,

p = the aggregate price of exported goods in dollars,

r = the average cost of servicing the external debt, and

t = the time index.

It is assumed that:

1   The instantaneous utility is a concave function of consumption: $u' > 0$ and $u'' < 0$, $u'(0) = \infty$ and $u'(\infty) = 0$.
2   The aggregate production is a concave function of capital and imported inputs: $f_K > 0$, $f_m > 0$, $f(0,m) = f(K,0) = 0$, $f_{KK} < 0$, $f_{mm} < 0$ and $f_{KK}f_{mm} - f_{Km}f_{mK} > 0$.
3   The average cost of servicing the external debt rises as the indebted country's reputation declines, that is, $r_R < 0$.
4   The rate of capital depreciation increases as the country's trustworthy reputation declines due to retaliatory measures implemented by lending countries, including a spare-part embargo, that is, $\delta_R < 0$.
5   Due to a greater degree of isolation and loss of access to world markets, the prices of imported goods rise and the prices of exported goods fall as the indebted country's reputation declines, that is, $q_R < 0$ and $p_R > 0$.
6   There exists an interior solution to the optimal-control problem. This assumption is compatible with the empirical evidence that, in most cases, repudiation is partial and retaliatory sanctions are limited rather than total or nil.

In this optimal-control problem, $c(t)$, $m(t)$, $x(t)$ and $v(t)$ are the control variables; and $K(t)$, $D(t)$ and $R(t)$ are the state variables. The maximum principle developed by Pontryagin et al. (1962) implies that if the control functions and the corresponding trajectories of the state variables maximise the objective function (18.1) subject to the state-transition equations (18.2) – (18.4), there exist continuously differentiable co-state functions $\lambda_1(t)$, $\lambda_2(t)$ and $\lambda_3(t)$ such that the optimal control functions and the corresponding state and co-state functions simultaneously satisfy the state-transition equations, the co-state transition (or adjoint) equations and the optimality conditions. These transition equations and optimality conditions can be derived by considering the Hamiltonian (H) associated with the constrained intertemporal decision problem described by equations (18.1) to (18.4):

$$H = e^{-\rho t}u(c) + \lambda_1[f(K,m) - c - x - \delta(R)K]$$
$$+ \lambda_2[q(R)m - p(R)x + r(R)(1-v)D]$$
$$- \lambda_3\beta(v - v^*)$$

(18.5)

where, for convenience, the time index t is omitted. In this context, the co-state variables λ_1, λ_2 and λ_3 can be interpreted as the shadow values (in utiles) of infinitesimal increments in the country's capital stock, amount of external debt and level of international reputation, respectively. The first term on the right-hand side (r.h.s.) indicates the direct contribution of current consumption to the overall level of utility, whereas the second, third and fourth terms on the r.h.s. display the indirect contributions of current net investment, borrowing and repudiation of external liabilities, respectively, to the sovereign's overall utility level through altering future consumption possibilities.

In addition to the state-transition equations, the necessary conditions include the adjoint equations

$$\dot{\lambda}_1 = -\lambda_1[f_K(K,m) - \delta(R)] \tag{18.6}$$

$$\dot{\lambda}_2 = -\lambda_2 r(R)(1 - v) \tag{18.7}$$

$$\dot{\lambda}_3 = \lambda_1 \delta_R K - \lambda_2[q_R m - p_R x + r_R(1 - v)D] \tag{18.8}$$

and the optimality conditions

$$H_c = e^{-\rho t}u'(c) - \lambda_1 = 0 \tag{18.9}$$

$$H_m = \lambda_1 f_m(K,m) + \lambda_2 q(R) = 0 \tag{18.10}$$

$$H_x = -\lambda_1 - \lambda_2 p(R) = 0 \tag{18.11}$$

$$H_v = -\lambda_2 r(R)D - \lambda_3 \beta = 0 \tag{18.12}$$

Finally, the transversality conditions require that, from the sovereign's perspective, there is no value to the terminal levels of capital, external debt and reputation. As long as the sovereign's rate of time preference is positive, these conditions are also satisfied in the case where the terminal levels of the state variables are positive.

The time differentials of the optimality conditions (18.9) – (18.12) yield singular-control equations describing the transitions of the control variables. The singular-control equations, the adjoint equations (18.6) – (18.8) and the state-transition equations (18.2) – (18.4) constitute a system of non-linear differential equations. Due to its size and complexity, it is impossible to solve this system and identify its asymptotic properties without additional strong assumptions and a substantial loss of generality. Thus, the following sections present only some essential features of the optimal paths of the control and state variables and the steady-state levels of these variables.

18.3   CHARACTERISTICS OF THE OPTIMAL
          TRAJECTORIES

The adjoint equation (18.6) requires that, along the optimal path, the rate of change in the shadow price of capital is equal to the difference between capital's rate of depreciation and the marginal product of capital. The optimality condition (18.9) indicates that at any instance within the planning horizon the shadow price of capital should be equal to the marginal utility from current consumption and thus reflects the trade-off between current consumption and future consumption.

The adjoint equation (18.7) requires that along the optimal path the rate of change in the shadow value of external debt is equal, in absolute terms, to the repudiation-free interest rate $(1 - v)r$. Furthermore, the optimality condition (18.11) implies that the ratio of the shadow prices of capital and external debt should be equal to the price of the country's exports, and in recalling the optimality condition (18.9):

$$\lambda_2 = -e^{-\rho t}u'(c) / p(R) \qquad (18.13)$$

By substituting (18.13) and (18.9) into the optimality condition (18.10) for λ_1 and λ_2 we obtain further that along the optimal path the marginal product of the imported inputs should be equal to the country's import–export price ratio:

$$f_m(K,m) = q(R) / p(R). \qquad (18.14)$$

Note further that since the country's import-export price ratio declines with R and since the marginal product of imported inputs is diminishing, the greater the country's trustworthy reputation the larger the amount of imported goods along the optimal path.

The optimality condition (18.12) implies that along the optimal path the rate of repudiation of external liabilities is such that the marginal gains (in utiles) from lowering the costs of servicing the country's external debt are offset by the adverse effect of the loss of reputation on present and future consumption and utility levels. By substituting equation (18.13) into the optimality condition (18.12), the shadow value of an infinitesimal increase in the country's reputation can be expressed as

$$\lambda_3 = r(R)De^{-rt}u'(c) / \beta p(R) \qquad (18.15)$$

By differentiating the optimality condition (18.9) with respect to t

$$-\rho e^{-\rho t}u'(c) + e^{-\rho t}u''(c)\dot{c} - \dot{\lambda}_1 = 0 \qquad (18.16)$$

and in recalling conditions (18.6) and (18.9)

$$\dot{c} = -[f_K(K,m) - \delta(R) - \rho]u'(c)/u''(c). \tag{18.17}$$

Similar to what optimal growth theory proposes (for example, Cass 1965), equation (18.17) implies that, given that the sovereign's marginal utility is diminishing, consumption increases, remains the same, or decreases over time if the marginal product of capital is greater, equal to, or smaller than the rental (or user) cost of capital ($\delta + \rho$). This effect of the marginal net return on capital is amplified by the degree of concavity of the sovereign's utility function. Note that in this framework, the marginal product of capital increases (decreases) with the amount of the imported inputs when K and m are complementaries (substitutes) in production, and the rental cost of capital declines with the country's level of reputation.

By taking the time differential of the optimality condition (18.11)

$$-\dot{\lambda}_1 - \dot{\lambda}_2 p(R) - \lambda_2 p_R(R)\dot{R} = 0 \tag{18.18}$$

and in recalling conditions (18.6), (18.7), (18.9) and (18.11) it can be shown that the transition of the country's international trustworthy reputation is given by

$$\dot{R} = \{(1-v)r(R) - [f_K(K,m) - \delta(R)]p(R)\} / p_R(R) \tag{18.19}$$

Since p_R is assumed to be positive, whenever the repudiation-free interest rate is greater, equal to, or smaller than the foreign exchange receipts from exporting the net marginal product of capital, the country's reputation increases, remains the same, or decreases, respectively. The change in the country's reputation is amplified by the vulnerability of the country's exports to retaliatory measures implemented by the lending countries as indicated by the export price derivative with respect to R. Note that for given levels of K and m, the higher the country's reputation the lower the repudiation-free interest rate and the greater the foreign exchange receipts from exporting the net marginal product of capital and hence the greater the country's inclination to repudiate and lower its reputation.

The time differential of the optimality condition (18.12) implies

$$-\dot{\lambda}_2 r(R)D - \lambda_2[r_R(R)D\dot{R} + r(R)\dot{D}] - \dot{\lambda}_3\beta = 0 \tag{18.20}$$

and by substituting conditions (18.7) and (18.8) into equation (18.20) for $\dot{\lambda}_2$ and $\dot{\lambda}_3$, respectively, and in recalling that along the optimal path λ_1 and λ_2 behave in accordance with condition (18.11), it can be shown that

$$r(R)^2(1-v)D - r_R(R)D\dot{R} - r(R)\dot{D}$$
$$+ \beta[q_R m - p_R x + r_R(1-v)D + p(R)\delta_R(R)K] = 0 \tag{18.21}$$

By dividing both sides of equation (18.21) by $r(R)D$ and rearranging terms, it can be shown that along the optimal path the instantaneous rate of change in the country's external debt is given by

$$\frac{\dot{D}}{D} = \frac{\beta}{r(R)}[(1-v)r_R + p(R)\delta_R(K/D)$$
$$+ (q_R m - p_R x)/D - r_R\dot{R}/\beta] + (1-v)r(R) \tag{18.22}$$

Equation (18.22) and the assumptions that $\delta_R < 0$, $q_R < 0$ and $p_R > 0$ indicate that the higher the country's leverage (D/K) and the lower the sensitivity of the country's import and export prices to changes in trustworthy reputation, the higher the optimal rate of external debt accumulation.

18.4   STEADY-STATE LEVELS OF REPUDIATION, REPUTATION, IMPORT, CAPITAL STOCK OUTPUT AND EXTERNAL DEBT

By setting $\dot{R} = 0$ in equations (18.4), (18.19) and (18.22), $\dot{c} = 0$ in equation (18.17), and $\dot{D} = 0$ in equation (18.22), we obtain that in steady state (*ss*):

$$v_{ss} = v* \tag{18.23}$$

$$(1-v_{ss})r(R_{ss}) - [f_K(K_{ss},m_{ss}) - \delta(R_{ss})]p(R_{ss}) = 0 \tag{18.24}$$

$$f_K(K_{ss},m_{ss}) = \delta(R_{ss}) + \rho \tag{18.25}$$

$$\frac{\beta}{r(R_{ss})}[(1-v_{ss})r_R(R_{ss}) + p(R_{ss})\delta_R(R_{ss})\,(K_{ss}/D_{ss})$$
$$+ (q_R(R_{ss})m_{ss} - p_R(R_{ss})x_{ss})/D_{ss}] + (1-v_{ss})r(R_{ss}) = 0 \tag{18.26}$$

The Steady-State Levels of Repudiation and Reputation

Equation (18.23) indicates that in steady state the country's rate of repudiation of external debt should be equal to the excusable rate. The substitution of (18.23) and (18.25) into equation (18.24) implies that the steady-state level of the country's reputation should be such that the repudiation-free interest rate is equal to the sovereign's rate of time preference times the stationary price of the country's exports:

$$(1-v^*)r(R_{ss}) = \rho p(R_{ss}) \tag{18.27}$$

By taking the total differential of equation (18.27) and in recalling that $0 \le v^* \le 1$, $r_R < 0$ and $p_R > 0$ we obtain that the higher the excusable repudiation rate and the rate of time preference, the lower the country's reputation in steady state:

$$\frac{dR_{ss}}{dv^*} = \frac{r(R_{ss})}{(1-v^*)r_R(R_{ss}) - \rho p_R(R_{ss})} < 0 \tag{18.28}$$

and

$$\frac{dR_{ss}}{d\rho} = \frac{p(R_{ss})}{(1-v^*)r_R(R_{ss}) - \rho p_R(R_{ss})} < 0 \tag{18.29}$$

The above derivatives suggest further that the more sensitive the average cost of servicing the external debt and the price of exports to changes in the country's reputation, the smaller the effect of an increase in either the excusable repudiation rate or the rate of time preference on the steady-state level of the country's trustworthy reputation.

In order to explore further the effects of the responses of r and p to changes in R on the country's reputation in steady state let us consider the following linear forms:

$$r = r_{max} - r_1 R \qquad\qquad r_{max}, r_1 > 0 \tag{18.30}$$

and

$$p = p_{min} + p_1 R \qquad\qquad p_{min}, p_1 > 0 \tag{18.31}$$

where r_{max} and p_{min} are the average cost of servicing the external debt and the aggregate price of exports when the country's reputation reaches the lowest level (that is, $R = 0$), respectively, and r_1 and p_1 indicate the sensitivities of the average contracted interest rate and price of export to changes in the country's reputation, respectively. The substitution of these forms into equation (18.27) leads to the following close-form solution to the country's stationary level of trustworthy reputation:

$$R_{ss} = \frac{(1-v^*)r_{max} - pp_{min}}{pp_1 + r_1(1-v^*)}$$

(18.32)

This solution implies

$$\frac{dR_{ss}}{dr_{max}} = \frac{(1-v^*)}{pr_1 + r_1(1-v^*)} > 0$$

(18.33)

$$\frac{dR_{ss}}{dp_{min}} = \frac{-p}{pr_1 + r_1(1-v^*)} < 0$$

(18.34)

$$\frac{dR_{ss}}{dr_1} = \frac{-(1-v^*)[(1-v^*)r_{max} - pp_{min}]}{[pp_1 + r_1(1-v^*)]^2} \lessgtr 0 \text{ as } (1-v^*)r_{max} \gtrless pp_{min}$$

(18.35)

$$\frac{dR_{ss}}{dp_1} = \frac{-p[(1-v^*)r_{max} - pp_{min}]}{[pp_1 + r_1(1-v^*)]^2} \lessgtr 0 \text{ as } (1-v^*)r_{max} \gtrless pp_{min}.$$

(18.36)

The Steady-State Levels of Imports, Capital and Production

In order to find the steady-state levels of imports (m_{ss}), capital (K_{ss}) and production (y_{ss}), consider the following Cobb-Douglas aggregate production function

$$y = K^{\alpha_1} m^{\alpha_2} \quad 0 < \alpha_1, \alpha_2 < 1$$

(18.37)

Then, in recalling equations (18.14) and (18.25), it can be shown that the marginal products of imported inputs and capital in steady state should be equal to:

$$\alpha_2 K_{ss}^{\alpha_1} m_{ss}^{\alpha_2 - 1} = q(R_{ss}) / p(R_{ss})$$

(18.38)

$$\alpha_1 K_{ss}^{\alpha_1 - 1} m_{ss}^{\alpha_2} = \delta(R_{ss}) + p$$

(18.39)

Equations (18.38) and (18.39) indicate that the steady-state levels of imports and capital are such that:

$$\frac{K_{ss}}{m_{ss}} = (\alpha_1 / \alpha_2) \frac{q(R_{ss}) / p(R_{ss})}{\delta(R_{ss}) + \rho} \tag{18.40}$$

$$m_{ss} = \left(\frac{\delta(R_{ss}) + \rho}{\alpha_1}\right)^{\frac{\alpha_1}{1-\alpha_2+\alpha_1\alpha_2}} \left(\frac{q(R_{ss})}{\alpha_2 p(R_{ss})}\right)^{\frac{1-\alpha_1}{1-\alpha_2+\alpha_1\alpha_2}} \tag{18.41}$$

$$K_{ss} = \left(\frac{\delta(R_{ss}) + \rho}{\alpha_1}\right)^{\frac{1-\alpha_2}{1-\alpha_2+\alpha_1\alpha_2}} \left(\frac{q(R_{ss})}{\alpha_2 p(R_{ss})}\right)^{\frac{2(1+\alpha_1\alpha_2)-\alpha_1}{\alpha_1(1-\alpha_2+\alpha_1\alpha_2)}} \tag{18.42}$$

The steady-state level of output can be found by substituting equations (18.41) and (18.42) in the aggregate production function.

Equation (18.40) implies that, for a given level of reputation, the steady-state ratio of capital to imported inputs in production:

1. increases with the capital–imports production elasticities ratio,
2. increases with the import–export price ratio in steady state,
3. decreases with the rate of depreciation of capital in steady state, and
4. decreases with the sovereign's rate of time preference.

Moreover, equations (18.41) and (18.42) indicate that, for a given level of trustworthy reputation, K_{ss}, m_{ss}, and subsequently y_{ss}, increase with:

1. the depreciation rate of capital,
2. the rate of time preference, and
3. the import–export price ratio.

Note, however, that the effect of the country's steady-state trustworthy reputation level on the capital–import ratio is not clear, since both the import–export price ratio and the capital depreciation rate, appearing in the numerator and denominator of equation (18.40), respectively, decline with R_{ss}. Therefore, if the import–export price ratio is more (less) sensitive than capital's depreciation rate to changes in R, the lower the country's trustworthy reputation the more (less) capital intensive the country's production process in steady state.

Note further that the effect of the rate of time-preference (that is, the degree of myopia) on the capital–import ratio in steady state is not obvious once the country's reputation is not held constant. On the one hand, and as indicated above, an increase in the rate of time-preference raises directly the rental costs of capital and hence moderates the steady-state capital–import ratio. On the other hand, and in view of equation (18.32), an increase in the rate of time preference lowers the country's reputation and hence affects indirectly the capital–import ratio in accordance with the relative sensitivity of the capital depreciation rate and the import–export price ratio. Thus, the full effect of the rate of time preference is clear only in the case where the import-export price ratio is less sensitive than the rate of capital depreciation to changes in the country's trustworthy reputation. In this case, both the direct and indirect effects of an increment in the rate of time preference are negative and hence reduce the stationary capital–import ratio. When the import–export price ratio is more sensitive than the depreciation rate to changes in the country's trustworthy reputation, the indirect effect of an increment in the rate of time preference on the stationary capital-import ratio in the production process is positive and offsets the direct effect.

The Steady-State Level of External Debt

By setting $\dot{D}$ and $\dot{R}$ to be equal to zero in equation (18.21), the country's external debt in steady state (D_{ss}) is given by

$$D_{ss} = \frac{[p_R(R_{ss})x_{ss} - q_R(R_{ss})m_{ss}] - p(R_{ss})\delta_R(R_{ss})K_{ss}}{(1-v^*)[r_R(R_{ss}) + r(R_{ss})^2 / \beta]} \tag{18.43}$$

In recalling the assumptions that p_R is positive and q_R and δ_R are negative, it is clear that the numerator is positive. However, in view of the assumption that the contracted interest rate declines as the country's reputation rises (that is, $r_R < 0$), the sign of the denominator of the term on the right-hand side of equation (18.43) is not clear and hence

$$D_{ss} \mathop{=}_{<}^{>} 0 \text{ as } r(R_{ss}) \mathop{=}_{<}^{>} \frac{\beta E_{ss}}{R_{ss}} \tag{18.44}$$

where E_{ss} is the stationary elasticity (in absolute terms) of the contracted interest rate with respect to the indebted country's trustworthy reputation. As can be expected, the more sensitive the country's trustworthy reputation to repudiation (that is, the larger the β) the smaller the country's external liabilities in steady state, and for a sufficiently large β and contracted interest rate elasticity it is possible that the initially indebted country will be a net creditor in steady state, provided that the steady-state is reached. Equation (18.43) indicates further that the size of D_{ss}, in absolute terms, increases with:

1. the country's steady-state levels of imports, exports, capital stock and the price of exports; and

2. the sensitivity of export prices, import prices and capital depreciation rate to changes in the country's trustworthy reputation.

It is important to note further that an increment in the excusable rate of repudiation increases directly the stationary level of external debt if $r_{ss} > \beta E/R_{ss}$. However, in recalling equation (18.28), the direct effect of v^* on D_{ss} is likely to be moderated indirectly by the deterioration in the country's stationary level of trustworthy reputation.

REFERENCES

Bulow, J. and K. Rogoff (1989), 'Sovereign Debt: Is to Forgive to Forget?', *American Economic Review*, **79**, 43–50.

Cass, D. (1965), 'Optimum Growth in an Aggregative Model of Capital Accumulation', *Review of Economic Studies*, **32**, 233–40.

Eaton, J. and M. Gersovitz (1981), 'Debt with Potential Repudiation: Theoretical and Empirical Analysis', *Review of Economic Studies*, **48**, 289–309.

Grossman, H. and J. Van Huyck (1988), 'Sovereign Debt as a Contingent Claim: Excusable Default, Repudiation, and Reputation', *American Economic Review*, **78**, 1088–97.

Kletzer, K.M. (1984), 'Asymmetries of Information and the LDC Borrowing with Sovereign Risk', *Economic Journal*, **94**, 287–307.

Krugman, P. (1988), 'Financing vs. Forgiving a Debt Overhang', *Journal of Development Economics*, **29**, 253–68.

Krugman, P. (1989), 'Market-Based Debt-Reduction Schemes', in Jacob A. Frenkel, M.P. Dooley and P. Wickham (eds), *Analytical Issues in Debt*, Washington, DC: International Monetary Fund (IMF), 258–78.

Pontryagin, L.S., V.G. Boltyanskii, R.V. Gamkrelidze, and E.F. Mishchenko (1962), *The Mathematical Theory of Optimal Process*, New York: Wiley.

Name index

Aghion, P. 36, 37, 38, 39
Alesina, A. 10, 16–17, 18, 132
Anderton, B. 273
Arbache, J. 132, 276
Arndt, H.W. 216
Arrow, K.J. 110
Asano, A. 27, 28–29, 31

Baranzini, M. 338
Barro, R.J. 18, 23, 28, 30, 339
Barros, R.P. 275
Bassett, W. 94, 95
Becker, G.S. 23, 109, 110
Beggs, J.J. 178
Bell, M. 193
Bénabou, R. 90, 91, 97, 102
Benhabib, J. 14, 280
Berman, E. 274, 292
Bernard, A. 302, 305
Berthélemy, J.C. 278
Bertola, G. 10
Beyer, H. 275
Bhagwati, J. 273
Borjas, G. 178, 273, 291
Bourguignon, F. 4, 98
Brander, J.A. 23
Breitung, J. 318
Bulow, J. 344

Caballero, R. 220
Calwell 215–16
Cameron, G. 277
Chiswick, B.R. 178
Coe, D.T. 311, 314
Cragg, M.I. 275
Currie, J. 276

Davis, D.R. 281
de Mello, L. 97, 98
Deininger, K. 10, 29–30, 93
Desjonqueres, T. 274

Dornbusch, R. 131

Easterly, W. 95
Eaton, J. 343
Edwards, S. 277
Ehrlich, I. 28–29
Ethier, W.J. 164

Feenstra, R.C. 273, 275–76, 282, 292
Feliciano, Z. 275
Fields, G.S. 175
Figini, P. 95, 97
Fitzgerald, V. 238
Flood, J. 193, 211
Forbes, K. 30, 36
Forster, C. 219
Freeman, R.B. 273, 302
Freund, R.J. 177
Friedman, M. 109, 133
Furman, J. 91

Galor, O. 19, 23, 24–26, 27, 29, 92
Gaston, N. 273, 302, 305
Goldin, C. 281
Gouveia, M. 94, 95
Green, F. 275
Greene, W.H. 205, 209
Greenhalgh, C. 272
Greenwood, M.J. 175, 192
Grossman, G. 273, 311
Grossman, H. 343
Guest, R. 40, 243

Hakkura, D. 312
Hammond, S. 177
Hanson, G .H. 275, 292
Haskel, J. 272, 273
Hirsch, S. 313

Im, K.S. 318

Subject index